Business and Global Governance

Over the past two decades, the role of business in global governance has become increasingly topical. Transnational business associations are progressively more visible in international policy debates and in intergovernmental institutions, and there is a heightened attention given to global policy-making in national and international business communities.

This text examines and explains the multiple modes of engagement between business and global governance; it presents a variety of theoretical approaches which can be used to analyse them, along with empirical illustrations. Featuring a range of leading US and European scholars, it is divided into three parts that summarize different modes of engagement. Each section is illustrated by two or three studies that represent a distinct theoretical take on the issue with empirical illustrations. The book examines:

- Business as master and purpose of global governance
- Business as subject and opponent to global governance
- Business as partner and facilitator of global governance

This book will be of interest to students and scholars of Business Studies, International Relations, International Politics and International Political Economy, as well as for practitioners – in the public and private sector.

Morten Ougaard is Professor of International Political Economy, and Director of the International Business and Politics Program at Copenhagen Business School, Denmark. He is the co-editor of *Towards a Global Polity* – also published by Routledge.

Anna Leander is Professor of International Political Economy, Copenhagen Business School, Denmark. She is the co-editor of *Constructivism and International Relations: Wendt and his Critics* – also published by Routledge.

Routledge/Warwick studies in globalisation

Edited by Leonard Seabrooke *and published in association with the Centre for the Study of Globalisation and Regionalisation, University of Warwick*

Editorial Board, Jason Sharman, *Griffith University, Australia,*
Diane Stone, *University of Warwick, UK and*
Catherine E. Weaver, *University of Texas at Austin*

What is globalisation and does it matter? How can we measure it? What are its policy implications? The Centre for the Study of Globalisation and Regionalisation at the University of Warwick is an international site for the study of key questions such as these in the theory and practice of globalisation and regionalisation. Its agenda is avowedly interdisciplinary. The work of the Centre will be showcased in this series.

This series comprises two strands:

Warwick Studies in Globalisation addresses the needs of students and teachers, and the titles will be published in hardback and paperback. Titles include:

Globalisation and the Asia-Pacific
Contested territories
Edited by Kris Olds, Peter Dicken, Philip F. Kelly, Lily Kong and Henry Wai-chung Yeung

Regulating the Global Information Society
Edited by Christopher Marsden

Banking on Knowledge
The genesis of the global development network
Edited by Diane Stone

Historical Materialism and Globalisation
Edited by Hazel Smith and Mark Rupert

Civil Society and Global Finance
Edited by Jan Aart Scholte with Albrecht Schnabel

Towards a Global Polity
Edited by Morten Ougaard and Richard Higgott

New Regionalisms in the Global Political Economy
Theories and cases
Edited by Shaun Breslin, Christopher W. Hughes, Nicola Phillips and Ben Rosamond

Development Issues in Global Governance
Public–private partnerships and market multilateralism
Benedicte Bull and Desmond McNeill

Globalizing Democracy
Political parties in emerging democracies
Edited by Peter Burnell

The Globalization of Political Violence
Globalization's shadow
Edited by Richard Devetak and Christopher W. Hughes

Regionalisation and Global Governance
The taming of globalisation?
Edited by Andrew F. Cooper, Christopher W. Hughes and Philippe De Lombaerde

Global Finance in Crisis
The politics of international regulatory change
Edited by Eric Helleiner, Stefano Pagliari and Hubert Zimmermann

Business and Global Governance
Edited by Morten Ougaard and Anna Leander

Routledge/Warwick Studies in Globalisation is a forum for innovative new research intended for a high-level specialist readership, and the titles will be available in hardback only. Titles include:

1. Non-State Actors and Authority in the Global System
Edited by Richard Higgott, Geoffrey Underhill and Andreas Bieler

2. Globalisation and Enlargement of the European Union
Austrian and Swedish social forces in the struggle over membership
Andreas Bieler

3. Rethinking Empowerment
Gender and development in a global/local world
Edited by Jane L. Parpart, Shirin M. Rai and Kathleen Staudt

4. Globalising Intellectual Property Rights
The TRIPs agreement
Duncan Matthews

5. Globalisation, Domestic Politics and Regionalism
The ASEAN free trade area
Helen E. S. Nesadurai

6. Microregionalism and Governance in East Asia
Katsuhiro Sasuga

7. Global Knowledge Networks and International Development
Edited by Diane Stone and Simon Maxwell

8. Globalisation and Economic Security in East Asia
Governance and institutions
Edited by Helen E. S Nesadurai

9. Regional Integration in East Asia and Europe
Convergence or divergence?
Edited by Bertrand Fort and Douglas Webber

Business and Global Governance

Edited by
Morten Ougaard
and Anna Leander

Routledge
Taylor & Francis Group

LONDON AND NEW YORK

CENTRE FOR THE
STUDY OF
GLOBALISATION AND
REGIONALISATION

First published 2010
by Routledge
2 Park Square Milton Park Abingdon, Oxon, OX14 4RN

Simultaneously published in the USA and Canada
by Routledge
270 Madison Avenue, New York, NY 10016

Routledge is an imprint of the Taylor & Francis Group,
an informa business

Typeset in Times New Roman by Glyph International Ltd.
Printed and bound in Great Britain by TJ International Ltd, Padstow,
Cornwall

British Library Cataloguing in Publication Data
A catalogue record for this book is available from the British Library

Library of Congress Cataloging in Publication Data
Business and global governance/edited by Morten Ougaard and
Anna Leander. – 1st ed.
p. cm. – (Routledge/Warwick studies in globalization)
Includes bibliographical references and index.
1. International business enterprises. 2. International cooperation.
I. Ougaard, Morten. II. Leander, Anna.
HD2755.5.B874 2010
338.8′8–dc22   2009049717

ISBN: 978-0-415-49336-9 (hbk)
ISBN: 978-0-415-49337-6 (pbk)
ISBN: 978-0-203-85026-8 (ebk)

Contents

Figures and tables

Figures

Table

Contributors

Benedicte Bull is Associate Professor at the Centre for Development and the Environment at the University of Oslo. She is the author of *Aid, Power and Privatization* (Edgard Elgar, 2005), *Development Issues in Global Governance: Public–Private Partnerships and Market Multilateralism* (Routledge, 2007, with Desmond McNeill), *International Development* (Sage, 2010, with Morten Bøås) and various articles published in, inter alia, *Third World Quarterly*, *Global Governance*, *New Political Economy*, *Journal of Latin American Studies* and *Governance & Regulation*.

Andrew F. Cooper is Associate Director and Distinguished Fellow at the Centre for International Governance Innovation (CIGI) and Professor in the Department of Political Science at the University of Waterloo, Ontario, Canada. In 2009 he held the Fulbright Research Chair in Public Diplomacy at the Annenberg School of Communications, University of Southern California. He has authored or edited some 20 books, including *Celebrity Diplomacy* (Paradigm, 2008).

A. Claire Cutler is Professor of International Relations and International Law in the Political Science Department at the University of Victoria, Victoria, British Columbia, Canada. She specializes in the intersection of international law and international politics and is engaged in developing a critical political economy analysis of public and private international law. Her current research project involves analysis of the privatization and commodification of international security.

Robert Falkner is Senior Lecturer in International Relations at the London School of Economics and Political Science. He is an Associate of the Grantham Research Institute on Climate Change and the Environment at the LSE and an Associate Fellow of the Energy, Environment and Development Programme at Chatham House. His most recent publications include *Business Power and Conflict in International Environmental Politics* (Palgrave, 2008) and *The International Politics of Genetically Modified Food: Diplomacy, Trade and Law* (ed.) (Palgrave, 2007).

Annegret Flohr at the Peace Research Institute Frankfurt and a PhD candidate at Technische Universität Darmstadt, Germany. Her research interests revolve around global governance, international law and the role of non-state actors in international politics. Her dissertation analyses the impact of self-regulation on international legalization in the banking sector and features case studies of the Wolfsberg and Equator principles. She is a co-author of 'The Role of Business in Global Governance' (Palgrave, 2010).

Hans Krause Hansen holds a PhD from the University of Copenhagen and is Associate Professor at the Department of Intercultural Communication and Management, Copenhagen Business School. His current research revolves around the study of private actors and private sector practices in global politics and focuses specifically on the role of corruption and anti-corruption in global governance.

Anna Leander is Professor at the Copenhagen Business School. She works with sociological approaches to international political economy and international relations and has focused on commercial security practices. She has recently published *Constructivism in International Relations* (with Stefano Guzzini) (Routledge, 2006) and 'Securing Sovereignty by Governing Security through Markets'. For further information see www.cbs.dk/staff/ale.

Christopher May is Professor of Political Economy and Associate Dean of the Faculty of Arts and Social Sciences at Lancaster University. He has published widely on intellectual property rights, including the first independent book-length study of the World Intellectual Property Organisation (Routledge, 2007). His latest book is an extensively revised second edition of *The Global Political Economy of Intellectual Property Rights: New Enclosures* (Routledge, 2009). He also edited *Global Corporate Power* (Lynne Rienner, 2005) and has published work on the music industry, digital rights management and the information society.

Craig N. Murphy is M. Margaret Ball Professor of International Relations at Wellesley College, Massachusetts, and past-president of the International Studies Association. His most recent books include (with JoAnne Yates) *The International Organization for Standardization: Global Governance through Voluntary Consensus* (Routledge, 2009) and *The UN Development Programme: A Better Way?* (Cambridge University Press, 2006).

Andreas Nölke is Professor of Political Science, in particular International Relations and International Political Economy, at Goethe University Frankfurt. He is co-editor of 'The Transnational Politics of Corporate Governance Regulation' (2007) and 'Transnational Private Governance and its Limits' (2008) and has published in journals such as *World Politics*, *Review of International Political Economy* and *Journal of Common Market Studies*.

Morten Ougaard is Professor of International Political Economy and Director of the BSc and MSc programs in International Business and Politics at Copenhagen

Business School. He co-edited *Towards a Global Polity* (Routledge, 2002) with Richard Higgot and his most recent book is *Political Globalization* (Palgrave,2004).

Lothar Rieth works as a Research Associate at the Department of Political Science, Technische Universität Darmstadt. His doctoral dissertation focused on 'Global Governance and Corporate Social Responsibility' and the effectiveness of self-regulatory initiatives. He has published a number of articles on the role of non-state actors and new modes of governance. Moreover, he is interested in new teaching methodologies, linking theory and practice. As an expert in the field of corporate social responsibility he provides policy advice to international and national institutions.

Sandra Schwindenhammer is a Research Associate in the Department of International Politics at FernUniversität in Hagen, Germany. From 2005 to 2008 she worked at the Department for International Relations at Technische Universität Darmstadt on the research project 'Corporations as Norm-entrepreneurs?' She holds a Master Degree and graduated in political science, sociology and law at Technische Universität Darmstadt in 2005. Her research focus lies on global governance, corporate social responsibility (CSR) and sustainability reporting. In her PhD dissertation, she is analysing the impact of home-state conditions on corporate contributions to governance in the Global Reporting Initiative.

Heather Taylor is a Research Associate specializing in International Political Economy at Goethe University Frankfurt. She has also worked at the University of Kassel, the Friedrich Ebert Foundation in Germany and most recently at the Sadar Patel Institute for Economic and Social Research in Ahmadabad, India. Her research is primarily focused on the impact of post-acquisition strategies of Indian MNEs on work systems and industrial relations and her publications include several book chapters and journal articles on these issues.

Eleni Tsingou is Research Fellow at the Centre for the Study of Globalisation and Regionalisation, University of Warwick, UK. Her research focuses on global banking regulation and transnational private governance, transnational policy communities and the global anti-money-laundering regime and the fight against terrorist financing, and her work has appeared in several edited collections. She is also Programme Manager of GARNET, an EU-funded project on 'Global Governance, Regionalisation and Regulation: The Role of the EU'.

Klaus Dieter Wolf is Deputy Director of the Peace Research Institute Frankfurt (PRIF). He holds the Chair for International Relations at Technische Universität Darmstadt, Germany, and is also one of the Principal Investigators of the Cluster of Excellence 'Formation of Normative Orders'. He was President of the German Political Science Association (DVPW) from 2003 to 2006. His fields of research include questions of legitimate governance beyond the state, with special emphasis on the role of non-state actors. His recent publications include *The Role of Business in Global Governance* (co-authored with

Annegret Flohr, Lothar Rieth and Sandra Schwindenhammer) and *Corporate Security Responsibility?* (co-edited with Nicole Deitelhoff).

JoAnne Yates is Sloan Distinguished Professor of Management and Deputy Dean of MIT's Sloan School of Management. Her most recent books include (with Craig N. Murphy) *The International Organization for Standardization: Global Governance through Voluntary Consensus* (Routledge, 2009) and *Structuring the Information Age: Life Insurance and Technology in the Twentieth Century* (Johns Hopkins University Press, 2005 and 2008).

Preface

This volume grew out of a workshop entitled: "Theorizing Business and Global Governance" at Copenhagen Business School in November 2007. The workshop had been in the making for some time, spurred both by our research interests and our teaching commitments. Working in the broad field of international political economy, we naturally were interested in many questions relating to business and global governance. We also took notice of the rich proliferation, in recent years, of research that has a focus on business and global governance and of the great theoretical diversity involved. In teaching, since 2003 we both have been involved in the creation and running of two new educational programs at the Copenhagen Business School: a Bachelor and a Master degree in International Business and Politics. These programs have strong elements of politics, international relations and international political economy, taught in combination with more conventional business school courses.

Out of these experiences came our conviction that it would be useful for scholars, and for advanced students in international relations programs and in business schools, to have a book that focused on business and global governance: a volume that would explore different aspects of the mutual engagement between business and global governance, present recent theoretical advances and contributions to the analysis of such aspects, and thereby also contribute to an overview and a more rounded picture of the business global governance nexus. With this in mind, we invited colleagues to the workshop and initiated the process that now has resulted in the present volume.

Along the way we have incurred a number of debts. One is to all the people who have commented and provided ideas to this project. This includes the participants in the original CBS workshop and the ISA panels that followed: the contributors to this volume as well as Brigitte Hamm, Helge Hveem, Jan Aart Scholte, Leonard Seabrooke and Arthur Mühlen-Schulte. We also want to acknowledge the constructive and helpful comments made by the students in the International Business and Politics Program who commented on a selection of the chapters. Finally, we are very grateful to Swati Chaudry and especially Øystein Lønsettig for diligent and careful editorial assistance. Another kind of debt is to those who have made this possible. This includes in particular the EU network of excellence,

GARNET, which supported the original idea and the CBS workshop, the CBS and particularly Dorte Salskov-Iversen, the head of our department – Intercultural Communication and Management – who agreed to host the workshop and, of course, Lynne Dunne, our patient and helpful editor.

Anna Leander and Morten Ougaard

1 Introducing business and global governance[1]

Morten Ougaard

Introduction

Business and global governance is an important and multifaceted topic. This is evident from even a cursory look at the current global agenda with the unfolding financial and economic crises, the politics of climate change, and the persistent problems of poverty and development. The influence of the financial industry on international regulation is blamed as one reason for the crisis; multilateral efforts at strengthening financial regulation have been launched by governments and international institutions; private credit rating agencies are criticized for the impact of their ratings, international bodies such as the G20 and the G8 are discussing how governments can stimulate business and restart growth without resorting to protectionism; much of the politics of climate change is about changing productive practices in the private sector; and, under headings like corporate social responsibility and public–private partnerships, efforts are made to mobilize business for addressing a range of problems concerned with development, human rights and environmental sustainability.

Unquestionably, business and global governance are central features of world society in the era of globalization. Over the last decades, international trade in goods and services has grown faster than world production, and foreign direct investment by transnational corporations (TNCs) has continued to rise, so that in 2008 "an estimated 79,000 TNCs control some 790,000 foreign affiliates in the world economy" and "the value added activity of foreign affiliates worldwide accounted for 11% of global GDP in 2007" (UNCTAD 2008: 9). The immensely increased global economic interconnectedness represented by private business is a profound characteristic of the contemporary world order. At the same time, the *Yearbook of International Organizations 2007/2008* listed 970 active intergovernmental international bodies and registered no less than 2376 "multilateral treaties and intergovernmental agreements" (Union of International Associations 2007: 2996). These numbers do not include less formalized and private arrangements such as voluntary codes of conduct, but they do provide a clear indicator of the extensive network of international and global governance arrangements existing in the global political economy.

Generally, across many policy areas, global governance arrangements address business practices with incentives, support and regulations; international institutions provide legal and institutional preconditions for international business; business has influence on governance arrangements, directly and indirectly; business practices may by themselves generate governance effects; and cooperation between businesses, other non-state actors and public institutions is seen as a solution to many problems. In short, as Levy and Kaplan put it: multinational corporations "have, *de facto*, become part of the fabric of global governance" (Levy and Kaplan 2008: 433) and the business and global governance nexus – the multiple ways in which business and global governance interact, impact on, and condition each other – is a multifaceted and increasingly important phenomenon.

This book is about analyzing different aspects of this business–global governance nexus. It aims to show how such aspects are identified, conceptualized and analyzed by different scholars who share the interest in business and global governance, but who approach it with diverse conceptual frameworks and from different theoretical perspectives. In other words, the book is based on theoretical pluralism and diversity, but unified by the shared ambition to advance theory building and empirical research on the mutual engagements between business and global governance. Thus the volume presents different theoretical takes on the ways in which business directly and indirectly impacts global governance arrangements, including perspectives on ways in which business practices by themselves have governance effects; it presents contributions to the analysis of how global regulations of business are created and changed, and it presents perspectives on ways in which businesses are mobilized as partners in global governance arrangements through voluntary efforts and partnership arrangements. These themes do not constitute separate theoretical perspectives on the topic; rather, they are different aspects of the business–global governance nexus that represent different emphases in scholars' research interests, each of which can be pursued from different theoretical positions.

First, however, this introduction will survey the literature for contributions to the analysis of business and global governance. On the one hand it only recently has become a central research theme in its own right, but on the other hand there is a long history of scholarly interest in aspects of the topic. This interest, however, appeared in different and separate scholarly communities, as evidenced by the following quotes from what arguably was the first comprehensive discussion of international governance arrangements pertaining to business, namely *The Rules of the Game in the Global Economy: Policy Regimes for International Business* (Preston and Windsor 1992; 1997). The authors set themselves the task of combining "themes and topics from two major fields of knowledge, international relations (a branch of political science) and international business." They described these two fields as follows:

> The international relations and international political economy literature is primarily theory-focused and state-centered; its principal emphasis is

on relationships among governments. [...] it gives little attention to the internal dynamics of industries and business enterprises. The international business literature is, of course, typically enterprise- or industry-centered, but its treatment of the surrounding policy environment is typically descriptive, institutional and static. It gives little attention to the origins and evolution of the various policy regimes governing international business operations, the connections among such regimes, or the role of business in shaping them.

(xiii–xiv)

This assessment was undoubtedly correct at the time, although the publication of *Rival States – Rival Firms* (Stopford *et al.* 1991) had signaled that things were beginning to change. Today business and global governance constitutes a rich and complex field of inquiry with many contributions from both of the literatures mentioned by Preston and Windsor.

What follows is an overview of major contributions to this field, providing a context for the following chapters. It is also intended as an introduction to each of these two bodies of literature to readers unfamiliar with one or both of them. First, the introduction takes a brief look at early beginnings in the 1960s and 1970s. Then it surveys the business literature, focusing on theories on international business strategies and investment decisions because of the utility of these contributions for understanding business interests towards national and international governance arrangements. It moves on to the diverse universe of international relations and international politics, looking at contributions to the analysis of international governance arrangements pertaining to business, under the headline "Policy regimes for international business" borrowed from Preston and Windsor (1992, 1997). The purpose here is not to recount the intense theoretical debates that have characterized this area, but rather to identify some of the main insights developed concerning the creation (or non-creation), evolution and change of such policy regimes. The context here is still what could be called the general theory of regimes and international institutions, and therefore the fourth section goes on to focus on contributions that have put the role of business in global governance more squarely at the center of interest. Finally, the introduction presents the subsequent chapters.

Beginnings

The interest in issues related to business and global governance can be traced back many decades. Although a dominant strand of research in international politics, realism, focused mainly on military and security matters – according to Hans Morgenthau (1973) "politics among nations" was a "struggle for power and peace" and not, for instance, for wealth and welfare – early on several debates and themes emerged with a focus on economic issues. Richard Cooper's *The Economics of Interdependence* (1968) marked the beginning of an interest in the international politics of economic issues, in particular the politics of trade and international monetary matters. It also introduced the notion of *interdependence* as an important feature of international relations, in addition and correction to realism's emphasis on *anarchy* as a defining feature.

Cooper's work was followed by several studies that focused on the politics of the international economy (Bergsten and Krause 1975; Kindleberger 1970; Spero 1977), studies of *economic aspects of foreign policy* such as Susan Strange's study of monetary aspects of British foreign policy (Strange 1971), and the study of policy problems presented to the US by the international expansion of American companies (Bergsten *et al.* 1978). Much of this work shared a state-centered focus with realism and dealt with the economy in aggregate terms – it was about national and international policies towards markets in goods and capital – but some also began to see private actors, including business, as relevant for international politics. Thus the economic and political activities of multinational corporations were one of several kinds of *transnational relations* singled out for study in Robert Keohane and Joseph Nye's *Transnational Relations and World Politics* (1972) and these authors maintained this element in their landmark study of *Power and Interdependence* (1977) which initiated what later became known as the *liberal institutionalist approach* to international relations. This book also gave central attention to the concept of *international regimes*, in particular regimes concerning economic matters, which became the central designator for international governance arrangements of the kind that later scholarship would group together under the heading of international and global governance.

In a related development, researchers also had begun to study the *transnational corporations* in their own right. Scholars were describing and classifying their internal organization and their strategies, seeking explanations for their strategic choices and more generally asking why they were becoming a steadily more salient feature in the world economy. An important figure in these early years was Stephen Hymer, "the undisputed pioneer" according to Peter Dicken (2003: 202). Among other things, Hymer mapped the major types of foreign operations: wholly-owned subsidiary, majority-owned subsidiary, joint venture, minority interest, licensing arrangement and tacit collusion (Hymer 1976: 65), and posed the central explanatory question of why companies chose one of these forms instead of arms-length market relations to suppliers or customers in foreign countries, suggesting that the answer had to do with control; for instance in order to reduce competition, to exploit advantages, to step over barriers between countries, or to avoid exchange rate risk (Hymer 1976: 33–48).

Another significant contribution to these early studies in multinational companies was Raymond Vernon's *Sovereignty at Bay* (1971) which among other things introduced the notion of *the product cycle* to explain patterns in FDI. A few years later, Barnet and Müller's *Global Reach* (1974) offered a rich description of TNC activities and a discussion of many policy issues, economic and political, posed by them for home and host countries. By then such issues had become quite contentious in political debates.

In the US, where opposition to the Vietnam War and other elements in US foreign policy was growing, critics such as Gabriel Kolko had argued that business interests and particularly the interests of American transnational corporations were the dominant force in shaping policy (Kolko 1969). In Europe, the French journalist and politician Jean-Jacques Servan-Schreiber warned in 1967 against *Le défi américain*, "the American challenge," pointing to the rapid growth in Europe of affiliates of American companies and expressing grave concerns about the consequences in terms of possible loss of autonomy and a competitive decline of European-owned business (Servan-Schreiber 1967). This was also a time in which developing countries grew increasingly critical of the international economic order in general and the role of transnational corporations in particular. In 1974 they utilized their voting power in the United Nations General Assembly to adopt the *Declaration on the Establishment of a New International Economic Order*, which, among other things, called for "Regulation and supervision of the activities of transnational corporations by taking measures in the interest of the national economies of the countries where such transnational corporations operate on the basis of the full sovereignty of those countries" (United Nations General Assembly 1974).

The practical consequences of this declaration remained negligible; the distance between the regulations sought by the Group of 77 and what developed countries would offer was far too wide. But the declaration signaled that transnational corporations had become thoroughly politicized, and that the impact of their activities for growth, development, welfare and other social objectives in home and host countries, developed as well as developing, had become subject to intense debate. So had also the question of whether and how they should and could be regulated nationally and internationally, discussed for instance in Barnet and Müller (1974) quoted above and in Robert O. Keohane and Van Doorn Ooms' "The multinational firm and international regulation" (1975).

In addition to these three sources of scholarly interest in business and global governance – studies of the politics of international economics, the study of transnational corporations, and the political debates surrounding the international economy and the regulation of TNCs – a fourth source deserves mention. This consisted of critical studies of the international political economy, mainly associated with Marxist theories of imperialism and theories of North–South dependency.

Going back to questions and modes of analysis initiated in the classical theories of imperialism, represented in particular by Hobson, Lenin and Luxembourg (which was being maintained and reproduced in a rather dogmatic fashion by Soviet scholarship), the study of imperialism experienced a renewal in Western Marxism, outside the orbit of communist party orthodoxy. A major area of interest was relations between developed and underdeveloped countries (as developing countries were called then), with Paul Baran's *The Political Economy of Growth* (1957) as an early contribution, later followed by, for instance, Samir Amin's *Accumulation on a World Scale* (1974) and Benjamin Cohen's *The Question of Imperialism: The Political Economy of Dominance and Dependence* (1973). A core question in these and other works was whether mechanisms of the global capitalist economy systematically worked to the disadvantage of the developing countries so that capitalist development would remain a development of underdevelopment. Such notions were not unique to Marxist theories of imperialism; they were also advanced by structural theories of development and dependency (e.g. Cardoso and Faletto 1979; Evans 1979) that focused on unequal international trade relations and on negative developmental consequences of foreign direct investment.

Other issues taken up by critical scholarship were the relations between Third World governments and transnational business (e.g. Evans 1979), a theme that fed into debates about the international regulation of TNCs, and US foreign policy which, for instance by Harry Magdoff in *The Age of Imperialism* (1969), was explained largely as a response to the expansionary drive inherent in American capitalism and transnational corporations. Furthermore, although there was a strong focus on North–South relations and in particular their economic aspects, studies were also made of relations among the developed capitalist countries including studies of the political dimension of these relations. For example, Ernest Mandel published analyses of the process of European integration which situated it in the context of the economic rivalry between Europe and the US (Mandel 1970), and of the international currency crises of the late 1960s and early 1970s (Mandel 1972).

Still, the analysis of international political phenomena in general and international governance arrangements in particular remained at best a sub-theme in critical and Marxist studies and there was a tendency to interpret them as reflective of economic developments. Thus it was largely justified when Keohane and Nye commented that there was no real theory of international regimes in the Marxist literature of the day (Keohane and Nye 1977: ix). Nevertheless, these strands of scholarship are still relevant as precursors to later studies of business and global governance for three reasons: first, for their contribution to bringing economic issues and transnational corporations on the agenda for the study of international relations; secondly, for their continued questioning of the social and developmental benefits of the existing international economic order; and finally, because of their emphasis on applying a systemic perspective to the international political economy, i.e. on seeing the capitalist world as an integrated economic and political system, which remains an important theoretical ambition.

Thus, by the mid-1970s several sub-themes in the business–global governance nexus had been brought onto the agenda for research: the study of international and transnational business enterprises in its own right, the study of international business-related policy regimes and governance arrangements, and the study of the impact of business on foreign policy and international politics. The following sections describe later developments in these areas.

Understanding international business

The literature on international business can, with some simplification, be divided into two major strands. One group consists of management-oriented research that seeks to guide business practices, here labeled the *business literature*, published in dedicated management journals and presented and synthesized in numerous textbooks (e.g. Bartlett et al. 2008; Lasserre 2007). On the other hand there are social science studies, oriented towards theory development *per se* and/or towards informing public policy and often being critical of business. Dicken's (2003) *Global Shift* is an excellent and comprehensive representative. There is, however, a fair amount of overlap and exchange between these two groups, to the extent that both of them conduct and build upon empirical observations of business practices. Hence both groups can and do use insights developed by the other, and many contributions have a dual use: they can be applied in explanatory analyses of why companies act as they do, and they can be useful for guiding business practitioners.

All of the business literature arguably is contributing to the analysis of one basic problem: how to maximize profits by combining in the best possible way the purchase of inputs – capital goods, raw materials and labor –, the organization of production processes, the distribution and sale of the resulting products or services, and the financing of the whole venture. For some business economists the core of this endeavor is formalized analysis based on micro-economic models, but many have found this insufficient, and business studies have branched out considerably into a varied set of subfields, applying theories and approaches from several social science disciplines. The ongoing evolution of TNC studies is also, naturally, a response to the dynamism of the subject: business enterprises are inherently expansive and innovative, in constant search of new opportunities to enhance their competitive position and maximize profits.

In the context of understanding the business and global governance nexus, some of the most relevant insights developed in these literatures are those that focus on overall business strategies and organizational forms. They are useful because they help one to understand how the TNC universe evolves and, in particular, because they are valuable tools for understanding the diverse, multifaceted and changing interests TNCs have in relation to national and international policies and regulatory frameworks.

Explaining foreign direct investment

An early contribution was the *product cycle theory*, originally developed in the analysis of business evolution in the US but brought to the study of international business by Raymond Vernon (1971). This theory was focused on investment in industrial production, whereas investment in raw materials extraction had other explanations. According to the theory, an industry goes through a cycle from innovation to maturity and finally decline as the product or technology is overtaken by new innovations. In the first stage the industry is developed in and produces for the home market, but as the industry matures the home market becomes saturated and expansion abroad begins. First this happens through exports, mediated by foreign agents, then the industry establishes its own sales outlets abroad, and eventually it becomes advantageous to establish production abroad through direct investment.

Empirically this cycle captured much of what was happening. But in itself it does not explain why companies choose to invest abroad rather than supplying foreign markets through exports or, for instance, licensing agreements with foreign producers. One answer to this given by Vernon was that it was a response to foreign competition; FDI would enable the company to exploit the cost advantages – such as cheaper labor – that foreign competitors had. Another pioneer in the study of TNCs, Stephen Hymer, gave a more general answer: companies chose direct investment in order to obtain and maintain *control*, which could be in order to reduce competition, to exploit their advantages in a more secure way, to step over barriers between countries such as high tariffs, and to avoid exchange rate risks (Hymer 1976).

Thinking along these lines has evolved considerably since then. An important contribution is John Dunning's *OLI paradigm*, also known as *the eclectic theory* of FDI (Dunning 2000, 2001). It is debated whether this really is a genuine theory or merely a list of explanatory factors, but it is undoubtedly a successful synthesis of several such factors that are frequently used in explanations of investment decisions (Dicken 2003; Dunning 2001). According to the theory, a direct investment is preferable to arms-length market relations with foreign suppliers or customers due to a combination of three kinds of advantages, namely *ownership-specific* advantages, *location-specific* advantages, and *internalization-specific* advantages.

Ownership or O-advantages are resources or assets the company controls that are not accessible to competitors. They can, for instance, be technology and patents, brands and trademarks, unique organizational and management capabilities and other kinds of know-how. *L-advantages* are specific to the *location* where the investment is done. They can derive from market size or geographical proximity to large markets, unique or cheap raw materials or energy sources, low labor costs or a workforce with particular skills, and political factors such as benign regulatory frameworks or tax levels. Finally, *internalization* advantages refer to the circumstances that make it preferable to *internalize* activities in the company's own organization rather than relying on market transactions or licensing agreements. I-advantages typically are about reducing transaction costs such as the costs of screening the market for reliable suppliers, of finding reliable partners for licensing agreements, or of developing sufficiently secure contracts with business partners.

Another, partly overlapping, way of examining international business expansion is to look for the *motivations* behind them. In the early days of TNC studies, a single distinction between raw materials and market-seeking investments was sufficient, but since then a more differentiated picture has emerged. A contemporary management text, for instance, discusses the following motives (Bartlett et al. 2008: 4–7):

– secure key supplies, e.g. minerals, agricultural inputs, energy sources;
– access low-cost factors of production, in particular labor;

- access advanced product and process technologies; and
- competitive positioning.

The last motive – competitive positioning – is related to the nature of business strategies in a world of oligopolistic competition. Here investment decisions may not only reflect "market attractiveness or cost–efficiency choices, but also the leverage such investments provided over competitors" (Bartlett et al. 2008: 7). An investment may not be attractive (i.e. profitable) in itself but may still be considered worthwhile because it helps to close a certain path of action to competitors. Thus international investments can be undertaken to "defend worldwide dominance" or "challenging the global leader," or to "protect domestic niches" (Bartlett et al. 2008: 207f).

Clusters and competitive environments

The first three of these motives – supplies, factors of production, technologies – are directly related to L-advantages. An important contribution to the understanding of these is the notion of *industrial clusters* (also called *business clusters*), introduced and popularized by Michael Porter (1990, 1998; see also Krugman 1991). Porter describes the phenomenon in the following terms: "Clusters are geographic concentrations of interconnected companies and institutions in a particular field." They "encompass an array of linked industries and other entities," for example "suppliers of specialized inputs such as components, machinery and services, and providers of specialized infrastructure," and they extend "to companies in industries related by skills, technologies, or common inputs." They also often include "governmental and other institutions – such as universities, standards-setting agencies, think tanks, vocational training providers, and trade associations – that provide specialized training, education, information, research, and technical support" (Porter 1998: 78).

Examples of successful clusters are found in Germany in "chemicals, metal-working, transportation and printing" where, in each case, "the nation is inter-nationally successful in finished goods, machinery used in producing the goods, specialized inputs and often related services" (Porter 1990: 149). Other examples are the film and entertainment cluster in Hollywood, the IT cluster in Silicon Valley, and the Danish bio-tech cluster linking the dairy, brewery and meat-processing industries with the pharmaceutical industry in a complex network of supply relationships, common inputs and common technologies and skills (Porter 1990: 150, fig. 4-5).

A key point in Porter's theory is that clusters have a strong internal dynamism: "Once a cluster forms, the whole group of industries becomes mutually supporting. Benefits flow forward, backwards, and horizontally" (Porter 1990: 151). These dynamic inter-linkages depend strongly on *geographical proximity* and therefore, more generally, competitive companies tend to have key activities located in successful clusters, so that "the phenomenon of industry clustering is so pervasive that it appears to be a central feature of advanced national economies" (Porter 1990: 149). This is significant for understanding the location decisions of TNCs: L-advantages are not only a question of raw materials, low-cost factors of production, or markets; companies also invest in order to tap into the general dynamism of a successful cluster and to access both tangible and intangible assets specific to it. This further makes clear, for instance, why certain locations are attractive for some companies and not for others: a successful fashion and apparel cluster and an IT cluster will attract rather different kinds of investment. The insights of cluster theory also help one to understand why the upgrading of production in less developed areas and countries is a complex issue.

Global value chains

In addition to the cluster approach, however, another geographical perspective on international economic activity has proven useful. This is the concept of *global value chains*, value-added chains or commodity chains; "different researchers use different terminology to discuss very similar ideas" (Gereffi et al. 2001: 2). According to one of the first presentations of this perspective, it is "a surprisingly easy yet powerful concept" (Kogut 1985a: 16). A finished product is the result of several stages in a process that goes from raw materials through the production of components to their assembly and on to marketing, sales, and retail distribution. In each of these steps value is added to the final product, but, significantly, some steps add more value than others. Moreover, companies engaged in oligopolistic competition tend to pursue strategies that allow them to obtain *rent*, in this context defined as profits above the market average, for instance by utilizing O-advantages (a terminology not used by Kogut) that are not available to competitors. Therefore companies will be particularly interested in those links in a value chain where the potential for rents is high.

Kogut combined this with an understanding of L-advantages (again without using Dunning's terminology), leading him to argue that the strategic challenge for an international company is to *combine* an assessment of the comparative advantage of nations – where is the best location for a specific link in the chain? – with the competitive advantage of the company – in which link does the company have the best potential for earning rents? Therefore, certain links in the value chain will be attractive for a company, but only if located in the right place, i.e. a strong cluster; and, conversely, a location will be attractive but only for specific links in a certain value chain.

This implies that on one hand there can be a tendency for companies to control the entire value chain to exploit I- and O-advantages, but on the other hand there can be an opposing tendency for companies to focus only on the highest value-added links in the chain, and to *out-source* the rest – or perhaps to focus on intermediate products that allow the extraction of rents from several value chains. This also underscores a point often emphasized by John Dunning, namely that the ways in which companies juggle these different concerns strategically are strongly dependent on context and vary significantly among them.

It also means that global value chains differ considerably. Generally, as a result of the substantial deepening of the international division of labor that has taken place over many decades, itself also partly a result of TNC activity, many finished products are now resulting from production processes that span many countries and regions of the world. For example, in 1999 Francis Snyder portrayed the production of Barbie Dolls, a fairly simple product, as follows: "China provides the factory space, labor and electricity, as well as cotton cloth for the dress." Hence the label says "Made in China." But

> Japan supplies the nylon hair, Saudi Arabia provides oil, Taiwan refines oil into ethylene for plastic pellets for the body, Japan, the US, and Europe supply almost all the machinery and tools, most of the moulds (the most expensive item) come from the US, Japan, or Hong Kong, the United States supplies cardboard packaging and paint pigments, and Hong Kong supplies the banking and insurance and carries out the delivery of the raw materials to factories in Guangdong Province in South China, together with the collection of the finished products and shipping. Two Barbie dolls are marketed every second in 140 countries around the world by Mattel Inc. of California.
>
> (Snyder 1999: 337)

In a similar but vastly more complex fashion, products like PCs, automobiles or airplanes involve raw materials, machinery, components, design and research services, as well as financial, insurance and consultancy services and other inputs that are sourced from multiple locations in many countries (see Dicken 2003 for an analysis of commodity chains in different industries).

How are value chains organized and governed? In early studies of TNCs this was answered with a simple distinction between *markets* and *hierarchies* in which some chains (or parts of chains) were characterized by market relations between independent business entities, whereas others were internalized in large corporations and governed by their hierarchical management structure. But analysts of value chains have found this insufficient. One reason is that even in the case of market relations some companies are much more influential than others so that "some firms in the chain set and/or enforce the parameters under which others in the chain operate" (Humphrey and Schmitz 2001: 2). Thus chains can be dominated by a "lead firm," and this insight led Gereffi (1994) to introduce the distinction between *producer-driven chains*, such as the automobile industry that is dominated by large car companies, and *buyer-driven chains*, exemplified by the Barbie Doll chain where the design and marketing company Martell owns the brand name but is not directly involved in the actual manufacturing of dolls.

In more general terms, then, the governance of a value chain is understood as the "inter-firm relationships and institutional mechanisms through which coordination of activities in the chain take place" (Gereffi et al. 2005). The analysis of such relationships and mechanisms has been further developed to capture the variation found between the two opposing poles of hierarchies and competitive situations with many suppliers and/or buyers. Thus, according to Gereffi, Humphrey and

Sturgeon, in addition to markets and hierarchies there is a variety of *network governance* types that differ in terms of the level of explicit coordination and power asymmetries among companies (Gereffi et al. 2005). Explicit coordination mechanisms found in such networks can be long-term contracts between buyers and suppliers where suppliers produce to the buyers' specifications, or licensing agreements. But coordination can also take place through enduring informal relationships between firms, based on trust and reputation, and perhaps "tied to dispersed family and social groups." The key point is that "co-ordination and control of global-scale production systems, despite their complexity, can be achieved without direct ownership" (Gereffi et al. 2005: 81).

Organizing transnational business

Seen from the perspective of an individual company, the organization of a value chain depends strongly on the choices made on how to enter foreign countries, what is known as *entry modes* in the business literature. Depending on the nature of the company's interest in a specific location, it will choose among the multiple available modes. Thus, according to one textbook discussion, in situations where the company wants a limited investment and is little concerned with control, it typically will rely on arm's length agreements with distributors or agents, or use licensing or franchising agreements or the like. A higher degree of control can be achieved by establishing, for instance, a marketing subsidiary, a procurement office, or a technical observatory, perhaps created to tap into know-how in a successful cluster. When it wants full control and a strong investment commitment, the choices will be a wholly or majority owned subsidiary, which can be established through a *greenfield investment* (building a new facility where none existed), by the acquisition of an existing company (*brownfield investment*), or by entering a *joint venture* with an existing company with majority ownership (Lasserre 2007: 195ff). These are merely typical forms; in practice business arrangements can be more complex and combine more than one of the modes mentioned here.

If the organization of value chains is a complex matter, this is also the case for the *internal* organization of a transnational company and its multiple relations to suppliers and customers. It is a constant management challenge to organize relations between headquarters, subsidiaries and partners in a way that maximizes flexibility, utilizes OLI advantages, and responds to changing framework conditions, with a view to maximizing long-term profits. In the words of a management textbook:

> The transnational company must create the ability to sense and analyze the numerous and often conflicting opportunities, pressures, and demands it faces worldwide. Strong *national subsidiary management* is needed to sense and represent the changing needs of local consumers and the increasing pressures from host governments; capable *global business management* is required to track the strategy of global competitors and provide the coordination to respond appropriately; and influential *worldwide functional management* is

needed to concentrate corporate knowledge, information, and expertise and facilitate their transfer among organizational units.

(Bartlett et al. 2008: 340)

Thus, within the company, it is a challenge to find the right balance between global and local decision-making authority and to decide whether the primary chain of command is defined along geographical lines (from global to regional to country managers), product lines (one global chain of command for each product), or functional specializations (i.e. one globally centralized organization for, respectively, research and development, procurement, production, marketing, accounting etc.). The business literature is rich in discussions of ways in which companies have addressed such issues more or less successfully.

The rise of the political manager

The theories and concepts presented here – the product cycle, the OLI paradigm, the motivations for investing abroad, the notions of industrial clusters and global value chains, strategic positioning in oligopolistic competition, entry modes and organizational challenges – are important contributions to the understanding of the evolution of transnational business. They are useful analytical tools for explaining individual investment decisions and for understanding overall business strategies. They are, naturally, to be seen in the context of the inherent growth and profit-maximizing imperatives of capitalist enterprise. Together these notions help elucidate how and why transnational business is a very diverse universe but also one that represents a force for continued economic growth and the ongoing integration of the world economy through a continuous deepening of the international division of labor.

In the context of business and global governance, however, these theories are relevant and important because they shed light on the fact that business interests in relation to political authorities and regulatory frameworks can be quite diverse because companies operate in many jurisdictions and in value chains that cross national borders. Companies can be interested in low labor costs, low taxation and lax regulation, but they can also be interested in government support, in public upgrading of industrial clusters through infrastructure, education and research, or in direct subsidies. Companies that have developed high standards in a particular area in the home countries may be better able to utilize their O and I advantages if they apply the same standards in host countries and may therefore improve their competitive position if host countries heighten their standards, and so on. Thus, while *regulatory arbitrage* – optimizing profits by playing on regulatory differences between countries – is an integrated element in the strategies of many large companies (see Kogut 1985b), the theories on TNC behavior explain why this is not necessarily or always leading to a regulatory *race to the bottom*.

In the same manner, business interests towards global governance arrangements can vary considerably. While it is true that most international businesses generally are oriented towards economic openness – free movement across borders of goods, services and capital – there are also many situations where companies and industries are interested in restrictions, protection and subsidies. What cannot be doubted, however, is that national and international business regulation and governance arrangements – the political and regulatory framework conditions – are of strategic interest to international business. One clear reflection of this is what Michael Useem called "the rise of the political manager" (Useem 1985). Useem argued that "company initiatives in the areas of social responsibility, public affairs, and political action have evolved from *ad hoc* responses to systematic strategies" (Useem 1984: 24), making such issues a distinct management discipline supported by dedicated textbooks (e.g. Baron 2002).

If business has obvious reasons to be interested in national and international governance arrangements, the converse is equally true. Many such arrangements relate to business, and a large body of literature has evolved that is relevant for the analysis of what Preston and Windsor (1997) called "policy regimes for international business."

Policy regimes for international business

Looming large in this literature is the sustained effort in research and theory building represented by the neo-liberal institutionalist study of international organizations and regimes. It can be said to represent an effort to build a "general theory of regimes," concerned with international institutions in all policy areas including but not limited to those relating to business, but naturally having relevance for the latter subset of international institutions.

Students of international relations will be familiar with the central role played by this effort and with the pioneering contributions from Keohane, Nye and Krasner (Keohane 1984, 1989; Keohane and Nye 1977; Krasner 1983). Equally well known are the debates between this strand of research and realism and constructivism, widely seen as the most important theoretical debates among students of international politics and international political economy (for overviews see Hasenclever et al. (2000), which also presents a synthesis, and Simmons and Martin (2002), and for a constructivist critique Ruggie (1998)). These debates are concerned with basic issues in social ontology, i.e. assumptions about society, states and other actors, and with different strategies for theory-building, for instance formal model-building and hypothesis-testing versus historical interpretation. In the present context there is no reason to recount these debates in any detail, although some of them must be touched upon, in particular the question of understanding state preferences towards international institutions. But the primary purpose is to point to some of the key insights developed in these contributions and the debates between them.

One important early step was to move beyond the study of formal international organizations and include a variety of more or less formalized cooperative arrangements between governments under the label of institutions. Thus in one definition international institutions include formal organizations, regimes and conventions, the latter understood in its sociological sense (Keohane 1989: 3–5).

This means for instance that what has been termed "soft law" (Abbott and Snidal 2000) is part of the object for study and, more generally, that many insights developed in this literature have relevance for all types of international governance arrangements.

Another key point that was central in the long-running debate with realism and neo-realism was that "institutions matter" and that therefore international politics cannot be reduced to a simple power play between sovereign states only concerned with relative gains. An important tactic in this debate was that even under the restrictive assumptions of neo-realism, it could be shown that international cooperation in institutions is rational behavior for egoistic states (Simmons and Martin 2002: 196). This tactic, along with efforts to formalize the argument in utilitarianist and similar terms, perhaps also gave neo-institutionalism an overly rationalistic flavor, thereby tending to background some of the substantive insights developed under less restrictive assumptions about states in this literature.

In addition to this basic point, that states have reasons to cooperate and to build, maintain and develop international institutions and regimes, it has further been argued that international organizations are not necessarily the simple instruments of governments; they are important in their own right and can have a capacity for agency and agendas of their own. Furthermore, it has been argued theoretically and demonstrated empirically that once created, such international institutions can have significant effects on state behavior and preferences.

Another important modification to a state-centered picture of international relations is the recognition that while cooperation among states to achieve common goals is the most important source of regime creation, it is not the only factor shaping regime creation and regime development. In this regard several additional factors have been acknowledged.

Thus it is acknowledged that domestic politics matter; state preferences are developed in political processes at the national level, where political parties, interest groups, the media, voters and other political players can be important. Furthermore, under the heading of "transnational relations" it is acknowledged, but perhaps not so often actually analyzed (Ruggie 2004), that a variety of non-state transnational actors such as NGOs, advocacy groups and economic interests groups including business can be important (Risse-Kappen 1995). Importantly, this category of actors can be operative and of consequence at the domestic level in many countries – seeking influence in several national capitals on an issue – as well as at the international level, lobbying international organizations and negotiations. And finally attention has been paid to the role of expert knowledge and epistemic communities, i.e. transnational networks of experts and professionals that share certain basic assumptions and standards for describing, analyzing and assessing policy issues, in such areas as health, the environment, or the international economy.

In sum, a more complex and nuanced picture has emerged of the multiplicity of forces and actors that interact with each other in creating, developing and transforming global governance arrangements, including arrangements that relate to business. In this picture, however, in spite of the important modifications, states and their interests still loom large, bringing to the forefront the question of what these interests are. At this point, the arguments forwarded by constructivists are central.

Understanding state interests and preferences

Constructivists have criticized both neo-realists and neo-institutionalists for basing their arguments on untenable assumptions about states being in rational pursuit of well-defined interests (Ruggie 1998). According to the critics, this entails a mechanical view in which material structures determine state behavior, and human agency as well as the role of ideational factors disappears. A better understanding therefore requires that identities, values, norms and ideas are taken into consideration. And these are not static; states adapt to changing international circumstances and domestic changes can have important consequences for how they relate to the external world. States can "redefine their interests or even their sense of self" (Ruggie 1998: 868). Furthermore, these are not only interpretations of interests mechanically imposed by material structures; they also have an element of constructed collective intentionality, a "we feeling" that contains shared aspirations and purposes (Ruggie 1998). States can change purposes, and there can be variations between states in the purposes pursued. None of this is captured by rationalist accounts that are based on the assumption that all states are similar.

This critique, however, has been countered by the argument that, rather than positing a contradiction between rationalist and constructivist approaches, it is possible and more productive to strive towards synthesis between the two, or at least between rationalism and what has been labeled "soft constructivism," i.e. a constructivism that accepts that societal and material structures *also* matter (Hasenclever et al. 2000; see also Fearon and Wendt 2002). In this context it is worth while to quote a statement by Robert Keohane:

> The rationalist – constructivist debate is not only old but mostly false. A coherent approach to the study of world politics must take into account rationalist, institutionalist, liberal domestic politics, and constructivist insights. The trick is how to synthesize these ways of looking at the world in a coherent way, not to run some sort of phony competition among them.
>
> (Keohane, in Schouten 2008)

It should be noted, though, that the constructivist challenge can be seen as a sound reaction against overly simplistic rationalist accounts (which probably have marked neo-realism more than institutionalism). To explain, consider again the discussion of business practices and management decision-making in the preceding section. In a very fundamental sense it is correct to claim that all business decisions are efforts to rationally maximize profits. But this has to be broken down into distinct sub-goals (purchasing raw materials, organizing production, developing new products, marketing, and so on), each of which is pursued separately. Added to this is the complexity of the situations in which businesses operate, the complexity of their operations, the level of uncertainty and risk involved, and tensions between short- and long-term consideration. This makes clear that the choices made and strategies developed by business managers involve the juggling of multiple concerns, often mutually conflicting, and that the managers' knowledge, skills, world-views, prejudices, values and so on by necessity play a role. This does not invalidate the basic principle of profit-maximizing rationality, but it does mean that this principle, while being indispensable for the understanding of business behavior, is insufficient and cannot stand alone as an abstract principle when explaining concrete business behavior.

A parallel argument can be made concerning the choices made by governments and other political actors. A simplistic notion of state interests, while not necessarily wrong, often will have limited analytical traction because of the complexities of the goals pursued and the possibility for conflicts among them. States can be concerned with security, economic growth, social stability, environmental issues, welfare and so on, and conflicts and trade-offs between such goals can be expected to be frequent occurrences. But the issue is by necessity even more complicated than in the business example because of the difficulties of identifying a basic, defining goal for states that is as precise and unambiguous as profit maximization is for business.

One could say that the principle of utility maximization plays the same role for states as the principle of profit maximization plays for business. But still this says nothing about the societal content in states' utility. In a sense, neo-institutionalists sidestep this issue, arguing that state preferences are exogenous to the theoretical models and that there is an inherent difficulty in specifying *ex ante* what the interests are (Simmons and Martin 2002: 196). But, on the other hand, institutionalists argue on the basis of the assumption that when states cooperate, it is to pursue common or at least compatible goals, so the question of what these goals are and whether anything can be said about them remains. In the words of Ruggie's version of constructivism, the question is one of values, intentions, aspirations and purposes. This does not mean that all considerations of material structures and rationality must be discarded; it rather means that rationality must be seen in relation to goals and interests that are constructed by agents in historically specific situations and contexts where pre-existing material structures, political institutions and dominant ideas have roles to play. Rationality, in this view, would mean that states – or rather political decision makers – strive to pursue such goals as effectively and rationally as possible.

The problem at hand, then, is about the shared intentionalities that lead states to cooperate in regime construction; it is a question about the social purposes that states pursue when constructing regimes for international business. This problem ties in with another issue, namely why it is that cooperation is easy to achieve in some policy areas and more difficult in others. To answer this, Michael Zürn suggested looking at the problem structure and situation structure of the issue at hand, the key idea being precisely that the *underlying constellation of interests* is important (Zürn 1992). If there is a high degree of compatibility between states' interests and aspirations, regime formation will be easier, whereas situations with a stronger element of conflicting interests are less likely to lead to regime formation. But while there is a convincing logic to this argument, it still begs the question of the specification of state interests.

Leaving aside for the purposes of the present discussion that rationalists prefer to talk about state interests and utility, while constructivists prefer a language of preferences, intentionalities, aspirations and purposes, the following section examines the societal specification of state purposes that have been suggested by various scholars.

The purposes of global business regulation

Answers to the question have been proposed both in rationalist terms based on economic reasoning and in a more inductive and constructivist manner. In the rationalist camp, Zacher and Sutton argued, in *Governing Global Networks. International Regimes for Transportation and Communications* (1996), that when "market failures exist to a significant degree, regimes directed at their 'correction' will probably increase welfare gains and hence the likelihood that all or a large majority of states will realize benefits. Consequently regimes will be accepted" (Zacher and Sutton 1996: 26). The underlying assumption is that a state's basic rationale is the maximization of societal welfare. Zacher and Sutton used the notions of market failures, externalities and public goods derived from economics to further specify state interests, and they demonstrated in empirical analysis that this understanding, combined with due acknowledgement of states' concerns with national autonomy, is useful for explaining global infrastructure regimes.

Susan Strange pointed to some of the same purposes but in a formulation that is open to a constructivist interpretation. She outlined a list of "responsibilities attributed to the state, and still claimed for it by many political leaders," including, *inter alia*, "correcting the tendency to cyclical booms and slumps," "providing a safety-net to the old and the young, the sick and disabled, and the un-employed," and "building of the economic infrastructure" (Strange 1996: 73–82). She further discussed international cooperation as a more or less successful pursuit of these goals in the international realm (Strange 1996: 184–190). Writing in the tradition of historical materialist state theory, Robinson argued that international institutions are created to perform the political functions necessary for the ongoing growth of global capitalism (Robinson 2004). Craig Murphy combined such insights with constructivist understandings in his study of the growth of international organizations (Murphy 1994, 2002), while Ougaard argued, also leaning towards rationalism, that global governance arrangements must be seen both as responses to the needs of the capitalist world economy and also as parts of a broader function of societal persistence that includes concerns with social and environmental sustainability (Ougaard 2004).

Focusing specifically on international governance arrangements that pertain to business, the question has been addressed in a more inductive fashion by looking empirically at business-related regimes and institutions as they have evolved in world society. As mentioned previously, Preston and Windsor's study of "policy regimes for international business" (1992, 1997) probably was the first overview of this nature. A few years later Braithwaite and Drahos published a larger and very comprehensive study of *Global Business Regulation* (Braithwaite and Drahos 2000) based on a broad, pragmatic and inductive approach, having numerous practitioners from private and public sectors identify significant fields of international business regulation and then conducting in-depth case studies of each of them. In each of the cases the authors discussed the extent to which regulations were globalized and examined the processes, actors, ideas and principles that have shaped them.

The purposes pursued by governments in these cases vary considerably, but on the basis of this work, and the previously mentioned studies, it is possible to group them into three broad clusters. In the first cluster are international institutions that purport to regulate state policies with a view to facilitating international commerce by reducing barriers to the movement of goods, services and capital. They are epitomized by the World Trade Organization and the OECD's agreements on the liberalization of capital flows. The immediate addressee of these regulations is not business, but their purpose is to promote the internationalization of business.

The second cluster consists of governance arrangements that provide institutional underpinnings for the global economy. They include an international monetary and banking system that enables and facilitates international payments, a legal framework that secures property rights and the enforcement of contracts, exemplified by the *United Nations Convention on Contracts for the International Sale of Goods* from 1980, regimes created to enable the smooth functioning of the global infrastructure, i.e. transportation and communications networks, and numerous international standards.

Finally, the third cluster consists of regulations that seek to influence business practices with a view to furthering other purposes not directly related to business. Such purposes can relate to public health, environmental quality and sustainability – an area of continuously growing salience including issues such as biodiversity, deforestation, trans-border pollution, and particularly the central problem of addressing climate change – human rights, security and public safety, and to social and educational aspects of economic development.

In sum, then, the universe of global business regulations or policy regimes for international business is large and varied, consisting of numerous governance arrangements created and developed to pursue diverse goals. The analysis of their development and change has led to a composite picture with several explanatory models and principles. On one hand, rationalist and functionalist arguments are forwarded that see these governance arrangements as emanating from the needs of the global economy and from needs arising from societal persistence and sustainability. On the other hand it is argued that such arrangements are always the products of human agency in political processes where a multitude of actors, public and private, with different and often conflicting interests, ideas and aspirations engage with each other. These perspectives can be seen as conflicting, but also as complementary in a way that suggests that both could be taken into account in analysis.

The above discussion has acknowledged the importance of non-state actors, including business, but still it has maintained a strong focus on states. This reflects the situation in much regime theory where the role of business is acknowledged but relatively seldom analyzed (Ruggie 2004). A growing number of scholars, however, particularly in international political economy (IPE), has put the role of business much more squarely at the center of interest, and to these we now turn.

Business in global governance

Compared to Preston and Windsor's assessment from 1992, there is now a large and growing literature on the role of business in global governance. It is theoretically diverse, working with different conceptual frameworks, different societal ontologies, for instance concerning the understanding of states, domestic political systems and the international political system, and based on different epistemological and methodological principles. It is not possible to discuss all of this theoretical variation in this survey, and instead the following will focus on aspects of the business–global governance nexus that in particular have drawn the interest of scholars; it attempts to portray the field according to the different emphases in research interests, rather than theoretical divergences. One such emphasis is the question of understanding how global regulations of business are created and changed and to what extent they have real impacts on business practices. Another (overlapping) theme that has generated much interest is the question of business power, not only in relation to business regulations but more generally an interest in direct and indirect impacts of business on global governance arrangements. Lastly, a third theme that has gained considerable momentum over the last decade is the focus on ways in which business is mobilized as partners in global governance arrangements through voluntary efforts and partnership arrangements.

The first of these themes, the analysis of global business regulation, is already introduced in the preceding section on business-related international regimes and institutions. What is to be added now is that, since Preston and Windsor's 1992 assessment, significant contributions have come from numerous empirical studies of cases of international and global business regulation. Thus, in addition to Braithwaite and Drahos's comprehensive study of a large number of such regulations (Braithwaite and Drahos 2000), analyses have been published of, for instance, international infrastructure regimes (Zacher and Sutton 1996), environmental regimes (Falkner 2008; Newell and Levy 2006; Orr 2007; Prakash 2000), international property rights (Sell 1999; Sell and Prakash 2004), the governance of communication and information technologies and the internet (McDowell 2006; Salter 1999), regulation of the financial sector (Pauly 2002; Porter 2007), accounting standards (Perry and Nölke 2006), taxation of transnational corporations (Webb 2006), the international governance of mineral markets (Kellow 2007; Webb 1999), regimes for maritime transport (Cutler 1999), and many more. Although the theoretical diversity mentioned above is very much present in this literature, there is a common agenda shared by a large part of it: it is concerned with the question of how international policy regimes for business have been created, modified, non-created, or unmade in political processes where state and non-state actors have interacted and where material structures, institutions and ideas have all been at play. Theoretical disagreements are often about the relative weight and significance of each of these factors and about the theorization of the interlinkages between them.

A special theme in this context is the interaction between competitive market dynamics, variations among national regulations, and the international harmonization of regulatory standards. The key question is whether the strategies of regulatory arbitrage open to corporations – locating activities where the regulatory environment is most beneficial – are leading to regulatory races to the bottom or to the top. And while the race-to-the-bottom view is quite widespread in popular conceptions, clear examples of the second are well documented, for instance in Braithwaite and Drahos's analysis of the international harmonization of auto safety standards (Braithwaite and Drahos 2000: 438–53). In a detailed examination of regulation of selected industries, Dale Murphy found examples of both: convergence towards "the lower common denominator" in the regulation of flags of convenience in the shipping industry and in offshore finance, and convergence towards a "higher common denominator" in the Montreal Protocol on CFS gases and in the Basle Accord on Capital Adequacy (which later events in the financial crisis have proven not high enough!). He also found examples of mixed cases (Murphy 2004).

In the analysis of policy regimes for business the question of *institutional forms* has also drawn increased interest. Realizing the limitations of conventional understandings of political processes – national decision-making and interstate bargaining – as well as regulatory forms – national legislation, international treaties and international law – scholars have paid much attention to the significance of less formalized networks among regulators and market participants, to new modes of transnational interaction between public and private actors, and to new "governance technologies" such as standards, voluntary codes, bench-marking, audits, and more.

In short, the "Why and How?" of international business regulation has become an important area of research, generating empirical analysis and theoretical developments. So has the partly overlapping agenda of understanding business impact on global governance – both the impact on business regulations, and also more generally on global governance as such. In this regard, several sub-themes have appeared in the literature.

The power of business

A first sub-theme is direct political action – lobbying – of business entities with the purpose of influencing global governance arrangements. The business actors involved can be individual firms, particularly large transnational corporations, but can also be business associations organized at the national, regional and international levels or international coalitions of business associations. The targets of their political activities can be national governments, with a view to influencing their policies in global institutions, but can also be international institutions directly. Indeed, it seems that business can have a considerable capacity to create organizations and coalitions that simultaneously lobby political institutions at all significant levels in the international politics of creating regimes for business. A well-documented example is the high-tech coalition created, with large American companies as leaders, to influence the negotiations of the WTO agreement on intellectual property rights by working at national levels in North America, Europe and Japan, the regional level in the EU and the global level at the WTO (Braithwaite and Drahos 2000; Sell 1999). Given the existence of numerous international business associations, both industry-specific organizations and peak associations such as the International Chamber of Commerce and the International Organization of Employers (see Euromonitor 2007), there is no doubt that direct political lobbying by business and business associations is an important phenomenon in global governance.

Part of the literature studying this phenomenon argues along traditional pluralist lines, where the focus is on observable political action and business is seen as one interest group among several (e.g. Ronit 2007). Thus these researchers apply to the international level of theoretical approach, interest group pluralism, which was originally developed for the analysis of domestic politics. But many scholars have been interested in a broader perspective on the impact of business on global governance. Thus a common theme in much literature is the notion that business is in a special position and is endowed with particular power resources (Falkner 2008; Fuchs 2007; Newell and Levy 2006; Strange 1996). It is argued that due to its centrality to economic growth and thereby to societal wealth and economic well-being in capitalist societies, business has structural economic power. Policy-makers have to factor in the impact on the viability and continued dynamism of private business when economic regimes and business regulations are created and developed. Therefore, even in the (perhaps unlikely) absence of direct lobbying, business interests would exert a powerful influence on global governance arrangements. Given the fact that important international institutions – and national governments – have economic growth as a central explicit goal, this argument carries much weight.

But there is more to arguments about structural business power. Thus it is pointed out that many instances of global business regulation involve highly complex and difficult technical issues – whether concerning production technologies, accounting standards, legal technicalities relating to intellectual property rights and so on – where private companies are almost alone in possessing the technical expertise required to develop and assess policy options. This means that even if business is merely one interest group among several, it speaks with a much stronger voice than others, and its cooperation is required for effectively dealing with the problems that regulators seek to solve (Falkner 2008; May 2006; Newell and Levy 2006).

In addition to these materially based sources of business power, influential arguments have been forwarded about ideological sources. Such notions have in particular been developed by Neo-Gramscian contributions to international political economy that have focused on the role of *hegemonic ideas* in shaping global governance (Cox 1987; Gill 1995). It is argued that powerful liberal and neo-liberal ideas constitute a dominant core of beliefs and assumptions, a world view, that informs policy-makers and political elites and shapes their understandings of what governance arrangements can do and should do. This world view has an inherent pro-business orientation and constitutes therefore yet another source of business power rooted in ideas and not in material structures.

In short, as summarized by Doris Fuchs, the literature has identified three kinds of business power: direct or instrumental power, structural economic power, and ideational power (Fuchs 2007). The strongest versions of arguments about business power go one step further and posit the existence of one dominant *transnational or global capitalist class* (Gill 1990; Pijl 1984, 1998; Rupert 2005; Sklair 2001) or *a transnational managerial class* that includes business and promotes business interests (Cox 1987). In these notions, the material and ideational sources of business power are combined with the capacity for political action through coalitions and interest organizations to create a picture of an international business community led by large transnational corporations that exert a dominant influence on national governments and global governance arrangements alike.

Notions of a transnational capitalist class, however, have not gained general acceptance. One reason is theoretical; the class perspective on capitalist society inherent in these notions is contended and not generally accepted by students of international political economy. Another reason is that, whether accepting a class perspective or not, it is debatable to posit *one* transnational capitalist class or one unified international business community. Business communities are, the argument goes, still primarily constituted at the national level and there are conflicts of interest between different national business communities. Furthermore, even at the national level there are significant divisions and conflicts of interests within business (Falkner 2008; Nölke and Taylor in this volume). Nevertheless, it is important to recognize that there is an enhanced business capacity for internationally organized political action, as evidenced by the growing number of international business associations (Gill 1990; Ougaard 2004; Pijl 1998).

Discussions of business power and influence in global governance often focus on *formalized* governance arrangements, in particular those emanating from intergovernmental organizations. But this is not a necessary delimitation, particularly if global governance is understood broadly as suggested in the opening section. Indeed, a distinct theme in recent literature has been notions of *private authority* and *private institutions* in global governance.

The editors and contributors to the volume *Private Authority and International Affairs* (Cutler *et al.* 1999:19) focused on "*private* international authority as a form or instance of governance," understood as situations where private actors are "empowered either explicitly or *implicitly* by governments and international organizations with the right to make decisions for others" (on private authority see also Hall and Biersteker 2002; Haufler 2006; Graz and Nölke 2008; Hansen and Salskov-Iversen 2008). While this definition implies an element of *delegation* from public authorities to the private sector, this delegation can be merely implicit so that decisions are made and implemented by private arrangements, making business a governance-conducting entity in its own right. Thus the notion of private authority calls attention to an important aspect of business in global governance that easily can be neglected if governance is associated only with governments and formal intergovernmental organizations.

A good example of private authority is the *Forest Stewardship Council*, studied by Philip Pattberg under the heading of *private institutions* in global governance (Pattberg 2007). Pattberg shows that this is a highly institutionalized private governance arrangement that brings together business and other non-state actors in a formalized setting that makes rules in the form of standards for sustainable forestry practices, and contributes to their implementation through certification schemes. In this case there is no explicit empowerment or delegation from governments; acceptance by public authorities is at most an implicit background factor.

Furthermore, even without such formalized private decision-making bodies, business can have distinct governance-related impacts. Thus scholars have argued that business practices in and by themselves can have very real governance effects on political institutions and society in general. Tim Sinclair, for instance, has analyzed how the commercial operation of credit rating agencies has significant implications for governments and international institutions (Sinclair 2005), Anna Leander has shown how the practices of private security companies have an impact on public understandings and policies in the security realm (Leander 2005), and the power relations inherent in global value chains and their governance implications have been analyzed by scholars in this tradition (e.g. Gibbon and Ponte 2005). In such cases the argument is that business practices *are* governance, in and by themselves.

Having now considered business as being subject to international regulations and the impact of business on global governance, we turn to the last aspect of the business and global governance nexus that increasingly is drawing scholarly interest, namely notions to the effect that business can be mobilized to serve public purposes, that business can be a *partner in global governance*.

Business: a partner in global governance

Especially noteworthy in recent years has been the field of *corporate social responsibility (CSR)*. Here a host of private-sector-driven codes of conduct, reporting standards and ethical trading and investment schemes has appeared and has drawn the interest of students of international political economy, asking questions about the causes of this development and the effectiveness of such codes for achieving the desired purposes (e.g. Haufler 2001; Levy and Kaplan 2008; Ougaard 2006; Pegg 2006; Vogel 2005; Wolf et al. 2007). At the same time, it should be noted, a rich business literature has developed that focuses on the questions of why, when and how companies engage in CSR practices, and whether such practices detract from or add to the bottom line (e.g. Prakash 2000. For an overview see Ougaard 2006, for comprehensive coverage Crane et al. 2008).

When considering these more recent themes in the literature on business and global governance, two clarifications are important because CSR is often seen as being based only on business self-regulation and voluntary efforts, and the two phenomena – voluntary self-regulation and CSR – are often conflated. But firstly, private sector self-regulation is also known from other areas, in particular from the setting and monitoring of business standards, for instance those concerning product or process technologies, or accounting standards (many examples are discussed in Braithwaite and Drahos 2000; see also Kerwer 2005, Murphy & Yates this volume). Business self-regulation is not only concerned with standards of social responsibility. Furthermore, private standard-setting is not necessarily voluntary; standards set by, for instance, private industry associations can be binding in practice.

Secondly, the reverse is also true: CSR is not only a private matter and a matter of voluntary efforts. At the core of the CSR phenomenon are efforts to mobilize companies to achieve goals that normally are considered outside the scope of business and rather are seen as the responsibility of public policies. CSR is about environmental sustainability, human rights, public health, development and poverty; it is about a "public role for the private sector" (Haufler 2001). Such efforts are promoted through purely private and voluntary codes, but they are also promoted through codes and standards set by international organizations such as the OECD guidelines for multinational enterprises (OECD 2008) and the core codes embodied in the UN Global Compact (United Nations Global Compact Office 2008), and they are promoted through various partnership arrangements between public and private actors, again with the Global Compact as an important example. The central feature is not any particular institutional form, but rather that business is mobilized as a *partner in global governance* for the purpose of achieving public purposes (see also Bull and McNeill 2007, Bull this volume). In one way this makes CSR similar to any other kind of business regulation: it is about impacting business practices through regulatory mechanisms. But there is an important difference: CSR is concerned with wider societal and environmental consequences of business activities and goes beyond the regulation of these activities per se. It is about more than doing business in a legal and ethical way, it is about business contributing more to society than employment and the sale of products and services.

To some extent the two literatures mentioned above – the IPE scholarship, often critical of business, and the "how is it done?" business literature – mirror each other: they are both concerned with the commercial drivers behind business adoption of CSR practices, and in their explanations they both tend to focus on factors such as reputation sensitivity, regulatory risk, activist risk, market expansion motives, and concerns with business legitimacy. Unsurprisingly, however, there is a wide divergence of views in these literatures. Normatively, opinions range from the classical liberal view that "the social responsibility of business is to increase its profits" (Friedman 1970: 33) to the view that "corporations were created and controlled by the state to serve the public good" (Kelly 2001: 165). In terms of evaluating and explaining the reality of business CSR practices, some see it largely as a commercially driven response to outside pressures and a scheme for enhancing business legitimacy and thereby business power, while others see it as a genuine reforming movement with real and beneficial contributions to public policy goals, even if these benefits are limited in scope as argued for instance by Robert Liubicic (1998). Still, a shared agenda for many contributions is the analysis of the reasons for, the drivers behind, and the potential and actual benefits of business as a partner in global governance.

In conclusion to this introductory survey, then, in the twin literatures of business studies and international relations many themes are now on the agenda for the study of the business and global governance nexus, understood as the multiple ways in which business and global governance interact, impact upon and condition each other. Business strategies and business interests in relation to national and international regulatory arrangements is one important concern; another is the analysis of the creation, shaping and modification of international business regulation and business-related regimes through the political interaction between state- and non-state actors including business. Business power, i.e. the direct and indirect impact of business on global governance including business self-regulation, private authority and the governance effects of business practices, has become an important research interest; and so has the mobilization of business for public purposes through codes of conduct, partnerships and trading schemes. The business–global governance nexus has become a rich field of study with much theoretical variation and diversity.

The volume

The purpose of this volume is to advance this agenda further. Thus it is not a book on business strategies per se, and it is not a book on international regimes and global governance per se; it is on the business and global governance nexus. The book does not reflect a particular theoretical agenda but a broad research agenda that is concerned with empirical examination and theoretical understanding of multiple aspects of business and global governance. The purpose is to present different theoretical advances and contributions to the analysis of this nexus, rather than developing one single theoretical perspective further. It is, in other words, based on theoretical pluralism combined with the ambition to explore different aspects of the mutual engagement between business and global governance. The focus and organizing principle, therefore, is on such aspects or emphases in research interests, rather than on engaging systematically with specific themes in theoretical debates. Not that we consider such debates unimportant, but rather that we believe that by taking this tack at this moment in time, in addition to the insights presented in each of the chapters that follow, this approach can also help facilitate dialog and exchange between different schools of thought, and, perhaps more importantly, it can contribute an overview and a more rounded picture of the business and global governance nexus.

To highlight the different emphases in research interest, reflecting different aspects of the business and global governance nexus, and for the sake of convenience, we have labeled them *business as master* of global governance, *business as subject* to global governance, and *business as partner* in global governance.

Under the heading of **business as master** we present contributions to theorizing and empirically investigating ways in which business exerts a powerful influence on global governance. The research interest in these contributions is to identify and examine modalities and types of business power that include, but go beyond, observable political activities directed at global governance institutions.

Christopher May examines *direct and indirect business influence in the World Intellectual Property Organization*. May argues that business influence too often is asserted rather than demonstrated in the literature and that to remedy this it is necessary to take a broader view of the question. He suggests that beyond the specific decision-making process on individual issues, power is articulated through the construction of "rules of the game" and norms that are presented as natural and neutral but in reality are heavily biased towards business interests. This leads May to suggest that a critical issue for further research in international political economy is the analysis of how such norms are constructed and reproduced.

Whereas May's chapter focuses on business influence on a formal governance institution, *Anna Leander* takes a different tack. She asks: What if business impact was not primarily about how it relates to public institutions? What if business mattered in its own right, if it was doing global governance? Presenting her own approach via a critique of formalism and atomism in studies of global governance, she develops a Bourdieu-inspired *practice analysis* of the *private security industry*. Leander shows how this perspective can open for an appreciation of the security governance effects of business practices that are both public and private, practices that produce ordering and hierarchies and transform contexts. She concludes by arguing that practice analysis opens for greater attention to the prevalence of resistance and potential for change in security practices.

In *Unthinking the GATS: A radical political economy critique of private transnational governance*, *Claire Cutler* applies a historical materialist perspective to the General Agreement on Trade in Services. She sees it as a regime of private accumulation and as a legitimizing mechanism that functions to serve transnational capitalism. Cutler moves on, however, to qualify this "business as master" argument by arguing that transnational business corporations are neither monolithic nor (drawing on Althusserian notions of subjectivity) perfectly interpellated as subjects of transnational capitalism and neo-liberal discipline. This understanding opens up for a praxis conception of transnational law as a theoretical–practical strategy for resisting neo-liberal discipline.

The second section, headlined **Business as subject to global governance**, consists of contributions to the analysis of the hows and whys of global business regulation. The shared research interest in these chapters is the creation and shaping of international and global governance arrangements that purport to change or modify business activities, whether through hard or soft regulations or other mechanisms. This of course also includes a concern with business power and influence, but the key emphasis here is not on developing arguments about business power per se, but rather on the understanding of how interactions between business and other actors and societal forces create, change, and implement governance arrangements directed at, or with implications for, business.

Thus, while recognizing that business has a powerful, even privileged position, *Robert Falkner* argues that it doesn't always get its way. Applying a *neo-pluralist perspective to global climate governance*, Falkner analyzes several limitations to business power: there are countervailing forces, prominently among them new transnational actors such as influential environmental non-governmental organizations as well as states that remain powerful gatekeepers in many policy areas. Just as important, if not even more, business cannot be assumed always to be a unified block; rather it is often divided on matters of international policy and corporate strategy. Thus conflicts within the business world are important when explaining the evolution of global climate governance.

Hans Krause Hansen's chapter analyzes *corruption governance*, i.e. attempts to curb the use of bribery in transactions between Western businesses and public sector agencies in global markets. It shows that this particular instance of international business regulation is driven by a multiplicity of actors – state, non-state and hybrid in-betweens – and moves on to examine the mechanisms through which the governance of corruption works. The chapter further argues, building on Foucauldian notions of *governmentality*, that understanding global business regulation is not only about analyzing how rules and norms are created, but also how they are enacted in practice. Corruption governance includes coercive strategies to regulate business conduct, promulgated by state and interstate organizations, but it also builds on strategies that are more indirect, diverse and multi-centered and that employ governance technologies of risk, performance and transparency.

Eleni Tsingou also examines a case of strong business influence in global governance, namely the Basle Accord's regulation of the financial sector. But she also takes up the broader issues of explaining how this governance arrangement came about and of assessing its legitimacy. Tsingou's theoretical approach is centered on *transnational governance networks* and policy communities, and she argues that the complete blurring of the distinction between private and public in this community is central to understanding the outcome. Written while the financial crisis unfolded and national and multilateral policy responses began to develop – "blatantly highlighting" the normative issues involved – the chapter also discusses the prospects for financial regulation and supervision, pointing to the resilience of the transnational governance network.

As argued in Falkner's discussion of business conflicts, one reason for diverging business interests is *differential regulatory impact*, meaning that the same international or global regulation will affect different companies differently.

Therefore, when analyzing the forces shaping global governance, it is important also to analyze variations in business responses to the global regulatory environment. In this regard the recent rise of *multinational companies from emerging economies* presents a novel and increasingly important challenge. *Andreas Nölke and Heather Taylor* address this question in their chapter. The purpose is to develop theoretically and empirically grounded hypotheses on how such companies, and their home governments, are likely to respond to and engage with the global governance arrangements they are subjected to. Given the large historical baggage of confrontations between North and South on economic issues, they ask whether this will still be a North–South conflict. They develop their (provisional and mixed) answers by applying a modified *Varieties of Capitalism approach*, extrapolating from the companies' regulatory environments to their expected preferences toward global regulations.

In the last section we present contributions whose emphasis is on the role business as a **partner in global governance**. This interest derives from the rise of CSR and public–private partnerships in the global political economy and from the questions about causes and consequences posed by these developments as outlined in a previous section, questions about the reasons for business involvement in these new practices, about the potential and limitations of mobilizing business for public purposes, and about larger systemic consequences of these developments.

Benedicte Bull examines *public–private partnerships (PPPs) in the United Nations* system. She identifies four main goals pursued by PPPs in varying combinations: resource mobilization, advocacy, policy development, and operational purposes. Bull then asks questions about the extent to which the achievement of these goals is limited by corporate interests and how much they entail modifications in corporate behavior. To frame this theoretically she develops the concept of *market multilateralism*, arguing that this is replacing the classical form of inter-state multilateralism and is characterized by the emergence of an international system that coordinates relations not only between states but also between private for-profit and non-profit organizations. Empirically she examines this new kind of multilateralism, its legitimacy and affinity with corporate interests, in the two cases of the *Global Alliance for Vaccines and Immunization* and the *UNESCO–Microsoft* partnership.

Efforts at mobilizing business as a partner in global governance often rely on *voluntary standard setting*, but this mode of governance is not new; it can be traced back to the consensus-based setting of industrial standards by engineers before 1900. Now this governance form is migrating to the areas of environmental and social responsibility, making it pertinent to ask what has driven it and why it has been so successful. This is the topic of the chapter on *ISO, the International Organization for Standardization*, co-authored by *Craig N. Murphy* and *JoAnne Yates*. They base their answer to these questions on two strands of theory, one that employs Bourdieu's concepts of economic, cultural and social capital in the context of social movements theory, and another that draws on game-theoretical reasoning to understand the role of leadership in "derived coordination problems." Based on a rich empirical account of the evolution and workings of

ISO, they conclude that it is precisely the "social movements" quality of the process supported by a specific type of leadership that has made the process workable and successful.

The UNESCO–Microsoft partnership is also, due to the high-profile public role of Bill Gates, representative of another conspicuous phenomenon, namely the involvement of *business celebrities* in global governance activities. These are not limited to philanthropy; they also include public advocacy in favor of humanitarian, environmental and developmental causes. This is the topic of *Andrew Cooper's* chapter on the "business face of celebrity diplomacy." Cooper discusses how this phenomenon challenges more conventional theoretical approaches to international political economy, examines motives behind it and the reasons why it can be of consequence for global governance, tracks recent developments in one of the arenas of choice for celebrity diplomacy, the *Davos World Economic Forum*, and assesses the viability and limitations of this contribution to global governance.

In the final chapter, *Anne Flohr, Lothar Rieth, Sandra Schwindenhammer and Klaus Dieter Wolf* analyze *variations in corporate norm-entrepreneurship*. Norm-entrepreneurship is differentiated from norm-consumership and is a more intense form of participation in global governance. The authors explain the observed variation in norm-entrepreneurship in a two-step argument. First they introduce the constructivist argument that corporate behavior is conditioned by the institutional patterns into which company managers are socialized. Second, they develop a modified Varieties of Capitalism approach to capture the relevant differences between countries. Rather than using the classical juxtaposition between liberal and coordinated market economies, they suggest that what matters is where the home country is located on a continuum from corporatist, non-adversarial and non-interventionist business–government relations to adversarial, non-corporatist or interventionist patterns of business government interactions. This alternative typology groups, for instance, the UK much closer to Germany than to the US, in contrast to the standard VoC approach that groups the UK and the US together and apart from Germany. The authors find empirical support for the hypothesis that companies from countries at the cooperative end of the continuum are more likely to engage in norm-entrepreneurship at the global level.

Note

1 I want to thank all the participants in the 2007 workshop on Business and Global Governance at CBS and particularly my colleagues Hans Krause Hansen and Anna Leander for many useful comments to earlier versions of this chapter.

References

Abbott, Kenneth W. and Duncan Snidal (2000) "Hard and Soft Law in International Governance," in *International Organization* 54(3), 421–56.

Amin, Samir (1974) *Accumulation on a World Scale*, New York: Monthly Review Press (French original: Paris, 1970).

Baran, Paul A. (1957) *The Political Economy of Growth* (New York: Monthly Review Press).

Barnet, Richard J. and Ronald E. Müller (1974) *Global Reach. The Power of the Multinational Corporation* (New York: Simon and Schuster).

Baron, David P. (2002) *Business and Its Environment*, Fourth Edition (Upper Saddle River: Prentice Hall).

Bartlett, Christopher, Sumantra Ghoshal and Paul Beamish (2008) *Transnational Management. Text, Cases, and Readings in Cross-Border Management*, Fifth Edition (Boston etc.: McGraw Hill).

Bergsten, C. Fred and Lawrence B. Krause (eds) (1975) *World Politics and International Economics* (Washington, DC: The Brookings Institution).

Bergsten, C. Fred, Thomas Horst and Theodore H. Moran (1978) *American Multinationals and American Interests* (Washington, DC: The Brookings Institution).

Braithwaite, John and Peter Drahos (2000) *Global Business Regulation* (Cambridge, UK: Cambridge University Press).

Bull, Benedicte and Desmond McNeill (2007) *Development Issues in Global Governance: Public–Private Partnerships and Market Multilateralism* (Abingdon and New York: Routledge).

Cardoso, Fernando Henrique and Enzo Faletto (1979) *Dependency and Development in Latin America* (Berkeley: University of California Press).

Cohen, Benjamin (1973) *The Question of Imperialism: The Political Economy of Dominance and Dependence* (New York: Basic Books).

Cooper, Richard N. (1968) *The Economics of Interdependence: Economic Policy in the Atlantic Community* (New York: McGraw-Hill).

Cox, Robert W. (1987) *Production, Power, and World Order. Social Forces in the Making of History* (New York: Columbia University Press).

Crane, Andrew, Abagail McWilliams, Dirk Matten, Jeremy Moon and Donald S. Siegel (eds) (2008) *Oxford Handbook of Corporate Social Responsibility* (Oxford: Oxford University Press).

Cutler, A. Claire (1999) "Private Authority in International Trade Relations: The Case of Maritime Transport," in A. Claire Cutler, Virginia Haufler and Tony Porter (eds) *Private Authority and International Affairs*, pp. 283–329 (Albany: State University of New York Press).

Cutler, A. Claire, Virginia Haufler and Tony Porter (eds) (1999) *Private Authority and International Affairs* (Albany: State University of New York Press).

Dicken, Peter (2003) *Global Shift. Fourth Edition. Reshaping the Global Economic Map in the 21st Century* (London, Thousand Oaks, New Delhi: SAGE Publications).

Dunning, John H. (2000) "The eclectic paradigm as an envelope for economic and business theories of MNE activity," in *International Business Review*, 9(1), 163–90.

Dunning, John H. (2001) "The Eclectic (OLI) Paradigm of International Production: Past, Present and Future," in *International Journal of the Economics of Business*, 8(2), 173–90.

Euromonitor (2007) *World Directory of Trade and Business Associations* (London: Euromonitor plc).

Evans, Peter B. (1979) *Dependent Development: The Alliance of Multinational, State and Local Capital in Brazil* (Princeton: Princeton University Press).

Falkner, Robert (2008) *Business Power and Conflict in International Environmental Politics* (Houndmills: Palgrave Macmillan).

Fearon, James and Alexander Wendt (2002) "Rationalism v. Constructivism: A Skeptical View" in Walter Carlsnaes, Thomas Risse and Beth A. Simmons (eds) *Handbook of International Relations*, pp. 52–72 (London etc.: Sage Publications).

Friedman, Milton (1970) "The Social Responsibility of Business is to Increase Its Profits," in *New York Times Magazine*, September 13.

Fuchs, Doris (2007) *Business Power in Global Governance* (Boulder and London: Lynne Rienner).

Gereffi, Gary (1994) "The Organization of Buyer-Driven Global Commodity Chains: How U.S. Retailers Shape Overseas Production Networks," in Gary Gereffi and Miguel Korzeniewicz (eds) *Commodity Chains and Global Capitalism*, pp. 95–122 (Westport and London: Greenwood Press).

Gereffi, Gary, John Humphrey, Raphael Kaplinsky and Timothy J. Sturgeon (2001) "Introduction: Globalization, Value Chains and Development," *IDS Bulletin* 32(3). Downloaded from www.ids.ac.uk/UserFiles/File/publications/classics/gereffi_et_al_32_3.pdf

Gereffi, Gary, John Humphrey and Timothy Sturgeon (2005) "The governance of global value chains," in *Review of International Political Economy*, 12(1), 78–104.

Gibbon, Peter and Stefano Ponte (2005) *Trading Down: Africa, Value Chains, and the Global Economy* (Philadelphia: Temple University Press).

Gill, Stephen (1990) *American Hegemony and the Trilateral Commission* (Cambridge, UK: Cambridge University Press).

Gill, Stephen (1995) "Globalisation, Market Civilisation and Disciplinary Neoliberalism," in *Millennium: Journal of International Studies*, 24(3), 399–423.

Graz, Jean-Christophe and Andreas Nölke (eds) (2008) *Transnational Private Governance and its Limits* (Abingdon and New York: Routledge).

Hall, Rodney Bruce and Thomas J. Biersteker (eds) (2002) *The Emergence of Private Authority in Global Governance* (Cambridge, UK: Cambridge University Press).

Hansen, Hans Krause and Dorte Salskov-Iversen (eds) (2008) *Critical Perspectives on Private Authority in Global Politics* (Basingstoke: Palgrave Macmillan).

Hasenclever, Andreas, Peter Mayer and Volker Rittberger (2000) "Integrating theories of International Regimes," in *Review of International Studies*, 26(1), 3–33.

Haufler, Virginia (2001) *A Public Role for the Private Sector. Industry Self-Regulation in a Global Economy* (Washington, DC: Carnegie Endowment for International Peace).

Haufler, Virginia (2006) "Global Governance and the Private Sector," in Christopher May (ed.) *Global Corporate Power. International Political Economy Yearbook*, Vol. 15, pp. 85–103 (New York: Lynne Rienner Publishers).

Humphrey, John and Hubert Schmitz (2001) "Governance in Global Value Chains," *IDS Bulletin*, 32(3).

Hymer, Stephen Herber (1976) *International Operations of National Firms. A study of direct foreign investment* (Cambridge, MA and London: MIT Press).

Kellow, Aynsley (2007) "Privilege and underprivilege: countervailing groups, policy and the mining industry at the global level," in Karsten Ronit (ed.) *Global Public Policy. Business and the countervailing powers of civil society*, pp. 110–31 (London and New York: Routledge).

Kelly, Marjorie (2001) *The Divine Right of Capital: Dethroning the Corporate Aristocracy* (San Francisco: Berrett-Koehler).

Keohane, Robert O. (1984) *After Hegemony. Cooperation and Discord in the World Political Economy* (Princeton: Princeton University Press).

Keohane, Robert O. (1989) *International Institutions and State Power. Essays in International Relations Theory* (Boulder, San Francisco and London: Westview Press).

Keohane, Robert O. and Joseph S. Nye (eds) (1972) *Transnational Relations and World Politics* (Cambridge, MA: Harvard University Press).

Keohane, Robert O. and Van Doorn Ooms (1975) "The multinational firm and international regulation," in C. Fred Bergsten and Lawrence B. Krause (eds) *World Politics and International Economics*, pp. 169–209 (Washington, DC: The Brookings Institution).

Keohane, Robert O. and Joseph S. Nye (1977) *Power and Interdependence. World Politics in Transition* (Boston: Little, Brown & Co).

Kerwer, Dieter (2005) "Rules that Many Use: Standards and Global Regulation," in *Governance*, 18(4), 611–32.

Kindleberger, Charles P. (1970) *Power and Money. The Economics of International Politics and the Politics of International Economics* (New York and London: Basic Books).

Kogut, Bruce (1985a) "Designing Global Strategies: Comparative and Competitive Value-Added Chains," in *Sloan Management Review*, 26(4), 15–28.

Kogut, Bruce (1985b) "Designing Global Strategies: Profiting from Operational Flexibility," in *Sloan Management Review*, 27(1), 27–38.

Kolko, Gabriel (1969) *The Roots of American Foreign Policy* (Boston: Beacon).

Krasner, Stephen D. (1983) "Structural Causes and Regime Consequences: Regimes as Intervening Variables," in Stephen D. Krasner (ed.) *International Regimes*, pp. 1–22 (Ithaca: University of Cornell Press).

Krugman, Paul (1991) "Increasing Returns and Economic Geography," in *The Journal of Political Economy*, 99(3), 483–99.

Lasserre, Philippe (2007) *Global Strategic Management*, Second Edition (Basingstoke: Palgrave Macmillan).

Leander, Anna (2005) "The Power to Construct International Security: On the Significance of Private Military Companies," in *Millennium*, 33, 803–25.

Levy, David P. and Rami Kaplan (2008) "Corporate Social Responsibility and Theories of Global Governance: Strategic Contestation in Global Issue Areas," in Andrew Crane, Abagail McWilliams, Dirk Matten, Jeremy Moon and Donald S. Siegel (eds) *The Oxford Handbook of Corporate Social Responsibility*, pp. 432–51 (Oxford: Oxford University Press).

Liubicic, Robert J. (1998) "Corporate Codes of Conduct and Product Labeling Schemes: The Limits and Possibilities of Promoting International Labor Rights through Private Initiatives," in *Law and Policy in International Business*, Fall, 111–58.

McDowell, Stephen D. (2006) "Commercial Control of Global Electronic Networks," in Christopher May (ed.) *Global Corporate Power. International Political Economy Yearbook*, Vol. 15, pp. 127–55 (New York: Lynne Rienner Publishers).

Magdoff, Harry (1969) *The Age of Imperialism: The Economics of U.S. Foreign Policy* (New York: Modern Reader Paperbacks).

Mandel, Ernest (1970) *Europe Versus America: Contradictions of Imperialism* (London: New Left Books).

Mandel, Ernest (1972) *Decline of the Dollar. Marxist View of the Monetary Crisis* (New York: Monad Press).

May, Christopher (2006) "Introduction," in Christopher May (ed.) *Global Corporate Power. International Political Economy Yearbook*, Vol. 15, pp. 1–20 (New York: Lynne Rienner Publishers).

Morgenthau, Hans J. 1973 (1948) *Politics Among Nations – the Struggle for Power and Peace*, Fifth Edition (New York: Alfred E. Knopf).

Murphy, Craig N. (1994) *International Organization and Industrial Change. Global Governance since 1850* (Cambridge: Polity Press).

Murphy, Craig N. (2002) "The Historical Processes of Establishing Institutions of Global Governance and the Nature of Global Polity," in Morten Ougaard and Richard Higgott (eds) *Towards a Global Polity* (London and New York: Routledge).

Murphy, Dale D. (2004) *The Structure of Regulatory Competition. Corporations and Public Policies in a Global Economy* (Oxford: Oxford University Press).

Newell, Peter and David Levy (2006) "The Political Economy of the Firm in Global Environmental Governance," in Christopher May (ed.) *Global Corporate Power. International Political Economy Yearbook*, Vol. 15, pp. 157–78 (New York: Lynne Rienner Publishers).

OECD (2008) *OECD Guidelines for Multinational Enterprises* (Paris: OECD).

Orr, Shannon K. (2007) "The evolution of climate policy – business and environmental organizations between alliance building and entrenchment," in Karsten Kronit (ed.) *Global Public Policy. Business and the countervailing powers of civil society*, pp. 154–73 (London and New York: Routledge).

Ougaard, Morten (2004) *Political Globalization. State, Power and Social Forces* (Houndmills: Palgrave).

Ougaard, Morten (2006) "Instituting the Power to Do Good?" in Christopher May (ed.) *Global Corporate Power. International Political Economy Yearbook*, Vol. 15, pp. 227–47 (New York: Lynne Rienner Publishers).

Pattberg, Philipp H. (2007) *Private Institutions and Global Governance. The New Politics of Environmental Sustainability* (Cheltenham: Edward Elgar).

Pauly, Louis W. (2002) "Global finance, political authority and the problem of legitimization," in Rodney Bruce Hall and Thomas J. Biersteker (eds) *The Emergence of Private Authority in Global Governance*, pp. 76–90 (Cambridge, UK: Cambridge University Press).

Pegg, Scott (2006) "World Leaders and Bottom Feeders: Diverse Strategies Toward Social Responsibility and Resource Extraction," in Christopher May (ed.) *Global Corporate Power. International Political Economy Yearbook*, Vol. 15, pp. 249–69 (New York: Lynne Rienner Publishers).

Perry, James, and Andreas Nölke (2006) "The transnational politics of global accounting standard harmonization," in *Review of International Political Economy*, 13(4), 559–86.

Pijl, Kees van der (1984) *The Making of an Atlantic Ruling Class* (London: Verso).

Pijl, Kees van der (1998) *Transnational Classes and International Relations* (London and New York: Routledge).

Porter, Michael E. (1990) *The Competitive Advantage of Nations* (New York: The Free Press).

Porter, Michael E. (1998) "Clusters and the New Economics of Competition," in *Harvard Business Review*, November–December, 77–90.

Porter, Tony (2007) "Governance and contestation in global finance," in Karsten Ronit (ed.) *Global Public Policy. Business and the countervailing powers of civil society*, pp. 89–109 (London and New York: Routledge).

Prakash, Aseem (2000) *Greening the Firm. The Politics of Corporate Environmentalism* (Cambridge, UK: Cambridge University Press).

Preston, Lee E. and Duane Windsor (1997) (First Edition 1992) *The Rules of the Game in the Global Economy: Policy Regimes for International Business*, Second Edition (Boston: Kluwer Academic Publishers).

Risse-Kappen, Thomas (1995) "Bringing transnational relations back in: introduction," in Thomas Risse-Kappen (ed.) *Bringing Transnational Relations back in. Non-state Actors, Domestic Structures and International Institutions*, pp. 3–33 (Cambridge, UK: Cambridge University Press).

Robinson, W. (2004) *A Theory of Global Capitalism. Production, Class, and State in a Transnational World* (Baltimore and London: The Johns Hopkins University Press).

Ronit, Karsten (2007) "Introduction: global public policy – the new policy arrangements of business and countervailing groups," in Karsten Ronit (ed.) *Global Public Policy. Business and the countervailing powers of civil society*, pp. 1–42 (London and New York: Routledge).

Ruggie, John Gerard (1998) "What makes the World Hang Together? Neo-utilitarianism and the Social Constructivist Challenge," in *International Organization*, 52(4), 855–85.

Ruggie, John Gerard (2004) "Reconstituting the Global Public Domain – Issues, Actors, and Practices," in *European Journal of International Relations*, 10(4), 499–531.

Rupert, Mark (2005) "Class powers and the politics of global governance," in Michael Barnett and Raymond Duvall (eds) *Power in Global Governance*, pp. 205–28 (New York: Cambridge University Press).

Salter, Liora (1999) "The Standards Regime for Communications and Information Technologies," in A. Claire Cutler, Virginia Haufler and Tony Porter (eds) *Private Authority and International Affairs*, pp. 97–127 (Albany: State University of New York Press).

Schouten, P. (2008) "Theory Talk #9: Robert Keohane on Institutions and the Need for Innovation in the Field," *Theory Talks*, http://www.theory-talks.org/2008/05/theory-talk-9.html (29-05-2008)

Sell, Susan (1999) "Multinational Corporations as Agents of Change: The Globalization of Intellectual Property Rights," in A. Claire Cutler, Virginia Haufler and Tony Porter (eds) *Private Authority and International Affairs*, pp. 169–92 (Albany: State University of New York Press).

Sell, Susan K. and Aseem Prakash (2004) "Using Ideas Strategically: The Contest Between Business and NGO Networks in Intellectual Property Rights," in *International Studies Quarterly*, 48(1), 143–75.

Servan-Schreiber, Jean-Jacques (1967) *Le défi américain* (Paris: Denoël).

Simmons, Beth A. and Lisa L. Martin (2002) "International Organizations and Institutions," in Walter Carlsnaes, Thomas Risse and Beth A. Simmons (eds) *Handbook of International Relations*, pp. 192–211 (London etc.: Sage Publications).

Sinclair, Timothy J. (2005) *The New Masters of Capital. American Bond Rating Agencies and the Politics of Creditworthiness* (Ithaca and London: Cornell University Press).

Sklair, Leslie (2001) *The Transnational Capitalist Class* (Oxford: Blackwell Publishers).

Snyder, Francis (1999) "Governing Economic Globalization: Global Legal Pluralism and European Law," in *European Law Journal*, 5(4), December, 334–74.

Spero, Joan Edelman (1977) *The Politics of International Economic Relations* (London: Allen & Unwin).

Stopford, John M., Susan Strange and John S. Henley (1991) *Rival States, Rival Firms: Competition for World Market Shares* (Cambridge, UK: Cambridge University Press).

Strange, Susan (1971) *The Sterling Problem and the Six* (London: Chatham House).

Strange, Susan (1996) *The Retreat of the State. The diffusion of power in the world economy* (Cambridge, UK: Cambridge University Press).

UNCTAD (United Nations Conference on Trade and Development) (2008) *World Investment Report 2008. Transnational Corporations and the Infrastructure Challenge* (New York and Geneva: United Nations).

Union of International Associations (2007) *Yearbook of International Organizations. Guide to Global and Civil Society Networks, Edition 44 2007/2008 Volume 1B* (München: K.G. Saur).

United Nations General Assembly (1974). *Declaration on the Establishment of a New International Economic Order*, at http://www.un-documents.net/s6r3201.htm, accessed December 28, 2008.

United Nations Global Compact Office (2008) *United Nations Global Compact: Corporate Citizenship in the World Economy* (New York: UN Global Compact Office).

Useem, Michael (1984) *The Inner Circle. Large Corporations and the Rise of Business Political Activity in the U.S. and U.K.*, New York and Oxford: Oxford University Press.

Useem, Michael (1985) "The Rise of the Political Manager," in *Sloan Management Review*, 27(1), 15–26.

Vernon, Raymond (1971) *Sovereignty at Bay. The Multinational Spread of U.S. Enterprises* (London: Longman Group).

Vogel, David (2005) *The Market for Virtue: The Potential and Limits of Corporate Social Responsibility* (Washington, DC: The Brookings Institution).

Webb, Michael C. (1999) "Private and Public Management of International Mineral Markets," in A. Claire Cutler, Virginia Haufler and Tony Porter (eds) *Private Authority and International Affairs*, pp. 53–95 (Albany: State University of New York Press).

Webb, Michael C. (2006) "Shaping International Corporate Taxation," in Christopher May (ed.) *Global Corporate Power. International Political Economy Yearbook*, Vol. 15, pp. 105–26 (New York: Lynne Rienner Publishers).

Wolf, Klaus Dieter, Nicole Dietelhof and Stefan Engert (2007) "Corporate Social Responsibility. Towards a Conceptual Framework for a Comparative Research Agenda," in *Cooperation and Conflict*, 42(3), 294–320.

Zacher, Mark W. and Brent A. Sutton (1996) *Governing Global Networks. International Regimes for Transportation and Telecommunications* (Cambridge, UK: Cambridge University Press).

Zürn, Michael (1992) *Interessen und Institutionen in der internationalen Politik: Grundlegung und Anwendungen des situationsstrukturellen Ansatzes* (Opladen: Leske & Budrich).

Part I

Business as master of global governance

2 Direct and indirect influence at the world intellectual property organization

Christopher May

There can be little doubt that corporations have significant influence on global politics. However, while much has been written about the role of corporations in national politics, which has identified the mechanisms by which commercial interests are articulated and furthered in states' internal political processes, there has been much less interest in exploring this issue in detail at the global level. Indeed, while much of the literature on the global political economy seeks to develop a position that regards corporations as being major sites of political power, and often then constructs a critique of such power, the analysis of any pervasive business interest is more often asserted and assumed rather than fully addressed analytically (May 2006). Authors such as John Pilger (2003: 17–47) have examined specific and worrying examples of corporations' political influence (in Pilger's account, their role in Indonesia), but have focused on corruption and covert pressure rather than more formal and legitimate modes of influence. However, these cases of unacceptable and illegal behavior are then, in the protest literature, generalized as the mode by which corporations have an undue influence on weakened or corrupt states, as well as on more developed countries' governments. Other popular analyses have focused on secret groups of corporate leaders (Ronson 2001) who seek to influence and corrupt policy makers, or have sought to assert that corporations have too close a relationship with our leaders (Hertz 2001) and therefore bypass democratic modes of accountability. This literature, and the campaigning materials it has spawned, sees corporations' behavior as intrinsically corrupting and illegitimate. It suggests that well-documented cases of corporate wrongdoing are merely the tip of the iceberg, generating considerable hyperbole but little extra knowledge of the more general and ongoing modes by which the interests of business are articulated within global mechanisms of governance.

In International Political Economy (IPE) we see a more balanced approach, but even here the empirical basis of discussions of the role of corporations in the global system remains relatively thin. Certainly Stephen Gill (2003) and Leslie Sklair (2001), to name two prominent critics, recognize the role that corporate leaders play in developing and maintaining a new global business elite interest, and some attempt has been made to map the networks through which these interests are articulated, reproduced and deployed (see for instance Carroll and Carson 2003). Although some see corporations' role as potentially constructive (for instance, in the moves against bribery and corruption, see Wrage and Wrage 2005), and others see corporations as presenting problems for democratic accountability (Koenig-Archibugi 2004), little work has developed a more detailed account of the manner in which corporations individually or collectively act within the international diplomatic realm, despite the starting point for such work that was established in John Stopford and Susan Strange's ground-breaking *Rival States, Rival Firms* (Stopford and Strange 1991). Here, corporations are seen as fully rounded non-state actors that have legitimate interests and interact with states on a number of levels to articulate a complex range of issues. This nuanced and empirically grounded vision of the influence of business on international (or now global) affairs seems to have been sadly lacking in more recent IPE scholarship on corporations, which has been long on generalized analysis but often short on specific detail.

In light of these shortcomings, and utilizing the case of the World Intellectual Property Organization, I seek to put some flesh on the bones of the argument that global corporations are able to influence the conduct and development of global affairs. This influence, many critics would argue, is conducted by clandestine means that are undemocratic and unaccountable. While I may have some sympathy with this view, it seems to be incumbent upon those who take this position to offer some evidence for their conclusions, in addition to merely assuming that political access (and corporate leaders do have excellent access to elite political groups) produces outcomes favorable to corporations. In other words, it is necessary to demonstrate that political shifts are prompted by corporate influence rather than merely the result of political deliberations in which corporations, like other interest groups, would remain legitimate interlocutors.

To explore this issue with a specific case, I examine the question of business influence at the World Intellectual Property Organization (WIPO). To do this, I draw on the notion of the "new constitutionalism" developed by Stephen Gill, to suggest that power is articulated (at least partly) through the construction of the "rules of the game," and that corporations play a major role in this process by both direct and indirect means. I will then offer a brief sketch of the current system of global regulation of intellectual property, identifying the conduits by which corporations have been able to influence and shape the governance agenda in this issue area. This leads me to suggest that the key research question for a critical IPE concerns the manner in which these norms are (re)produced. Here I move beyond an analysis that suggests that it is clearly in the interest of capitalists for these norms to be constructed in the manner they are, and ask how this is achieved in practical terms. Having explored the modes of construction deployed by corporations at the WIPO and more generally in the governance structure around (but not exclusively constituted by) the Trade Related Aspects of Intellectual Property Rights (TRIPs) agreement, I conclude by suggesting this case highlights the processes by which agenda construction in global governance is politicized through norm (re)production.

Business power from a critical perspective

Business groups and individual corporations have for at least three decades recognized the need for the development and deployment of what Doris Fuchs has termed "discursive power" (Fuchs 2007). This is the power to be able to define norms and values that serve a particular interest as being emerging or ascendant *general* norms and values, alongside a developed capacity to (re)produce these norms beyond the immediate confines of corporate interrelations. However, while this discursive power may be articulated through the media and communicative channels with corporations mobilizing large communications and advertising budgets, at least in the field of intellectual property rights (IPRs), corporations have also sought to establish, or perhaps more accurately maintain, a specific set of narratives around the roots of innovation and creativity through more direct means. In this sense, corporations and their allied analysts, scholars and researchers have sought to develop a perception of the "rules of the game" that limits the discussion of corporate practice, and the criticism thereof, to a relatively narrow field of acceptable issues. Perhaps more importantly, corporations' representatives have been active in seeking to define the new millennium's global political economy in ways that follow the interests of a specific (corporate) form of practice.

For Fuchs (2007), the power of corporations in global governance can be disaggregated into: instrumental power, which I will refer to below as direct means of influence; structural power, revolving around rule-making which can be rather more indirect, as the rules concerned require legislation and thus corporate influence is often actually linked to national jurisdictions; and discursive power, linked to the manner in which certain settlements are politically legitimated outside the formal processes of policy adoption. Although further research can largely identify the extent of direct/instrumental power of corporations, it is this discursive, legitimating element that actually underpins the direct influence. However, the operation of such discursive-based legitimization is also much harder to easily identify in the global realm. Here, the work of Stephen Gill, it seems to me, offers a useful starting point for understanding how corporations have depoliticized the issues around IPRs.

The legal modes developed by specific actors in the contemporary global system are at the center of Gill's analysis. He argues that, rather than a relatively neutral set of spatial processes, globalization has involved the establishment of a "market civilization" that represents the latest phase of the expansion of a neo-liberal capitalism that finds its origins in the nineteenth-century international system, or domestically further back with the nascent liberal state that emerged in Britain in the seventeenth century (Gill 1998: 27–29; Gill 2003: 118). Although this is a complex process that has a number of important facets, one of its central elements has been the increasing marketization of social relations, and their consolidation through specific legal forms. Thus, drawing from Foucault, Gill sees this process of marketization as being furthered and supported by a set of "disciplinary practices" (Gill 2003: 130), central to which is the use of legal institutions to structure and shape both state and international political forms of regulation and governance. Gill defines this "new constitutionalism" as

> A macro-political dimension of the process whereby the nature and purpose of the public sphere in the OECD has been redefined in a more globalised and abstract frame of reference … [It is] the political project of attempting to make transnational liberalism, and if possible liberal democracy, the sole model for future development.
>
> (Gill 2003: 131–2)

> It mandates a particular set of state policies geared to maintaining business confidence through the delivery of a consistent and credible climate for investment and thus for the accumulation of capital. … It stresses the rule of law … [and expands] state activity to provide greater legal and other protections for business.
>
> (Gill 1998: 38)

Emphasizing "market efficiency; discipline and confidence; economic policy credibility and consistency; and limitation[s] on democratic decision-making processes," this new discipline establishes "binding constraints" on fiscal and economic policy (Gill 2003: 132). Perhaps most importantly, this "new constitutionalism" seeks to confer privileged rights of citizenship on global corporate capital.[1]

As Gill notes, "traditional notions of constitutionalism are associated with political rights, obligations and freedoms, and procedures that give an institutional form to the state" (Gill 2003: 132). However, this new constitutionalism is carried forward at the global level and, rather than focusing on the rights and obligations of the global citizenry as related to some form of globalized governing body (or bodies), it is concerned with a much smaller groups; global capital and its operating agents, national and multinational corporations. A key aspect of this constitutionalism is to hold separate the political and economic realms for the purposes of globalized governance, ensuring that the economic remains uncontaminated by the political. And it is this discourse of non-contamination that business groups are voracious at furthering. Therefore, for instance, at the WIPO, during the debates around the Development Agenda, corporations and business groups were constantly lobbying against the introduction of the question of development as an unwarranted *politicization* of the organization's activities (May 2007b).

Another important element of Gill's notion of "new constitutionalism" is the manner in which specific forms of capitalist social relations are normalized through multilateral agreements on the rights of property owners and investors, and the institutionalization in domestic legislation of these rights; specifically, in this case, via the TRIPs agreement and through the activities of the WIPO which have both been heavily influenced by corporate actions and interventions. Although requiring the recognition and protection of non-national property, requiring unrestricted access to national markets, and establishing compensation ("damages") for state actions that impede these rights, such benefits are all set out in supposedly neutral, technical, trading and investment agreements. This assumption of technocratic governance rather than political balancing is a constant refrain from corporations, both directly via lobbying, but also through their involvement in programs at the WIPO, as will be discussed below.

Legal codification "locks in" specific free market policies, and the agreements Gill focuses on do not merely recognize and codify already existing and politically legitimized rights, but are rather intended to provide and establish rights for global capital that previously had been incomplete and unevenly enforced, and in some cases to establish rights that previously did not exist in any formal manner. Perhaps most importantly, for Gill, these legal mechanisms are intended to shield global capital from local, popular democracy (threats "from below"), to insulate property rights from either democratic or oligarchic interference (Gill 1998: 25, 30). Political choices are masked or cloaked by their presentation as legal requirements, and where Gill's approach is especially useful in his identification of globalized legal instruments not as the result of domination and political hegemony, but rather as the method by which such hegemony is both established and maintained.

Here the international legal sphere is not the ground on which political disputes and conflicts are settled, but rather is the manner in which powerful (class) interests shape the forms of political economic relations that *can* be established, the norms of behavior in the global system. Gill's approach recognizes that the more general legal context underpins political economic power and hegemony even as disputes and conflicts play out within the limited field this legal system maps out. If hegemony in Gill's analysis, following Antonio Gramsci, and in parallel to Fuchs's analysis of discursive power, is about the construction of a common sense as uncontroversial, at the very same time that it serves and privileges the interests of one specific class, then the new constitutionalism in the realm of intellectual property rights (IPRs) is constructing the particular (and highly politicized) settlement around IPRs as non-political.

This supports the still widely articulated assertion that the global governance of IPRs is, broadly speaking, a technical issue. Certainly there are political disputes and conflicts within the governance regime as it currently stands, combining aspects of the World Trade Organization's legal structure and elements that have been retained by the World Intellectual Property Organization (WIPO). However, as I have often argued in the past, the governance of IPRs is itself actually a highly politicized realm,[2] but this is the very identification that is resisted and criticized by business interests and corporations.

Corporations and intellectual property

As Susan Sell and I have laid out elsewhere at some length, the history of intellectual property has been a history of political contest, dispute and bargaining (May and Sell 2005). At the forefront of these political debates for the last half millennium have been commercial interests; originally these were represented by guilds (the British Stationers for instance) and other collective organizations such as trade associations, but as corporations established their socio-economic position, and as they grew larger, specific commercial interests began to represent themselves. Trade associations and other corporate-based organizations continue to seek to influence governments, but large corporations themselves also have sought to directly influence government, especially where they enjoy a dominant market position. Perhaps the key mechanism for individual corporate influence, in the realm of intellectual property, has been the numerous attempts (some very successful) to encourage the adoption of specific corporate technologies or protocols as industry standards, supported by governmental bodies. Therefore, corporate influence has usually taken place in two dimensions: in some areas of political-legal debate the corporation has represented its own interest (in specific intellectual property court cases), while at other times corporations have used their considerable political economic resources to lobby and support politicians/legislators to move the law of intellectual property in specific directions. Moreover, the notion that corporations should be encouraged through the award of intellectual property rights has often been presented as a central part of the "logic" of modern capitalism.

The narratives of justification that have underpinned intellectual property for much of its existence have always included, drawing on the work of John Locke, a claim that the grant of (intellectual) property rights both rewards previous effort but equally also stimulates further innovation and economic activity (May and Sell 2005: chapter two). Thus, Adam Smith in his *Lectures on Jurisprudence* (published in 1766) saw patents as a "rare example of a harmless exclusive privilege" that had clear benefits as regards the support of invention (MacLeod 1988: 197). And in his famous *Inquiry into the Nature and Causes of the Wealth of Nations* (first published in 1776) Smith justified patents and copyrights as monopolies on the grounds that they were "the easiest and most natural way in which the state can recompense [companies] for hazarding a dangerous and expensive experiment, of which the publick is afterwards to reap the benefit" (Smith 1776 [1993]: 418). These views were echoed and consolidated in the subsequent two centuries, leading to their central role in underpinning the Trade Related Aspects of Intellectual Property Rights (TRIPs) agreement under the auspices of the World Trade Organization.

Paradoxically, now that intellectual property has finally been incorporated into the mechanisms of global governance, the corporate interest seems to tell two very different stories about the history of development. As far as IPRs are concerned, the long contested, nationally based and differentiated history of the development of intellectual property should be ignored; developing countries should immediately adopt the standards that have only relatively recently been adopted in the richest, most developed economies. Thus, while it has taken the best part of 500 years for the now developed countries to establish the contemporary forms of intellectual property, rather than also work through this developmental trajectory, developing countries should immediately adopt a robust and wide-ranging commodification of knowledge and information for their own good. Conversely, in the realm of wages, corporations and their representatives argue that remuneration must reflect the local levels of development to accord for differences in productivity and skills, while the prices paid for local inputs should reflect local market conditions. Differential treatment is fine when it reflects the corporate interest, but is not acceptable when it might threaten important sources of corporate profitability.

This is not to say that all IPRs are illegitimate or problematic: intellectual property as a policy device was developed by various governments (from Venice in the fifteenth century to the US in the eighteenth and nineteenth) to serve specific social or public ends, and as such may certainly have a role to play in contemporary global society. Intellectual property has always been a mechanism to encourage and reward innovation in technology and other socially useful creative endeavors, on the grounds that this would serve national governments' ends in stimulating and expanding social economic activity and development. However, the manner in which IPRs have often been deployed by corporations has not always achieved these ends in any meaningful manner, and as such in domestic law the rules protecting IPRs are frequently hedged around with exceptions and allowances that for corporations, at least, are perceived as mechanisms for reducing profitability, not for protecting the public interest in access to information and knowledge. In the last twenty years, the discussion of these conflicting interests has moved decisively into the international, or now global, political arena.

The global governance of intellectual property: between the WTO and the WIPO

Although the current global governance regime for IPRs is centered on the World Trade Organization's TRIPs agreement, for over a century the political economy of the global protection of IPRs was separate from any negotiations over international trade. In the 1970s, this non-trade regulatory regime was finally fully consolidated through the establishment of the World Intellectual Property Organization as a UN specialized agency. This organization has its roots in the nineteenth century, with the 1883 Paris Convention for the Protection of Industrial Property (for patents, trademarks and industrial designs) and the 1886 Berne Convention for the Protection of Literary and Artistic Works (for copyrights). Initially, a joint secretariat was established in 1893 and placed under supervision of the Swiss government with offices in Berne, finally moving to Geneva in 1960. During its first decades the organization oversaw the slow development of further international treaties attending to various elements of the (international) regulation of intellectual property.[3]

As new states gained independence during the post-1945 period of accelerated decolonization, some joined the *Bureaux Internationaux réunis pour la protection de la propriété intellectuelle* (BIRPI) by signing onto one or other of the treaties it oversaw. While expanding the potential international reach of intellectual property, when these new members attended conferences organized by the BIRPI their delegations were often sharply critical of the manner in which patents and other intellectual properties were being utilized in the international system. Indeed, criticisms from developing countries would repeatedly surface, and be effectively sidelined for the next thirty years. Thus, once the membership started to expand, the happy (relative) consensus of the early years was not only more often challenged, but the BIRPI (like the WIPO after its establishment) needed to spend more resources and effort maintaining the semblance of consensus over the regulation and further extension of regulation of intellectual property.

Until the 1960s, although the *Bureaux* was an international agency, its operations were the responsibility of one member; the Swiss government. Recognizing this anomaly, a new convention consolidating the previous governance arrangements into a formal international organization was adopted in 1967 at the BIRPI's Stockholm conference. This effectively facilitated the establishment of the WIPO, because the responsibility for the budget, program and activities of the organization was formally assumed by its initial twenty members, removing this responsibility from the Swiss.

This process of institutional development was driven by Arpad Bogsch, first as Deputy Director of the BIRPI from 1963, then as Deputy Director General of the WIPO on its formation, and finally as Director General from 1973 to his retirement in 1997. Bogsch strove to establish the WIPO as a universal organization for the protection of IPRs and believed that the link with the UN was crucial to this end; his first major move as the new Director General was to initiate proceedings to gain specialized agency status. Indeed, the organizational structure of the WIPO was established so that it already resembled a UN specialized agency, making the assumption of this status in 1974 easy to complete. The *Bureaux* and specifically Bogsch believed that working inside the UN system would also encourage more developing countries to join the organization (Bogsch 1992: 28). However, widening the membership prompted some concerns among the European, United States' and Japanese delegations as they were worried (rightly, as it turned out) that these new members might question the key *promotional* aspects of the WIPO's activities.

Nevertheless, the link with the United Nations strengthened the WIPO's international position: it was able both to gain diplomatic advantage from being a member of the UN system and to demonstrate its central role in the realm of global economic governance. On becoming a specialized agency of the UN the WIPO had already nearly doubled its membership to thirty-six signatories of its establishing Convention; in the next decade this rose to a total of 104 members and in 2007 reached 184. However, unlike other UN organizations, the WIPO is largely funded by fees that the private sector (predominantly corporations) pays for the use of services related to the Patent Co-operation Treaty, freeing it from many of the budget-related pressures that shape and sometimes constrain other UN agencies' activities. While the member countries do make a small contribution to the running costs, this is minimal compared to the WIPO's fee and administration income. This reliance on private sector income to fund and maintain its operations has been a cause for concern among some of the organization's members and has prompted concerns, articulated in the proposed Development Agenda, that the WIPO is too accommodating to specific business interests.

The formal agreement with the UN set out how the two organizations would coordinate their activities and cooperate over their strategic direction (article 2), with an obligation by the WIPO to follow any recommendations of the UN and work with other agencies to develop resources to tackle problems identified by the WIPO and the other specialized agencies (article 5). Other commitments related to information and documents (article 6), the provision of statistics (article 7) and technical assistance (article 9), as well as setting out its diplomatic status within the UN (article 17), which extended considerable diplomatic benefits to the organization's staff.[4]

Importantly, the WIPO was explicitly obliged to work with the UN Conference on Trade and Development (UNCTAD), the UN Development Programme (UNDP) and the UN Industrial Development Organization (UNIDO) to promote and facilitate "the transfer of technology to developing countries in such a manner as to assist these countries in attaining *their* objectives in the fields of science and technology and trade and development" (article 10, emphasis added). The question of how the WIPO's activities have interacted with, and have reflected (or perhaps more accurately have often not reflected), developing countries' priorities has become a major element of the criticisms leveled at the WIPO, and a central concern in the discussions around the Development Agenda.

Prior to the establishment of the TRIPs agreement as part of the new WTO in 1995, the WIPO had been responsible for both the negotiation and oversight of international treaties on intellectual property. The organization's relative ineffectiveness in enforcing the various treaties it hosted led to significant pressure for the private sector to include intellectual property under the new multilateral trade organization established at the WTO (May and Sell 2005: chapter seven). After the establishment of the WTO, the development of legal precedent and practice through cases brought before the WTO's dispute settlement body had some impact on the context in which the WIPO operated, although in the first ten years of the TRIPs agreement the Appellate Body has, in the words of Frederick Abbott (2005: 84), "pursued a cautious approach, warning against expansive interpretations of TRIPs obligations." Nevertheless, the WIPO's promotional and support role has been further enhanced following requests by members of the WTO for support, in response to the pressures applied through the WTO's dispute settlement mechanism and other bilateral measures to expand compliance with the TRIPs agreement's required domestic legislative standards.

Perhaps more importantly, the establishment of the Doha round of multilateral trade negotiations as a "Development Round" raised the possibility of integrating developmental concerns into the mainstream of trade negotiations. However, while there have been some highly publicized rhetorical victories, such as the Doha Declaration on the TRIPs agreement and Public Health, this has also been viewed as a smokescreen that has done little to shift the enforcement of IPRs to a more developmental-sensitive mode of governance (Sell 2007). The establishment of a group of developing countries which have identified common interests, at variance with those of the most strident supporters of the TRIPs agreement, was at least partly prompted by the high-profile debates and arguments about the enforcement of patents on medicines in the context of public health emergencies. This is the political grouping that now seeks to shift the priorities of the WIPO, recognizing that while the WIPO is no longer involved with enforcement, it retains a significant role in the maintenance of the legal practices underpinning the TRIPs agreement and the promotion of global norms of regulation of IPRs.

Since the conclusion of the Uruguay Round, and the shifting of responsibility for enforcement, the WIPO's three principal areas of operation are: registration; technical support; and development of further governance measures. The first of these activities is primarily concerned with the administration of the Patent Co-operation Treaty (PCT); this involves the processing of applications under the PCT and as such is a direct service to owners of, and applicants for, patents in various jurisdictions. Alongside this PCT-related activity the WIPO also processes the international registration of trademarks (under the Madrid System), acts as a depository for internationally deployed industrial designs (under the Hague Agreement) and acts as a registry for applications for appellations of origin (under the Lisbon Agreement). These activities provide the majority of the funds for the rest of the WIPO's undertakings, and have allowed the WIPO to maintain a relative independence.

The second area of activities concerns technical support and assistance to help members build the capacity to manage the protection and regulation of IPRs, and to fulfill their international obligations due to membership of the WTO or where particular members of the WIPO have agreed bilateral trade or investment treaties that involve undertakings regarding the protection of intellectual property. This support ranges from information dissemination activities, including collections of members' existing laws for guidance to policy makers developing new legislation, to a wide-ranging education and training program. Since 1993 the WIPO's own Academy in Geneva has offered a diverse range of residential courses and more recently has developed an extensive on-line learning program. This is intended to "enable the participants after returning to their respective countries, to become active in the formulation of government policies on intellectual property questions" (WIPO 1997: 30). The third area of the WIPO's activities involves the promotion of compliance with existing treaties, including those now encompassed by the TRIPs agreement, as well as the updating and revision of these treaties in response to members' requirements, and the organization of negotiations towards the development of new treaties in the realm of intellectual property. Most obviously this aspect of the organization's current activities has been taken up with its multifaceted response to the increasingly global reach of digitized communication.

Therefore, although it no longer has any significant role in the enforcement of treaty compliance, the WIPO still plays a major role in the regulation and recognition of globalized intellectual property rights. While it is now joined by the WTO, which has its own TRIPS Council as a venue for political discussion and deliberation about the global regulation of intellectual property, the WIPO remains an important element in global intellectual property politics. It is a recognition of this continued importance that prompted a number of its members to seek to shift its priorities in the new millennium. However, as many of the debates around the proposed Development Agenda for the WIPO have argued,[5] the private sector, and specifically large multinational corporations, appear to have undue influence on the governance mechanisms for IPRs at the global level. Perhaps more importantly, these corporations seem to have a major impact on the manner in which the norms underpinning the recognition of property rights in knowledge and information are (re)produced through the technical assistance and capacity-building activities of the WIPO and its partners and/or contractors. The influence of business interests can be detected in the positions adopted by various national delegations to the WTO and the WIPO, in the practices of the WIPO's own secretariat and staff, and in the wider realm of political dialogue over global governance.

It is the multifaceted ability to inform the construction and maintenance of a normative commitment to a certain position as regards the commodification of knowledge, both directly and indirectly, that represents the range of influence that business brings to bear on the political economy of IPRs. This is to say that not only do corporations support a specific normative settlement at the WIPO, the organization itself socializes corporations into this "mind-set" as well. This suggests our explanation of the continuing (re)production of a narrative of IPRs that privileges corporate interests cannot merely focus on the ability to deploy political resources and influence in Geneva.

Norms in global governance: making property in knowledge normal

Certainly the western notion of IPRs does not closely reflect customary practice in many developing countries, and thus the legal innovations that may be required to establish compliance with the TRIPs agreement can be relatively difficult to sustain. As Graeme Dinwoodie notes: "It is economic and social contexts that *sustain* these laws [of intellectual property], and if a similar social setting does not exist, merely harmonising [legal] texts may be of little value" (Dinwoodie 2000: 311–12, emphasis added). Supporting the rights that are at the core of the TRIPs agreement is a particular set of norms regarding the treatment of knowledge as property. And, since the inclusion of the TRIPs agreement in the final settlement establishing the WTO, it has become obvious to many corporations and others who benefit from such commodification that merely asserting the advantages of this approach to making property from knowledge and information is insufficient. Increasingly the question of normative (re)production has moved center stage.

The norms that underpin the entire agreement are based on the notion that the private ownership of knowledge as property is a major spur to continued economic development and social welfare; public benefits are achieved through the reward of private rights. This emphasizes the development of knowledge as an individualized endeavor, and the legitimate reward of individualized effort through "ownership" of property. Although IPRs always balance private rewards to reward with public rights of access through time limits on rights, or the scope of protection allowed, the TRIPs agreement downplays historic public realm strategies, such as "fair use" in copyright or the compulsory license of patented goods, utilized when monopoly pricing damages public welfare. Instead, the social value of private rights is emphasized and privileged throughout the TRIPs agreement to the obvious advantage of the owners of such rights, the majority of which are corporations in the richest, most developed countries of the global political economy.

The TRIPs agreement is grounded in a robust norm of commodification of knowledge and information. Although the agreement is potentially quite flexible, as evidenced by the negotiations over the Doha Ministerial Declaration on the TRIPs agreement and Public Health, the forces that support a reading of the agreement that privileges private rights are difficult to overcome in a more general sense. Moreover, the Doha declaration itself, despite extensive negotiations, *only* reasserted the broad thrust of the original text's invocation of health emergencies as legitimate reasons for the compulsory licensing of pharmaceuticals, and did not extend or expand the flexibilities that might already be found in the TRIPs agreement as originally constituted. It took two years of further negotiations in the TRIPs Council to produce the more recent agreement on suspending the prohibition of the cross-border trade in generic drugs, to aid countries lacking domestic drug manufacturing capacity, and even this has done little in the subsequent period to transform the flow of medicines to the Global South, although recent actions by the Canadian government may well initiate the process of change more widely. This struggle over the issue of patented medicines exemplifies the strength of the ownership norms within TRIPs, and the political weight of those countries which support them, revealing the implicit influence of the corporate lobby in one form or another.

These norms of property in knowledge and information are hardly universal; thus well-funded capacity building and "awareness raising" programs have aimed to realign normative attitudes to IPRs. The World Bank, WTO, WIPO and a number of other multilateral, national and private agencies are expending significant effort to "help" developing countries establish compliance with TRIPs. Paradoxically, as Peter Drahos has demonstrated, in an attempt to ensure their clients are not caught up in costly trade disputes with the US stemming from the Special 301 section of the Omnibus Trade and Tariff Act, 1988, the WIPO has encouraged developing countries to adopt legislation that goes beyond the formal requirements of the TRIPs agreement (Drahos 2002: 777). Not least of all, this reflects the statutory authority on which the US Special 301 provisions are based, which notes that "a country can be found to deny adequate and effective intellectual property protection *even if it is in compliance* with its obligations under the TRIPs agreement" (USTR 2003: 9, emphasis added). In the wake of bilateral trade agreements with the US, many developing countries have required "TRIPs-plus" legislation.

Although article 41 of the TRIPs agreement clearly states that accession does not require "a judicial system for the enforcement of intellectual property rights *distinct* from that for the enforcement of laws in general" (emphasis added), the agreement does imply the adoption of a particular legal culture as regards intellectual property. Supporting the treatment of knowledge as property underpins the developed countries' use of the TRIPs agreement to continually "ratchet up" the protection of IPRs' owners' rights. This is not neutral, nor merely technical, but rather is a normative position into which WTO members' governments, policy makers and their enforcement agencies are to be socialized. This legal culture is by no means uncontested and therefore there is a continuing "need" for capacity building to ensure developing countries enact suitable and compliant legislation for IPRs.

Once the issue of normative (re)production is raised, the question of who benefits from such norm-maintenance and socialization activities becomes important for a critical IPE analysis. Given the need for corporations to control their assets (so they can have clear property rights which allow alienability), and that most owners of IPRs across the global system are in fact corporations, the immediate conclusion must be that a key group that benefits from the construction of norms of property in knowledge and information must be corporations. Now, certainly, these norms include a well-developed set of narratives around the individual and social benefits of makiing knowledge and information into property (May 2010: chapters one and two), but the aggregate benefits of this commodification are also, most certainly, enjoyed by the commercial/business sector.

This leads to the central question I am concerned with here: How do corporations (re)produce the norms of commodification that underpin the contemporary system of global governance of IPRs? One set of answers has been developed in regard to the ability of a small group of corporations to push forward the multilateral negotiations that led to the establishment of the TRIPs agreement (Sell 2003: chapter five). Ravi Ramamurti (2005: 351–57) summarized the important and extensive role of Pfizer in this process as involving four strategic elements that encompass a much more general typology of corporate modes of influence. Firstly, Pfizer sought to infiltrate its high-level managers into policy-making bodies worldwide. This involved chairing fora and advisory groups as well as supporting the protection of IPRs in other associations with which they were affiliated. Secondly, Pfizer deployed considerable time and resources on building and managing coalitions between corporations to ensure that the "line" taken with governments was consistent and could therefore be used to lead policy makers in the direction that Pfizer and its allies desired. Thirdly, and perhaps more specifically, Pfizer and their associates were able to utilize the strong position of the US in trade negotiations to further their ends – which of course also encouraged non-US corporations to seek ways of influencing the Pfizer-led alliance, thereby further strengthening the alliance's ability to mobilize private sector resources elsewhere. Finally, as Ramamurti also points out, the Pfizer-led group was instrumental in arguing for a shift in fora, from the WIPO to the WTO. Interestingly, of course, now that the TRIPs council has become moribund, and the WTO has been subject to considerable pressure from developing countries, the private sector has sought to support renewed negotiations at the WIPO, on the Substantive Patent Law Treaty for instance, while at the same time firmly resisting attempts to "mainstream development" at the organization.

More generally, the answer to how corporations (re)produce intellectual property norms is that this process encompasses both direct and indirect means:

- Direct means include: lobbying of national trade and legal negotiators both as individual corporations and through trade groups; the representation of business interests in negotiations by private-sector-linked non-governmental organizations.
- Indirect means include: the funding of research groups and advocacy groups that seek to promote the expansion of the realm of IPRs; the deployment of discursive resources (through advertising especially) to underpin "paradigm maintenance" around the social utility of IPRs; the continual representation to the media of damage done to both business and society by counterfeiting and "piracy."

The key issue here is the relatively widely held common-sense view that firstly intellectual property is a technical and complex issue that can only really be dealt with by experts. This is compounded by a second commonly held view, that intellectual property is built on basic values of reward for effort and support for progress. However, these values are not "natural" or organic social beliefs; rather, they are a set of norms that require constant political attention for their maintenance and (re)production.

One clear element of the program to (re)produce norms of knowledge and information commodification, which I have discussed elsewhere, is the capacity building and technical assistance provided by the WIPO, the WTO and other organizations, all focused on underpinning and supporting the maintainability of the norms underlying IPRs at the global level (May 2004a). One of the key purposes of this program has been to ensure that there are few, if any, avenues for developing a mainstream alternative vision of how knowledge and informational resources might, or should, be governed, outside the TRIPs mind-set.

This "mind-set" does not command significant support outside the developed world; hence, the potential tensions that capacity building attempts to ameliorate are hardly likely to be transitory, nor merely focused on governmental organizations; efforts at norm (re)production come up against the real problems that TRIPs-compliance produces in many developing countries. The TRIPs-mandated settlement on governance of intellectual property stresses and privileges the rights and needs of knowledge "owners" – mainly corporations – while denuding the "democratic" public realm of substantial knowledge and information resources. In the governance of IPRs these privileges have been enlarged and supported in developing countries by extensive capacity building programs in the legislative realm and by supporting enforcement practices. Indeed, capacity building and technical assistance are intended to ensure the world is safe for the information- and knowledge-suffused modern capitalism that has developed in the richest countries in the last decades. Although it may offer benefits for some sectors in the developing world, generally, while developing countries continue to use more information and knowledge-based products than they produce, compliance with the TRIPs agreement remains a mechanism for transferring wealth from the poor to the rich, and mostly to the corporate sector in these rich(est) countries.

Critical IPE, the (re)production of norms and power in global governance

If it is relatively easy to see the linkages between organizations such as the WIPO and formal programs of normative (re)production, a more fundamental question is: how have the norms, which are beneficial to the corporate owners of IPRs, been established and politically maintained? Moreover, what role do corporations themselves play in this process? As Fuchs notes, one of the reasons that corporations have managed to expand their influence over debates around the forms of political economic relations is that the policy discourse has moved firmly into a narrative of competitiveness, economic growth and efficiency, all aspects of social practice that corporations have claimed as reflecting their own particular competences and skills (Fuchs 2007: 153). If the direct means of influencing the WIPO's programs are relatively easy to detect, both through the provision of expertise that is deployed in the WIPO's technical assistance activities and via the WIPO's dependence on private sector income, more generally we need to explain why the narrative of property in knowledge and information remains so powerful. Here the relations between the WIPO and corporations are more complex, not least as the WIPO runs programs for corporations setting out how they can best take advantage of IPRs.

Many of the formal business-related programs that the WIPO has developed are concerned with aiding small and medium sized enterprises (SMEs) to use the global system of IPRs established by the TRIPs agreement. However, as in other areas, this aid moves beyond the merely technical and facilitative. The WIPO Worldwide Academy offers a number of executive programs that focus on managing intellectual property. Indeed, much of the content of the widely circulated (electronically published) WIPO magazine is taken up with case studies of successful IPR-related business strategies and the use of IPRs to underpin specific forms of business development. Here, facilitation and assistance move towards promotion and socialization (May 2007a). Therefore, while these programs are undoubtedly within the remit of the WIPO, what is presented to SMEs, and to corporations more generally, is a set of IPR-related solutions to business problems, and this reflects the involvement of corporations in the programs themselves. Frequently the WIPO deploys private sector consultants, drawn from the corporate sector in their training programs, leading to a specific business viewpoint being reinforced with the imprimatur of a UN specialized agency.

The most important result of the direct and indirect influence on the global governance of IPRs, and specifically the manner by which this has been articulated at the WIPO, has been to normalize a very specific set of practices and procedures around the commodification of knowledge and information. This is to say that the power of global corporations or global business has been manifest not through a direct deployment of resources in this issue area, but through a well-managed process of consolidating the "rules of the game" and constraining contending and alternative models of dealing with the utilization and distribution of knowledge by rendering these alternatives as non-sensical or lacking in technical finesse. That the field of intellectual property politics has become an area of significant global interest should be no surprise given the clear expansion of value in intangible, knowledge-based assets and their increasing importance to other sectors. That those who have benefited from the existing system should seek to maintain the status quo and expand their benefits should also hardly surprise us.

If, as Erik Reinert has recently argued, emulation is the key development policy that has historically underpinned economic development in countries outside any particular period's core rich countries (Reinert 2007), then we can expect that, whatever the rhetoric, the mechanisms that facilitate emulation are likely to be subject to political interest. Both developed and underdeveloped countries seek to utilize the means of emulation for their own ends: for developing countries this means obtaining free, or at least cheap, access to the raw materials of emulation (knowledge resources, primarily); for developed countries, whatever their expressed stance, emergent economic competition is never likely to be welcomed. However, while for states competition may be unwelcome, there may be other political issues at stake; currently the rhetoric of failed states and poverty-induced terrorism suggests that fostering development may have some useful security pay-offs, directing energies into enrichment rather than conflict and terror. However, corporations have few of these wider concerns and are much more concerned with the stifling and constraint of competitors; here emulation as a development strategy is a direct threat to market domination and capital accumulation. Hence, although state trade negotiators may be subject to a wide range of political concerns, for their corporate advisers only competitive success is salient, and therefore, in the governance of IPRs, the voice of corporations has been particularly evident, as we would expect.

This has been most clearly manifest in the construction of the norms of protection that have been developed and articulated in the last two decades' negotiations around the establishment of global governance mechanisms for IPRs. At the WIPO this influence has been both direct and indirect, and perhaps most interestingly has been instrumental in the shift of role for the WIPO. Combining the political pressure around forum shifting, and the internal politics of expanding the programs for the promotion of IPRs, corporate influence at the WIPO has changed the organization's role from regulatory to advisory and facilitative. Moreover, this influence has often successfully sought to constrain and shape the forms of advice and facilitation that the WIPO delivers. Interestingly, the debates around the Development Agenda suggest that this influence is increasingly being brought out into the open and challenged; indeed, the next five years may well see a re-balancing at the WIPO, with the developing country members seeking to reassert control of the organization in order to resist the current corporate agenda of IPR promotion. This political project is aimed at establishing, in the realm of the global governance of IPRs, that the claim that this issue is merely technical and not political is itself an important political claim by business and as such should be the subject of debate and deliberation.

Notes

1 See the discussion of corporate citizenship in Goldman and Palan (2006) and May (2010b)
2 See, for instance, May (2004a, 2004b, 2010a)
3 Much of this section summarizes material from May (2007a).
4 See Agreement between the United Nations and the World Intellectual Property Organization, available at: <http://www.wipo.int/treaties/en/agreement>
5 The Development Agenda is discussed in May (2007b).

References

Abbott, Frederick (2005) "Toward a New Era of Objective Assessment in the Field of TRIPs *and* Variable Geometry for the Preservation of Multilateralism," *Journal of International Economic Law*, Vol. 8, No. 1: 77–100.

Bogsch, Arpad (1992) *The First Twenty-Five Years of the World Intellectual Property Organisation from 1967 to 1992* [WIPO Publication No. 881 (E)] (Geneva: International Bureau of Intellectual Property).

Carroll, William K. and Colin Carson (2003) "The network of global corporations and elite policy groups: a structure for transnational capitalist class formation?" *Global Networks*, Vol. 3, No.1: 29–57.

Dinwoodie, Graeme (2000) "The Integration of International and Domestic Intellectual Property Lawmaking," *Columbia VLA Journal of Law and the Arts*, Vol. 23, No.3/4: 307–14.

Drahos, Peter (2002) "Developing Countries and International Intellectual Property Standard Setting," *Journal of World Intellectual Property*, Vol. 5, No. 5: 765–89.

Fuchs, Doris (2007) *Business Power in Global Governance* (Boulder: Lynne Rienner).

Gill, Stephen (1998) "New Constitutionalism, Democratisation and Global Political Economy," *Pacifica Review*, Vol. 10, No. 1 (February): 23–38.

—— (2003) *Power and Resistance in the New World Order* (Basingstoke: Palgrave Macmillan).

Goldman, Ian and Ronen Palan (2006) "Corporate Citizenship," in Christopher May (ed.) *Global Corporate Power* (IPE Yearbook 15) (Boulder: Lynne Rienner Publishers).

Hertz, Noreena (2001) *The Silent Takeover: Global Capitalism and the Death of Democracy* (London: William Heinemann).

Koenig-Archibugi, Mathias (2004) "Transnational Corporations and Public Account-ability," *Government and Opposition*, Vol. 39, No. 2 (Spring): 234–59.

MacLeod, Christine (1988) *Inventing the Industrial Revolution: The English patent system, 1660–1800* (Cambridge: Cambridge University Press).

May, Christopher (2004a) "Capacity building and the (re)production of intellectual property rights," *Third World Quarterly*, Vol. 25, No. 5: 821–37.

—— (2004b) "Cosmopolitan Legalism Meets 'Thin Community': Problems in the Global Governance of Intellectual Property," *Government and Opposition: An International Journal of Comparative Politics*, Vol. 39, No. 3 (Summer): 393–422.

——— (2006) "Introduction," in: C. May, *Global Corporate Power* (IPE Yearbook, Volume 15) (Boulder: Lynne Rienner).

——— (2007a) *The World Intellectual Property Organisation: Resurgence and the Development Agenda* (Global Institutions series) (London: Routledge).

——— (2007b) "The World Intellectual Property Organisation and the Development Agenda," *Global Governance: A Review of Multilateralism and International Organizations*, Vol. 13, No. 2 (April–June): 161–70.

——— (2010a) *The Global Political Economy of Intellectual Property Rights: New enclosures* (Revised second edition) (London: Routledge).

——— (2010b) "The corruption of the public interest: intellectual property and the corporation as a rights holding 'citizen'," in Tony Porter and Karsten Ronit (eds) *Business and Democracy* (Albany, NY: State University of New York Press – forthcoming).

May, Christopher and Susan Sell (2005) *Intellectual Property Rights: A Critical History* (Boulder: Lynne Rienner).

Pilger, John (2003) *The New Rulers of the World* (London: Verso).

Ramamurti, Ravi (2005) "Global Regulatory Convergence: The case of intellectual property rights," in Robert Grosse (ed.) *International Business and Government Relations in the 21st Century* (Cambridge: Cambridge University Press).

Reinert, Erik S. (2007) *How Rich Countries Got Rich ... and Why Poor Countries Stay Poor* (London: Constable and Robinson).

Ronson, John (2001) *Them* (London: Picador).

Sell, Susan (2003) *Private Power, Public Law: The Globalisation of Intellectual Property Rights* (Cambridge: Cambridge University Press).

——— (2007) "Intellectual Property and the Doha Development Agenda," in Donna Lee and Rorden Wilkinson (eds) *The WTO After Hong Kong* (London: Routledge).

Sklair, Leslie (2001) *The Transnational Capital Class* (Oxford: Blackwell).

Smith, Adam (1776 [1993]) *An Inquiry into the Nature and Causes of the Wealth of Nations* (edited with an introduction and commentary by K. Sutherland) (Oxford: Oxford University Press).

Stopford, John and Susan Strange (1991) *Rival States, Rival Firms: Competition for world market shares* (Cambridge: Cambridge University Press).

USTR (Office of the United States Trade Representative) (2003) *2003 Special 301 Report* (Washington, DC: USTR) [available at <http://www.ustr.gov/sectors/intellectual.shtml> (8 May 2003)].

WIPO (World Intellectual Property Organization) (1997) *Introduction to Intellectual Property Theory and Practice* (London: Kluwer Law International).

Wrage, Stephen and Alexandra Wrage (2005) "Multinational Enterprises as 'Moral Entrepreneurs' in a Global Prohibition Regime Against Corruption," *International Studies Perspectives*, Vol.6: 316–24.

3 Practices (re)producing orders

Understanding the role of business in global security governance[1]

Anna Leander

To recognize that business can have a significant role in global governance of security and military matters seems rather difficult. A key reason is the way global governance is understood. Global governance often boils down to what is done by a set of public institutions at the international level. But what if the role of business in shaping global politics was not primarily about how it relates to public institutions? What if business mattered in its own right; if it was doing global governance? And what if this doing was altering the way activities in specific areas were ordered; *possibly without* altering formal public arrangements or influencing state behavior? In short, what if business practices produced global governance?

This chapter argues that this is the case in the global governance of security but that this has proved difficult to analyze. The chapter departs from a suggestion that the influence of a twofold – formalist and atomist – conceptual "blinder" explains why this is so. It proceeds, in the second section, to show that an analysis of global governance as practice[2] can remove this blinder: By focusing attention on the production of hierarchical orders, it can place business squarely at the center of analysis and move away from formalism. By focusing on the inter-subjective and contextual nature of order, it then accounts for the broader implications of the rise of private companies and moves away from atomism. The final section insists that a focus on practices directs attention to change. It is well suited both for explaining the emergence of private actors in global security governance and for thinking about potential future changes in its current role.

Blinders obscuring business's part in global security governance

A decade ago, the private military/security business[3] was much smaller than today, and largely unknown. Today the hype surrounding the private market for force has produced innumerable publications, meetings, documentaries, articles and investigations and few will be unaware of its existence. Yet, academia resembles Lampedusa's Sicily: the more things change the more they remain the same. The private military/security business figures in the margins (if at all) of most scholars' writings on global security governance. Those who look at the business often consider it a means in the hands of states rather than something that significantly alters global security governance (Shearer 1998; Stoker 2008). The reason is the blinders that hamper studies of private business in global security governance studies. Two blinders have been particularly effective: formalism and atomism. The argument for studying global governance as practice is that it removes these two blinders.

A. Formalism

The most effective way of preventing private business from appearing as an independent actor in global security governance is "formalism," or an understanding of global governance as a matter of public or legal processes.[4] In the security field, scholars look at institutionalized negotiation and bargaining surrounding decisions relevant to security governance, shifts in legal authority, or developments in the formal control of the state over the use of force.[5] This work is important. However, it also has serious drawbacks. The focus on law and public process can easily become a Procrustean bed for thinking about the private military/security business in global governance. Procrustes (the stretcher) had an iron bed into which he invited every passer-by to lie down. If the guest proved too tall, he would amputate the excess length; if the victim was found too short, he was then stretched out on the rack until he fit, the bed having been adjusted by Procrustes beforehand. Formalism tends to treat the study of business in global governance in the security field in similar fashion.

First, a formalistic approach to global governance leads to cutting off or leaving out central aspects of how business comes to be part of global governance. By reducing global governance to its formal expressions it neglects ways in which business participates in or alters global governance fundamentally without necessarily causing any legal or procedural changes. In the security field, this influence is of particular significance. The reason is that the state monopoly on the "legitimate use of force" is so profoundly anchored in thinking and practice that it is very unlikely to change. Yet the privatization of security has placed private military/security business in charge of much of the practice of security governance (still decided upon by states). Companies interpret rules, implement them, write them, and often in fact formulate them (Fainaru 2008). Privatization has also altered the way states understand what it means to have a monopoly on the legitimate use of force (Leander 2009f). However, these changes have left the formal state "monopoly of the legitimate use of force" unaltered (Leander 2005). The trouble with the formalist focus in this situation is that it discourages analysis of the important political implications of market developments. In Procrustean fashion it cuts them out of the picture and impoverishes our understanding of security governance.

Second, formalism hampers analysis by triggering Procrustean stretching. In the case of the role of private business in security government this stretching centrally involves the notions of public and private to which everything is forcefully fitted. By positing that the private military/security business is a "private" actor and the state a "public" one, observers can ignore the disturbing developments signaling that this is not the case and hence get a stylized but inaccurate picture of the role that (private) business plays in (public) governance. The lines between the public and the private are not only "blurred"; the public and private are enmeshed. State actors are integrated into the private realm and behave accordingly, and *vice versa*. For example, civilian technicians assisting the collection of surveillance data during operations missions, civilian maintainers providing battlefield maintenance of a TOW missile, the M1A1, the Bradley or the Patriot missile and contractors supporting the gathering and interpreting of data from the Joint Air Forces Control Center and feeding intelligence and targeting information to operators are not simply "private" actors. They are also an integral part of the (public) armed forces. They are both public and private *at the same time*. Military lawyers are continuously struggling with how to deal with this dual status (Heaton 2005; Zamparelli 1999). Similarly, vice president Cheney in the US (like many other public officials[6]) is not simply a public actor. He holds private positions, including being president of the board of a major military contractor (KBR).[7] He is a public and a private person at *the same time*. Like the contractor on the battlefield, Cheney signals the *enmeshing* of the private and the public.

Positing that business is private and state is public may have the virtue of saving a formalistic legal framework. But it stretches the categories in a way that hampers inquiry by obscuring the ambivalent status of actors and its implications. It distorts the understanding of security governance by upholding an elusive distinction and the connotations tied to it. On a practical level, the effect of this Procrustean category stretching is an inability to identify, let alone face, the issues raised by the growing role of private business in security governance.[8]

B. Atomism

A second blinder that makes it difficult to analyze the role of private business in global security governance is the focus on single cases at the expense of social relationships or intersubjective meanings. This focus is linked to the (no doubt important) wish to hold firms accountable (Kierpaul 2008). However, it also tends to preempt inquiry into how the creation of a collective institution, the market, reshapes governance. This is not a plea for neglecting the particulars or the rationalities of actors in a single case but rather one for the necessity to contextualize – "to reassemble the social" (Latour 2005) – to make sense both of the single case *and* of what it says (or not) about the role of business in global security governance.

For analyzing private business in global security governance, it is important to focus on the broader questions surrounding the effects of evolving discourses, social hierarchies and relationships. Yet there has been a strong tendency to focus on case studies either of specific companies or of specific incidences. The good reason for this is the need for empirically anchored arguments, strongly encouraged by editors and reviewers. However, the trouble is when the analysis stops at the case. Considering the Nisour incident, where Blackwater contractors killed 17 civilians on 16 September 2007, makes clear why. An analysis of this case in isolation can show that Blackwater contractors broke some rules and respected others. However, it gives little leverage for understanding why they acted as they did and why they were there in the first place, as pointed out by Singer (2007a) in his analysis of the Nisour incident. Confining analysis to the single incidence gives even less leverage to shed light on global security governance. Such leverage is gained by placing the incidence in the more general context of security privatization and outsourcing, and even more broadly in the context of shifting understandings of the forms and aims of security governance that have accompanied the shift to neo-liberal forms of security governance. The atomist framing of problems militates against such efforts to reassemble the social world.

Shaking off atomism in the study of the private military/security business is complicated by the temptation to privilege the controversial, scandalous, large scale and spectacular over the uncontentious, normal and small scale. The scandals make for better stories, but they also raise important normative, legal and political questions. Hence, scandals such as those surrounding the CACI involvement in the Abu Ghraib interrogations, the Aegis "trophy video" featuring contractors shooting randomly at civilian cars while "driving in Iraq" or the DynCorp sex-ring involving 12-year-olds in Bosnia have (understandably) attracted much attention and critique (for accounts see e.g. Human Rights First 2008; War on Want 2006).

This prioritization has two regrettable consequences for the analysis of private companies. First, it skews the understanding of business in global governance. The scandals are important, of course, as are the questions they raise. However, they obviously do not form a sufficient basis for thinking about the role of firms in global security governance. Analysis needs to go on to consider also what respectable firms, staffed with law-abiding people and acting in accordance with the political and social norms of their context entail for security governance. The difficulty is that the focus on scandal draws attention away from the normal and well-behaved market; crowding out analysis of its effects. As a consequence, industry advocates and lobbyists become the sole interpreters of the normal situation, with regrettably little critical intervention facing them (Leander 2008a).

Second, and no doubt unwittingly, the focus on scandals leaves the impression that all we need to do is to prevent the bad eggs from spoiling the basket (as US Secretary of Defense Robert Gates at the time of the Nisour Square incident expressed it). The focus on scandals therefore contributes actively to building the wide consensus around the importance of improving "regulation." However, it also contributes to the endemic glossing over of the profound disagreements that exist with regard to the aims of that regulation; in particular, the fundamental disagreement about the acceptability of commodifying military/security services (Leander 2009d).

That one might miss the forest for staring at the trees is not new, but it is often forgotten in the analysis of business in global security governance. To think about business in global security governance we have to re-assemble the social and think about collective institutions and inter-subjective meanings. It is also imperative to move beyond formal rules and definitions and to grasp the role of business in global governance. The main reason to move into the world of practices is that it does both things. The remainder of this chapter gives some indications of how.[9]

Breaking with formalism: global governance as practice

Global governance is sometimes treated as "government" by international institutions or by states in the international realm. This notion of global governance is often widened to encompass hybrid public–private institutions that may be less formalized and the emphasis is then put on "governance" rather than "government" (Rosenau 2002). Focusing on practices leads even further away from the formal institutions as global governance becomes the hierarchical order produced through practices – through what states, public officials but also companies and individuals do. The question of global governance becomes what "rules of the game," "governing of conducts" or "governmentality" are (re)produced in practices (e.g. de Goede 2006; Larner and Walters 2004). Placing governmentality rather than "government" or "governance" at the heart of the study of global governance makes the relevance of the public/private, inside/outside or formal/informal a matter of investigation: not something posited as point of departure. This breaks with formalism and paves the way for placing private business squarely in the study of security orders.

A. Practices producing ordering

Looking at global governance through the practice lens directs attention to the many things that private firms do in global security governance and to the kind of ordering, or governance, these "practices" (re)produce.

Order is reflected and produced in what people and institutions do. Therefore a starting point for thinking about business in global governance of, for instance, security is to look at what kind of activities they engage in; at the "micro-practices" of companies and at how these relate to practices of other actors. In the case of security, for example, looking at what companies do is a first step towards understanding what role they play in global security governance. In 2007, there were more contractors contractors working for the Pentagon than there were US troops in Iraq (Isenberg 2008). Looking at what these companies do, how they do it and how their actions relate to those of other security institutions (the armed forces, the police, the various informal and "rebel" groups) is an inroad for understanding the degree to which global security governance practice involves private companies.

At the very least one can argue that companies have a "street level" role in producing global security governance. But their activities also alter the rules governing the use of force. The enmeshment of the public and private spheres has placed contract law at the heart of formal regulation; it has created endemic uncertainty about the civilian/combatant status of a whole wide range of actors and about conventional military hierarchies and the applications of martial law. Regulators are trying to catch up with these changes in practices, as is signaled by the intensity of legal discussion but also in legal initiatives such as the US Uniform Code of Military Justice, the Military Extraterritorial Jurisdiction Act or the ICRC-sponsored *Montreux Document* (ICRC 2008; IPOA 2007; Singer 2007b; Waits 2008). For the discussion here it is important to underline that these changes follow changes in governance practices. The plea for a focus on practices is a plea for the analytical and political significance of capturing these changes independently of whether or not regulators react to them. It is a plea for recognizing that what companies *do* (re)produces specific orders.

But order is not only inherent in the doings of people and institutions; it is also (re)produced in discourses and images they and others convey (Campbell 2007; Lacy 2008; Williams 2003). Writing, telling and depicting also play an important role in (re)producing order. They express and shape understanding of global security governance; including ideas about what issues are at stake and what courses of action are available. This is no less true when it comes to thinking about private business in global security governance. The images of the bodies of four Blackwater employees lynched in Fallujah (31 March 2004) and displayed hanging on a bridge were pivotal to the onset of the "Fallujah offensive;" they have shaped understandings of global security governance and the role of private security firms in it. But less noted and perhaps more significant are the consequences of the public statements, advertisements, newspaper articles, interviews, documentaries and films made by and about private security companies and their role in specific conflicts (Leander and van Munster 2007). Studying these images, ideas, branding efforts and media reflections as discursive practices and thinking about how they (re)produce specific roles for private business in global governance is a second way of working with practices (Radin 1996; Leander 2009b).

Finally, practices may not only be about doings and images, they may also be about objects and technologies. "Things can authorize, make possible, encourage, make available, allow, suggest, influence, hinder, prohibit and so on" (Latour 2006: 104). Objects and technologies may be "actants" in the practices that produce order. This certainly is true when it comes to thinking about the role of private firms in global security governance. The so-called revolution in military affairs has been driven largely by "actants," including unmanned armed vehicles of different kinds and the increased reliance on "off-the-shelf," "dual use" technologies. It has also made outsourcing and privatization central to most armed forces (Singer 2009). Similarly, simulation in technology has been an actant not only in tying in the market for video games with the training for the armed forces, but also in the sense of reshaping military practice (Der Derian 2009; Lenoir 2000).

Looking at practices to understand global governance involves looking at what kind of order a specific practice (re)produces. This can be done by singling out doings, depictions or actants. But it often involves tying together a combination of these and looking at how they form *dispositifs* (devices in Foucault's terminology), *agencements* (Deleuze and Guattari) or *assemblages* (Latour) that uphold specific orders (for a discussion see Schatzki 2002). By contrast to many IPE approaches to global governance, the point of entry to a question about the role of business in global governance is hence *not* how companies take part in more or less institutionalized and formal governance arrangements, but how the practices they engage in become part of the "assemblages" that order (i.e. govern) global security. How these practices relate to practices by armed forces, the UN or the media is a question to be answered rather than something that can be posited from the outset. This leads to the second key aspect of analyzing global governance as a practical order: its attention to hierarchies and power relations.

B. Practices producing hierarchies

To mention the relative significance of companies, institutions and armed forces is another way of saying that there are hierarchies in practices. Thinking about global governance as an ordering practice is centrally about clarifying this. The central role of symbolic power and violence directs attention to the role categories and connotations play in producing hierarchies. By the same token it highlights the extent to which notions such as public/private, formal/informal or inside/outside are variable and malleable. It destabilizes them, making them part of the analysis rather than relying on them as points of departure for the analysis. In other words, it effectively removes the formalist blinder.

Inherent in the analysis of practices is an idea that power and hierarchies are continuously produced in the constantly changing interactions that make up the social world. They therefore have to be extrapolated from these relationships (see e.g. Latour 2006: 118–19).[10] Doings, sayings/picturing and technological actants systematically favor some actors and institutions over others. Symbolic violence or power is pivotal in producing this systematic bias and the resulting hierarchies. The reason is that "intersubjectively shared" views (or "the social stock of knowledge," "discourses" or the "*habitus*"[11]) is fundamental in shaping practices. They decide how people understand the context, their interests and their options, but also how they interpret actions by others. Consequently, shaping or being favored by these intersubjectively shared understandings – i.e. having *symbolic power* (Bourdieu 1993) – becomes fundamental for the establishment of hierarchies. Symbolic power effectively obfuscates and hides the power and hierarchies produced in practice by making them appear natural and neutral. It is also essential for understanding why those on the receiving end continue to engage and be complicit in practices that do "*symbolic violence*" to them (Bourgeois 2002; Braud 2003).

Thinking about hierarchies as imbued with symbolic power or violence pushes the analyst to look at what role categories (such as private/public, national/international, state/market) and the connotations categories play in the practices and how they (as part of the intersubjectively shared understandings) participate in producing hierarchies. The point is not that categories are unimportant or have been superseded. Some categorizations may be essential and prove relatively stable. Looking at practices clarifies which ones, how and why. For example, in global governance (and beyond) the inside/outside and public/private categorizations are so profoundly anchored that few (if any) practices are unaffected by them (Bauman 2001; Walker 1993). In security governance, professionals, but also academics, commentators and policy-makers, constantly mobilize the symbolic resources tied to being public and/or private for their own purposes. Private categorization further serves as a matrix structuring thought, analysis, doings, picturing, and sayings in the field. The categories are the taken for granted, the *doxa*, of the field. Formalistic thinking is problematic precisely because it obscures the systematic bias and the "matrix effect" of categorizations (Leander 2009a). By assuming that categories are fixed and unproblematic it creates a "blind spot" in the analysis (Teubner 2006). Thinking in terms of practices logically directs attention to that blind spot, lifting the formalist blinder.

Analogously, the analysis of practices remains open with respect to the significance of material and the institutional in hierarchical orderings, including global security governance. Unlike most other IPE/IR approaches, those analyzing global governance as practice cannot assign a predetermined role to the material (in the guise of, for example, money, arms or natural resources) or to institutions (the UN, the foreign ministry or the armed forces). This makes them difficult to fit into the standard presentations of the discipline where the schools are defined by what they attach most importance to in the analysis: realists focus on states, liberals on interests and non-state actors, Marxians on class relations, constructivists on "ideas" (for such accounts see e.g. Cohn 2009; Jackson and Sørensen 2007; O'Brien and Williams 2007). However, refusing to assign fixed roles does not entail that those studying practices suggest that institutions or material factors are unimportant for order and hierarchies. Whether or not a specific institution or materiality matters – and how – is decided in the practice itself. It is part of the shared understanding (re)produced in the practice.

For example, financial resources are significant to the extent that they are valued in a practice. In security governance the economic clout of companies such as DynCorp shapes order and hierarchy. It allows the company to hire competent staff, advertise, lobby, develop technology and finance a human rights lawyer to participate in public debate surrounding the company, all of which bolsters the company's standing in the field. However, thinking back two decades makes clear that materiality (in this form) matters only because the practice has made it acceptable for companies to advertise, lobby and promote specific technologies and important for them to employ human rights lawyers.

Thinking about the role of business in global governance (of security) in terms of practices has the advantage that it directs our attention to the substantive ordering practices that govern security and to the hierarchies they (re)produce. Formal procedural developments (or material resources) are part of this account, but explaining them is not the main aim. For many political theorists and lawyers this may be disappointing. They are more interested in normative questions about how legitimate authority can be created, exercised and controlled than in the empirical question of its exercise (Flathman 1980). From a sociological or an IPE perspective these priorities are often inversed. Understanding empirical and substantial authority and the potential for action and change is a frequent and recurring aim. For this purpose, thinking in terms of practices is effective as it removes the formalist blinder that otherwise obscures the analysis.

Breaking with atomism: contextualizing practices

Analyzing global governance as a practice further has the advantage of removing the atomist blinder. Practices are confined; specific doings, saying, picturing and technologies ("micro-practices," "everyday social life") are analyzed. One can study global security governance as the ordering (re)produced for example by the practices of South African and Ugandan contractors in Iraq, the advertisements of Gray Security in Africa, or the work of the British Association of Private Security Companies on the role of gender in private security companies. This said, studies of practices are inherently situated in a wider context. They are "cases" of something (Klotz 2008). The practices of the South African and Ugandan contractors are cases of global security governance. Deployed in this way, studies of practices inevitably speak back to the more general context to refine and improve understanding of them. By the same token they lift the atomist blinder by removing the temptation to study cases, and particularly scandalous ones, in isolation.

A. Contextual practices

Practices are always contextual.[12] They are situated, framed and shaped by developments that go on elsewhere. These have to be taken into consideration if an ordering practice – and the hierarchies and power relations it (re)produces – is to be analyzed. The practices of African soldiers can only be made sense of with reference to the context in which they occur. To think that one can understand a practice by narrowing enquiry is a mistake.

At the most general level, practices are contextual because the context profoundly shapes and influences the practice. The context defines a large share of what is natural, acceptable and doable and consequently weighs heavily on "symbolic power." The recent ascension of business in global governance of security, for example, only makes sense against the backdrop of broader developments. New public management thinking and the (Foucauldian) "neo-liberal governmentality" it expresses, the obsession with risk (turn towards "risk society") and the end of the cold war have been particularly important in this respect (Minow 2003). They have led to profound alterations of general understandings about the role of business in global governance, which are generally relevant also for security governance. They have altered the terms on which companies engage in security – from being illegitimate mercenaries, companies are now broadly considered legitimate service providers. Mercenaries have become market actors (Chesterman and Lehnardt 2007; Leander 2007, 2009d). The context, in other words, sets the basic understanding that informs the practice, it shapes the rules of the game and it creates systematic biases in favor of some and against others. Analyzing the practices of African contractors in Iraq requires some notion of these basic conditions. Their presence, activities, relations to their employers, to the Iraqi institutions/law and to other laws/institutions are molded by this context. Hence to analyze their practices and the way these order security requires contextualization.

More than this, contextualizing is necessary to understand the strategies, interests and choices of those who engage in a practice. It is not only about general rules of the game and points of departure. The general context may become part of behavior, as part of taken-for-granted attitudes and habits that are not consciously reflected on and are slow to change. A strong statist imprint on security is (re)produced in soldiering where national belonging, military grade and branch, and a conventional ethos of protection are omnipresent. However, and at the same time, there is no reason to think that those engaged in a practice cannot (or do not) manipulate ideas and biases from a more general context to their own advantage. The South African contractors (working privately) effectively mobilize the (old) statist understanding of military valor – highlighting their military qualifications, their ranking and their attachment to legitimate states – and a (new) market discourse that emphasizes decentralized knowledge and cost effectiveness and a capacity to manage risks anchored in market-based experience across the African continent (e.g. Eben Barlow, quoted in Seery 2007).

The recognition of this dual role of context (as shaping *both* the general taken-for-granted rules *and* as being instrumentalized in strategies and actions) underlines that it may not be essential to know whether ideas are "really" taken for granted or not. We do not need to get into people's heads and minds to show that they are unconsciously shaped by ideas. It is far more pertinent to understand what the general notions that can be drawn in and manipulated are, and especially whether or not actors have any chance of altering hierarchies (re)produced in practices by drawing on them.

Contextualizing is an integral and unavoidable part of the analysis of practices. It is necessary for understanding the basic conditions of any practice, the rules of the game as well as the strategies of actors. To understand an ordering practice and its power relations, contextualization is necessary. Looking at global security governance and the role of business in it hence leads away from atomism because contextualization is part and parcel of any analysis. But, more than this, the analysis of practices leads away from atomism also in a second way: practices are usually analyzed as talking back to and transforming contexts.

B. Global governance practices transforming contexts

Contexts are themselves made up of the practices that (re)produce them. If we think about the current context that favors decentralized governance through (quasi-) markets, that context is produced through a great number of practices by companies, the media, the military consultancy industry, armed forces, defense and foreign ministries but also in governments, educational institutions, and the public services.[13] The implication is that analysis of these practices is a way of improving, refining and perhaps altering understandings of the current pro-market, "neo-liberal" context.[14] The study of a practice ordering global governance in security must be informed by context but it will also talk back at context. Those who study practices often do take the step to explicitly reflect on what the analysis of an ordering practice and its hierarchies tells us about context.

When talking back at context, the accent is frequently placed on the "re" in (re)produce. Focus is then directed at how specific practices underpin and reinforce (possibly also reshape) existing orders. For example, in the case of practices producing global governance in security the evaluation practices of private companies, consultants, rating agencies, but also national (e.g. GAO) and international institutions (e.g. the UN's Brahimi report) create a bias for private firms through the indicators and criteria they use in evaluations and through the skewed application of these to private companies (Löwenheim 2008; Markusen 2003). This in turn reinforces the tendency to rely even more on markets in security, which places private companies in an even more central role in the practices that produce the global governance of security.

Evaluation practices in security are, in other words, an example of how practices reflect a pro-market logic which they *also* confirm/reinforce. They speak back at the context. Evaluation practices become a "self-fulfilling prophecy"; an old idea that has been revived in recent constructivist IPE/IR work (Guzzini 2003, 2010; Guzzini and Leander 2006). But more than this, the UN Brahimi report or the GAO evaluations and their results are not confined to shaping governance in security. They are discussed and debated in politics at large. They become part of the arguments and ideas that shape other practices that also uphold pro-market governance. The practice of evaluation speaks back at the context and (*re*)produces it. Most scholars working on practices do reflect on this by asking, for example, whether this reproduction differs significantly from what is usually said. This is often the key claim to making theoretical/general scientific contribution.

Practices also talk back at contexts in ways that emphasize the "producing" – rather than the "re" – in (re)producing. Focus is then not directed at how practices mirror and stabilize existing logics but at how they create new ones; on how new doings, sayings, depiction and technologies can alter the general context of a practice. For example, the rapidly growing use of computer simulations in training has transformed soldiering as well as strategy and hence the practice ordering security provision, tying it into a number of new areas and expanding the scope of activities (Singer 2009). Similarly, the advertising practices and lobby practices of private companies, as well as their status as public experts on security, have been pivotal to enlarging the scope of what falls within the realm of security to be handled mainly by security professionals (Leander 2007).

The consequence is that new technologies, sayings and doings have reshaped the context. The boundaries of security practices have been moved outwards in many areas, encroaching on other practices and displacing them. For example, security has crowded out other concerns in post-conflict reconstruction, as is reflected in the rapid expansion of the resources and energy flowing into Security Sector Reform and Disarmament Demobilization and Reintegration as opposed to conventional infrastructure programs or development aid (Abrahamsen and Williams 2006; Cockayne 2006; Spearin 2008). It has redefined what political practice in post-conflict context is and who should play a role in it. It has "militarized" politics. "Performativity" – rather than "self-fulfilling prophecy" – may be a useful term for these processes by which a new context is actually performed into being.[15]

Practices are never isolated; they take place in a context by which they are formed and which they in turn (re)produce/refashion. By implication, "contextualizing" practices is not an optional add-on that may or may not be included in the analysis. It is integral to it. It is a condition for understanding the practice and hence the orders and hierarchies it produces. In that sense thinking in terms of practices forcefully lifts the blinder of atomism. This is true of practices that order global governance and the role of business in global governance. Practices are tied directly to contexts. They can consolidate, transform and change them. But they may also be at the origin of new contexts. Analyzing the processes and mechanisms by which this takes place is a – if not *the* – motivation for studying practices.

The rise (and possible decline) of business in global governance

Change (or at least revealing the potential for change) figures prominently on the social and political science agenda. This may be because of a conservative concern with the perversity, futility and jeopardy of change or because of a critical ambition to make science reveal "emancipatory" potential (Hirschman 1991; Patomäki 2002). When it comes to thinking about the role of business in the global governance of security, comprehending change must figure centrally. The role of private business has moved from being marginal and tightly controlled by states to becoming independent and prominent. The final point this chapter wants to underscore is that, in addition to lifting conventional blinders that hamper the analysis of the private military/security business, a practice perspective on global governance also provides considerable leverage for examining change. This leverage is provided by the centrality of "resistance" and "reflexivity" to the approach.

A. Practices of resistance/resistant practices

Because work on practices emphasizes the constant reproduction of orderings it is correspondingly good at highlighting resistance to order and hence the potential for change. With regard to discussions about the evolving role of private company practices as a form of global governance in security, these insights can be useful both for explaining the ascendance of private companies and for thinking about the fragility of this change.

Resistance is built in as inherent in practices. First, because looking at practices involves emphasizing a lack of fixity. People studying practices favor the use of verbs and shun nouns in social analysis to undermine the immobility that comes with structure, discourse and actor. They are therefore often thought of as "post-structuralists" (having moved beyond structural thinking), working with "productive power" (rather than resources) and the formation of "subjectivities" (rather than actors). In Bourdieu's terminology fields are sites of struggle as much as sites of positions.[16] If orderings and hierarchies are not permanent creations, hovering outside and above actors but constantly created in practice through interactions, it is not only possible but probable that those in a practice should try to conserve or change them to their own benefit and that competing – possibly incompatible – understandings of a practice should be clashing within any given practice. Resistance and potential for change is hence something inherent and normal, in contrast to much IPE/IR where change is analyzed as a break with normality the likelihood of which can be captured by analyzing "scope conditions" or "critical junctures" (see Frieden and Lake 1995; Frieden 2007).

This omnipresence of resistance and potential change provides analytical leverage for explaining changes in power and hierarchies. It keeps dissent and diverging understandings in the analysis. It can hence see the sources of change, including during normality.[17] This has made work on practices better at explaining the ascent of private companies in global governance of security. An emphasis on the multiplicity of conflicts surrounding the role of companies in various security practices, also before the end of the Cold War, makes it easier to comprehend the radical transformations in public discourses. In some areas the status and involvement of private firms in security had changed markedly already before the end of the Cold War.

For example, in logistics, technological developments and altered economic governance had already made companies central independent actors even though little formal change had occurred (Lovering 2000). A practice perspective captures this, which makes the "normalization" of the governance practices in security following the end of the Cold War appear less radical and surprising than it does to most other IPE/IR perspectives (Patomäki 2008; Leander 2008b). Analogously, because analyzing resistance is integral to the analysis of practices, those working on practices are less prone to overstating the permanence and immobility of the order. They have for example been more cautious in confirming the inevitability and irreversibility of private companies in the global governance of security than other commentators (Leander 2009f). Looking at practices brings out the resistance against this ascendance and the diverging views on it, and hence sustains awareness of its fragility and possible reversal.

Resistance, in other words, figures centrally in the analysis of change in global governance conceived as practice. It provides inroads for understanding change and putting it in perspective. But more than this, it provides the point of departure for imagining possible futures. Looking at practices as centrally involving resistance and dissent is also a way of identifying potentially influential alternatives. Researchers working on practices are probably better equipped to predict (or devise scenarios) than are most conventional IPE/IR theorists, as emphasized by those who did see the end of the Cold War coming (e.g. Evangelista 1999; Hopf 2002; Kaldor 2003).

B. Reflexivity and change

Reflexivity is a second key way that practice theories have of explaining and conceptualizing change. Reflexivity generally refers to bending back and reflecting on one's own doing or sayings or writing. In IPE it is usually associated with Robert Cox, who remarked that since "science is always for someone" it is important to be reflexive about who one's own scientific work is for.[18] However, reflexivity is central in all "constructivist" thinking in IPE, including practice theory (Bourdieu 2004; Leander 2002; 2008c). The reason is that meaning (produced in practices, including those of the academic) is "constitutive" of social relations. Since this is the case, reflexivity about meaning is a key avenue for understanding change.

One way to link reflexivity and change is through those observing, analyzing, describing and depicting the world (second-order observations). The practices of observers play an important role in producing the meaning that constitutes the social world. This is the backdrop against which one must understand the focus on expert institutions, practices in the World Bank, the IMF or amongst academic economists and the exhortation that these observers should be aware of the power effects their knowledge produces (see e.g. Cameron and Palan 2004; Fourcade-Gourinchas 2006; Dezalay and Barth 2002).

In the practices of global governance in security, this focus on evolving knowledge practices could explain the viability of an Orwellian discourse on private security companies in global governance. The lobby organization trying to extend the role of private military companies internationally calls itself the "International Peace Operations Association" (IPOA), calls the military service business "the Peace and Stability Industry", and edits a journal called the *Journal of International Peace Operations*. Looking reflexively at knowledge production helps clarify how this has become possible by highlighting how changed understandings about the appropriate role of military markets, the nature of military expertise and the role of these in multilateral operations among experts (including in academia) are necessary for these labels to be credible. It could also trigger critical reflection; strengthening "resistance" and competing discourses.

A second link between reflexivity and change in the analysis of global governance as practice is through reflexivity at the level of those engaged in practices (first-order observation). In fact, reflexivity or bending back on one's own practice is not only something that matters at the level of academics and other observers or that only these people engage in. Those in a practice are engaged in (often more sophisticated) reflexivity about their own practice. In global security governance reflexivity is pivotal for understanding developments both past and ahead. The reports by human rights activists, the concerns of lawyers in the armed forces and the wish of companies and their employees to clarify their obligations and rights, have been crucial in reshaping the legal practices and informal norms governing the involvement of private companies in conflicts (for a range of examples, see Leander 2009e). This reflexivity in turn spurs critique of power relations, it may bolster existing competing discourses, but it may also create new ones. In so doing, reflexivity becomes a key ingredient of change in the constant reproduction of ordering hierarchies.

The dividing line separating second-order reflexivity and reflexivity of those engaged in a practice is fuzzy. But the dividing line is not significant. The point is that reflexivity is integral to the analysis of change in practices. Similarly to resistance, reflexivity highlights that there are alternatives to existing orders and hierarchies. Highlighting resistance and reflexivity is usually about "unveiling" power relations and facilitating change. However, an analysis of practices has little to say about whether change will be an improvement. It is less helpful for thinking normatively than for understanding the practices producing norms, the hierarchy entailed by norms and the direction in which norms may evolve.

Conclusion

Global governance in this chapter has been treated as a hierarchical ordering (re)produced in practices. The chapter has insisted (as summarized in the table below) that shifting to a "practice approach" makes the evolving role of business in global governance (of security) less elusive and a that there are a range of relatively well established concepts that can be deployed to think about this role.

Summary Table: The Evolving Role of Business in Global Security Governance...

Is *elusive for* *conventional IR/IPE* because of	Can be captured by *practice approaches* because they look at	*Key Concepts* used in practice approaches
Formalism	Political orderings	Assemblages /dispositifs / agencements
	Hierarchical	Symbolic power /violence
Atomism	Contextually (**re-**) produced	Self-fulfilling prophecy
	Contextually (re-) **produced**	Performativity
Immobilism	Multiple and contradictory Practices	Resistance
	Multiple and contradictory Discourses	Reflexivity (1st and 2nd Order)

To be able to capture the role of business in global security governance is an important achievement. However, it comes at a cost: the analysis of global governance as practice does not allow for grand statements based on studies informed by the timeless categories of the social sciences.[19] This price may be worth paying. If the analysis improves our understanding of power relations in specific areas of global governance (such as security) it may not be so important that it cannot make grand and general statements about business in global governance. If practice analysis can help debunk such statements that often serve more to hide and legitimize power relations than to reveal them, one might even consider that the price is cheap.

Notes

1 Thanks to Lothar Brock, Benedicte Bull, Nicole Deitelhoff, Clair Cutler, Anna Geis, Hans Krause Hansen, Morten Ougaard and the students in the Global Political Economy course at CBS (fall 2008) for helpful comments on an earlier version of this chapter.

2 The "practice turn" in the social sciences has resulted in a rapidly growing body of literature. I refer mainly to the thinking of Bourdieu, Foucault, and the actor network (ANT) theorist Latour. But clearly practice theory can also be inspired by Wittgenstein or Berger and Luckmann. For useful overviews see Schatzki (2000) and for a critique Turner (1994).

3 Military/security business refers to firms providing military or security services (including direct provision of security, logistical support, training and intelligence) in the context of armed conflict. References on this topic have been reduced to a minimum. For fuller discussions and references please refer to Leander (2009b, 2009e).

4 For a more extensive discussion of formalism see Cutler (2002: 35 ff).

5 For illustrations of this see e.g. Avant (2005), Krahmann (2005), Singer (2003: chapters 6 and 7) or Verkuil (2007)..

6 For a vivid account of how this works in the DRC context see the UN report on the conflict in the area (United Nations 2001).

7 For an introduction to a series of books documenting Cheney's professional activities in the public and private sectors, see Didion (2006). For discussions on his role in the development of the private military sector in the US see ICIJ (2002).

8 For a more elaborate argument on this point, see Leander (2009a).

9 For elaborations of this argument see Abrahamsen and Williams (2009); Leander (2008c, 2009b, 2009c).

10 As Latour underlines, contrasting work on practices with "critical" sociology: practices reveal "the visible and modifiable means used to produce power [while] sociology – and critical sociology in particular – has all too often substituted these by an invisible, immobile, and homogenous world of power in itself" (Latour 2006: 123).

11 These expressions refer to different traditions in work on practices and therefore also differ in substantive ways. However, at the level discussed here they converge.

12 Context in practice theory is itself (surprise!) not predefined by theory (as a structure or a discourse) but by the nature of the practice. As Latour insists, "I have always found it hard to believe that it was necessary to absorb the exact same types of actors, the same entities, the same kinds of beings and the same forms of existence, in the same type of collections as those used by Comte, Durkeheim, Weber or Parsons" (Latour 2006: 375). Consequently, what exactly context is depends: "when a context is made out of entities of the same sort as those of which it is the context, I call it a texture. When this stuff differs, I call it a contexture" as Schatzki explains, leaving it up to the scholar to decide what is relevant in any specific study (Schatzki 2002).

13 The hierarchy among these practices is itself a subject of long discussion. Bourdieu for example clearly suggests that some practices – those in metafields such as the state or education – are more important than others (see e.g. Bourdieu 2000).

14 Neo-liberal is used here in a Foucauldian sense referring to a specific, historically situated form of governmentality (way of understanding government). See in particular Foucault (2004).

15 In IPE/IR performativity has been tied mainly to work on gender (Butler 1990) and on securitization (it is central to Austin's speech act theory). However, there is considerable work in the field of economic sociology that could be of more direct relevance to analysis of markets and market practices, including particularly MacKenzie (2006) and MacKenzie et al. (2007).

16 Bourdieu was very critical of the "post structuralists" and preferred to label himself a "structuralist constructivist." For a discussion and comparison see Callewaert (2006).

17 Bourdieu and Foucault both grant exceptional circumstances a limited role in explaining change. Foucault's large macro changes (from punishment to discipline, for example) take place for reasons that are not tied to any crisis or any exceptional circumstance. Even more provocatively, Bourdieu explicitly highlights the limited impact of major crisis. The state *nobility* has successfully (re)produced itself since and through the French Revolution, which is usually supposed to have eliminated it (Bourdieu 1998).

18 As with most critical theorists, Cox turned this statement into a normative one that science should be emancipatory, reveal power and pave the way for change. But it is a common view in academia. Strange, for example, considered revealing power the moral obligation created by academic privileges.

19 One of the arguments Bruno Latour gives for not renaming his theory is that the acronym ANT suitably conveys the kind of work shouldered by those working with the approach (Latour 2005: 69). Similarly, Bourdieu repeatedly expressed his disdain for those who refused to engage in hard and time-consuming empirical work.

References

Abrahamsen, R. and Williams, M.C. (2006) "Security sector reform: bringing the private in," *Conflict, Security & Development*, 6: 1–23.

—— (2009) "Security Beyond the State: Global Security Assemblages in International Politics," *International Political Sociology*, 3: 1–17.

Avant, D. (2005) *The Market for Force: The Consequences of Privatizing Security* (Cambridge: Cambridge University Press).

Bauman, Z. (2001) "Reconnaissance Wars of the Planetary Frontierland," *Theory, Culture & Society*, 19: 81–90.

Bourdieu, P. (1993) *Language and Symbolic Power* (Harvard: Harvard University Press).

—— (1998) *State Nobility: Elite Schools in the Field of Power* (Cambridge: Polity Press).

—— (2000) *Propos sur le Champ Politique, avec une Introduction de Philippe Fritsch* (Lyon: Presses Universitaires de Lyon).

—— (2004) *Science of Science and Reflexivity* (Chicago: University of Chicago Press).

Bourgeois, P. (2002) "La violence en temps de guerre et en temps de paix. Leçons de l'après-guerre froide: l'exemple du Salvador," *Cultures et Conflits*: 81–116.

Braud, P. (2003) "Violence symbolique et mal-être identitaire," *Raisons Poliques*: 33–48.

Butler, J. (1990) *Gender Trouble. Feminism and the Subversion of Identity* (New York: Routledge).

Callewaert, S. (2006) "Bourdieu, Critic of Foucault: The Case of Empirical Social Science against Double-Game-Philosophy," *Theory, Culture & Society*, 23: 73–98.

Cameron, A. and Palan, P.R. (2004) *The Imagined Economies of Globalization* (London et al.: Sage).

Campbell, D. (2007) "Geopolitics and Visuality: Sighting the Darfur Conflict," *Political Geography*, 26: 357–82.

Chesterman, S. and Lehnardt, C. (eds) (2007) *From Mercenaries to Markets: The Rise and Regulation of Private Military Companies* (Oxford: Oxford University Press).

Cockayne, J. (2006) "Commercial Security in the Humanitarian Space," in *International Peace Academy*. New York: (available at: www.ipacademy.org/pdfs/COMMERCIAL_SECURITY_FINAL.pdf).

Cohn, T.H. (2009) *Global Political Economy: Theory and Practice* (New York: Longman).

Cutler, C.A. (2002) "Private international regimes and interfirm cooperation," in R.B. Hall and T.J. Biersteker (eds) *The Emergence of Private Authority in Global Governance*, pp. 23–40 (Cambridge: Cambridge University Press).

de Goede, M. (2006) "International Political Economy and the Promises of Poststructural-ism," in M. de Goede (ed.) *International Political Economy and Poststructural Politics*, pp. 1–20 (Basingstoke and New York: Palgrave).

Der Derian, J. (2009) *Virtuous War: Mapping the Military-Industrial-Media-Entertainment Network* (New York: Routledge).

Dezalay, Y. and Barth, B.G. (2002) *The Internationalization of Palace Wars: Lawyers, Economists and the Contest to Transform Latin American States* (Chicago and London: The University of Chicago Press).

Didion, J. (2006) "Cheney: The Fatal Touch," *New York Review of Books*, 53.

Evangelista, M. (1999) *Unarmed Forces: The Transnational Movement to End the Cold War* (Ithaca: Cornell University Press).

Fainaru, S. (2008) *Big Boy Rules: In the Company of America's Mercenaries Fighting in Iraq* (Cambridge: Da Capo Press).

Flathman, R.E. (1980) *The Practice of Political Authority: Authority and the Authoritative* (Chicago: Chicago University Press).

Foucault, M. (2004) *Sécurité, territoire, population. Cours au Collège de France (1977–1978)* (Paris: Gallimard, Seuil).

Fourcade-Gourinchas, M. (2006) "The Construction of a Global Profession: The Transnationalization of Economics," *American Journal of Sociology*, 112: 149–95.

Frieden, J. (2007) *Global Capitalism: Its Fall and Rise in the Twentieth Century* (New York: W.W. Northon).

Frieden, J. and Lake, D. (1995) *International Political Economy: Perspectives on Global Power and Wealth* (New York: Routledge).

Guzzini, S. (2003) "'Self-fulfilling geopolitics?', or: the social production of foreign policy expertise in Europe," in *Danish Institute of International Affairs. WorkingPapers no. 23*, Copenhagen.

Guzzini, S. (ed.) (2010) *Geopolitics Redux? 1989 and the revival of geopolitical thought in Europe*.

Guzzini, S. and Leander, A. (2006) "Wendt's constructivism: a relentless quest for synthesis," in S. Guzzini and A. Leander (eds) *Constructivism and International Relations: Wendt and his critics*, pp. 73–92 (London and New York: Routledge).

Heaton, J.R. (2005) "Civilians at War: Reexamining the Status of Civilians Accompanying the Armed Forces," *Air Force Law Review*, 57: 157–208.

Hirschman, A.O. (1991) *The Rhetoric of Reaction. Perversity, Futility, Jeopardy* (Cambridge (MA) and London: The Belknap Press of the Harvard University Press).

Hopf, T. (2002) *Social Construction of International Politics: Identities and Foreign Policies, Moscow, 1955 and 1999* (Ithaca: Cornell University Press).

Human Rights First (2008) "Private Security Contractors at War: Ending the Culture of Impunity," in Washington: Human Rights *First* (available at: www.humanrightsfirst.org).

ICIJ (International Consortium of Investigative Journalists) (2002) *Making a Killing: The Business of War*, Washington, DC: ICIJ (available at: www.publicintegrity.org/dtaweb/ICIJ_BOW.ASP?Section = Chapter&ChapNum = 1).

ICRC (2008) "Montreux Document on Pertinent International Legal Obligations and Good Practices for States related to Operations of Private Military and Security Companies during Armed Conflict," in Geneva (available at: www.icrc.org/web/eng/siteeng0.nsf/htmlall/montreux-document-170908).

IPOA (2007) Peace Operations and the Law. *International Peace Operations Association Quarterly* 2 (available at: http://peaceops.com/web/).

Isenberg, D. (2008) *Shadow Force: Private Security Contractors in Iraq* (New York: Praeger).

Jackson, R. and Sørensen, G. (2007) *Introduction to International Relations: Theories and Approaches* (2nd revised edition) (Oxford: Oxford University Press).

Kaldor, M. (2003) *Global Civil Society: An Answer to War* (Cambridge: Polity Press).

Kierpaul, I. (2008) "The Rush to Bring Private Military Contractors to Justice: The Mad Scramble of Congress, Lawyers, and Law Students after Abu Ghraib," *The University of Toledo Law Review*, 39: 407–35.

Klotz, A. (2008) "Case Selection," in A. Klotz and P. Depaak (eds) *Qualitative Methods in International Relations: A Pluralist Guide*, pp. 43–58 (Basingstoke: Palgrave Macmillan).

Krahmann, E. (2005) "Controlling Private Military Companies in the UK and Germany: Between Partnership and Regulation," *European Security*, 13: 277–95.

Lacy, M. (2008) "Designer Security: Control Society and MoMA's SAFE: Design Takes on Risk," *Security Dialogue*, 39: 333–57.

Larner, W. and Walters, W.P. (2004) *Global Governmentality: Governing International Spaces* (London: Routledge).

Latour, B. (2005) *Re-assembling the Social. An Introduction to Actor Network Theory* (Oxford: Oxford University Press).

—— (2006) *Changer de société, refaire de la sociologie (Re-assembling the Social. An Introduction to Actor Network Theory)* (Paris: La Découverte).

Leander, A. (2002) "Do we really need reflexivity in IPE? Bourdieu's two reasons for answering affirmatively (contribution to a colloquium on Pierre Bourdieu)," *Review of International Political Economy*, 9: 601–9.

—— (2005) "The Power to Construct International Security: On the Significance of Private Military Companies," *Millennium*, 33: 803–26.

—— (2006) *Eroding State Authority? Private Military Companies and the Legitimate Use of Force* (Rome: Centro Militare di Studi Strategici).

—— (2007) "Regulating the Role of PMCs in Shaping Security and Politics," in S. Chesterman and C. Lehnardt (eds) *From Mercenaries to Markets: The Rise and Regulation of Private Military Companies*, pp. 49–64 (Oxford: Oxford University Press).

—— (2008a) "Portraits in Practice: The Politics of Outsourcing Security," *Underreview forthcoming* (available at: http://www.cbs.dk/content/view/pub/38570).

—— (2008b) "Scenarios and Science in IR/IPE. Review Symposium on Heikki Patomäki's 'The Political Economy of Global Security'," *Cooperation and Conflict*, 43: 447–67.

—— (2008c) "Thinking Tools," in A. Klotz and P. Depaak (eds) *Qualitative Methods in International Relations: A Pluralist Guide*, pp. 11–28 (Basingstoke: Palgrave Macmillan).

—— (2009a) "Chimeras with Obscure Powers: Hybrid States and the Public–Private Distinction," in *The International Studies Association Workshop: The Chimerical State and the Public–Private Hybridization of the 21st Century State* (New York).

—— (2009b) "Commercial Security Practices," in P.J. Burgess (ed) *Handbook of New Security Studies* (London and New York: Routledge).

—— (2009c) "*Habitus* and Field," *Blackwell: International Studies Compendium Project*.

—— (2009d) "New Roles for External Actors? Disagreements about International Regulation of Private Armies," in K. Aggestam and A. Björkdal (eds) *War and Peace in Transition: Changing Roles for External Actors*, pp. 32–52 (Lund: Nordic Academic Press).

—— (2009e) "The Privatization of Security," in M. Dunn Cavelty and V. Mauer (eds) *The Routledge Handbook of Security Studies* (London and New York: Routledge).

—— (2009f) "Securing Sovereignty by Governing Security through Markets," in R. Adler-Nissen and T. Gammeltoft-Hansen (eds) *Sovereignty Games: Instrumentalising State Sovereignty in Europe and Beyond*, pp. 151–70 (London: Palgrave).

Leander, A. and van Munster, R. (2007) "Private Security Contractors in Darfur: Reflecting and Reinforcing Neo-Liberal Governmentality," *International Relations*, 21: 201–16.

Lenoir, T. (2000) "All But War Is Simulation: The Military–Entertainment Complex," *Configurations*, 8: 289–335.

Lovering, J. (2000) "Loose Cannons: Creating the Arms Industry of the Twenty-first Century," in M. Kaldor (ed.) *Global Insecurity*, pp. 147–76 (London: Pinter).

Löwenheim, O. (2008) "Examining the State: A Foucauldian perspective on international 'governance indicators'," *Third World Quarterly*, 29: 255–74.

MacKenzie, D. (2006) *An Engine, Not a Camera. How Financial Models Shape Markets* (Cambridge, MA: MIT Press).

MacKenzie, D., Muneisa, F. and Siu, L. (eds) (2007) *Do Economists Make Markets? On the Performativity of Economics* (Princeton: Princeton University Press).

Markusen, A.R. (2003) "The Case Against Privatizing National Security," *Governance: An International Journal of Policy, Administration, and Institutions*, 16: 471–501.

Minow, M. (2003) "Public and Private Partnerships: Accounting for the New Religion," *Harvard Law Review*, 116: 1229–70.

O'Brien, R. and Williams, M. (2007) *Global Political Economy: Evolution and Dynamics* (Houndmills and New York: Palgrave Macmillan).

Patomäki, H. (2002) *After International Relations: Critical Realism and the (Re)construction of World Politics* (London and New York: Routledge).

—— (2008) *The Political Economy of Global Security. War Future and Changes in Global Governance* (London and New York: Routledge).

Radin, M.J. (1996) *Contested Commodities: The Trouble with Trade in Sex, Children, Body Parts and Other Things* (Harvard: Harvard University Press).

Rosenau, J.N. (2002) "Governance in a New Global Order," in D. Held and A.G. McGrew (eds) *Governing Globalization: Power, Authority and Global Governance*, pp. 70–86 (Oxford: Polity Press).

Schatzki, T.R. (2002) *The Site of the Social: A Philosophical Account of the Constitution of Social Life and Change* (Penn State University Press).

Schatzki, T.R., Knorr-Cetina, K. and von Savigny, E. (eds) (2000) *The Practice Turn in Contemporary Theory* (New York: Routledge).

Seery, B. (2007) "Bullets, bombs and business," in *The Star*, 5 November.

Shearer, D. (1998) "Outsourcing War," *Foreign Policy*, Fall: 68–81.

Singer, P.W. (2003) *Corporate Warriors. The Rise of the Privatized Military Industry* (Ithaca and London: Cornell University Press).

—— (2007a) "Can't Win with 'Em, Can't Go to War without 'Em: Private Military Contractors and Counterinsurgency," *Foreign Policy at Brookings. Policy Papers*.

—— (2007b) "The Law Catches Up to Private Militaries (and embeds too)," *DefenseTech* (available at: http://www.defensetech.org/archives/003123.html).

—— (2009) *Wired for War: The Robotics Revolution and Conflict in the 21st Century* (New York: Penguin Press).

Spearin, C. (2008) "Private, Armed and Humanitarian? States, NGOs, International Private Security Companies and Shifting Humanitarianism," *Security Dialogue*, 39: 363–82.

Stoker, D. (ed.) (2008) *From Mercenaries to Privatization, 1815–2007* (New York: Routledge).

Teubner, G. (2006) "In the Blind Spot: The Hybridization of Contracting," *Theoretical Inquiries in Law*, 8: 51–72.

Turner, S. (1994) *The social theory of practices* (Chicago: Chicago University Press).

United Nations (2001) *Report of the Panel of Experts on the Illegal Exploitation of Natural Resources and Other Forms of Wealth of the Democratic Republic of Congo (S/2001/357)*, New York: UN Security Council.

Verkuil, P. (2007) *Outsourcing Sovereignty: Why Privatization of Government Functions Threatens Democracy and What We Can Do about It* (Cambridge: Cambridge University Press).

Waits, E.K. (2008) "Avoiding the 'Legal Bermuda Triangle': The Military Extraterritorial Jurisdiction Act's Unprecedented Expansion of U.S. Criminal Jurisdiction over Foreign Nationals," *Arizona Journal of International and Comparative Law*, 23: 493–540.

Walker, R.B.J. (1993) *Inside/Outside: International relations as political theory* (Cambridge: Cambridge University Press).

War on Want (2006) *Corporate Mercenaries*, London: War on Want (available at: www.waronwant.org/Corporate%20Mercenaries%2013275.twl).

Williams, M.C. (2003) "Words, Images, Enemies: Securitization and International Politics," *International Studies Quarterly*, 47: 511–29.

Zamparelli, C.S.J. (1999) "Competitive sourcing and privatization: Contractors on the battlefield," *Air Force Journal of Logistics*, XXIII: 1–17.

4 Unthinking the GATS

A radical political economy critique of private transnational governance

A. Claire Cutler

This chapter develops a radical political economy critique of the role of governance devolving to private business corporations under the multilateral trade agreement, the General Agreement on Trade in Services (GATS). This agreement contributes to profound changes in state–society relations by de-centering states as "masters" of their households and as the constitutive "subjects" of international law. In their place are powerful transnational business corporations who, through the GATS, are interpellated as self-governing, neoliberal subjects, whose subjectivity lies not with any particular state but with a new master, that of transnational capitalism and the nascent transnational and neoliberal business civilization.

The paper begins by situating the GATS as an instance of private transnational governance that functions, materially and institutionally, as a regime of private accumulation, and ideologically as a legitimating mechanism. The origin of the GATS is discussed and the process by which transnational corporations de-center the state as "subject" is theorized. The paper argues, however, that transnational business corporations are neither monolithic nor perfectly interpellated as subjects of transnational capitalism and neoliberal discipline, and provides an illustration from the global governance of water services. It concludes that such imperfections open up space for "unthinking" the GATS and advances a praxis conception of transnational law as a fertile theoretical-practical strategy for resisting the discipline of neoliberal market civilization. The analysis suggests the possibility for individual agency to rethink and reshape the conditions that give rise to corporate power and subjectivity in the world today.

The GATS and subjectivity in transnational governance

An understanding of the power of business corporations in the governance of trade in services involves analysis of the political and legal doctrines that empower them as "subjects" of an increasingly transnationalized and privatized politico-legal order. The traditional starting point in international relations and international law is that the state is the main "subject" of political and legal significance (Cutler 2001). Indeed, the analytical and theoretical foundations of both disciplines accept the state as an unproblematic identity, according only derivative political or legal significance to non-state entities such as transnational business corporations. In international relations the dominant theorizations, neorealism and neoliberalism, rest upon statist analytical foundations, while in international law the doctrine of legal positivism restricts legal subjectivity and, indeed, historical significance or effectivity, to states. For conventional theorists, the transnational business corporation, like the individual, is regarded as an "object" and not an effective "subject" of international law (Higgins 1985; Johns 1994). However, less conventional approaches challenge these views by illustrating the power of transnational business corporations to profoundly affect political and legal choices and outcomes, operating as *de facto* "subjects" of international law even though they lack formal legal recognition (Cutler 2001, 2003).

Indeed, so significant are the power and influence of transnational corporations in structuring the global political economy materially, institutionally, and ideologically, that historical materialists resist using the term *international governance*, preferring that of *transnational governance* (Overbeek *et al.* 2007). The idea here is that the transnational corporation has not so much replaced or eclipsed the state, but rather has contributed to processes of re-regulation that reorder state–society relations and in so doing de-center the state as subject, recasting the authority of both business and government in governance. The term *governance without government* (Czempiel and Rosenau 1992) is commonly utilized to capture the enhanced political and legal significance of non-state actors, and there has been a burgeoning of studies of the private authority wielded by transnational business corporations (Cutler 2003; Cutler *et al.* 1999; Graz and Nölke 2008; Hall with Biersteker 2002; Overbeek *et al.* 2007).

The growing political and legal significance of transnational business corporations is being recorded in many diverse areas, including the regulation of economic matters such as finance, banking, accounting, auditing, insurance, credit-rating, trade, investment, taxation, money laundering, securities, technical standards, and corporate social responsibilities in labor, human rights, and environmental relations, as well as military and security relations (Djelic and Sahlin-Andersson 2006; May 2006). A common thread running through all these areas is the increasing intensity and extensity of corporate power and authority resulting from the privatization and marketization of law, regulation, and governance that has taken place throughout the world in past decades. Indeed, this tightening of the nexus between business and governance is symptomatic of deeper structural and discursive connections between capitalism and law. Capitalism does not simply self-generate or reproduce itself, but requires material, institutional, and ideological contexts to support and reproduce its hegemony. Privatized transnational governance provides precisely these contexts and is opening up new vistas for capital accumulation in the deregulated and privatized economies of eastern and central Europe, the Americas, Asia, and Africa (Harvey 2005).

The General Agreement on Trade in Services (GATS), negotiated within the World Trade Organization (WTO) as part of the Uruguay Round of multilateral trade negotiations, is an integral element of privatized transnational governance. The GATS negotiations were driven by powerful transnational service corporations. American-based service industries and their offices abroad in telecommunications, finance, and insurance led lobbying efforts to incorporate services into the trade regime and shaped the debates over services regulation (Cafruny 1989; Hoekman and Kostecki 2001).[1]

The GATS has generally unrecognized potential for transforming state–society relations in a most elemental and significant way by reaching deep inside the domestic sphere of states. This is because it embraces the liberalization of myriad basic services and limits a government's ability to impose public policy regulations or legal restrictions on service operations that are found to be discriminatory. It is important to note that, first and foremost, the GATS is a legal document that creates binding and enforceable rights and obligations. While no state can be forced into signing the GATS, once a state signs on, it is legally bound by the terms of the agreement. This is significant because the GATS imports market-based criteria for services provision, disembedding such activity from local social and political controls. In doing so, the GATS facilitates the privatization and commodification of services whose provision in the past was regarded by states as of domestic concern, thus raising essential public policy matters relating to health, safety, environmental protection, domestic development and the like.

Moreover, the GATS grants to foreign private business corporations the same rights as domestic providers have to operate in services provision, leading to a delocalization and transnationalization of services provision. The GATS fundamentally transforms how cross-border services are conceptualized and regulated. Services ranging over business services (legal, accounting, taxation, architectural, engineering, urban planning, medical and dental, veterinary, midwifery, nursing, physiotherapy, computer consulting and data processing, research and development, real estate, rental/leasing, advertising, management, fishing, mining, manufacturing, photography, packaging, printing), communication services (courier, telecommunications, audiovisual, radio, television, sound recording, motion pictures), construction and related engineering services, distribution services, educational services, environmental services (sewage, refuse disposal, sanitary), financial services (insurance, banking), health-related and social services (hospitals), tourism and travel services, recreational, cultural and sporting services (entertainment, news, libraries, sports), and transport services (maritime, internal waterways, air, space, rail, road, pipeline) are slated for liberalization and privatization under the GATS (WTO 1991).

The GATS imports into the regulation of services provision the same disciplines that characterize the regulation of trade in goods under the GATT/WTO regime, in effect treating services provision as tradable commodities. In doing so, it commodifies the service relationship and "disregards the social context of provision, the lived experiences of the poor and dismisses and/or reinforces the way in which deprivations are constituted" (Higgott and Weber 2005). Indeed, the adoption of GATT/WTO language and disciplines and the "shift to trade discourse" for services regulation is described as "a revolution in social ontology: it redefined how governments thought about the nature of services, their movement across borders, their roles in society, and the objectives and principles according to which they should be governed" (Drake and Nicolaïdes 1992). In fact, the characterization of services provision as trade in services is "an artificial construct" that implies the equivalence of trade in goods and trade in services and obscures a recognition of the distinctive and personal nature of providing services as an integral part of daily living and caring that extends "into families, communities, and societies" and serves "purposes that are intrinsically social, as well as environmental, cultural, and economic" (Kelsey 2003: 267). Technical, legal language operationalizing commitments to progressive liberalization and non-discrimination are adopted to govern the policies of states concerning services regulation, involving four modes of delivery. Mode one deals with cross-border supply, mode two addresses consumption abroad, mode three concerns establishing a commercial presence, and mode four regulates the temporary presence of services personnel. The third mode is possibly the most controversial since it effectively sets up rules governing foreign direct investment and is generally regarded as the corporate solution to the failure of the Organization for Economic Cooperation and Development's Multilateral Agreement on Investment. The fourth mode, in contrast, is of greatest concern to developing states that generate considerable remittances from citizens working abroad.

The adoption of the trade in goods paradigm for the regulation of services provision brings along with it the entire corpus of trade law and liberal assumptions concerning the superiority of regulation through free-market principles and related presumptions concerning the equality of bargaining partners in exchange relation-ships and the economic benefits flowing from exchanges, based upon the doctrine of comparative advantage. The GATS functions like a constitution, locking governments into their commitments and further reform.[2] However, as Jane Kelsey (2003) illustrates, the language of non-discrimination and liberalization conceals the inequalities in the bargaining power of developed and developing states and the unequal gains flowing from liberalizing services provision. The GATS was initially resisted by many states, particularly developing states. Most developed states favored mode three commitments to benefit their transnational corporations, but wanted to limit mode four freedoms in order to restrict the influx of foreign workers. In contrast, developing states were reluctant to bind themselves under mode three, but wanted access to foreign labor markets under mode four. In the end, however, even the developing states accepted the four modes, although practice so far reveals that developed states are driving the liberalizing process and concentrating their efforts, predictably, on mode three activities.

How is it that states agreed to accept limits on their policy and legislative independence concerning the regulation of matters regarded as hitting so close to home? Even more problematic, how is it that developing states agreed to accept limitations that have profound implications for their policy autonomy and development prospects? How is it that these states agreed to liberalizing and privatizing services, which effectively cedes subjectivity to foreign corporate services providers? The answer to these questions takes us into the terrain of the constitution of the modern subject as a prelude to examining the constitution, through the GATS, of the transnational business corporation as the contemporary neoliberal subject.

Law and the modern corporate subject

The constitution of the corporation as the modern subject involves a number of developments establishing the corporate form as a dominant legal form and, indeed, a necessary condition for capital accumulation and expansion. In this regard, law and key, influential individuals and groups have exercised significant regulatory power through relations of both consent and coercion. It was noted earlier that capitalism does not establish hegemony or reproduce of its own accord, but requires particular supports. Analyses inspired by the works of Antonio Gramsci (1971) identify the hegemony of capitalism with material, institutional, and ideological conditions that create a favorable climate for the ruling class through achieving a blend of coercion and consent in society (Cox with Sinclair 1996; Gill 1993, 2008). Gramsci insisted that hegemony, the process by which the ruling class establishes the conditions necessary for achieving control, cannot be secured through coercion alone, but requires ideologically capturing popular support and conditioning or legitimating this support as the articulation of the public interest and common sense. In his famous equation "state = political society + civil society," "in other words hegemony protected by the armour of coercion," Gramsci (1971: 263) located hegemony in civil society. The state is thus regarded as combining relations of coercion, associated with the military and state laws, with consent, associated with the voluntary relations of civil society. But hegemony, as in the balance between consent and coercion, he insisted, emerges from civil society. Gramsci (ibid.) used the terms "ethical state," "civil society," and "regulated society" interchangeably to capture the possibility of the withering away of the coercive State by degrees in a society "capable of accepting the law spontaneously, freely, and not through coercion, as imposed by another class, as something external to consciousness."

In this, the praxis conception of law, which was developed in a fragmentary way by Gramsci, is central to achieving a blend of consent and coercion (see Cutler 2008: 216). The praxis conception regards law as operating dialectically by giving rise to both oppressive and emancipatory potentials. The role of "organic intellectuals" is crucial for "creating a social conformism which is useful to the ruling group's line of development" (Gramsci 1971: 247). Organic intellectuals advance the private interests of the ruling class as societal and common interests, thereby assisting in generating popular belief in the legitimacy of the bourgeois order. In this process, capitalist law operates with a "double face" (Cain 1983), creating both coercive and consensual social relations and forming a bourgeois conception of law wherein the "bourgeois class poses itself as an organism in continuous movement, capable of absorbing the entire civil society, assimilating it to its own cultural and economic level" (Gramsci 1971: 260). However, what Gramsci does not address is: how, in the absence of a change in material circumstances, does the subaltern consciously consent to and accept the subjugated position of "subaltern" in this ethical state? This is significant, for, as noted above, this is not a process that is "external to consciousness" (Gramsci 1971: 263).

While this problem will be taken up later, analyses of the origins of the GATS reveal the central role played by "organic intellectuals," who galvanized support for advancing a neoliberal, deregulatory ethos as the *grundnorm* for the regulation of services provision. The GATS agenda was initially driven by powerful transnational corporations and, later, by key international organizations and agencies, and by influential states such as the United States. Drake and Nicolaïdes (1992: 39) describe them as an "epistemic community" comprised of private firms, states, and international organizations committed to the ideological framework of neoliberal market civilization. They included academics, lawyers, industry specialists, journalists, government officials, and representatives from many major transnational corporations, as well as representatives from states and international organizations. Functioning as organic intellectuals, they legitimated the liberalization and privatization of services provision as common sense and as serving the common interest. As organic intellectuals they created the ideological climate for the commodification of services provision by presenting their positions as "scientifically objective" and true, with benefits for "the international community as a whole" (Drake and Nicolaïdes 1992). Invoking neoliberal theory and political economy, these organic intellectuals presented deregulation of services sectors and liberalization as the way forward to prosperity and happiness. In doing so, they gained support and legitimacy from complementary policies adopted by influential international institutions, such as the United Nations, World Bank, and International Monetary Fund, which had for some time been advancing the "public" goods generated by deregulatory and privatization policies.

Unfortunately, Gramsci does not assist in understanding the specific ways in which organic intellectuals and the law serve to refashion "private" matters as "public" interests and concerns or manage to achieve the consent of subaltern peoples and groups. Nor did he get inside the relationship between law and capitalism or establish its transnational reach. The works of Louis Althusser go part way in helping to understand how it is that individuals or states would willingly consent to subordination.

Althusser (1971) began from the position that capitalism would not inevitably produce itself, but required certain dispositions, institutions, structures, and social sites, which he termed "apparatuses," as conditions of existence. In this, he believed that the agency of individuals constituted as willing *subjects* is crucial, as too are the various state apparatuses. The *political apparatus* is comprised of the state, which he termed the "repressive state apparatus" (RSA), and includes the government, administration, military, police, prisons, and the courts. The *ideological state apparatuses* (ISAs) include schools, the family, trade unions, the press, culture, religion and religious institutions, and function ideologically to inculcate people into ways of thinking about and understanding their relationship to society and submitting to the rules of the established order. The distinction between the two is that RSA "functions massively and predominantly *by repression,*" while ISAs "function *by ideology*" (ibid.: 138). Althusser emphasizes that "[t]o my knowledge, *no class can hold State power over a long period without at the same time exercising its hegemony over and in State Ideological Apparatuses*" (ibid.: 139). Thus far, Althusser is more or less at one with Gramsci (1971: 12), who also emphasized the role of schools and other social institutions in the formation of the intellectuals who would function as "deputies" of the ruling class. In fact, Althusser (1971: 136, note 7), in his efforts to capture the material influence of ideology, footnotes Gramsci as being "the only one who went any distance in the road I am taking. He had the 'remarkable' idea that the State could not be reduced to the (Repressive) State Apparatus, but included, as he put it, a certain number of institutions from 'civil society': the Church, the Schools, the trade unions, etc. Unfortunately, Gramsci did not systematize his institutions, which remained in the state of acute but fragmentary notes."

Althusser went further to develop an understanding of the processes by which identities are formed by the material structures of capitalism as *individuals* are filtered through institutions that function ideologically to shape and inculcate them into willing *subjects* of capitalism. Particular emphasis is given to the ideological significance of schools, which, he argued, have replaced churches as the central institutions that through the development of practices and rituals reproduce capitalism by developing "skilled" and conscientious subjects. Althusser speaks of these practices and rituals inscribed in these ideological institutions as "recruiting" individuals and transforming them into subjects through the process of "*interpellation* or hailing" (Althusser 1971: 162–63). The theory of *interpellation* seeks to capture the role that ideology plays in constituting individuals as subjects who are aware of and identify with their own subjectivity and, thereby, participate consensually in the (re)production of capitalism.[3] In the much celebrated essay "Ideology and Ideological State Apparatuses," Althusser (1971: 169) notes the "ambiguity of the term *subject*": in ordinary use it means "a free subjectivity, a centre of initiatives, author of and responsible for its actions." But, *subject* also means "a subjected being, who submits to a higher authority, and is therefore stripped of all freedom except that of freely accepting his submission" (ibid.). This ambiguity, he says, with an illustration from the interpellation of Christians, reflects "the effect which produces it: the individual is interpellated as a (free) subject in order that he shall submit freely to the commandments of the Subject."[4] Althusser begins with the formulation that: "*all ideology hails or interpellates concrete individuals as concrete subjects*, by the functioning of the category of the subject" (ibid.: 162). Note that first there is the concrete *individual* who, upon interpellation by ideology, emerges as a concrete *subject*. It is the process of interpellation that creates the subject: the subject does not preexist the hailing for it is the call that constitutes ("recruits," "transforms") the subject *qua* subject (ibid.: 163). Althusser developed the theory of interpellation through an allegory involving a scene in a street where an individual is hailed by a police officer: "Hey, you there!" The hailed individual turns around and "By this mere one-hundred-and-eighty-degree physical conversion, he becomes a *subject*" (ibid.: 163). The individual becomes a subject, in terms of being subjected, because he recognizes that it "is really him who is being hailed." Althusser continues (ibid.: 163) that this recognition is strange and cannot be explained solely through a guilty conscience, but he doesn't explain why this is so. In an insightful reading of Althusser, Judith Butler (1997: 107) interprets the call "as a demand to align oneself with the law, a turning around (to face the law, to find a face for the law?), and an entrance into the language of self-ascription – 'Here I am' – through the appropriation of guilt." She continues (ibid.) that the act of turning around is not the response to a demand, but rather an act that is both "conditioned by the 'voice' of the law" and by the responsiveness of the one hailed. The turn thus embodies the ambiguity of the *subject* in that it invokes both meanings: one subject to the rule of law and one exercising reflexivity and agency in turning to the law. This assists in understanding why Althusser (1971: 163), although presenting interpellation as a sequential process of hailing and turning, notes that "in reality these things happen without any succession. The existence of ideology and the hailing or interpellation of individuals as subjects are one and the same thing." As will be argued later, this simultaneity of subjection and reflexivity also opens up space for the exercise of human agency.

Butler notes (1997: 116) that the linkage in Althusser of conscience and consciousness to the subject's mastery of the practices and rituals in which he or she is interpellated highlights the double meaning of the *subject* and the simultaneity of the master and subject ascription. But this still raises the question of why the individual accepts the ascription and willingly submits to the law, whether guilty or not. Butler (ibid.: 107) asks: why does the subject (really, the individual) turn and, if the turning is what constitutes the subject, how does the subject know to turn? She argues that the doctrine of interpellation thus "appears to presuppose a prior and unelaborated doctrine of conscience" (ibid.:109).

It is possible to read Althusser's theory of interpellation as embodying a theory of consciousness that, while only implicit, may be usefully developed to understand why the subject appears to willingly accept subjection. This involves consideration of Althusser's understanding of ideology, for it is ideology that he insists constitutes the *subject*. Althusser notes that the hailing of the individual appears to take place "outside ideology" in the street, but "really takes place in ideology" (Althusser 1971: 163). He further observes (ibid.: 169) that "the vast majority of (good) subjects work all right 'all by themselves', i.e. by ideology. ... They are inserted into practices governed by the rituals of the ISAs" and thus require little intervention. But (ibid.: 170) he notes that this is "not 'naturally' so", for their recognition of freedom is a "misrecognition" (*méconnaissance*), because they are "ignorant" of what is taking place. Althusser (ibid.: 148) argues that the "mechanisms which produce this vital result for the capitalist regime [the reproduction of "the relations of exploited to exploiters and exploiters to exploited"] are naturally covered up and concealed by the universally reigning ideology." Ideology, being "the system of the ideas and representations which dominate the mind of man or a social group," (ibid.: 149) does not represent the actual or real position of the subject, but an idealized, imaginary situation because the subject's consciousness has been framed and, indeed, constituted by the very ideology that mystifies the real conditions of existence. It is thus necessary to get behind ideology in order "to outline a discourse which tries to break with ideology" (ibid.: 162).

The theory of consciousness implicit in this account of identity formation takes as its point of departure Karl Marx's theory of commodity fetishism. In *Capital* (Marx [1867] 1976) and other texts Marx shows that the logic of subject formation is parallel to the logic of commodity formation.[5] The interpellation of the modern subject is thus connected to the production and reproduction of the capitalist system. Insofar as the system relies upon fetishized commodity relations, the modern subject will possess a fetishized consciousness. The theory of commodity fetishism is based on the insight that social relations take on a specific form under capitalist production, entailing, as the latter does, the alienation of the worker from the fruit of his/her labor, the commodity. Theorizing that commodities have both use-value and exchange-value, Marx argued that upon entry into the market and becoming commodities differences in the use-value of things disappear as they are equalized through their exchange value, which is translated into monetary terms. This severs the link between the worker and the product of his/her labor and infuses the product, now a commodity, with the appearance of independence from its producer and with a life and value of its own. Marx [1867] (1976: 163–64) described this as the fetishism of commodities, to which he attributed "metaphysical subtleties" and an "enigmatic character."

Marx did not develop his understanding of the significance of law to capitalism beyond an acute awareness of the significance of new forms of property to the internal logic and expansion of capitalism (see Cutler 2008: 210 ff). However, others have sought to integrate or isolate the role of law in commodity fetishism, developing the idea of the fetishism of law, as the legal form mirrors the commodity form under capitalism (see Miéville 2005; Pashukanis 1978). Elsewhere (Cutler 2005; 2008) I develop the commodity form theory of law to capture the tendency of legal regulation to take on a particular form that parallels and is coextensive with the fetishized commodity form under transnational capitalism.

The commodity form theory of law recognizes that legal concepts are embodied in regulations that establish the institutional, material, and ideological conditions of existence for capitalism. Legal forms articulate enforceable interests in property and contract and give rise to social relations that recognize legal agency and subjectivity and that enable the continued reproduction of capitalist activity. These legal forms instantiate relations of coercion and alienation that flow more generally from the fetishization of commodity production and exchange. As Marx (1976: 178) observes, the "juridical relation" between the owner and purchaser of a commodity "is a relation between two wills which mirrors the economic relation. The content of this juridical relation…is itself determined by the economic relation." Insofar as the economic form is an alienated and fetishized form, so too will be the legal form. In this, the role of transnational corporations in creating systems of private transnational governance may be examined as an integral dimension of law operating in a commodified and fetishized form.

Law in its commodity form *interpellates* the corporation as the neoliberal subject and the bearer of private property rights, because "the commodity form needs the legal form to create subjects that can realize the value of the commodity through its exchange in the market" (Fletcher 2003: 221). To Althusser, the law belongs to both state and ideological apparatuses and is an integral institution in the interpellation of individuals as subjects who are aware of and identify with their own subjectivity and participate in the production of capitalism.[6]

This theorization challenges both the classical treatment of the subject as *a priori* and as a cause, as well as the belief held by many that ideology is not a historically effective social force but rather a reflection of underlying material causes. Both challenges speak to contemporary theoretical debates concerning the primacy of structure or agent, as well as disputes between material and ideational accounts of world order.[7] However, for the purpose of this discussion, the concept of interpellation is utilized to assist in understanding how law in its commodity form operates.

In the context of national law, capitalist legal forms create the business corporation as a legal subject and as an autonomous, rights-bearing identity, which is a condition of existence of capitalist production and exchange. National laws vest corporations with the legal personality required to enter into valid employment and commercial contracts and empower them to resolve their disputes, enforce their agreements, and settle their accounts in a secure legal framework. Interpellation is the process by which capitalist legal forms create legal subjects, vest them with legal entitlements and responsibilities, and thus constitute concrete individuals or corporations as subjects who recognize themselves as such.

However, when we turn to consider transnational law, the interpellation of the corporate neoliberal subject must be accounted for otherwise. There is no solidarist transnational state or transnational civil society, and only weak counterparts functioning as state and ideological apparatuses. It is useful to look for inspiration to Gramsci's understandings of hegemony and historical blocs, combined with the Althusserian conception of interpellation, to develop a theory of emergent transnational apparatuses. As noted earlier, Gramsci conceived of hegemony as consensual domination, whereby the ruling class established dominance through force as well as through obtaining the consent of the subaltern class. He developed the idea of the "extended state" as comprising both political society (government, military, courts) and civil society (family, schools, churches) and located hegemony in civil society (Gramsci 1971: 12, 263). The state was regarded as combining relations of coercion and consent, involving the repressive and also consensual ideological state apparatuses. In the contemporary context, William Robinson (2004: 88) locates an "incipient" transnational state apparatus "in a set of emerging transnational institutions" and "an emerging network that comprises transformed and externally integrated national states, *together with* the supranational economic and political forums, and has not yet acquired any centralized institutional form."[8] He continues (2004: 101) that the "supranational organizations function in consonance with transformed nation-states. They are staffed by transnational functionaries who find their counterparts in transnational functionaries who staff national states. These *transnational state cadre* act as midwives of capitalist globalization." While Robinson does not develop the conception of transnational civil society, we might develop the logic further by identifying transnational business corporations, non-governmental civil society organizations, transnational religious movements and the like as elements of an incipient transnational civil society.

Crucial, however, to the constitution of transnational hegemony is the interpellation of the corporation as the neoliberal subject and the bearer of transnational capitalist private property relations through the institutions and ideology of transnational law, in which private transnational governance is a dominant characteristic. Here, experts such as transnational lawyers, accountants, bankers, and insurers function as organic intellectuals, developing the foundation for the consent of civil society to the ruling group. Gramsci (1971: 12) argued that this consent is "spontaneous" amongst the masses in that it is "'historically' caused by the prestige (and consequent confidence) which the dominant group enjoys because of its position and function in the world of production." Private transnational governance may be thus analyzed as a mechanism of accumulation and legitimation through the agency of experts and organic intellectuals who interpellate the business corporation as the neoliberal subject and thereby create the conditions of possibility for the continuing reproduction of transnational capitalism. Transnational business corporations thus emerge simultaneously as masters and subjects of the nascent transnational market civilization.

Imperfect subjects and unthinking the GATS

Conceptualizing transnational business corporations as both masters and subjects raises interesting possibilities for rethinking the GATS and reassessing and resisting the authority accorded to these powerful actors. Indeed, the above analysis of interpellation reveals suggestive insights when applied to the role of transnational corporations in the global political economy today. The GATS may be conceived as an illustration of the fetishized legal form taken by the commodity form under transnational capitalism. The GATS establishes and, indeed, naturalizes the commodification of services as an integral dimension of the reconfiguration of state apparatuses under transnational capitalism. In commodifying the provision of services, the GATS shifts authority from states to markets, while simultaneously subordinating provision of local services to the discipline of transnational corporations. The transnational corporations engaged in providing the services that drove the creation of the GATS regime, and are working on its expansion, are interpellated as the masters and the subjects of the emerging neoliberal historical bloc. As both architects and servants of the mode of production of transnational capitalism, transnational services corporations are the bearers and organic intellectuals of neoliberal ideology. As Stephen Gill notes, disciplinary neoliberalism is the new overriding socio-economic form, extending processes of commodification and alienation through a "politico-legal framework" for the reconstitution of capital on a world scale that integrates domestic societies and markets, globally, into a "new constitutionalism" (Gill 2008: 138–139).

Importantly, this theorization problematizes the exclusive legal subjectivity of states and challenges classical treatments of the corporation as an "object" under international law and as an apolitical, private actor standing outside history. It posits the corporation as becoming a subject, meaning an active agent of history, through interpellation by the various structures or apparatuses of the state and society under transnational capitalism. It also challenges the belief held by many that ideology is not a historically effective social force, but rather a mere reflection of underlying productive or material causes. This theory reasserts the historical and material significance of ideology, as against economically determinist Marxist accounts, and tries to capture the complexity of the relationship between corporate agency and capitalist structures, nationally and transnationally. This has great relevance for international relations theory and understandings that reject that ideational phenomena, such as norms, are causal influences and regard them, along with similarly regarded superstructural phenomena such as international law, as epiphenomenal. It is also relevant for debates over structure and agency in international relations and the prospects for resistance against the hegemony of neoliberal market discipline.

In this regard it is instructive to note Judith Butler's (1997: 13) account of interpellation as a process involving both submission and freedom. It involves submission of the individual or corporation to the power of capitalist social relations, but it simultaneously involves an exercise of free will when the power "is wielded by the subject, a situation that gives rise to the reverse perspective that power is the effect of the subject, and that power is the subject's effect." Power, which appeared "outside" the subject, is at once internalized and takes on the appearance of the willed effect of the subject (Butler 1997: 14). Butler submits that the point of submission involves a turn to the law that embodies free will that is not exhausted in the act of turning. She thus contemplates a residue or space for resistance of the subject to subjection. This suggests that the interpellation of the subject is not total, but incomplete. In the context of the GATS it suggests that there may well be alternatives to the dominance of transnational business corporations in regulating the services sector and ways of resisting the commodification and privatization of services provision.

The prospect for resistance is usefully explored in the context of the privatization and commodification of water, which has been a global trend for the past decade or more, advocated as it is by the World Bank, the International Monetary Fund, the OECD, and other global governance institutions (Holland 2005). Transnational water corporations have been very active in driving the agenda of water liberalization and have entered into partnerships with international financial institutions, including the Global Water Partnership and the World Water Council, both founded in 1996. These partnerships promote the neoliberal agenda of privatization and commodification in a broader context of environmental sustainability and poverty reduction. However, as Higgott and Weber (2005: 448) show, this agenda subverts development goals by re-inscribing inequality through a "market-oriented structure of ownership that disregards the social relations through which ownership patterns and processes of dispossession are legitimised."[9]

Indeed, the trend to privatize water services may be seen in the context of the extensive and intensive expansion of capitalism and movement to dispossess water resources. William Robinson (2004: 6–7) argues that capitalism is growing extensively, in terms of bringing new societies into its orbit, and intensively by commodifying human activities and natural resources hitherto deemed outside of capitalism's reach. Intensive expansion leads to the ever-deeper commodification of social life and expanding dispossession of natural resources. Relatedly, Erik Swyngedouw (2005: 87) regards water privatization as a new strategy for capital accumulation and "a process through which nature's goods become integrated into global circuits of capital; local common goods are expropriated, transferred to the private sector and inserted in the global money and capital flows, stock market assets, and portfolio holdings. A local/global choreography is forged that is premised upon mobilizing local H_2O, turning it into money, and inserting this within transnational flows of circulating capital. Consequently, local resource systems become part of the strategic checkerboard of global companies." This, he argues (ibid.: 91–92), is generating a new form of privatized governance.

Water privatization has generated much conflict, as is evident in the water wars in South America,[10] and is very much at issue under the GATS (Lang 2005). There is concern that the GATS might require states to allow foreign operators in their water sectors and limit the states' regulatory capacities. While Lang (2005) resists the position that the GATS requires water privatization, he argues that it sets up an ideological framework that constrains political choices by normalizing, rationalizing, and hence naturalizing the commodification and privatization of water. The reconceptualization of foreign investment and participation in a state's water sector as "trade in services" "can have the effect of changing the terrain on which debate about water privatization is carried out" (Lang 2005: 412). This can happen by shifting the debate away from one about water privatization to a less controversial and, indeed, generally supported one of services trade liberalization. Lang notes further (ibid.: 413) that "liberal trade theory has an immense intellectual capital behind it, benefits from a high degree of legitimacy built up over a long history, and is supported and deployed by powerful and entrenched economic and political forces."

This shift can make it difficult to resist privatization and make proponents of public management appear anti-trade liberalization, protectionist, and opposed to narratives about progressive modernization through the market. This is relevant in accession negotiations for transition economies. It also influences who participates in the water privatization debate and can have the effect of broadening participation by powerful water services corporations, as happened in the case of the corporations driving water privatization in Europe (Lang 2005: 417). However, Lang (ibid.) notes that placing water privatization on the international agenda by the European Commission also opened up space for contestation and resistance.[11] Indeed, in response to opposition from union and civil society groups, the European Commission in 2006 removed water for human use from its services liberalization requests, while the major water corporations attempted to distance themselves from the debate. This is regarded as "a success for civil society groups, trade unions and many others, both in Europe and around the world, who have been campaigning against the inclusion of water services in the GATS agreement as they saw the EU agenda as a threat to public water delivery" (Deckwirth 2006). Notably, Thames Water, owned by the German transnational RWE, broke ranks with European water corporations and announced at the World Water Forum in Kyoto that it did not support the GATS negotiations on water services. Water privatization runs counter to the increasing international recognition of access to water as an essential human need and a universal human right, and a number of developing countries have re-evaluated its inclusion in the GATS.

It is, therefore, understandable that the Sir Paul Lever, CEO for Thames Water, resisted "potential damage to our reputation" from the water controversy (Lever 2008: 6).[12] Clare Joy (2008), a member of World Development Movement, an NGO opposing the inclusion of water in the GATS, observes that a number of factors conspired to make developing countries slow to respond to the significant problems that they would face under the GATS regime. Inadequate access to information clarifying the regulatory implications of the GATS, lack of capacity to participate in and respond to GATS negotiations, and the negotiating culture of "horse-trading" in the WTO regime diminished their ability to resist the GATS. Significantly, though, resistance has occurred, suggesting that the interpellation of the corporate neoliberal subject is far from hegemonic.

Louise Amoore (2005: 2) observes that theorizing global resistance "confronts the difficulty that, as a concept and a set of practices, it does itself resist being singularly defined or pinned down." However, she continues (ibid.: 3) that its contested nature means that we must always consider resistance "in relation to power and to politics." Resistance to the commodification of services provision thus requires unthinking the GATS by revealing the power relations and politics constituting it materially, institutionally, and ideologically. This involves engaging in a radical political economy critique that lays bare the constitutive significance of powerful services corporations and their simultaneous interpellation as modern neoliberal subjects and masters of transnational capitalism and the consequent de-centering of the state. In this, the praxis conception of law is relevant. As a dialectical formulation, a praxis conception of transnational law contemplates the law as embodying forces of both domination and emancipation (Cutler 2005, 2008).

Transnational law globalizes fetishized commodity relations, but its grasp is not complete or totalizing. Indeed, there are fractures in the discipline of transnational neoliberal law and the commodity form of capitalism. The GATS as a legal instrument has the potential to work toward oppressive or emancipatory ends. Resistance from trade unions and other civil society groups was able to challenge the inclusion of water for human use in the GATS negotiation, although other water uses remain open to negotiation and there is no guarantee that water for human use will not emerge again as a negotiable service. However, many of the developing countries who initially agreed to the GATS have changed their positions and might well block any future efforts to put water back on the GATS agenda. It remains to be seen how far commodification under the GATS will go. This turns very much upon the extent to which transnational corporations will function as masters of capital and facilitate the further expansion of capitalism through a deepening of the GATS discipline. Importantly, capitalism, in its "need of a constantly expanding market for its products chases the bourgeoisie over the whole surface of the globe. It must nestle everywhere, settle everywhere, establish connections everywhere" (Marx and Engels [1848] 1983: 207). Developing a critical understanding of the significance of transnational business corporations and their laws in the global expansion of capitalism is central to an understanding of the role of business in the world today.

This chapter has argued that transnational business corporations are central players in the global political economy today, with significant regulatory authority. However, their authority is neither total nor monolithic, for they are incompletely constituted as juridical subjects, as successful instances of resistance to neoliberal discipline and the commodification of water resources illustrate.

Notes

1 Efforts to liberalize foreign services markets began in the US in the 1970s as the financial services sector and insurance industry lobbied for inclusion of services under the GATT (Sell 2002: 166). Leading financial and professional services corporations included American Express and Arthur Anderson (Hoekman and Kostecki 2001: 250). The US Coalition of Services Industries (USCSI) was created in 1982 by the Vice-President of American Express to lobby for including trade in services on the agenda of world trade talks. USCSI worked closely with the US Trade Representative and Department of Commerce and in 1986, when the Uruguay Round was launched, a Group on the Negotiations on Services was formed and negotiations on services formally began. In preparation for the GATS 2000 negotiations, the Financial Leaders Group was created to organize European services industries, creating the European Services Network in 1999, later renamed the European Services Forum. European water corporations had a major role in the formulation of the EU's position in services negotiations (Wesselius 2002).
2 Jackson (1988) notes that constructing a constitution for regulating trade in services was the aim of the Uruguay Round negotiations on services.
3 Interpellate has many meanings. Interpellation can mean a right of a parliament to submit formal questions to the government. In philosophy it means the calling forth or bringing into being/identity an individual or category.
4 God is the "Subject *par excellence*" (Althusser 1971: 167).
5 In *The Holy Family*, written with Engels in 1844, Marx develops an analysis of Proudhon that articulates the distinction between social relations and their alienated, material form under capitalism and the institution of private property. In *The Poverty of Philosophy*, written in 1847, Marx distinguishes between social relations of production and their material expression. Then, in *A Contribution to the Critique of Political Economy*, published in 1859, he articulates the concept of commodity fetishism, which is fully developed in Chapter 1, Book I of *Capital*.
6 It is instructive to note that Althusser (1971: 138) did not find the distinction between the public and private spheres to be determinative, for both interpellate the subject: "It is unimportant whether the institutions in which they [the State ideological apparatuses] are realized are 'public' or 'private'. What matters is how they function. Private institutions can perfectly well 'function' as Ideological State Apparatuses. A reasonably thorough

analysis of any one of the ISAs proves it." He here cites Gramsci's observation that the public–private distinction is not a natural or organic distinction, but is simply an analytical construct of bourgeois law. For Althusser (ibid.), the state is in fact "the precondition for any distinction between public and private." For analysis of this point in the context of private and public international law, see Cutler (1997).

7 Althusser (1971) developed the concept of interpellation to capture the material impact of ideology and the complex process by which the individual comes to accept and reproduce capitalist exploitation. In this regard, his thinking has much relevance for the field of international relations, where significant neorealist theorizations reject that ideational phenomena, such as norms, and alleged superstructural phenomena, such as international law, are causal. These theories also challenge individual agency.

8 Included are the International Monetary Fund, the World Bank, the World Trade Organization and regional banks, the Group of Seven countries, the Group of Twenty-Two countries, the United Nations system, the Organization for Economic Cooperation and Development, the European Union, and the Conference on Security and Cooperation in Europe.

9 See Castro (2008) for the summary of an empirical analysis of water privatization policies in nine countries in Africa, Europe, and Latin America that reveals the general failure of such policies to provide the necessary financial resources for water management or to reduce social inequality in these countries. The study reveals that between 1990 and 2005 private sector investment in water services was concentrated on Latin America, the Caribbean, East Asia, and Pacific regions (89.1%) with little or no investment in the poorest regions of the world. Within regions, the bulk of investment went to a few countries, such as Argentina, the Philippines, Malaysia, and Turkey, with significantly less going to Mexico, Brazil, and China.

10 The wave of water privatizations began in 1989 when water utilities in England and Wales were privatized under the Thatcher government. However, the promotion of private sector participation in water management was already on the agenda of international organizations and financial institutions for developing countries as a result of the general failure of public sector water management (Castro 2008). In the 1990s the focus was on the developing countries (Spronk 2007). In 1998, as part of a more general privatization initiative, Bolivia gave a contract for water service in the city of Cochabamba to a consortium of private water companies who immediately raised water rates dramatically. In 2000 a general strike, transportation stoppage, and mass demonstrations occurred. After several protests and resistance to martial law, demands from people worldwide for the consortium to leave Cochabamba forced it in the end to abandon the project. The government repealed the privatization legislation and the consortium sued it under a Bilateral Investment Treaty, but the matter was in the end settled (see Holland 2005; Olivera and Lewis 2004). Similar water disputes have occurred in Brazil, Argentina, South Africa, Mexico, and India. International efforts to address the regulation of water date back to the 1977 United Nations Conference on Water, and include the World Water Forums held in 1997 (Marrakech), 2000 (The Hague), 2003 (Kyoto), and 2006 (Mexico), as well as the Bonn International Freshwater Conference (2001). In 2005 the United Nations launched the Decade for Action "Water for Life." The Fifth World Water Forum was held in Istanbul in 2009.

11 In 2002 a list of draft EU services liberalization requests was leaked to NGOs. The list included a broad range of services, including water. This prompted the organization of NGO anti-GATS and demands for transparency on GATS preparations in many countries throughout the world, generating a global movement (see Barlow and Clarke 2002). This anti-GATS sentiment spread beyond NGOs and trade unions to include towns and municipalities throughout the world that have been declared "GATS-free zones."

12 However, Lever also noted his company's preference for investing in countries offering more stable investment climates.

References

Althusser, Louis (1971) "Ideology and Ideological State Apparatuses: Notes Towards an Investigation," in *Lenin and Philosophy,* translated by Ben Brewster, pp. 121–73 (London: New Left Books).

Amoore, Louise (2005) "Introduction: Global resistance – global politics," in Amoore (ed.) *The Global Resistance Reader*, pp. 1–11 (New York: Routledge).

Barlow, Maude and Tony Clarke (2002) *Blue Gold: the Battle Against Corporate Theft of the World's Water* (New York: The New Press).

Butler, Judith (1997) *The Psychic Life of Power: Theories in Subjection* (Stanford: Stanford University Press).

Cafruny, A. (1989) "Economic Conflicts and the Transformation of the Atlantic Order: The US, Europe and the Liberalisation of Agriculture and Services," in *Atlantic Relations: Beyond the Reagan Era*, pp. 126–137 (New York: St Martin's Press).

Cain, Maureen (1983) "Gramsci, the state and the place of law," in Sugarman, D. (ed.) *Legality, Ideology and the State*, pp. 95–117 (London: Academic Press).

Castro, J.E. (2008) "Neoliberal water and sanitation policies as a failed development strategy: lessons from developing countries," in *Progress in Development Studies*, 8(1): 63–83.

Cox, Robert with Timothy Sinclair (1996) *Approaches to World Order* (Cambridge University Press).

Cutler, A. Claire (1997) "Artifice, Ideology, and Paradox: The Public/Private Distinction in International Law," in *Review of International Political Economy*, 4(2): 261–85.

—— (2001) "Critical Reflections on Westphalian Assumptions of International Law and Organization: A Crisis of Legitimacy," in *Review of International Studies*, 27(2): 133–50.

—— (2003) *Private Power and Global Authority: Transnational Merchant Law in the Global Political Economy* (Cambridge University Press).

—— (2005) "Gramsci, Law, and the Culture of Global Capitalism," in *Critical Review of International Social and Political Philosophy*, 8(4): 527–42.

—— (2008) "Toward a radical political economy critique of transnational economic law," in Marks, Susan (ed.) *International Law on the Left: Revisiting Marxist Legacies*, pp. 199–219 (Cambridge University Press).

Cutler, A. Claire, Virginia Haufler and Tony Porter (eds) (1999) *Private Authority and International Affairs* (New York: Suny Press).

Czempiel, E. and James Rosenau (1992) *Global Changes and Theoretical Challenges: Approaches to World Politics for the 1990s* (Lexington Books).

Deckwirth, Christina (2006) "Water almost out of GATS?" *A Corporate Europe Observatory Briefing.* http://www.corporateeurope.org/water/gatswater2006.pdf

Djelic, Marie-Laure and Kerstin Sahlin-Andersson (eds) (2006) *Transnational Governance* (Cambridge University Press).

Drake, W. and C. Nicolaïdes (1992) "Ideas, interests and institutionalism: 'trade in services' and the Uruguay Round," in *International Organization*, 46(1): 37–100.

Fletcher, Ruth (2003) "Legal Forms and Reproductive Norms," in *Social & Legal Studies*, 12(2): 217–41.

Gill, Stephen (ed.) (1993) *Gramsci, historical materialism and international relations* (Cambridge University Press).

—— (2008) *Power and Resistance in the New World Order* (New York: Palgrave Macmillan).

Gramsci, Antonio (1971) *Selections from the Prison Notebooks of Antonio Gramsci*, edited and translated by Quintin Hoare and Geoffrey Nowell Smith (New York: International Publishers).

Graz, J.C. and A. Nölke (eds) (2008) *Transnational Private Governance and Its Limits* (London and New York: Routledge).

Hall, Rodney with Thomas Biersteker (eds) (2002) *The Emergence of Private Authority in Global Governance* (Cambridge University Press).

Harvey, David (2005) *The New Imperialism* (Oxford and New York: Oxford University Press).

Higgins, Rosalyn (1985) "Conceptual thinking about the individual in international law," in Richard Falk, Franz Kratochwil and Saul Mendolvitz (eds) *International law: A contemporary perspective*, pp. 476–493 (Boulder: Westview Press).

Higgott, Richard and Heloise Weber (2005) "GATS in context: development, an evolving *lex mercatoria* and the Doha Agenda," in *Review of International Political Economy*, 12(3): 434–55.

Hoekman, Bernard and Michel Kostecki (2001) *The Political Economy of the World Trading System: The WTO and Beyond* (Oxford University Press).

Holland, Ann-Christin (2005) *The Water Business: Corporations versus People* (London: Zed Books).

Jackson, J. (1988) "Constructing a Constitution for Trade in Services," in *World Economy*, 11(2): 89–202.

Johns, Fleur (1994) "The Invisibility of the Transnational Corporation: An Analysis of International Law and Legal Theory," in *Melbourne International Law Review*, 19(4): 893–923.

Joy, Clare (2008) "Debating GATS: public accountability, access to information and citizen's participation," in *Progress in Development Studies*, 1: 23–49.

Kelsey, Jane (2003) "Legal fetishism and the contradictions of the GATS," in *Globalization, Societies, and Education*, 1(3): 267–80.

Lang, Andrew (2005) "Beyond Formal Obligation: The Trade Regime and the Making of Political Priorities," in *Leiden Journal of International Law*, 18: 403–24.

Lever, Sir Paul (2008) "Water and the GATS," in *Progress in Development Studies*, 1: 59–61.

Marx, Karl ([1867] 1976) *Capital: A Critique of Political Economy*, vol 1, translated by B. Fowkes (London: Penguin).

Marx, Karl and F. Engels ([1848] 1983) *The Communist Manifesto*, published in *The Portable Karl Marx*, edited and translated by Eugene Kamenka (New York: Penguin Books).

May, Christopher (ed.) (2006) *Global Corporate Power* (Boulder and London: Lynne Rienner).

Miéville, China (2005) *Between Equal Rights: A Marxist Theory of International Law* (Leiden and Boston: Brill).

Olivera, Oscar and Tom Lewis (2004) *Cochabamb! Water War in Bolivia* (Cambridge, MA: South End Press).

Overbeek, Hank, Bastiaan van Apeldoorn and Andreas Nölke (eds) (2007) *The Transnational Politics of Corporate Governance Regulation* (London and New York: Routledge).

Pashukanis, Evgeni (1978) *Law and Marxism: A General Theory* (London: Pluto Press).

Robinson, William (2004) *A Theory of Global Capitalism: Production, Class, and State in a Transnational World* (Baltimore and London: Johns Hopkins University Press).

Sell, Susan (2002) *Private Power, Public Law* (Cambridge University Press).

Spronk, Susan (2007) "The Politics of Water Privatization in the Third World," in *Review of Radical Political Economics*, 39: 126–31.

Swyngedouw, Erik (2005) "Dispossessing H_2O: the contested terrain of water privatization," in *Capitalism Nature Socialism*, 16(1): 81–98.

Wesselius, Erik (2002) "Behind the GATS 2000: Corporate Power at Work," *Transnational Institute*, Briefing Series No. 2002/6, Amsterdam.

WTO (World Trade Organization) (1991) Services Sectoral Classification List, MTN.GNS/W/120, 10 July, Publication # 98–0000.

Part II

Business as subject to global governance

5 Business and global climate governance

A neo-pluralist perspective

Robert Falkner

Introduction

Business plays a critical role in global climate politics; this is widely agreed upon in international relations and political economy. Whether we should view business primarily as blocking political progress or as providing necessary solutions remains a matter of debate and contention. Analysts also remain divided on how we should assess the power of business in climate politics. For some, corporations are just one type of interest group that competes with others for influence in the political process. Others see business actors as relying on structural power, which serves to constrain the options available to politicians and diplomats. This chapter puts forward a neo-pluralist perspective on business in global climate governance. It argues that business is in a powerful, even privileged, position internationally, but doesn't always get its way. The process of international climate politics is more fluid and open-ended than may seem at first sight, and while business interests can predominate they don't always pull in the same direction, nor do they control the global environmental agenda.

The notion that business is in a privileged position was most famously given expression by Charles Lindblom over two decades ago. In his seminal book *Politics and Markets*, Lindblom famously declared that "businessmen occupy a privileged position" (1977: 175) in liberal democracies. In doing so, he sought to correct a central weakness of the pluralist tradition in political science, which had treated business as just one among many interest groups that vied for influence in an open and pluralistic democratic process. Business was different from other interest groups, as critics of pluralism had argued, because the wellbeing of society and the economy depended on investment, technological innovation and economic growth. Business performance was central to the functioning of market economies and had to be "induced rather than commanded" (ibid.: 176). Governments, therefore, often had to defer to business leadership and share their authority with corporate actors. Lindblom thus laid the foundations of a neo-pluralist perspective that continues to reverberate in contemporary discussions of interest group politics and business power (for an overview, see McFarland 2004).

Politics and Markets did not address the international dimensions of business power or the rise of environmentalism as a counter-balance to business.

This chapter builds on Lindblom's insights and extends them to the international level and to global environmental politics. It is based on a book-length treatment of the neo-pluralist approach to studying business in global governance (Falkner 2008) and offers a corrective to statist and structuralist perspectives that have characterized much International Political Economy writing on international business in the past. This chapter advances two related arguments about the international role and power of business. It seeks to highlight the many ways in which corporate actors operate from a privileged position *vis-à-vis* states and NGOs when it comes to setting global environmental standards and implementing environmental agreements. Due to their central role in directing investment and technological innovation, companies can set the parameters of what is politically feasible in international environmental protection. Yet business actors do not always act in unison, and references to an underlying business or class interest fail to explain the competitive dynamics that characterize business involvement in international politics. Business conflict opens up political space for other actors – states, international organizations and social movements – to press for global change. The bond that holds these two arguments together is the neo-pluralist perspective on business power that is developed in more detail below.

The analysis is structured as follows. The next section gives an overview of the neo-pluralist perspective on business in global governance. This is then applied to the case of climate change politics by tracing in outline the evolution of the climate regime from the 1992 UN Framework Convention to the 1997 Kyoto Protocol and beyond. The concluding section summarizes the argument and highlights the implications for the study of business in global governance.

The neo-pluralist perspective on business in global governance

One of the striking features of international environmental politics is the profound change in business involvement in the international process. In the early days of global environmentalism, during the 1960s and 1970s, the political role of corporations was limited to occasional, and largely reactive, interventions to prevent burdensome regulations. More recently, a growing number of corporations have begun to integrate environmental objectives into their business operations and have developed more proactive forms of corporate environmental strategy (Hoffman 1997). Some firms have actively sought to influence, and even support, the creation of international environmental regimes (e.g. the Montreal Protocol on ozone layer depletion) and are now actively engaged in the provision of environmental governance mechanisms outside the states system, so-called "private environmental governance" (Falkner 2003).

As a consequence of this evolution of business roles, a diverse set of business interests and approaches has emerged. Some corporations continue to oppose international environmental regulations as an unwarranted burden on their operations, while others now openly support higher international regulatory standards. Undoubtedly, some of the so-called "greening" of industry is little more than empty rhetoric. But in many ways it signifies a more profound and potentially lasting trend with significant implications for global governance, and corporations can now be found on different sides of global debates, arguing against *and* for environmental regulation. How powerful are corporations in international environmental politics? To what extent are they able to shape the emerging global governance architecture for environment? And how does the divergence of business interests affect corporate influence overall?

The neo-pluralist perspective on business power

Although business power has become a central concern in International Political Economy (IPE) (May 2006), it remains a contested concept. Economic globalization and the growth in transnational relations have underlined the fact that non-state actors such as corporations play a more visible role in international relations, but debate continues on whether they make a difference to outcomes of international processes, and, if so, in what ways. A standard approach to the study of business power has been to treat business actors as interest groups that seek to influence policy outcomes within the state. This pluralist perspective, originally developed in the context of domestic politics but applicable to international relations as well, was criticized for assuming naively that the international policy process offers a level playing field for all interest groups. As structuralists have pointed out, corporations play a critical role in the economy, as providers of employment and sources of growth and innovation, and their consent is needed if profound changes to the working of the global economy are to be achieved through international regulation.

Neo-pluralists are reflective of the structural power of business but emphasize the political agency of firms. They agree with structuralists that business is in a privileged position, but acknowledge the diversity of business interests and the potential for conflict within the business community over matters of political strategy. Neo-pluralism provides a perspective on business power as a multi-faceted and multi-dimensional phenomenon, and argues that it needs to be established in the context of specific issue areas and fields of activity. Countervailing forces, which are located in the international and transnational spheres, limit corporate influence, as do divisions within the business sector itself. Indeed, the potential for what has become known as "business conflict" (Nowell 1996), that is the cleavages between different firms and industrial sectors with regard to international politics, prevents an understanding of business actors as belonging to a monolithic block. Neo-pluralists hold that the unity of business interests and strategy is a matter of empirical study, not theoretical conjecture. Likewise, the existence of structural business power needs to be established empirically and cannot prejudge the question of how powerful business actors are in specific international contexts. In other words, not all business actors are engaged in international politics; not all of those that are share the same interest; and not all of those that seek to influence international politics succeed.

To understand why business power is limited, and why international political processes should be presumed to be open-ended, we need to briefly consider the countervailing forces that prevent business influence from becoming dominant. They can be found in the resilience of state power and the proliferation of new transnational political actors, but most importantly in the heterogeneity of the business sector itself. Neo-pluralism's key insight in the international context is that the diversity of business interests, combined with the persistence of business conflict, serves to limit business power overall.

Countervailing forces can be found outside and within the business world. With regard to the former, states not only retain their status as loci of authority in core state functions such as security, but also remain powerful gatekeepers and providers in other policy areas that are more open to the influence of non-state actors (Drezner 2007). Furthermore, new transnational actors have come to challenge the legitimacy and authority of business actors even in domains where they can be said to be in a privileged position. New channels of transnational communication and campaigning have empowered social actors, even though they often rely on only limited financial resources and lack access to established policy networks (Tarrow 2005). Particularly in the environmental field, grass-roots and transnational campaigns by activist groups have undermined the legitimacy of multinational firms and induced change in corporate behavior (Wapner 1996). To be sure, interest group competition in transnational and international realms is rarely conducted on a level playing field. Global political space is not entirely pluralistic, but existing balances of power between different transnational actors vary across policy domains and are more fluid and unstable in an era of globalization, leading to a more open-ended process of global politics.

The pluralist message is further reinforced when we consider dissent and conflict within the business sector. The straightforward but important insight that neo-pluralism offers is that business is often divided on matters of international policy and corporate strategy, and that business should therefore not be treated as a solidly uniform block. The corporate sector may, of course, in some vague sense, represent a capitalist class interest, but this claim amounts to little more than a truism that is of limited analytical value in the empirical study of business influence in specific policy contexts. Indeed, if we want to understand the sources and limits of business power and influence, we need to disaggregate the business sector and analyze its constituent parts, often down to the level of the firm. For particular business interests to exercise a dominant influence, achieving business unity is an important but highly demanding condition. Business conflict thus serves as an important brake on business influence in international politics.

Business conflict in international environmental politics

One variant of this line of thinking is the "business school model" in IPE (Skidmore 1995; Skidmore-Hess 1996). Societal approaches that focus on the domestic origins of foreign policy have been at the forefront of this development. By identifying cleavages that exist within the business sector, Frieden (1988) and

Milner (1988) have explained the shifting patterns of business support for free trade and protectionist policies in the US and elsewhere. Rogowski (1989) uses factor endowments theory to analyze how the gains and losses from international trade are distributed between different economic sectors, and how those distributional effects in turn influence business preferences in trade policy. Business factionalism is a pervasive phenomenon in the study of foreign policy, particularly in the US where domestic and internationalist coalitions compete for influence over state policy (see the contributions in Cox 1996).

The main focus of the business school model has been to explain outcomes in foreign policy and international politics from the bottom up. By reversing the perspective, we can also capture the ambiguous effect that globalization has had on business actors. While international business has been the main beneficiary of ever greater economic integration, it has also become more exposed to new political demands and pressures that globalized politics has created. The nature of the international political process has changed due to globalization, resulting in a more open and fluid process of policy-making that involves an ever greater number and diversity of actors. Whether it is the international politics of trade and finance or new issue areas such as blood diamonds or genetically modified food, business actors are now faced with a large number of civil society actors that seek to create new international norms and affect corporate behavior directly by challenging the power and legitimacy of business (Vernon 1998). The advent of new information technologies has significantly reduced the costs of "presence" and "voice" in global politics, and transnational campaign groups have skillfully leveraged their social and discursive power through the use of symbolic politics. As political globalization progresses, established positions of power and influence are being challenged and redefined. This, as Cerny points out, reaffirms the neo-pluralist insight that

> those social, economic and political actors with the greatest access to material and social resources generally marshal those resources in uneven and complex ways in order to pursue their own interests as effectively as possible in what is still a relatively open political process. They predominate, but they do not necessarily control.
>
> (Cerny 2003: 156)

It should be noted that to place business conflict at the heart of the neo-pluralist perspective does not mean that such conflict is assumed to be the predominant pattern of behavior among firms. Indeed, business actors routinely seek to limit the potential for conflict and competition in an effort to stabilize the organizational field in which they operate. Students of business organization have long argued that the desire to reduce price competition and stabilize organizational fields is central to the strategy particularly of large multinational enterprises (Fligstein 1990; Spar 2001). Likewise, business actors will seek to minimize differences and tensions between them in their efforts to shape international political outcomes. On issues that affect most corporations in an equal way, business unity will be easier to achieve. But on other issues that have differential effects on individual firms – and regulatory politics is one such area – business disunity and conflict is a latent reality. It is therefore analytically preferable to treat the question of business unity as an empirical question, not as a given.

Business conflict arises in international environmental politics because of the *differential effects* that international regulatory measures have on individual companies or industries. Environmental regulations can take on many different forms and include a variety of mechanisms, including process and product standards, international monitoring or certification schemes, identification and documentation requirements for international trade and information exchange, targets and timetables for the reduction or elimination of harmful emissions, and emission trading schemes, among others. What they all share in common is that they rarely have a uniform effect on business as a whole, but target specific groups of corporations or industrial sectors, create new markets or transform existing ones. The aim of regulations is to change corporate behavior in a specific and targeted way, and it is this that creates uneven effects on business overall, potentially leading to a divergence of business interests, and even conflict. Business actors can therefore be expected to form interests and political strategies on international environmental politics that seek to limit the costs of regulation or maximize its benefits.

Several types of business conflict can be identified with regard to international regulation, norm setting and regime building: First, as suggested by studies on international trade policy (Frieden 1988; Milner 1988), a basic dividing line exists *between international and national firms*. International firms are more likely to support international rule-setting and the harmonization of national regulations. National firms have traditionally favored protectionism in trade policy and are more likely to oppose international rule-setting in environmental affairs. Firms that operate in different national markets and depend on the unhindered flow of goods will place a higher value on creating a level playing field than those that are concerned primarily with national markets and competition from abroad. This does not mean that international firms will always support international environmental regulation. They are likely to do so only where it provides them with a competitive advantage, by reducing the transaction costs of operating in multiple regulatory environments, and by raising the regulatory costs of competitor firms that operate in countries with lower environmental standards. This divide can be seen in the politics of ozone layer protection, where the highly globalized chemical industry was the first sector to support international restrictions on ozone-depleting substances, while many domestic industries that used these substances remained opposed to international restrictions for much longer (Falkner 2005). Vogel (1995) has referred to this effect as "trading up", where international firms promote the adoption of higher environmental standards in an effort to create a global level playing field.

A second, and closely related, form of business conflict can arise *between technological leaders and laggards* in the same industry or economic sector, be it nationally or internationally organized. In this case, the dividing line is found between competitors in a given market segment that are likely to experience differential effects of regulation due to their uneven ability to comply with new standards. If market leaders can hope to lower their compliance costs relative to their competitors, then an increase in regulatory standards and compliance costs may shift the competitive balance in their favor, thus making regulation more acceptable to them. The degree to which companies can respond to new environmental regulations through technological innovation will thus be an important factor in determining their overall political strategy. In some cases, regulation can produce new markets based on technological innovation that would otherwise not have been commercially viable, and technological leaders can therefore use regulatory politics to create new business models and achieve competitive advantage (Porter and van der Linde 1995).

A third form of business conflict can arise *between companies that operate in different economic sectors along supply chains*. Wherever regulations target specific products or production processes, they will affect all companies along the supply or production chain, which links suppliers of input factors, producers and retailers together. The important point to note is that regulation is likely to have differential effects on the companies that operate along this chain, leading to divisions and competition between them. While companies operating at the consumer end of the chain (e.g. retailers) may support higher regulatory standards as part of their strategy to maintain consumer confidence or enhance their reputation, companies providing raw material inputs or intermediary products further down the chain may end up facing higher production costs without gaining any reputational benefits. For example, supermarkets in Europe and North America have generally supported higher food and environmental safety standards in food production, but smaller producers, particularly in developing countries, have experienced difficulties in meeting those standards in a cost-effective manner. European supermarkets were the first to ban genetically modified food from their shelves, against the wishes of biotechnology firms and agricultural exporters in North America (Falkner 2008, chapter 5).

In sum, business conflict is an important feature of business involvement in international environmental politics. Whether it exists in reality or is only a latent threat to business unity depends on the nature of regulatory policies under consideration and the strategies that different companies form. For business conflict to become politically significant, business actors need to be able to identify the differential effects of regulations and integrate these perceptions into coherent political strategies. We thus need to consider the strategies that business actors form with regard to international environmental politics, and the ways in which these intersect with the strategies of states and non-state actors. The following section provides an empirical case study of business conflict in global governance, examining business involvement in climate change politics.

Business and the global politics of climate change

Climate change is one of the most intractable environmental problems the world faces today. A vast range of industrial sectors are involved in producing and emitting greenhouse gas (GHG) emissions, and many different economic and technological changes are required to slow down the global warming trend. Unlike in other environmental cases such as ozone layer depletion, no technical fixes are available to quickly replace fossil fuels. The central role that oil and coal play in modern industrial systems has limited the scope for rapid climate action. It has also enhanced the veto power of recalcitrant business interests. Thus, it would seem, at first sight, as if the fossil fuel industry's structural position in the global economy is the central blocking force in climate politics (Newell and Paterson 1998).

Indeed, the first business reactions to the scientific discovery of man-made climate change were overwhelmingly negative, focusing on the uncertainties involved in climate science. As pressure grew to address the issue internationally, corporate representatives highlighted the economic costs of taking action and the threat to international competitiveness. Slowly but steadily, a more diverse field of business interests and strategies has emerged. However, powerful business actors continue to resist international climate action until today.

Nevertheless, business conflict and competition have started to change corporate involvement as well as the dynamics of international climate politics. The political field has become more fluid today, and a range of new political alliances between business actors, leading states and environmental campaign groups have sprung up that seek to advance the goal of reducing GHG emissions. Within the Kyoto Protocol and beyond, an increasingly pluralistic field of political activity has emerged, involving an ever greater diversity of business interests and strategies. Business power is a central fact of climate politics, having held back effective international action in the past, but business conflict has opened up avenues for new political strategies.

The UN Framework Convention on Climate Change: business unity, for now

During the negotiations on the 1992 UNFCCC, the business lobby was dominated by powerful fossil fuel industry interests. Shortly after the creation of the Intergovernmental Panel of Climate Change in 1988, over 40 corporations and business associations created the Global Climate Coalition (GCC), the world's first dedicated climate change lobbying group. The GCC was initially focused on the US political scene, and as the international efforts to create a climate treaty gathered momentum, it re-oriented itself to become the premier industry lobbying group at the international level (Pulver 2002: 61). Led by US companies, it emphasized the uncertainties that plagued climate science and demanded full scientific proof before mandatory restrictions on GHG emissions be adopted. It highlighted the costs of taking precautionary action against global warming and warned against the implications for international competitiveness. The GCC's anti-regulatory arguments fell on fertile ground particularly in the US, where key representatives of the Bush administration were ideologically opposed to international environmental regulation (Hopgood 1998: 155–68).

By contrast, the EU entered the UNFCCC negotiations with a more proactive stance and adopted a mandatory target of stabilizing industrialized countries' GHG emissions by the year 2000 at 1990 levels (Skjærseth 1994: 26–27). European business leaders were more conciliatory than their US counterparts, but the EU's position clearly went beyond what the European business constituency was willing to support at that point. The European Commission's proposal for a tax on carbon-based energy, in particular, put the EU in an international leadership position but antagonized a wide range of energy-intensive firms. Leading industrial firms in Europe found it easy to mobilize a broad business front against the tax proposal and put up one of the toughest fights against a European regulatory proposal – "the most ferocious lobbying ever seen in Brussels", as *The Economist* commented (1992; see also Ikwue and Skea 1994). In the end, the EU settled with a compromise proposal for a carbon/energy tax that was conditional on the adoption of similar measures in other industrialized countries. The measure never won the required support and remains one of the unfulfilled promises of the EU's early climate policy.

Despite transatlantic differences in corporate outlook and lobbying style, leading businesses from the major industrialized countries were largely united in opposing a strong international climate treaty with mandatory GHG emission reductions. The oil and coal industry dominated business lobbying in this phase, and was able to rally a wide range of manufacturing firms behind its cause. Many other business sectors with a lesser stake in the climate debate were either not involved in the international process or were indifferent, partly because the regulatory debate was focused initially on the major energy producers and users. That the final compromise on the UNFCCC excluded binding targets and timetables can therefore be seen as a major success for the fossil fuel lobby. The vast majority of business actors involved in the talks had warned against mandated emission reductions, and, apart from the nascent energy efficiency and renewable energy sectors, no major global firm or industry spoke out in support of a global limit on GHG emissions (Grubb *et al.* 1999: 257). But despite its impressive show of unity, the fossil fuel industry was unable to prevent an international accord on climate change, as many in the industry would no doubt have preferred. As some business observers had warned, the framework convention set a precedent for a future tightening of international commitments. The global environmental movement and progressive state leaders were able to define the agenda in ways that promoted a precautionary approach – and there was no guarantee that the fossil fuel lobby could maintain a united business front in a changing political environment.

The Kyoto Protocol: the anti-regulatory business front crumbles

The first signs of a crack in the business lobby had already emerged at UNCED, but it was in the run-up to the Kyoto Protocol negotiations that new, pro-regulatory, business interests came to leave a mark on international climate policy. The newly created International Climate Change Partnership (ICCP), which counted influential chemical and electronics manufacturing firms among its members, put forward a more moderate industry position. In contrast to the fossil fuel industry, the ICCP recognized the threat of global warming and the need to act against it. Still, it advocated a cautious regulatory strategy, one that took into account the long lead times needed to find and adopt new technologies (Giorgetti 1999).

Soon after Rio, further divisions within the corporate sector emerged, including within the core group of fossil fuel industries. Whereas most American oil and coal firms remained opposed to any binding climate targets, Royal Dutch/Shell and British Petroleum (BP), Europe's leading oil firms, began to take a more conciliatory stance from 1995 onwards. A Shell executive announced at the 1995 World Energy Congress that the world needed to start preparing for the orderly transition to renewable forms of energy while continuing to use conventional fossil fuels (Gelbspan 1997: 86). And in October 1996, the American subsidiary of BP withdrew from the Global Climate Coalition, in a move that signaled the deepest rift yet within the fossil fuel sector. The switch in strategy was confirmed in a high-profile speech by BP's then chairman John Browne in May 1997, in which he acknowledged the growing scientific consensus on climate change, advocated taking precautionary action against it and announced a major investment initiative in solar energy (Pulver 2007; Rowlands 2000; Skjærseth and Skodvin 2003).

The most radical departure from the anti-regulatory business lobby occurred in a sector that was set to be one of the major losers of global warming: insurance. The world's largest reinsurance companies, Munich Re and Swiss Re, for some time had been concerned about their exposure to rising insurance costs caused by more extreme weather patterns. As early as 1992, both Munich Re and Swiss Re claimed that in the long run climate change posed the risk of bankruptcy for the global insurance industry (Schmidheiny and BCSD 1992: 64–66). As a sign of the industry's growing involvement in climate debates, in 1995 fourteen insurance companies from around the world signed a Statement of Environmental Commitment by the Insurance Industry, in which they committed themselves to a more systematic inclusion of environmental concerns, including climate change, into their risk and investment assessments (UNEP 1995; Paterson 2001).

These changes in corporate strategy had two positive impacts on international climate politics. First, they laid to rest the claim that a united business front stood against mandatory emission restrictions, and that significant reductions in GHG emissions were economically and technologically impossible to achieve. This helped to shift the regulatory discourse into a more precautionary direction. Second, the growing diversity of corporate climate strategies opened up avenues for new political alliances between corporate leaders, NGOs and state officials in support of an international climate accord with binding targets. Indeed, the negotiations on the Kyoto Protocol would be the scene for a range of initiatives from such progressive alliances.

Business conflict, however, also had its limits. The pro-regulatory forces within the business sector, especially the renewable energy sector, are economically less significant and lack the fossil fuel industry's well-organized and richly funded organizational basis (Sawin 2004). The insurance industry may have greater economic clout overall, particularly as a global investor, but it has found it difficult to shift its large-scale share ownership out of the fossil fuel sector and into renewables, thus curtailing its structural power (Paterson 2001). Furthermore, its lobbying effort has proved to be ineffective, held back by political naivety and inexperience with the complex machinery of climate diplomacy (Salt 1998).

The growing split in the business sector was in full show at the first meeting of the Conference of the Parties to the UN Framework Convention, held in Berlin in 1995. The GCC continued to oppose any move towards specific obligations while the insurance industry openly supported demands for a strong protocol. The middle ground was occupied by groups such as ICCP and the US Business Council for a Sustainable Energy Future, which played a more constructive role but warned against hasty decisions on the timing of future commitments. Observers felt that the arrival of more moderate business interests at the negotiations had transformed industry lobbying (Dunn 1995: 442). Governments willing to push for binding targets no longer faced a hostile and united business front, but could now draw more moderate voices into a constructive dialogue on how to reduce the technical and economic costs of climate action. The conference concluded with a decision to set up a two-year negotiation process on a climate protocol, which would include specific commitments by industrialized countries.

Faced with growing international resistance to its hard-line strategy, the US fossil fuel sector focused its lobbying effort on the domestic scene to prevent a change in US climate policy. It had good reason to do so. After the publication of the 1995 scientific report of the Intergovernmental Panel on Climate Change, which pointed to growing scientific evidence of man-made global warming, the US delegation began to signal more strongly than ever before that it was willing to negotiate mandatory targets. Alarmed by the apparent change in US strategy, US fossil fuel firms lambasted the administration for ignoring the economic costs of such a move and mobilized opposition on Capitol Hill against international climate commitments. The real battle was now over whether the new negotiating position of the US could find support among US senators. With both the Senate and the House of Representatives under control by Republicans after their 1994 landslide victory, industry was confident that Congress would rein in US negotiators. Following intense business lobbying, the US Senate passed a resolution in July 1997 (Senate Resolution 98, also known as the "Byrd–Hagel Resolution"), in which it expressed its fundamental opposition to any international climate treaty that would cause serious harm to the US economy and that did not include specific commitments to limit GHG emissions by developing countries (International Environment Reporter 1997a). The 95–0 vote on the resolution left no doubt about the US Senate's objection to a climate treaty as proposed by the EU that would create binding targets solely for the major polluters in the industrialized world.

Given the complexity of climate science and the high economic and political stakes involved in GHG emission reductions, few could have predicted the outcome of the Kyoto Protocol negotiations. At the start of the talks in November

1997, the US, together with Japan, Canada, Australia and New Zealand, once again urged the EU to lower its demands for emission reductions (International Environment Reporter 1997b). The US succeeded in inserting so-called flexibility elements into the draft treaty, such as the CDM (Clean Development Mechanism) and emissions trading, but was unable to win support for binding targets that included developing countries. Against domestic business opposition, the US delegation eventually agreed to a commitment for industrialized countries to reduce GHG emissions by, on average, 5.2 percent below 1990 levels, and within the commitment period of 2008–12. The outcome of the Kyoto talks disappointed environmentalists but went beyond what many business lobbyists had argued for. Whether the treaty would ever enter into force and whether the US in particular would ratify it was far from clear.

Business power and conflict after Kyoto

Business reactions would prove to be of critical importance to the future success of the Kyoto Protocol. For one, business lobbying at the domestic level played a critical role in delaying or preventing ratification in a number of countries, such as the US, Canada and Australia. Moreover, even in those countries that successfully ratified the treaty, business participation and cooperation were central to the implementation of the agreement. In this, industry's technological power, i.e. its ability to direct investment and innovation, would become a decisive factor in determining the ability of states to steer their economy into a carbon-reduced future. In a sense, therefore, there were close parallels between the climate treaty and the Montreal Protocol on ozone layer depletion. The Montreal Protocol was likewise aimed at changing production and consumption patterns that were central to modern industrial societies; and its success also depended on aligning corporate interests and patterns of business competition with the treaty's environmental objectives (Falkner 2005). But, unlike ozone layer depletion, climate change poses far more complex problems that no single company or industry can hope to solve through technological innovation. There are no substitutes that can fully replace fossil fuel-based energy, either in the short or medium term, particularly against the background of growing energy demand in emerging economies. Furthermore, reducing the economy's carbon intensity will require changes in production processes and products as well as consumptive patterns across all major industrial sectors. Technological innovation will thus be of central importance to climate action, but no single economic actor, or group of actors, possesses the same kind of technological power as DuPont and the chemical industry did in ozone politics.

Some of the first industry reactions to Kyoto were encouraging. Several business leaders, particularly in Europe, expressed guarded support for the treaty (Inter Press Service 1997; Business Wire 1997). Even though the North American fossil fuel industry remained united in its opposition, it soon became apparent that many other companies were beginning to re-define their corporate strategies in light of the successful conclusion of the Kyoto negotiations. The very fact that an agreement had been reached shifted expectations regarding future carbon restrictions and made climate-related business risks more tangible. Given the uncertainty that this involved for long-term investment plans, particularly those of the energy sector (World Energy Council 2007), businesses, including those in the US, began to factor in the costs of climate action and demanded a stable regulatory environment for climate policy (Houlder 1998). Ford Motor Company, DaimlerChrysler, GM and Texaco left the Global Climate Coalition between December 1999 and February 2000, sending a further signal to policy-makers that business was no longer united (International Environment Reporter 2000a, 2000b).

A striking feature of the international climate politics after Kyoto was the growing divergence between EU and US approaches. Whereas the EU took practical steps to implement the agreement and threw its weight behind efforts to ensure its entry into force, the US failed to introduce domestic policies in line with its international commitment and became increasingly detached from the Kyoto Protocol, culminating in President George W. Bush's decision in 2001 to withdraw from the Protocol. By this time, it seemed that the obstructionist stance of the US fossil fuel industry had paid off. Despite failure to prevent an international climate treaty, the US oil and coal industries were able to undermine international climate efforts by mobilizing what was widely acknowledged to be America's *de facto* veto power in climate politics. As Dunn argues, "[t]he diverging policy paths of North America and Europe have both shaped and been shaped by the strategies of firms headquartered with their borders" (Dunn 2002: 28).

But closer analysis of post-Kyoto climate politics reveals that the Bush administration's hard-line stance against Kyoto did not reflect overall US business interests. If anything, corporate climate strategies became more diverse even in the US, and the ground started to shift in favor of US engagement with international climate action long before the end of the Bush administration. Indeed, as developments in recent years have shown, the White House and Republican leaders in Congress became increasingly isolated amidst a groundswell of support for climate action among municipal, state-level and corporate actors in the United States. The relationship between oil and coal interests and the Bush administration proved to be particularly close and provided core anti-Kyoto business interests with a privileged position among competing interest groups. But this position came under attack as soon as the combination of domestic political change, sub-national environmental leadership and corporate support for climate action began to alter the climate agenda in US politics (Rabe 2004).

The growing number of state-level, municipal and private climate initiatives (e.g. Cities for Climate Protection; Carbon Disclosure Project; Chicago Climate Exchange; see Selin and VanDeveer 2007) has had two effects on business perceptions and strategy in the US. The fragmentation of US climate policy has increased concerns among corporations that they will have to operate in a more uneven and uncertain regulatory environment, while growing support for sub-national climate action has raised expectations that climate policy at federal level is likely to shift towards stricter measures (Donnelly 2007).

Will the change in business strategy that has become apparent across major US industries directly translate into political change in the US, and thereby strengthen the international climate regime? The business sector has undoubtedly played a powerful role in shaping America's climate policy and, initially, helped to prevent US participation in the Kyoto Protocol. Now that the business sector has grown more divided and the fossil fuel industry's influence has declined, should we expect an early and decisive shift in US policy under President Obama? At first sight, the business conflict model would suggest that growing divisions among previously united business actors open up political space for new political coalitions in favor of policy change. But it would be a case of misplaced economic determinism to argue that this outcome is inevitable. While many leading US business leaders have started to lend their support to mandatory emission reductions, others remain skeptical, and while the ground has shifted in US politics, the balance of competing business interests remains uncertain. Business conflict has opened up political space, but viewed from a neo-pluralist perspective the future direction of US climate policy remains uncertain and subject to shifting political alliances and discourses.

The indeterminacy of climate policy notwithstanding, the overall significance of change in corporate strategy is clear. At a discursive level, it has helped to move the debate from whether there is sufficient scientific evidence of man-made global warming to the question of how societies and industries might best respond to climate change. As doubters of climate science are becoming less vociferous, more and more businesses are positioning themselves as climate leaders in their sectors, hoping to gain a first-mover advantage or seeking to create synergies between climate action and other corporate strategies (Cogan 2006; Hoffman 2006). Whether these initiatives can have a significant impact remains to be seen, but the discursive shift they have promoted is in itself noteworthy. The World Energy Council recently captured this new business sentiment in a policy statement of March 2007, in which it stated that leading electricity companies agree that "addressing climate change now will be less risky and costly to the world economy than postponing action", and that "[t]aking bold, early steps to curb greenhouse gas emissions appears to be profitable for business, government and consumers" (World Energy Council 2007: 1).

Conclusions

The case of climate change reveals an unambiguous trend towards greater business involvement in international environmental politics, with mixed effects on the possibility of effective international action. Early on in the international process, a formidable alliance of corporate actors arose that was threatened most directly by proposed restrictions on greenhouse gas emissions: industries heavily dependent on the production or consumption of fossil fuels. Led by the oil multinationals, this fossil fuel industry became the dominant business lobby group in the 1992 'Earth Summit' negotiations on the UNFCCC. Other business sectors with a different set of interests also started to engage more in the international debate during the

1990s, though their international presence never came to rival that of the fossil fuel industry's main lobbying organizations, the Global Climate Coalition and the Climate Council. They were either lacking in economic strength (e.g. renewable energy firms) or failed to develop an effective and sustained political strategy (e.g. the insurance industry). Thus, it was only when the fossil fuel lobby began to disintegrate in the mid-1990s that diversity in business representation and lobbying by more pro-regulatory business interests increased significantly, with new groupings such as the International Climate Change Partnership and the World Business Council on Sustainable Development taking a more conciliatory stance.

The evolution of business lobbying on climate change demonstrates how business representation has increased at the international level while becoming more diverse as the global environmental agenda has expanded. International regulation creates differential effects on business, in climate change as much as in other environmental areas. As the number of politically engaged business actors increases, so does the potential for divisions within the business community. Business conflict has had important political consequences. It undermines business power overall and opens up the space for pro-regulatory alliances between states, firms and NGOs. However, whether latent divisions in the business sector develop into business conflict, and whether such conflict significantly changes international political dynamics, depends on the relative strength of competing business interests and other contingent factors.

The field of climate change politics provides important lessons for wider debates on how to think about business power and its limits. In seeking to influence international outcomes, business actors rely on multiple dimensions of power: relational, structural and discursive. Relational power, the ability to prevail over other actors in situations of conflict, has been clearly visible in the environmental field wherever business actors have lobbied governments and sought to influence the design of international regimes. Overall, the business sector possesses superior financial resources and strong organizational capacity, particularly when compared to environmental NGOs, and is well placed to exploit the privileged access it has to key governmental actors. However, these power resources have not necessarily translated into a predominant position in international environmental politics. They have been challenged by NGOs' ability to overcome their financial constraints through more effective transnational networking and mobilization. The key role that environmental ministries play in MEA (Multilateral Environmental Agreement) negotiations has also deprived business of the advantage of close working relationships with more business-friendly government officials. The issue-specific characteristics of environmental negotiations and the rise of a new and often imaginative form of transnational activism have thus served to curtail the business sector's relational power.

Our analysis would be too limited if we did not also take into account the business sector's central position in the global economy, which gives rise to structural business power. It is in this area that the business sector is credited by some with a dominant, even privileged, position as it controls decisions on investment and technological innovation. The case of climate change has shown how this dimension of power plays into the dynamics of international policy-making. Corporations possess structural power in the traditional sense, in that policy-makers need to consider the broader economic impact that proposed restrictions on GHG emissions will have. They also possess what can be described as *technological power*, in that corporations largely shape perceptions of which policy options are technologically and economically feasible. In this sense, corporations indirectly shape international outcomes, by setting parameters for policy-makers (for a related argument in the case of ozone politics, see Falkner 2005). But the analysis also suggests that structural power needs to be translated into the international process through the agency of firms, and that we need to consider the contingent ways in which business actors bring structural power to bear. Divisions among them greatly limit the sector's overall structural power, and have in many cases opened up opportunities to overcome structural barriers through political agency. Likewise, the discursive power of the business sectors has been undermined by a lack of business unity and challenged by environmental campaign groups that call into question the legitimacy of business actors.

The neo-pluralist perspective advanced in this paper not only urges us to study business power in its empirical manifestations within issue-specific contexts; it also draws our attention to the close connections that exist between business power and business conflict. As can be seen in international environmental politics, inter-firm and inter-sectoral conflict is always a latent reality, and frequently serves to limit business power overall. Whether business conflict manifests itself and comes to shape business involvement in international politics depends on several factors, including the nature of the issue at hand, industry structures and the specific effects of regulatory politics. It is also influenced by the agency of other actors who seek to exploit the political opportunities of business conflict. Political pressure and social protest thus play an important role in creating the conditions for business conflict to emerge.

The business conflict model holds important lessons for political leaders and civil society actors who seek to steer society and the economy in the direction of greater environmental sustainability. It suggests that the dynamics of economic competition and the potential for conflict between corporations may enhance the capacity of campaign groups to exert pressure on companies and bring about a change in corporate behavior. Social movement theorists speak of "industry opportunity structures" (Schurman 2004) that empower activist groups in their political campaigns. Where the potential for business conflict exists, e.g. between market leaders and laggards, or between companies operating at different points in transnational production chains, activist groups have sought to exploit these divisions and create political alliances with companies more likely to support stricter international standards.

Environmental activist groups have traditionally targeted states and international organizations in order to promote international norms and rules that bind economic actors and force change upon them. While this remains an important avenue for creating global governance, social movements have long come to realize that it is not the only, or even most promising, strategic option available to them. A growing number of activists have engaged in what Wapner (1996) calls "world civic politics", which involves targeting multinational corporations directly and creating governance structures outside the states system. Here again, neo-pluralism shows how business conflict provides activists with access points and powerful levers that allow them to pressure companies into change. It opens opportunities for such groups to engage and cooperate with more progressive companies in an effort to change markets and establish norms for good corporate behavior.

As Cerny has observed, political globalization that accompanies global economic integration has resulted in a situation where outcomes "are determined not by simple coercion and/or structural power but, even more significantly, by how coalitions and networks are built in real time conditions among a plurality of actors" (Cerny 2003: 156). Indeed, the proliferation of political alliances between diverse sets of actors, involving states, NGOs and business actors, makes for a more pluralistic and open-ended international politics of the environment. It does not create a level playing field for competition among equals. Significant power imbalances persist, and structural business power can constrain the search for political solutions to environmental problems. But business does not determine outcomes in international politics, nor can it control the global environmental agenda.

References

Business Wire (1997) 'CAPP Gravely Concerned about Kyoto Agreement,' 12 December.

Cerny, P.G. (2003) 'The Uneven Pluralization of World Politics,' in A. Hülsemeyer (ed.) *Globalization in the Twenty-First Century: Convergence or Divergence?* (Basingstoke: Palgrave Macmillan), pp. 153–75.

Cogan, D.G. (2006) *Corporate Governance and Climate Change: Making the Connection* (Boston, MA: Ceres).

Cox, R.W. (ed.) (1996) *Business and the State in International Relations* (Boulder, CO: Westview Press).

Donnelly, J. (2007) 'Debate over Global Warming is Shifting,' *Boston Globe*, 15 February.

Drezner, D.W. (2007) *All Politics is Global: Explaining International Regulatory Regimes* (Princeton, NJ: Princeton University Press).

Dunn, S. (1995) 'The Berlin Climate Change Summit: Implications for International Environmental Law,' *International Environment Reporter*, 18(11): 439–44.

—— (2002) 'Down to Business on Climate Change: an Overview of Corporate Strategies,' *Greener Management International* (39): 27–41.

Falkner, R. (2003) 'Private Environmental Governance and International Relations: Exploring the Links,' *Global Environmental Politics*, 3(2): 72–87.

—— (2005) 'The Business of Ozone Layer Protection: Corporate Power in Regime Evolution,' in D.L. Levy and P.J. Newell (eds) *The Business of Global Environmental Governance* (Cambridge, MA: MIT Press), pp. 105–34.

—— (2008) *Business Power and Conflict in International Environmental Politics* (Basingstoke: Palgrave Macmillan).

Fligstein, N. (1990) *The Transformation of Corporate Control* (Cambridge, MA: Harvard University Press).

Frieden, J. (1988) 'Sectoral Conflict and U.S. Foreign Economic Policy, 1914–40,' *International Organization*, 42(1): 59–90.

Gelbspan, R. (1997) *The Heat Is On: The High Stakes Battle Over Earth's Threatened Climate* (Reading, MA: Addison Wesley).

Giorgetti, C. (1999) 'From Rio to Kyoto: A Study of the Involvement of Non-governmental Organizations in the Negotiations on Climate Change,' *New York University Environmental Law Journal*, 7(2): 201–45.

Grubb, M., with D. Brack and C. Vrolijk (1999) *The Kyoto Protocol: A Guide and Assessment* (London: Earthscan).

Hoffman, A.J. (1997) *From Heresy to Dogma: An Institutional History of Corporate Environmentalism* (San Francisco: The New Lexington Press).

——(2006) 'Getting Ahead of the Curve: Corporate Strategies that Address Climate Change,' prepared for the Pew Center on Global Climate Change, University of Michigan, October.

Hopgood, S. (1998) *American Foreign Environmental Policy and the Power of the State* (Oxford: Oxford University Press).

Houlder, V. (1998) 'Business Grapples with Climate Change,' *The Financial Times*, 11 November.

Ikwue, T. and J. Skea (1994) 'Business and the Genesis of the European Community Carbon Tax Proposal,' *Business Strategy and the Environment*, 3(2): 1–11.

International Environment Reporter (1997a) 'Senate Approves Resolution 95–0 Calling for Binding Controls on Developing Nations,' 6 August, pp. 752–53.

——(1997b) 'U.S., Japan, Other Nations Agree to Urge EU to Modify Proposal on Greenhouse Gas Cuts,' 15 October, p. 951.

——(2000a) 'DaimlerChrysler Leaves Industry Coalition Opposed to Legal Requirements to Cut GHGs,' 19 January, p. 59.

——(2000b) 'Texaco Leaves Industry Coalition, Maintains Opposition to Kyoto Pact,' 15 March, pp. 244–45.

Inter Press Service (1997) 'European Oil Companies React to Kyoto Deal', 15 December.

Lindblom, C.E. (1977) *Politics and Markets: The World's Political-Economic Systems* (New York: Basic Books).

McFarland, A.S. (2004) *Neopluralism: The Evolution of Political Process Theory* (Lawrence: University Press of Kansas).

May, C. (ed.) (2006) *Global Corporate Power* (Boulder, CO: Lynne Rienner).

Milner, H.V. (1988) *Resisting Protectionism: Global Industries and the Politics of International Trade* (Princeton, NJ: Princeton University Press).

Newell, P. and Paterson, M. (1998) 'A Climate for Business: Global Warming, the State and Capital,' *Review of International Political Economy*, 5(4): 679–703.

Nowell, G.P. (1996) 'International Relations Theories: Approaches to Business and the State,' in R.W. Cox (ed.) *Business and the State in International Relations* (Boulder, CO: Westview Press), pp. 181–97.

Paterson, M. (2001) 'Risky Business: Insurance Companies in Global Warming Politics,' *Global Environmental Politics*, 1(4): 18–42.

Porter, M. and C. van der Linde (1995) 'Green and Competitive: Ending the Stalemate,' *Harvard Business Review*, 73(5): 120–33.

Pulver, S. (2002) 'Organizing Business: Industry NGOs in the Climate Debates,' *Greener Management International* (39): 55–67.

——(2007) 'Making Sense of Corporate Environmentalism: An Environmental Contestation Approach to Analyzing the Causes and Consequences of the Climate Change Policy Split in the Oil Industry,' *Organization and Environment*, 20(1): 1–40.

Rabe, B.G. (2004) *Statehouse and Greenhouse: The Emerging Politics of American Climate Change Policy* (Washington, DC: Brookings Institution Press).

Rogowski, R. (1989) *Commerce and Coalitions: How Trade Affects Domestic Political Alignments* (Princeton, NJ: Princeton University Press).

Rowlands, I.H. (2000) 'Beauty and the Beast? BP's and Exxon's Positions on Global Climate Change,' *Environmental and Planning*, 18: 339–54.

Salt, J. (1998) 'Kyoto and the Insurance Industry: an Insider's Perspective,' *Environmental Politics*, 7(2): 161–65.

Sawin, J.L. (2004) 'Mainstreaming Renewable Energy in the 21st Century,' Worldwatch Paper #169, Worldwatch Institute, May.

Schmidheiny, S. and BCSD (1992) *Changing Course: A Global Business Perspective on Development and the Environment* (Cambridge, MA: MIT Press).

Schurman, R. (2004) 'Fighting "Frankenfoods": Industry Opportunity Structures and the Efficacy of the Anti-Biotech Movement in Western Europe,' *Social Problems*, 51(2): 243–68.

Selin, H. and S.D. VanDeveer (2007) 'Political Science and Prediction: What's Next for U.S. Climate Change Policy?' *Review of Policy Research*, 24(1): 1–27.

Skidmore, D. (1995) 'The Business of International Politics,' *Mershon International Studies Review*, 39(2): 246–54.

Skidmore-Hess, D. (1996) 'Business Conflict and Theories of the State,' in R.W. Cox (ed.) *Business and the State in International Relations* (Boulder, CO: Westview Press), pp. 199–216.

Skjærseth, J.B. (1994) 'The Climate Policy of the EC: Too Hot to Handle?' *Journal of Common Market Studies*, 32(1): 25–45.

Skjærseth, J.B. and T. Skodvin (2003) *Climate Change and the Oil Industry: Common Problem, Varying Strategies* (Manchester: Manchester University Press).

Spar, D.L. (2001) *Pirates, Prophets and Pioneers: Business and Politics along the Technological Frontier* (New York: Random House).

Tarrow, S. (2005) *The New Transnational Activism* (Cambridge: Cambridge University Press).

The Economist (1992) 'Europe's Industries Play Dirty,' 9 May, pp. 91–92.

UNEP (1995) 'Statement of Environmental Commitment by the Insurance Industry,' Geneva.

Vernon, R. (1998) *In the Hurricane's Eye: The Troubled Prospects of Multinational Enterprises* (Cambridge, MA: Harvard University Press).

Vogel, D. (1995) *Trading Up. Consumer and Environmental Regulation in a Global Economy* (Cambridge, MA: Harvard University Press).

Wapner, P. (1996) *Environmental Activism and World Civic Politics* (Albany, NY: State University of New York Press).

World Energy Council (2007) 'The Energy Industry Unveils its Blueprint for Tackling Climate Change,' WEC Statement, London, March.

6 Governing corruption through the global corporation[1]

Hans Krause Hansen

Introduction

Only a couple of decades ago, attempts to curb corruption were national in nature and revolved around the sporadic measures taken by less than wholehearted governments. But comprehensive initiatives aimed at fighting corruption have proliferated since the early 1990s, spearheaded by the World Bank, the OECD, the United Nations, and NGOs such as Transparency International. These efforts have been translated into numerous international anti-corruption conventions. Many more initiatives have been launched during the present decade, including multi-stakeholder partnerships, business-driven anti-corruption networks, and anti-corruption tools and compliance programs developed by private consultancy firms and software producers.

That the fight against corruption has clearly moved beyond the national realm is itself an interesting development, which feeds into ongoing discussions about global governance. But what is also intriguing is the fact that business has begun to participate in these cross-cutting efforts at governing corruption. Drawing on theories on governance and governmentality, this chapter will investigate key institutional shifts and regulatory forms that have put corruption governance on the global policy agenda, and it will analyze the substance of business engagement in global corruption governance. In particular it will argue that charting the complex ways in which efforts at curbing corruption are linked to contemporary business concerns with the management of risk, performance and transparency provides a key entry point for understanding how business practices are intertwined with global governance.

Corruption governance

Corruption comes about in many ways, taking shape of exchanges that violate standards framed in legal and moral terms: bribery, extortion, nepotism, fraud, illegal financing of political parties, to mention just a few examples. It is widely acknowledged today that corruption is not confined to developing countries and emerging markets but has global ramifications (e.g. Campos and Pradhan 2007; Rose-Ackerman 1999). Corruption *governance* is fundamentally about curbing and preventing, within and beyond national space, the misuse of public office and other forms of entrusted power for private benefit. This chapter refers more narrowly to attempts to curb the use of bribery in the exchanges between Western businesses and public sector agencies on global markets. It is well documented that corporations have often become enmeshed in dense networks of agents, intermediaries, local state officials and political leaders through whom monetary and other services have been negotiated in exchange for deals and concessions. These transactions are complex because they often include mechanisms of reciprocity or loyalty based on friendship, kinship and patronage (Blundo and Sardan 2006; Rodríquez *et al.* 2006; Wrage and Wrage 2005).

The key feature of corruption governance is not that it acts directly on such transactions, but rather that it seeks to *govern* the conduct of the categories of actors that purportedly are engaged in or affected by them: industries, corporations, intermediaries, public sector agencies, international organizations, and so on. Conceptually, we can approach such governance or regulation in several ways. One is to draw inspiration from literatures on global governance and regulation and focus on the actors and forms of regulation involved. From this vantage point, the global governance of corruption is viewed as multilayered and pluralistic, structurally complex and geometrically variable, with national governments operating as "strategic sites for suturing together these various infrastructures of governance and legitimizing regulation beyond the state" (Held and McGrew 2002: 9). Another way is to explore how bribery has come to be constructed as a problem to be acted upon, including how this is being done in everyday organizational practices. From this lens, which draws on insights from Foucauldian studies, government always takes a very practical form and is irreducible to the state, suggesting the existence of multiple beliefs and tools of governing as well as a wide range of sites from which government may emanate, such as corporations, industries, systems of education, etc. (Larner and Walters 2004; Rose and Miller 1992).

The two approaches have much in common as they contest state-centrism in the analysis of power and authority. As such, they are both relevant in the context of this book which focuses on how business is both an object and a subject of global governance. But they also differ. The first position tends to study various forms of regulation of pre-defined issue areas and on different scales, struggling with grand questions relating to the fate of *sovereignty, who rules*, and the distinctions between the *public* and *private*, the *national* and *international* (e.g. Haufler 2006; Slaughter 2004). There is often the underlying assumption that governance is something new, to be distinguished from a recent past when social life was governed through the interventions of powerful and bureaucratized state governments.

The second position attempts to steer clear of the *institutional* or *functional* accounts of the state, which are often implied in the first position. Instead, the focus is on specific *practices of governing* located in a wide variety of sites. This includes the practical ways in which particular issues are being problematized and acted upon by actors whose location on the public and private, national and international continuum cannot always easily be defined in advance. In practice, the exercise of power is not so much a matter of imposing sovereign will as it is a process of enrolling the cooperation of actors into particular projects. Networks, nodes and centers that exercise government at a distance play an important role, shaping the conduct of actors *vis-à-vis* one another and equipping them with dispositions and instruments for self-regulation.

This chapter draws on insights from both positions. The following section focuses specifically on the regulation of business from the first perspective and demonstrates how international business has gradually become the object of anti-corruption regulatory efforts on a global scale. The section identifies various modes of business regulation in the trajectory of corruption governance. The subsequent section proposes that examining corruption governance through the second perspective, and more precisely through the lens of studies of governmentality, can make visible important aspects of the regulatory processes and practices that remain largely unexplored when drawing on the first position. Departing from a brief and critical overview of selected insights from this tradition, this section sets out to provide an understanding of the rationalities and techniques of governance deployed by business in the name of anti-corruption, illuminating how this agenda becomes aligned to wider business attempts to reduce risks, to improve corporate performance, and to handle growing public demands for transparency. Here, business comes out not only as an object of global governance efforts but also as a subject, one that aims to align the wider anti-corruption agenda to its business strategies and attempts to conduct itself and others. The final section outlines some implications of the study.

Corruption governance as business regulation

From the lens of the first position outlined above, corruption governance is, as in other contemporary issue areas, to a significant degree the tale of increasing regulatory complexity driven by a multiplicity of actors. Drawing on a distinction between four modes of regulation (Haufler 2006), it may be said to target and involve private actors through *traditional regulation* developed and enforced by sovereign governments acting on their own or together with other governments. It also takes place through *industry self-regulation* based on best practices and codes of conduct developed in the private and other sectors, as well as through the *co-regulation* of public and private sectors. Finally, corruption governance is also about *stakeholder regulation*.

The first building block of global corruption governance was in fact laid by a traditional and national regulatory initiative: the passage of the US Foreign Corrupt Practices Act (FCPA) in 1977. The FCPA criminalizes bribery on the part of US citizens and firms conducting business overseas. It introduces mandatory company self-regulation by requiring corporations to set up internal control mechanisms and to improve their accounting practices. The FCPA thus sets standards for combating corruption that are based on an extraterritoriality principle, and it changes the focus from the demand-side of corruption – government and bureaucracy – to the supply-side – corporations.

During the 1980s, US corporations lobbied the US government to seek international cooperation in suppressing bribes with a view to creating a level playing field, and by the 1990s the OECD was increasingly being used as a platform for extending the principles of the FCPA to the international business community. The 1990s mark the beginning of the development of international conventions against corruption (Getz 2006; Webb 2005). The OECD Convention on Combating Bribery of Foreign Public Officials in International Business Transactions from 1997 is drawing heavily on the FCPA. Bribing a foreign public official is now a crime to be punished in all OECD countries. Nor can bribes any longer be written off as tax deduction. The OECD Convention seeks to ensure enforcement of legal requirements through a comprehensive monitoring system based on peer-reviewing. The system is managed by a special government-mandated Working Group on Bribery in International Business Transactions, which surveys member countries' progress in implementing the Convention and monitors their compliance. On the other hand, the United Nations Convention against Corruption, signed in 2003 and being the most comprehensive anti-corruption instrument to date by including initiatives concerning asset recovery and provisions on private to public bribery, has little to offer in terms of implementation and monitoring. The same goes for regional initiatives such as the Organization of American States' Inter-American Convention Against Corruption, which is in fact the first binding multilateral agreement on corruption, signed in 1996 (Webb 2005).

Recent research on these legal efforts emphasizes their interesting prospects for the international fight against corruption. In assessing international conventions, Webb (2005: 228) argues that these have helped "elevate anti-corruption action to the international stage." Specifically, it is possible to observe an increase in the enforcement of the OECD convention in recent years, particularly in France, Germany and the US, while there is still little or no enforcement in Japan, the UK and Canada (Transparency International 2008). What is also clear is that US authorities have become significantly more active in the present decade, increasing the number of FCPA cases against corporations for criminal conduct occurring within and outside the US. Once convicted, corporations are now rewarded with reduction in sanctions in terms of fines and prison terms if they cooperate with the authorities and take steps to develop and implement anti-corruption programs (Ayres *et al.* 2007).

But corruption governance includes more than traditional regulation. Industry self-regulation emerges when international regulation is absent, partial or ineffective, whereas co-regulation emerges as a way to "achieve public regulatory aims with private sector efficiency" (Haufler 2006: 93–95). Both forms can emerge as a response to international governmental strategies to steer corporate conduct towards public goals without appearing to interfere directly or too much in corporate autonomy. In corruption governance, both forms can be found in the emergence of standards, best practices and codes of conduct, which are developed by business associations, echoing existing international anti-corruption activities and legislation while pointing to the need to reshape these efforts. One example is the International Chamber of Commerce (ICC), which has developed rules that encourage business to confront issues of extortion and bribery and provides it with input to become engaged with international initiatives to fight corruption:

> [These rules] outline the basic measures companies should take to prevent corruption [and they are] intended as a method of self-regulation by international business. Although they are without direct legal effect, the Rules of Conduct constitute what is considered good commercial practice in the matters to which they relate.
>
> (ICC 2008)

The ICC is equally interested in shaping "policy action to be taken at national and international level to strengthen the administrative and regulatory framework to fight corruption" (ICC 2008). Also business-driven is the Partnering Against Corruption Initiative (PACI), organized under the World Economic Forum (WEF), whose mission is to "develop multi-industry principles and practices that will result in a competitive level playing field, based on integrity, fairness and ethical conduct." PACI aims to "place the private sector in a unique position to guide governments' and international organizations' strategies and policies on anti-corruption" (World Economic Forum 2008).

A fourth category of business regulation includes multi-stakeholder regulation. Here different actors – public and private, national and international – set out to develop regulatory frameworks, to establish standards and goals, frameworks for decision-making, and procedures for achieving the standards. One important attempt at stakeholder regulation in corruption governance is the UN Global Compact. Its (tenth) principle against corruption is intended to send "a strong worldwide signal that the private sector shares responsibility for the challenges of eliminating corruption" (United Nations 2008). Noteworthy is also the recent Extractive Industries Transparency Initiative (EITI), whose objective is to "strengthen governance by improving transparency and accountability in the extractives sector" (EITI 2008). EITI is a cross-sectorial arrangement, involving governments, companies, civil society groups, investors and international organizations. EITI is related to another initiative, Publish What You Pay (PWYP). Launched in 2002 by George Soros, PWYP is a coalition of NGOs which campaigns for the mandatory disclosure of taxes, royalties and other payments by oil, gas and mining companies to governments and public agencies

Stakeholder regulation involves advocacy and non-profit groups. In the field of anti-corruption the presence of Transparency International in many of these schemes provides a good example of how anti-corruption *mobilization* can translate into new organizational forms and set-ups. Throughout the 1980s and early 1990s, it was a dominant belief that doing business in the South was impossible without paying bribes. But forces within the World Bank, including the persons behind what was later to be known as Transparency International, began to challenge this belief by exposing the World Bank's silence on corruption in development projects. Founded in 1993, Transparency International is today a central activist and watchdog in the international fight against corruption, encouraging coalition building across sectors and educational activities. The organization has a decentralized structure and stimulates the continuous mobilization and lobbying of political and economic elites worldwide (Holzner and Holzner 2006). It is deeply involved in the development of anti-corruption policies and strategies in international organizations and cooperates closely with a panoply of business associations. To some observers, the activities of Transparency International tie into wider political agendas, "contributing to a broadly neoliberal program of government" (Hindess 2005: 1390).

Corruption governance as the management of risk, performance and transparency

As we have seen, the governance of corruption today can be analyzed as driven by a multiplicity of actors – state, non-state and hybrid in-betweens – and a variety of regulatory arrangements spanning from traditional to other forms of regulation. One question that emerges from examining corruption governance from this vantage point is whether central responsibilities of the fight against corruption are being delegated from states, the primary locations of criminal law implementation and enforcement, to non-state actors, including business. The possible delegation from states towards non-state actors such as business is undoubtedly an important issue (Cutler *et al.* 1999; Hall and Biersteker 2002; Hansen and Salskov-Iversen 2008). But it does not capture how corruption is constituted as a problem and how measures taken against it are designed and enacted.

Drawing on inspiration from Foucault (1991), studies of governmentality typically make an analytical distinction between political rationalities and governance technologies, which captures precisely this. The first refers to the thoughts and representations involved as problems and fields of intervention are defined in policies, programs, plans and so on. The second captures the ways that problems and fields defined by political rationalities are dealt with, involving technologies of "seeing," such as practices of measurement, standardization and surveillance, which emanate from different centers of power, including the state and its agencies (Scott 1998; Sharma and Gupta 2005). The deployment of such technologies enables governance at a distance. Obviously, this is by no means a simple process as it relies on the "translations" that social actors make of policies and programs, and on how they align them to their own projects. If translation enables alignment with political projects and programs, facilitating the enrolment of chains of actors who "translate" power from one locale to another, such translation can never be perfect; this suggests that in practice power is to a considerable degree often out of the control of the powerful (Braithwaite and Drahos 2000: 482; Dean 1999; Latour 1986; Rose 1999; Rose and Miller 1992).

The concept of governmentality forms the starting point for a growing body of research concerned with the manifestations and implications of neoliberal forms of governance. Criminologists have used governmentality as a lens to study governance relations across the conventional boundaries that separate public from private, state from economy, and state from community. Scholars working within this tradition have examined the proliferation of private policing and risk governance in the context of neoliberal rule, which relies on markets and the private sector, presupposes a higher degree of independence, responsibility and involvement of institutions and individuals than previous regimes, and, not least, introduces performance technologies such as evaluation and rankings (Ericson 2007; Garland 1997; O'Malley 2004; Power 2007; Valverde and Mopas 2004: 236).

While much of the governmentality literature previously confined itself to the study of governance at a distance within nation-states, scholars have begun to explore the political rationalities and technologies of governing "global" spaces – *global governmentality* (Larner and Walters 2004; Neumann and Sending 2007; Walters and Haahr 2005). Such spaces are not self-evident objects, which is often implied in studies of global governance, but rather the consequence of the building up of networks from the bottom: "The 'government of space' – even 'globalization' itself – is simply a description of one actor's ability (or perhaps many actors' abilities) to produce some sort of connectability between networks" (Kendall 2004: 64). There has also been a growing interest in exploring how certain mentalities of rule developed in Western contexts subsequently travel to non-Western destinations where they are translated into a variety of practical purposes, quite often at odds with the original conception yet relying on the enrolment of transborder networks and alliances (e.g. Abrahamsen 2004; Hansen and Salskov-Iversen 2005; 2008; Löwenheim 2008).

With very few recent exceptions (e.g. Fougner 2008; Rose-Redwood 2006), this literature rarely explores the question of governmentality taking the point of departure in non-state actors, specifically international business. The following sections contributes to this emerging research area by examining some of the governance rationalities and technologies deployed by business in current anti-corruption efforts. This provides us with a picture of how corruption is being problematized and becomes the object of multiple business activities and interventions. Hence, from this perspective, business is not only an object of various modes of regulation as described in the previous section, but also its subject, a subject whose practices, shaped by particular rationalities and technologies of governance, contribute to global governance.

In the field of corruption governance as such, three partially overlapping rationalities and governance technologies stand out as particularly important for business activities: *Risk, performance* and *transparency*. While the deployment of risk technologies rests on the diagnosis of business environments as – in various ways – challenging, the deployment of performance technologies aims to enhance business competitiveness. The deployment of technologies of transparency emerges from growing concerns amongst business as regards legal and public demands for openness, corporate social responsibility and ethical conduct. In this process, business is becoming linked to specific sources and networks of knowledge and expertise concerning corruption governance, including not only state actors, international organizations and civil society organizations, but also commercial actors. Business efforts to tackle corruption are latched on to purposes that do not necessarily reinforce the anti-corruption agenda per se, but rather commercial and other objectives, including monitoring and surveillance.

Risk

Risk involves the assessment of processes, sectors and zones falling within pre-established "at-risk" categories. These assessments make up knowledge hierarchies on the basis of which strategic decisions and interventions can be made. Risk is not a static, objective phenomenon, but is being continuously created, negotiated and redefined in social networks and through processes of meaning-making: "Nothing is a risk in itself; there is no risk in reality. But on the other hand, anything *can* be a risk: it all depends on how one analyzes the danger, considers the event" (Ewald 1991: 199). From the perspective of business, the governance of corruption relies on the deployment of various forms of risk technology based on the diagnosis of risks. Such technologies are made available by a wide range of risk information providers. One example is Control Risks, a large, private risk consultancy that was founded in the 1970s and now operates in 18 countries, offering advice and assistance to corporate, governmental and non-governmental organizations. Its expanding activities reflect how corruption risk analysis has become increasingly important for organizations as they have moved into new territories. According to Control Risks, managers and business developers "need to know how different legal and regulatory environments, political rivalries and potential instability will affect the business." On the local level "you have to consider the effects your operations may have on specific communities." The point is that business operations take place "within a global context of legislation, regulation and local and international pressure groups, where corporate governance and reputation is of paramount importance. Understanding, monitoring and preparing for these risks can provide a real competitive edge" (Control Risks 2008).

The higher the regulative standards and the greater the perceived dangers are, the more comprehensive must be the risk technologies deployed to act upon these dangers. This is not merely a question of getting to know the "facts" about a local context, but of combining the information from a wide range of sources. Reaching some common ground for making strategic decisions requires the mobilization and enrolment of a whole net of actors and sources of expertise, operating on different levels and in different territories (Dicken *et al.* 2001). Like most risk consultancies, Consult Risk is specifically focused on the question of how international companies may best deal with local contacts and partners when they move into new territories and jurisdictions. Observes John Bray, Director at the company:

> In the past, foreign partners have often argued that they have no legal or moral responsibility if local partners or agents pay bribes without their direct knowledge or explicit approval. Indeed, they may employ local partners

precisely because of their ability to serve as a "buffer", protecting them from questionable local business practices…[but]…the risks will increase as the enforcement of anti-corruption laws become more effective. Local knowledge is of course essential, and it is important to build up trust between business partners. However, this trust must be based on a common understanding of what kinds of business practice are and are not acceptable. International companies cannot adequately protect their own interests unless they understand and can monitor what local partners do on their behalf.

(Bray 2006: 108)

The key solution here, according to Michael Price of Statoil, is to conduct Integrity Due Diligence. This risk technology is defined as

the process of mitigating risk arising from association with a third party who may be or may have been engaged in unethical or illegal practices. The risk may exist as a direct liability by the company through its association, or it may take the form of reputation damage as guilt by association.

(Price 2006:119)

Dealing with local agents must be based on a careful check of who these agents really are. This includes investigating whether they have close family relationships to key official figures and/or to competing companies, and whether payment is required to be in cash via third-party or suspicious bank accounts. Such enquiries strengthen the quality of documentation required for an international company to enter the market in question. If an arrangement with an agent is finally set up, it should include a statement "that the agent understand and will comply with the company's anti-corruption rules and procedures" (Bray 2006: 112).

Conducting integrity due diligence involves the mobilization of a comprehensive network of actors and associated expertise, including credit rating organizations and multilateral financial institutions with political clout. Credit ratings developed by specialized companies concerning the potential partner in question must be checked, including checking for bankruptcy (Price 2006: 121). For example, it is important to determine whether relevant companies and partners are blacklisted and appear on the list of debarred companies and individuals, developed by the World Bank, published on its website and referred to in its Anti-Corruption Guidelines. According to the Bank, more than 330 firms and individuals have been sanctioned by the bank for engaging in fraud and corruption in Bank-financed projects since 1999. Debarred organizations are excluded from World Bank-financed contracts. This sanction is determined via an administrative process in which the Integrity Department investigates the facts of a case, which then forms the basis for a decision by the Sanctions Committee. A report may also be submitted to relevant national authorities. The report has no legal status. It is nevertheless made available to governments, who may then undertake criminal investigation into the matter to find out whether any national laws have been violated (World Bank 2008).

Conducting integrity due diligence is presented as essential for international business, but it is not without problems. First, there has been a growing demand for support services related to the required investigations and business intelligence efforts, a situation which "has unfortunately encouraged some unqualified individuals to pass themselves off as specialists" (Price 2006: 121). A second problem relates to the high costs of conducting due diligence.

For small and medium-sized international companies who are living with tight budgets and thus unable to conduct thorough risk analysis there are certain remedies, however. Drawing on the latest innovations in information technologies, and with the support from the official development aid agencies of a number of Western countries, the private consultancy Global Advice Network (GAN) has recently developed a Business Anti-Corruption Portal. Available on the portal are tools such as references to international and national legislation and model codes of conduct based on Transparency International Business Principles and the ICC Code of Conduct. Tools for carrying out due diligence are also available, such as updated country profiles with "detailed information of strategic importance for businesses," which can be combined with the risk assessment tools that can be downloaded from the website (Business Anti-Corruption Portal 2008).

While the comprehensive instruments available on the portal are available for companies for free, GAN also offers basic and more specific anti-corruption training courses for employees. In this market the GAN is not alone. Many more companies have emerged, offering off-line courses and software systems. Like GAN, the content of courses and systems draws on material developed by Transparency International. Transparency International's products are key ingredients in corruption risk technologies, such as educational programs aimed at raising awareness, anti-corruption methodologies, and risk assessment. The comprehensive guidebook titled *National Integrity Systems: the TI Source Book* contains tools and practical advice enabling activists to develop and apply strategies for transparency and accountability. The *Global Corruption Report* offers more detailed evidence of public perceptions of corruption as well as accounts of failed and successful attempts to tackle corruption worldwide (Hindess 2005; Larmour 2006).

Another example includes Transparency International's collaboration with Enablon, a software provider responsible for the development of Anti-Bribery Solution (ABS). This software system is designed to enhance corporate performance by helping employees to assess the adequacy of their anti-bribery systems. On its website, Enablon writes the following:

> Enablon joins forces with Transparency International, the global coalition against corruption, to create a unique anti-bribery software solution. Enablon ABS enables companies to effectively implement, manage and track anti-bribery programmes ... Based on the Business Principles for Countering Bribery, developed by Transparency International with the cooperation of global companies and other stakeholders, ABS incorporates good practice

for countering bribery, including the experience gained from field tests, workshops and discussions with leading companies.

(Enablon 2008)

Obviously, many other companies operate in the field of anti-corruption, offering specialized tools and knowledge to firms and organizations as to how to prevent corruption, but without cooperating directly with Transparency International. Sai Global is a company that offers a best practice and awareness-raising courses. A specific online course entitled "The Bribery of Public Officials" has been designed to "engage learners and allow them to apply their knowledge." The objective of this course is to "introduce learners to the various anti-bribery laws, and train them to recognize situations in which bribery may be taking place" (Sai Global 2008).

As we can see, technologies of minimizing corruption risks do not go after specific "wrongdoers." Even if international and national legislations forbid bribery and steps have been taken to impose a sanctions regime through the World Bank's debarment list, which publicly blacklists specific individuals and companies, fighting corruption is generally a matter of corruption avoidance. Its practical effectuation entails governance at a distance. Indirect techniques, based on knowledge hierarchies established by specialized expertise, act on business itself and its environments to ensure that preventive measures are taken towards the perceived danger. However, there is, of course, no guarantee that a technique such as due diligence will achieve the desired effect on a full scale. Because if an intermediary is sufficiently sophisticated,

he can keep his image very clean while still paying bribes through relatives, off-shore accounts, or shell companies. It's never possible to say with confidence that you've done enough due diligence, but the constraints of business require you to stop at some point.

(Center for International Business Enterprise 2008)

Performance

Given that the objective of the private sector is, and has always been, to minimize risk and losses, corruption risk technologies are of course closely connected to the question of performance. The corruption governance today offers a veritable battery of *performance technologies* – comprehensive systems of ranking and benchmarking, performance indicators, auditing, best practice schemes and other modes of external verification. Such technologies not only provide companies and organizations with important strategic knowledge about where and how to – or how *not* to – invest their energies and resources. Importantly, some of the technologies also provide corporations with new opportunities to improve their competitiveness in that they benchmark the level of performance in the field of anti-corruption itself. This is an example of how performance technologies such as benchmarking can encourage corporations "to constantly reinvent themselves and remobilize their efforts" (Larner and Le Heron 2004: 215). Making comparisons establishes knowledge hierarchies that differentiate between good and bad performers, reflecting the aspirations of being internationally competitive. This is participation at a distance: it relies on various forms of calculative practices, which in turn are shaped by scientific expertise (ibid.: 212).

Sophisticated ranking and benchmarking schemes are being used by several public and private agencies. Transparency International cooperates intensively with research institutions and is the main force behind the continuous production of measures for assessing corruption and toolkits and methods for preventing and tackling it. These include the Corruption Perceptions Index (CPI) that ranks countries according to perceptions of their corruption. The CPI is a poll of polls, based on the perceptions of businessmen, journalists, academics, investment and risk analysts. TI has also developed the Bribe Payer's Index that compares the supply-side proclivity in various societies to pay bribes elsewhere. The long range of Transparency International outlets, including the results of the different surveys conducted, are not only frequently quoted in public media but also widely used and referred to by governments, international organizations and, as we saw in the above, the risk industry. Not only are governments aware of their rank in the indices, they occasionally also condemn the arrogance of TI when they are ranked among states that are perceived amongst the most corrupt. These indices, themselves an instantiation of knowledge hierarchies-based single number rankings of entire countries, are deployed by business and governments. Their influence is hard to ignore, in particular amongst low-ranked governments in developing countries, as the findings of the rankings are incorporated into the decision-making processes concerning significant financial and political matters (Holzner and Holzner 2006: 191; Löwenheim 2008: 261).

One example of a company specializing in the production of relevant indicators and benchmarks with a view to company performance in corruption governance includes the FTSE Group. The company is owned by the Financial Times and the London Stock Exchange. It is entirely devoted to the development of indices with a specific view to generating market and business information for consultants, asset owners, asset managers, investment banks, stock exchanges and brokers. The rationale behind the FTSE indices is that practices that do not meet the standards within different areas can have damaging effects on a company's brand values. Thus, investors are believed to be interested in knowing how different risks are managed by companies and whether or not they meet the standards set to mitigate the risks. A few years ago the company developed a special FTSE4Good Index Series, designed to measure the performance of companies in terms of "globally recognized corporate responsibility standards." The FTSE carried out consultations with corporations, fund managers, government representatives, non-governmental organizations, business associations and private investors. It finally decided to launch an additional set of FTSE4Good Index criteria covering the issue of bribery. The point of departure was taken in the Business Principles for Countering Bribery, launched by Transparency International in 2003. The new index identifies the companies in the current FTSE4Good list that have the highest levels of risk of engaging in bribery through three main filters: country, sector, and public contract. For example, a company that does business in a *country* that scores less than 4 on the TI CPI and 0 or negative on the World Bank Governance Indicators list, and is operating in an *industrial sector* that is likely to have the highest level of exposure to risk of engaging in bribery, such as oil, gas, pharmaceuticals or telecommunications, while being involved with *government contracts or license*, is considered as having the highest level of exposure to risk of engaging in bribery.

For a high-risk company to remain in the FTSE4Good Index, it must develop an anti-bribery program, with specific policy, management and reporting components. These components include the prohibition of giving and taking bribes, commitment to obey all relevant laws, and efforts to make its policy publicly available. Anti-bribery policy must be communicated to employees, and these must be trained, just as compliance mechanisms, secure communication channels and procedures to remedy non-compliance must be in place and publicly communicated. High-risk companies that are currently not in the FTSE4Good Index series will have to comply fully with the criteria to gain inclusion (FTSE 2007).

Engaging in the game of performance standards and benchmarking in corruption governance through an index such as the FTSE4Good is likely to impinge on company processes and hierarchies. The preoccupation with difference and differentiation makes benchmarking a highly selective and liminal technique that links up those organizations understood to have value according to the indicators designed, while discarding the rest. One can enter and get expelled from the rankings, and the number takes a life of its own. How the numbers are produced is less important than how they travel and they work they do. Should any contestation of the specific benchmarking exercise occur, contestation itself can in fact naturalize the exercise, "for even to engage in discussions about the inadequacy (flawed methodologies and so on) or appropriateness (for example, quantitative versus qualitative measures) of benchmarking techniques is enough to give them some materiality" (Larner and Le Heron 2004: 215–19).

By implication, in order to adjust to and appropriate the standards promoted by an index such as FTSE4Good, corporations can draw on yet another segment of specialized consultancy expertise. The company LRN, for example, presents itself as a "global leader in ethics and compliance management and education." Its seeks to offer "a full range of education, applications and services to help our clients advance an ethical culture while effectively managing their governance, ethics and compliance processes everywhere they operate" (LRN 2008). Here, the required attention to legal compliance on the part of high-risk companies on the FTSE4Good list can be supported through the languages and techniques of learning and business ethics.

Transparency

If one of the defining elements of corruption is secrecy, one of the defining elements of corruption governance today is the demand for openness in the conduct of organizations, public and private. Openness implies the recognition of the existence of a public sphere through which social practices can be problematized and rendered visible for the purposes of public scrutiny, criticism and improvement. Demands for openness can to a considerable degree be viewed as a response to specific political events, but they are also interlinked with the emergence of the notions of ethically and socially responsible business (Barry 2004).

Corruption governance involves the use of two different technologies of transparency. The first concerns the ongoing and direct exposure of practices and events deemed "corrupt" in public mass media and is driven primarily by investigative journalism. Public revelations about misconduct of entrusted positions are the foundation for scandals. Corruption scandals make visible the norms of conduct by testifying to the boundaries of what is acceptable or not from a particular point of view (Thompson 2000). Corruption scandals abounded throughout the second half of the 20th century, spurred by leaks, news coverage and analysis in public media. By the turn of the century, particularly the United States and Europe experienced a wave of business scandals. Media revelations of the activities of celebrity CEOs led to the destruction of many companies and jobs, including some of the leading accounting firms involved in the scandals. Consequently, important changes in corporate governance structures were made. The Sarbanes–Oxley Act of 2002 – US legislation developed in response to the scandals – now imposes heavy punishment for absence of transparency. Among other things, the Act establishes the Public Company Accounting Oversight Board, with which accounting firms must register. The Act holds various professions responsible for financial reports and introduces new provisions on how to disclose company information to the public. It also introduces criminal penalties for attempts to commit fraud, sets up sentencing guidelines, defines protection for whistle blowers, and directs other institutions to create rules concerning disclosure (Holzner and Holzner 2006: 223).

The complex relationship between public corruption scandals and legislation brings us to the second and partly interlinked set of technologies of transparency: the mushrooming initiatives, emanating from both within and without of corporations, to establish mechanisms that on the one hand make the reporting of suspicious behaviors possible, and on the other hand ensure that the establishment of the mechanisms themselves is reported, facilitating trust in the company.

Internal mechanisms include the creation of employee helplines within companies – an instrument that is also known under the less flattering term of whistle-blowing. This tool is offered by consultancies devoted to the promotion of ethics and compliance in companies. For example, the company Business Controls, Inc. is offering a web-based system to help firms to respond to employee inquires, termed "Anonymous Incident Reporting System" (Business Controls 2008).

As Tabuena and Mondini, managers in Deloitte Financial Advisory Service, point out, the popularity of this instrument is growing on an international scale along with the globalization of company business practices. But it has at the same time led to legal and regulatory concerns in countries such as France and Germany, a fact which is "now causing concern for many multinational public companies that must comply with US Sarbanes Oxley law and related rules" (Tabuena and Mondini 2006: 92). There are culturally different approaches to whistle-blowing, echoing the practices of previously authoritarian regimes, and the effectiveness of such an anonymous reporting system relies on the employees being aware of its existence, the de facto endorsement of it by the company leadership, and the existence of follow-up mechanisms that ensure that allegations are addressed and investigated and that sanctions are applied if needed. In addition to addressing the problem of corruption, the system can in fact "be a successful management tool" which makes possible that "underlying concerns" can be "safely raised and addressed, employee satisfaction and retention improved," supporting "a culture of compliance and ethical behavior" (ibid.: 95).

While whistle-blowing addresses company affairs in an internal system of information and feedback processes, there are also forms of reporting that are primarily externally oriented and reflect a variety of aims amongst companies, as well as stakeholder expectations. Such mechanisms include the detailed public statements of policies and operating procedures, available on corporations' websites, which explain company policies. Reporting on the compliance with anti-corruption codes of conduct and mandatory regulation has become more common, also with a view to satisfying business association membership requirements and, importantly, to meet pre-qualification requirements. For one thing, companies with anti-corruption programs may require their suppliers to have established comparable programs; but also multilateral development banks and export credit agencies are increasingly placing pre-qualification requirements related to anti-corruption practices before issuing loans, to ensure that a company certifies that no persons or entities acting for or on behalf of it engages in bribery (Wilkinson 2006: 98).

In this sense, reporting is a technology of both performance and transparency. Reporting on company anti-corruption measures, such as anti-corruption policy plans, risk assessment, adequate organization and management systems to implement policies, performance targets and indicators, as well as monitoring systems and mechanisms to ensure stakeholder responses, offers the public a window through which the company can be scrutinized, making possible the strategic assessment by external stakeholders and forces as regards the credibility and value of the company. This is endorsed by institutional actors such as the United Nations Global Compact. Participants in the compact are encouraged to take the lead in reporting, to demonstrate their progress and to share their experience.

In addition to this, company reporting on anti-corruption is itself subject to quality control through independent assessment, that is, an additional reporting exercise on company self-reporting. This purportedly independent second-layer verification process can be an important factor in building the credibility of the company, and it draws on a wide range of professions and techniques of standard-setting. Again, it seems that the scaling up of corruption governance is implying the existence of an entire anti-corruption industry (Everett *et al.* 2007; Michael 2004) devoted to helping companies to avoid loss of credibility, driven by professional associations and consulting firms that address a number issues at the interface between sustainability, business ethics, corporate social responsibility and corruption (Wilkinson 2006: 96).

Conclusions and perspectives

Corruption governance includes coercive strategies to regulate business conduct, promulgated by state and interstate organizations, but also strategies that are much more indirect, diverse and multi-centered. By drawing on a governmentality framework it has been made clear that key technologies of anti-corruption deployed by business and other actors include risk, performance and transparency, with substrata of managerial techniques and practices such as due diligence investigations, rankings and benchmarking schemes, whistle-blowing systems, as well as public reporting. The deployment of many of these technologies has increased considerably since the turn of the century (Berenbeim 2006; PWC 2007). And companies have come to rely on a wide variety of experts and sources of knowledge on the matter – public, private and non-profit agencies – including the multiple and interconnected agencies and organizations doing the rating, ranking and benchmarking that penetrate risk, performance and transparency technologies – clearly a key characteristic of corruption governance.

Like the congenial issues of corporate social responsibility and business ethics, the fight against corruption can be seen as a source of business innovation and opportunity, if not competitive advantage. From this perspective, business should be proactive in the field of anti-corruption, recognizing that a transparent business environment based on a level playing field will work to its favor: the high cost of pursuing anti-corruption and compliance will pay off in the long run (Porter and Kramer 2006; Wrage and Wrage 2005). This line of thought, while potentially providing constructive input to business strategizing, tends to obscure the fact that technologies of risk, performance and transparency and their associated managerial techniques are not merely neutral tools to satisfy business competitiveness aspirations. These technologies are embedded in relations of power and provide mechanisms of inclusion and exclusion that determine who is to be included in and excluded from the far-flung networks of actors involved in business. In fact, these technologies, which are not limited to business but can also be deployed by public sector and civil society organizations, are linked to political and normalizing projects that differentiate between practices by judging them against legal and ethical standards, and by charting their distribution in terms of the performance of specific actors and countries.

Consequently, if business engagement in anti-corruption suggests a linkage between competitiveness aspirations and a wider project of normalization, this is a linkage that extends far beyond the factory gates of Western companies and well into the foreign territories where these companies operate. The knowledge hierarchies on the basis of which decisions are made concerning investment targets – countries – are likely to impinge on those countries, their people and their institutions. Business governs at a distance, enrolling clients, agents, competitors and political authorities on foreign markets into wider networks in which such values are being articulated. Here there is some relevant research to be done in the future as regards the resistance towards anti-corruption activities deployed by Western corporations in developing countries and emerging markets. Recent research suggests that many corporations do not merely passively react to the challenges posed by corruption in a host country. Increasingly, companies "shape and change structural properties of business systems of which they are a part through their own practices ... that they recursively organize" (Luo 2006: 761). Only further empirical research can help determine how such governance at a distance is taking place, the alignment or resistance to the anti-corruption project of those acting down the line, and what its outcomes might eventually be.

Note

1 I thank the two editors as well as Lars Bo Kaspersen, Jan Aart Scholte, Grahame Thompson and Steen Valentin for their valuable comments to previous drafts of this chapter.

References

Abrahamsen, R. (2004) "The power of partnerships in global governance," *Third World Quarterly*, 25(8): 1453–67.

Ayres, M., Davis, J., Healy, N. and Wrage, A. (2007) "Developments in U.S. and International Efforts to Prevent Corruption," *International Lawyer*, 41(2): 597–611.

Barry, A. (2004) "Ethical Capitalism" in Larner, W. and Walters, W. (eds) *Global Governmentality. Governing International Spaces* (London: Routledge).

Berenbeim, R.E. (2006) *Resisting Corruption. How Company Programs are Changing*, The Conference Board, New York, accessible at www.conference-board.org.

Blundo, G. and Olivier de Sardan, J.P. (2006) *Everyday Corruption and the State: Citizens and Public Opinion in Africa* (London: Zed Books).

Braithwaite, J. and Drahos, P. (2000) *Global Business Regulation* (Cambridge: Cambridge University Press).

Bray, J. (2006) "Agents, consultants and joint-venture partners in international business transactions" in The Global Compact: *Business against corruption. Case stories and examples* (New York: United Nations Global Compact Office).

Business Anti-Corruption Portal (2008) "Introduction to the Business Anti-corruption Portal," http://www.business-anti-corruption.com/normal.asp?pageid = 46 (accessed 12 December 2008).

Business Controls (2008) "Anonymous Employee Reporting System," http://www.businesscontrols.com/incidentreporting/anonymousincidentreporting.html (accessed 12 December 2008).

Campos, J.E and Pradhan, S. (eds) (2007) *The Many Faces of Corruption. Tracking Vulnerabilities at the Sector Level* (Washington, DC: The World Bank).

Center for International Business Enterprise (2008): "Shedding Light on Corrupt Practices: Transparency Counteracts Bribery. An Interview with Alexandra Wrage," www.cipe.org (accessed 31 July 2008).

Control Risks (2008) "Political & security risk analysis," http://www.controlrisks.com/default.aspx?page = 315 (accessed 12 December 2008).

Cutler, A.C., Haufler, V. and Porter, T. (eds) (1999) *Private Authority and International Affairs* (Albany, NY: State University of New York Press).

Dean, M. (1999) *Governmentality: Power and Rule in Modern Society* (London: Sage).

Dicken, P., Kelly, P.F., Olds, K. and Yeung, H.W.-C. (2001) "Chains and Networks, Territories and Scales: Towards a Relational Framework for Analyzing the Global Economy," *Global Networks. A Journal of Transnational Affairs*, 1(2): 89–112.

EITI (2008) "EITI Overview," http://eitransparency.org/ (accessed 10 December 2008).

Enablon (2008) "Enablon ABS," http://enablon.com/products/corporate-responsibility-ehs-management/anti-bribery-solution/functionalities.aspx (accessed 12 December 2008).

Ericson, R.V. (2007) *Crime in an Insecure World* (Cambridge: Polity Press).

Everett, J, Neu, D. and Rahaman, A.S. (2007) "Accounting and the global fight against corruption," *Accounting, Organizations and Society*, 32: 513–42.

Ewald, F. (1991) "Insurance and risk," in Burchell, G., Gordon, C. and Miller, P. (eds) *The Foucault Effect: Studies in Governmentality* (London: Harvester Wheatsheaf).

Foucault, M. (1991) "Governmentality," in Burchell, G., Gordon, C. and Miller, P. (eds) *The Foucault Effect: Studies in Governmentality* (London: Harvester Wheatsheaf).

Fougner, T. (2008) "Neoliberal Governance of States: The Role of Competitiveness Indexing and Benchmarking," *Millennium: Journal of International Studies*, 37(2): 303–26.

FTSE (2007) "Counting Bribery Criteria," www. ftse.com (accessed 18 October 2007).

Garland, D. (1997) "Governmentality and the problem of crime," *Theoretical Criminology*, 1(2):173–214.

Getz, K.A. (2006) "The Effectiveness of Global Prohibition Regimes. Corruption and the Anti-bribery Convention," *Business & Society*, 45(3): 254–81.

Hall, R.B. and Biersteker, T. (eds) (2002) *The Emergence of Private Authority in Global Governance* (Cambridge: Cambridge University Press).

Hansen, H.K. and Salskov-Iversen, D. (2005) "Remodeling the Transnational Political Realm: Partnerships, Benchmarking Schemes and the Digitalization of Governance," *Alternatives. Global, Local, Political*, 30(2): 141–64. – (2008) *Critical Perspectives on Private Authority in Global Politics* (Basingstoke: Palgrave MacMillan).

Haufler, V. (2006) "Global Governance in the Private Sector," in C. May (ed.):*Global Corporate Power* (Boulder, CO: Lynne Rienner Publishers).

Held, D. and McGrew, A. (eds) (2002) *Governing Globalisation. Power, Authority and Global Governance* (Cambridge: Polity Press).

Hindess, B. (2005) "Investigating International Anti-corruption," *Third World Quarterly*, 26(8): 1389–98.

Holzner, B. and L. Holzner (2006): *Transparency in Global Change. The Vanguard of the Open Society* (Pittsburgh, PA: University of Pittsburgh Press).

ICC (2008) "ICC tools for self-regulation," http://www.iccwbo.org/policy/anticorruption/id870/index.html (accessed 10 December2008).

Kendall, G. (2004) "Global networks, international networks, actor networks," in Larner, W. and Walters, W. (eds) *Global Governmentality. Governing International Spaces* (London: Routledge).

Larmour, P. (2006) "Civilizing techniques: Transparency international and the spread of anti-corruption," in Bowden, B. and Seabrooke, L. (eds) *Global Standards of Market Civilization* (London: Routledge).

Larner, W. and Le Heron, R. (2004) "Global benchmarking. Participating 'at a distance' in the globalizing economy," in Larner, W. and Walters, W. (eds) *Global Governmentality. Governing International Spaces* (London: Routledge).

Larner, W. and Walters, W. (eds) (2004) *Global Governmentality. Governing International Spaces* (London: Routledge).

Latour, B. (1986) "The Powers of Association," in J. Law (ed.) *Power, Action and Belief* (London: Routledge and Kegan Paul).

Löwenheim, O. (2008) "Examining the State: A Foucauldian perspective on international 'governance indicators'," *Third World Quarterly*, 29(2): 255–74.

LRN (2008) "Solutions to inspire principled performance," http://www.lrn.com/solutions/solutions-to-inspire-principled-performance.html (accessed 12 December 2008).

Luo, Y. (2006) "Political behavior, social responsibility, and perceived corruption: a structuration perspective," *Journal of International Business*, 37: 747–66.

Michael, B. (2004) "Explaining Organizational Change in International Development: The Role of Complexity in Anti-Corruption Work," *Journal of International Development*, 16: 1067–88.

Neumann, I.B. and Sending, O.J. (2007) "'The International' as Governmentality," *Millennium: Journal of International Studies*, 35(2): 677–701.

O'Malley, P. (2004) *Risk, Uncertainty and Government* (London: The Glasshouse Press).

Porter, M. and Kramer, M.R. (2006) "Strategy & Society: The Link Between Competitive Advantage and Corporate Social Responsibility," *Harvard Business Review*, December: 78–92.

Power, M. (2007) *Organized Uncertainty. Designing a World of Risk Management* (Oxford: Oxford University Press).

Price, M. (2006) "Case story: Integrity Due Diligence," in The Global Compact: *Business against corruption. Case stories and example* (New York: United Nations Global Compact Office).

PWC – PricewaterhouseCoopers (2007) *Economic crime 2007: people, culture and controls. The 4th biennial Global Economic Crime Survey*, accessed on pwc.com/crimesurvey.

Rodríquez, P., Siegel, D.S, Hillman, A. and Eden, L. (2006) "Three lenses on the multinational enterprise: politics, corruption, and corporate social responsibility," *Journal of International Business Studies*, 37: 733–46.

Rose, N. (1999) *Powers of Freedom: Reframing Political Thought* (Cambridge: Cambridge University Press).

Rose, N. and Miller, P. (1992) "Political power beyond the state: problematics of government," *British Journal of Sociology*, 43(2): 173–205.

Rose-Ackerman, S. (1999) *Corruption and Government. Causes, Consequences and Reform* (Cambridge: Cambridge University Press).

Rose-Redwood, R.S. (2006): "Governmentality, geography and the geo-coded world," *Progess in Human Geography*, 30(4): 469–86.

Sai Global (2008) "Anti-bribery Training," http://www.saiglobal.com (accessed 12 December 2008).

Scott, J.C. (1998) *Seeing Like a State. How Certain Schemes to Improve the Human Condition Have Failed* (New Haven, CT: Yale University Press).

Sharma, S. and Gupta, A. (eds) (2005) *The Anthropology of the State. A Reader* (Malden: Blackwell Publishing).

Slaughter, A.-M. (2004) "Disaggregated Sovereignty: Towards the Public Accountability of Global Government Networks," *Government and Opposition*, 39(2): 125–55.

Tabuena, J.A. and Mondini, C. (2006) "Internal reporting and whistle-blowing," in The Global Compact: *Business against corruption. Case stories and examples* (New York: United Nations Global Compact Office) (accessible on www.unglobalcompact.org).

Thompson, J.B. (2000) *Political Scandal. Power and Visibility in the Media Age* (Cambridge: Polity Press).

Transparency International (2008) *Progress Report, 2008 OECD Anti-bribery Convention* (accessible on www.transparency.org).

United Nations (2008) "Transparency and Anti-corruption," http://www.unglobalcompact. org/AboutTheGC/TheTenPrinciples/anti-corruption.html (accessed 10 December 2008).

Valverde, M. and Mopas, M. (2004) "Insecurity and the dream of targeted governance," in Larner, W. and Walters, W. (eds) *Global Governmentality. Governing International Spaces* (London: Routledge).

Walters, W. and Haahr, J.H. (2005) *Governing Europe. Discourse, Governmentality and European Integration* (London: Routledge).

Webb, P. (2005) "The United Nations Convention Against Corruption. Global Achievement or Missed Opportunity?" *Journal of International Law*, 8(1): 191–229.

Wilkinson, P. (2006) "Reporting on countering corruption," in The Global Compact: *Business against corruption. Case stories and examples* (New York: United Nations Global Compact Office) (accessible on www.unglobalcompact.org).

World Bank (2008) "Fraud and Corruption," http://web.worldbank.org/external/default/ main?contentMDK = 64069844&menuPK = 116730&pagePK = 64148989&piPK = 64148984&querycontentMDK = 64069700&theSitePK = 84266 (accessed 12 December 2008).

World Economic Forum (2008) "Partnering Against Corruption Initiative," http://www. weforum.org/en/initiatives/paci/index.htm (accessed 10 December 2008).

Wrage, S. and Wrage, A. (2005) "Multinational Enterprises as 'Moral Entrepreneurs' in a Global Prohibition Regime Against Corruption," *International Studies Perspectives*, 6: 316–24.

7 Transnational governance networks in the regulation of finance

The making of global regulation and supervision standards in the banking industry

Eleni Tsingou

Regulation and supervision of the financial industry formally aim to promote the integrity and efficient operation of the financial system and ensure that participant protection is safeguarded. Financial markets have traditionally been more global than other aspects of business activity, and this intensified global dimension has highlighted the importance of systemic stability as a policy goal and made the financial sector subject to international regulation.

However, as blatantly highlighted by the credit crisis starting in 2007, financial regulation and supervision have been found to be inadequate and often perverse, tending to mirror private sector preferences and privilege large financial institutions and core market players. In the relatively narrow and esoteric world of global finance, this raises serious issues with regard to efficiency, effectiveness and financial stability, and in the broader world of the social scientist, this state of affairs also leaves many questions regarding responsibility, accountability and the appropriateness of regulation open to much interpretation.

This chapter is primarily interested in explaining how and why current governance arrangements came about, how the regulations to which business is subjected were shaped. The goal is to provide an account of the "making of" regulation and supervision in the (global) banking industry. Many commentators on the events of 2007–09 have been quick to point the finger at the industry, with no less a figure than Martin Wolf calling banking "the world's most irresponsible industry" early in the crisis (Financial Times 2007). But in order to understand how governance is generated in global finance, we need to look at a bigger picture and study a much wider range of actors involved in financial policy processes.

The analysis in this chapter is therefore guided by the following questions: (i) how are financial governance arrangements generated? (ii) how are private sector interests internalized in the policy process? and (iii) to what extent are the resulting arrangements acceptable, as public policy but also to the actors involved? The chapter looks at the role of private (business) actors in influencing policy outcomes, but also at the ways in which these actors acquire authority and governance functions. I argue that in order to explain financial regulation and supervision, we need a better understanding of the development of transnational policy communities or transnational governance networks (be they executive or elite) which transcend traditional public–private distinctions.

The chapter focuses on the regulatory and supervisory regime developing around the Basel process, and in particular the Basel II accord. The accord follows the 1988 Basel Capital Accord which first defined minimum capital requirements for banks at a coordinated global level and aimed to better reflect financial activity, following decades of innovation and improved understanding of various types of risk, as well as the evolving role of supervisory authorities. Using the key elements of the regime as illustration, the chapter analyses how regulation is generated in this particular field (at the global, regional and national levels) while identifying the ways in which business actors have key roles in governance arrangements and have, in turn, changed how financial governance has been understood since the 1980s. The chapter closes with a discussion on the implications of the role of transnational governance networks for our understanding of global governance, including some thoughts on the potential for reform and change in the face of crisis. The key argument is that the move to more market-oriented and more transnational forms of governance is the result of governance by network, which in turn has brought about a process of capture by private interests of the crucial public policy functions of regulation and supervision. Understanding this process not only accounts for the financial governance arrangements of the past twenty years, but further identifies some of the regulatory gaps and failures at the heart of the crisis and explains how policy reform options have been defined and constrained.

Financial sector regulation and supervision: trends, policies and interests

A close examination of financial market activities and their governance reveals a significant degree of transnationalization as well as a considerable place for private sector interests and concerns in the prevailing arrangements. Large global financial institutions have increasingly more in common with each other across borders than with the more domestically oriented (often smaller and less sophisticated) entities of their home markets. Similarly, their regulators and supervisors cooperate on an international basis to develop regulatory and monitoring frameworks which, as is the case with the work of the Basel Committee on Banking Supervision (Basel Committee), become predominant; but they do not always enjoy the same level of agreement over sets of public policy priorities with other public sector officials in their home jurisdictions. This state of affairs has developed over time against the background of a well-established engagement with neoliberal economic practice, which has brought private sector concerns to the forefront of policy-making. At the same time, securitization and financial innovation have expanded the scope of financial sector activity, in many cases beyond the reach of formal regulatory oversight. These are the principal phenomena at work here.

To understand how and why these processes occurred, the following analysis seeks to explain how a small number of core financial institutions whose activities are global have become increasingly important in terms of governance (regulation and supervision) as they highlight the multitude of markets in which institutions operate, the variety of products that institutions use, their mobility, as well as the complex links that have formed among and between themselves, local markets and the global financial system as a whole. A parallel development has seen financial policy viewed in technical/economist terms and quite distinct from public policy; all the while, it has become extensively harmonized at the transnational level (Cerny 2002; Picciotto and Haines 1999).

As for the institutional framework, it can be said to be one of coordinated standard-setting: the Basel Committee, the International Organization of Securities Commissions (IOSCO) and the International Association of Insurers Supervisors (IAIS) act as formal coordination mechanisms while, less formally, governance is generated through the interaction of the regulators and supervisors of core (G-10) countries, the private sector (private financial institutions and transnational business associations) and a community of experts (primarily from the discipline of Economics). This set-up corresponds to the framework built by Hewson and Sinclair on the emerging global governance, which focuses on marketized institutions, professional or specialized knowledge and the structural element of complex infrastructural technologies (Hewson and Sinclair 1999: 17–18).

In the present context, however, global financial governance is better explained through an integrative analysis of economic and financial activity that includes a range of actors that exercise varying degrees of authority; it also refers to a "mix of private and public categories" (Pauly 2002: 77). Thus, while the study in this chapter clearly shows that state-centrism tends to obscure the phenomena under investigation, it also indicates that pluralism or interest-based approaches miss the underlying agreement among the policy community at large.

Explaining financial governance: the role of transnational governance networks

Empirically, the analysis focuses on the emergence and development of an executive network or policy community which brings together key financial actors (from the world of global finance at large, including public, private, think tank and academia), formed gradually over the past 30 years to bring much-needed technical expertise and coordination to policy-making and to address issues arising from liberalization and intensive financial innovation from the 1980s onwards. The analysis looks in particular at policies and actors revolving around the Basel process. The development of the Basel Committee[1] as an influential actor in global financial governance and the articulation of respective state interests have been well documented (Kapstein 1991; Wood 2005). Recent work has also focused on state preference for standard-setting bodies such as the Basel Committee in questions of banking regulation rather than international financial institutions such as, for example, the International Monetary Fund (Drezner 2007), or has explored diffusion mechanisms in the production of international agreements and standards as linked to understandings of the self-interest of states (Simmons *et al.* 2008);

these approaches, however, do not discuss the conditions under which diffusion takes place. Most promisingly, there have been discussions of the activities of the Basel Committee in terms of network governance (Marcussen 2007). The latter analysis in particular shows that this governance by committee has intensified (as seen in the proliferation of standards) but has also become more extensive, with a core of standard setters but a significant "periphery of concerned parties" (ibid.: 217).

This chapter argues that additional insights are gained by integrating the role of private actors more comprehensively; private actors have been instrumental in shaping both the process of governance and the final policy content of Basel II.² This is not a straight story of private sector influence, however. Rather, the argument is that private actors are now an integral part of the policy community/network and that their role has evolved from one of input and potential influence to one of key drafters of the policy script. According to this approach, agreement over governance arrangements is reached through a process of continuous interaction of public and private actors and the sanctioning of private sector preference and practice, underscored by a framework of shared understanding about the nature of regulation and supervision. As a result, an examination of the patterns of global financial governance should move beyond the relative merits of public or private regulatory and supervisory procedures and focus on the choice of priorities embraced by the transnational policy network as well as the implications of such a choice.

This analysis takes explicitly into account the role of economic ideas and professional development. "Economic ideas provide agents with an interpretative framework [… and] both a 'scientific' and a 'normative' account of the existing economy and polity, and a vision that specifies how these elements *should* be constructed" (Blyth 2002: 11). Arguments about the role of epistemic communities and elites have gone some way towards explaining how there comes to be a significant degree of *shared* understanding about which ideas matter among policy communities (Cerny 1996; Haas 1992; Stone 1996). Professional development within the policy communities, whereby ideas take hold through a "traditional" trajectory of specific educational patterns, employment in international organizations and ultimately senior roles in national public governments and administration, is also to be noted (see, for example, Chwieroth 2007).

Taking these insights into consideration, this analysis moves beyond existing literature on domestic policy networks, as well as work on policy transfer (see, for example, Dolowitz and Marsh 2000). It is also distinct from accounts still very much rooted in transgovernmentalism and thus little interested in conceptualizing private sector interaction (for recent work on this topic, see Slaughter and Zaring 2006) or explanations of the technical and increasingly legalistic nature of standard setting (see, for example, Cohen 2008). It is much closer to the work of Stone (2004), who includes in her account networks operating in "emerging venues of global governance" and offers insights into distinguishing epistemic communities from advocacy networks or global public policy networks. Indeed, her approach allows for multi-actor networks which have collective (often *de facto*) authority based on their stakeholder status, deal with cross-border issues as well as questions arising from the absence of state-based responsibilities, and take lessons from the experience of network members (ibid.: 562). In more recent work, Stone has developed this notion further in order to conceptualize networks "creating spaces of assembly in the global agora," understood as a normatively neutral political and social space, "a public space, although [...] one where authority is diffuse, decision-making is dispersed and semi-privatized and sovereignty is muddled by recognition of joint responsibility and collective action" (Stone 2008: 35). Elsewhere, Morgan (2001) writes of transnational policy communities based on "structured interactions," where "individuals come to know each other within a specific transnational social space through distinctive and identifiable processes that lead in the direction of 'shared understandings' and shared meanings" (Morgan 2001: 117–18).

The analysis in this chapter builds on these approaches but looks at the policy process in a more comprehensive manner by investigating how policy is generated and not just who or which the relevant actors are. To do so, it develops a concept of a transnational policy community which does not explicitly distinguish between public and private and which understands its constituency at the transnational level. In the process, the role of the private sector is legitimized and its preferences internalized – and the conditions for regulatory capture are in place. There is, however, nothing explicitly deliberate about this. Expertise, financial resources and the clout of elites matter – so does, in the period under investigation and in the community at large (and especially among the regulators), an impetus to isolate financial governance from the realm of governments and politics.

In the next section, a number of questions relating to the emergence and role of transnational governance networks are addressed: How and why do they form? How do they evolve and find their niche? How do they consolidate as actors with precise policy functions in global financial governance? And what are the consequences of this diffusion of authority? The section sheds light on these issues by looking specifically at the governance of global banking activity and in particular the Basel II requirements.

Basel II – or how private interests become public policy

The main formal regulatory tool in the global regulation of financial institutions, Basel II, agreed in 2004[3] after a long period of consultation and gradually coming into effect, can be interpreted as the perfect example of regulatory and supervisory capture: it benefits big players, does not include tough regulation and its complex approaches are a clear market entry barrier. Basel II was developed on the basis of a three-pillar framework and with the understanding that banking rules must reflect the needs and sophistication of financial institutions. The pillars, minimum capital requirements, supervisory review and market discipline formally aim to deliver an accord more suitable to financial practices (Basel Committee 2004).

The first pillar (and by far the meatiest part of the accord) deals with minimum capital requirements. It offers provisions for banks, with the approval of their supervisors, to self-assess capital adequacy requirements on the basis of the complexity of their activities and the status of their internal risk-management systems. The largest global conglomerates, arguably the most sophisticated but also the least risk-averse, are to be subject to market-based regulatory arrangements – in essence, internal risk-management practices are institutionalized and financial institutions which can show that they have well-developed internal systems are relieved from additional (and possibly costly) regulatory requirements. The second pillar focuses on the supervisory review process, proposing practices that allow supervisors to evaluate banks' risk-management techniques and internal procedures and encouraging ongoing dialogue between the private and the public sectors. This has long been the practice in the United States, but the inclusion of the pillar in Basel II formalizes the practice of market-based supervision and encourages bank-by-bank risk analysis instead of broad supervisory principles, rules and direction.[4] Finally, the third pillar aims to strengthen disclosure requirements and market discipline by improving transparency provisions to market participants, including access to qualitative information on risk management and measurement, and hence on the capital adequacy of the institution.

In developing Basel II, it can be said that banking regulators and supervisors had three key aims. In the first place, the Basel Committee wished to be responsive to the needs of institutions and designed a capital requirements framework that relied on best practice in internal systems for identifying and measuring exposure to risk, all the while acknowledging that different firms require different types of treatment. Secondly, the Committee set up a framework for active supervision of banks' internal practices, eschewing rules for a risk-based system of examinations, case-by-case assessments and partnership among the regulators and the regulated. Thirdly, the Committee attempted to encourage market discipline mechanisms, by providing guidelines for improved disclosure and transparency. Throughout the process, the private sector was extensively consulted, both formally and privately, and the final document was a product of these consultations.[5] In so doing, the Basel Committee has assisted the consolidation of a system of regulation and supervision which has the interests of transnational financial institutions at its core.

The consultation process itself is indicative of the importance of consensus and the key role of the private sector in terms of input and guidance. What is also significant, however, is the way in which the first proposals came about. Indeed, in the run-up to the publication of the first Basel II proposals in 1999, the Group of Thirty (G-30), a private organization that brings together 30 senior public and private sector officials in a part-think tank, part-interest group and part-club setting, produced a report with a series of guidelines for the design of an enhanced regulatory and supervisory framework (Group of Thirty 1997).[6] The report called for global institutions to "take the lead in developing a global framework for comprehensive and effective management controls, in cooperation with supervisors and as a continuing exercise" (ibid.: 12), a proposal that highlighted the importance of sound internal risk-management structures and underlined the value of technical expertise. The group also produced instructions on dialogue between public officials and industry practitioners, adapted remuneration schemes for supervisors in order to ensure up-to-date skills, coordination of supervision and incentives offered to financial institutions, such as for differentiating between good and bad performers. The report's authors were, in their own view, representative of the financial policy community at large (albeit defined mostly in North American–European terms), exhibiting a high comfort level with the principle that the private sector needs to be more involved in its own supervision and that supervision principles should adjust to an environment of transnational financial operations.

The G-30 did not embark on this project independently. A few months prior to the publication of the G-30 study, the Institute of International Finance (IIF), a global lobbying banking association that concentrates its efforts on international agreements such as Basel II, issued its *Report of the Task Force on Conglomerate Supervision* which advocated developments in supervision along the same lines as the G-30 (Institute of International Finance 1997). The IIF's recommendations included a focus on *globally active financial institutions*, a transition to supervisory practices based on risk analysis, coordination among supervisors and upgrading of their technical ability, and increased use of disclosure as a market regulatory tool. In the late 1990s, the transnational financial policy community clearly favored increased and consistent private sector involvement and was actively involved in identifying possible policy proposals to that effect; indeed, it is widely acknowledged that the G-30 report was an exercise in testing the waters and a useful start to the revision of the Basel accord.[7]

These informal or semi-formal private sector exercises led to intensified and, arguably, institutionalized policy functions for private actors in the development and eventual content of Basel II, as exemplified most strikingly through the influence of the IIF in the process. The organization played an active consultative role in the drafting, revision and final version of Basel II. Beyond its formal role in the extensive consultation process, the IIF was regularly sounded out and offered consistent feedback, including by providing expertise on highly technical issues; it also, more informally, offered an up-to-date and uniform review of private sector preferences and reactions. The end result has been that IIF preferences for market-generated standards and market-based oversight solutions have been internalized in the Basel process, and that, consequently, large sophisticated banks have been the best placed and best suited to the ensuing proposals.[8] The IIF represents a wide variety of institutions (in terms of both size and geographical scope) but, in essence, its positions, especially on questions relating to the Basel process, have reflected those of the big financial players. The predominance of the interests of those players is manifest in the final text of Basel II. But the consultative process itself is indicative of the growing policy role of the IIF: the interaction had no typical pattern but took the form of standard responses to official documents and press releases, private letters, as well as face-to-face meetings. These informal meetings in particular allowed for an exchange of views with senior Basel Committee members and proved consistently fruitful in moving the accord forward. It is widely acknowledged that such informal procedures, including consultation about what constitutes best practice, while not formally documented, are an essential part of the process.

But why and how do these informal processes emerge and become key parts of governance arrangements? The first (uncontroversial) point is that the principal source of influence of such networks is their elite status and technical expertise and, more generally, the power of ideas and that of those who control them. This is best illustrated when examining the policy network at work, as in the case of the G-30, or, more broadly, when looking at the web of influence and authority that can be traced around it and the actors involved, including the IIF and formal public bodies such as the committees and associations hosted by the Bank for International Settlements, and especially the Basel Committee of G-10 regulators and supervisors. Crucially, such networks are fora of interaction but also sites of (narrow) policy-making and standard production (through studies, surveys, reports, task force findings, etc.). The G-30, which started the ball rolling on Basel II as explained above, points to how private organizations can find their niche and claim authority. Groups of eminent people making pronouncements on broad macroeconomic issues might be respected but are both too numerous and difficult to take into account in policy terms. Instead, by focusing on the mechanics of financial market operations, the G-30 was firstly able to make a meaningful contribution to subjects that were relatively obscure, technical or specialized. Established in 1978, it made its name through a 15-year study of clearance and settlements systems and its reputation was further consolidated with the publication of a seminal study of over-the-counter derivatives instruments which to this day is a key text in best practice (Group of Thirty 1993).

Over time, the group has operated on two levels. The private level is one of special meetings and off-the-record informality, part of a socialization exercise that allows the key men[9] of global finance to forge valuable relationships and consolidate the network; the G-30 is, of course, just one site in this process. The second level, the public work, is the main reason the group deserves attention. Through its studies and reports, the G-30 has essentially aimed at (i) addressing the experts (almost exclusively) in technical terms (as in the clearance and settlement study), (ii) defining a "new" policy issue and establishing the parameters of the regulatory debate (as in the derivatives study and, more recently, work on re-insurance), and (iii) testing new policy initiatives (such as in the financial conglomerates study leading to Basel II and ongoing work on regulatory systems and crises).

So, this trend towards public–private sector interaction and the adoption of a largely private interest agenda by a developing transnational policy network on specific technical issues can also have implications for general policy preferences. Originally specialized and technical work can promote the adoption of principles and practices that can substantially alter the nature of financial regulation and supervision, resulting in the development of a private regime of self-regulation and self-supervision in global finance. One indication of this development is the promotion of flexibility and the endorsement of often voluntary best practice standards as opposed to rules-based regulation. Further evidence is provided by the widespread reliance on the internal risk assessment models of financial institutions for the purposes of supervision, as exemplified by Basel II. In this instance, the "nuts and bolts" of financial market governance can eventually affect higher policy issues, including financial matters that are potentially controversial and touch upon vital public policy areas. The evidence also shows that this trend, along with developments in liberalization and innovation that have made financial markets more complex, encourages a bias in favor of treating financial issues in technical terms and minimizing scrutiny of activities and policies.[10] This is not necessarily the result of an elaborate private sector strategy; rather, it is possible that giving or delegating a role to the private sector encourages the latter to position itself at the forefront of policy-making and use its advantage of being one step ahead of public authorities on financial market processes, i.e. translating power into governance arrangements. Regular public–private sector interaction leads to issue-specific policy outcomes but also to long-term policy directions that may initially be unintended. In this context, this analysis goes further than recent work which focuses on delegation of authority to the private sector (Abdelal 2007); in particular, it highlights that delegation is an incremental process with long-term (unintended) consequences that may or may not be reversible.

Indeed, what becomes clear in the making of Basel II is the lack of obvious "advocacy" – this is very much a network which prefers to shun the limelight and is not averse to a certain understanding of the status quo (i.e. global finance evolves but its regulation and supervision should remain at the service of financial developments). Secondly, and strikingly, this is a community where public and private are blurred beyond notions of preferences, economic ideology or narrowly defined regulatory capture. The individuals making up this network (as exemplified by the G-30) have a long history of moving between the public and private sectors (and sometimes academia) during their distinguished careers. This "revolving doors" situation is most prevalent in the United States but can also increasingly be found in Europe. This question has yet to be studied in detail but it is relevant when thinking about the level of agreement on what is appropriate regulation and supervision among network members.[11]

Business and the governance of finance

Determining the influence and impact of business is notoriously challenging. Recent work by Fuchs (2007) goes some way in establishing a useful framework of analysis, and collections by Cutler *et al.* (1999) and Graz and Nölke (2008) have also significantly enhanced our understanding of private authority and governance, especially on a sectoral basis.[12] In this section I investigate how, in thinking of "business as subject to governance," we can conceptualize the role of business in global financial governance more broadly.

In the first place, the analysis deals with indirect business influence in global governance institutions, namely the formal and informal patterns of interaction between transnational governance networks and the activities of the Basel Committee. It should be noted, however, that the Basel Committee is not a formal global institution as such – it has been a G-10 institution and its proposals are not legally binding – though, in practice, it has long been global in its reach in terms of adoption of principles, as well as monitoring and compliance. As the empirical case has indicated, the private sector exerts influence in relatively traditional ways (lobbying through the IIF, participating in the Basel II consultation process, establishing informal contacts), yet the actual promotion of private sector interests and priorities takes place in a more subtle manner through the ongoing activities of the transnational financial governance network of which the private sector is an integral part.

Corporate practice can, of course, also be a form of global governance in its own right. This is an important element in financial governance and supervision as exemplified in the details of the Basel II accord, as well as in regulatory and supervisory debates more broadly. The past fifteen years have seen the proliferation of "best practice" standards as a way to retain flexibility and encourage innovation, as well as self-regulation and self-supervision as a form of financial governance; the latter is formally sanctioned by public authorities at the national and global levels. The role of rating agencies, whether in Basel II or in the 2007-09 credit crisis, is also particularly relevant in understanding how business practice can become a form of governance, as is the part that accounting standards have played in supporting the bubble and accentuating the subsequent collapse.[13] At the same time, we are seeing a conceptually different type of "actorness" at work: business is at the heart of a developing transnational governance network which acts as a mechanism of global governance. Within this framework, elite interaction (and, crucially, the extent of "revolving door" practices in global finance, especially in the Anglo-American world), as well as the training and socialization process, provide a significant degree of cohesiveness in the preferences, priorities and goals of the governance network.

In a broader sense, the private sector's semi-formal and ongoing policy role has adapted and shifted expectations on what is feasible, acceptable and desirable in the regulation and supervision of global finance. This policy role has been widely accepted against a background of finance as a technical and expert discipline and a widespread admission that the public sector does not have the means (in knowledge and remuneration terms) to provide rules and guidelines unassisted. The role is further enhanced by a subtle but important adoption of a "risk-assessment" model of regulation and supervision, which in principle quantifies and models all types of risk, and which is a far cry from anything resembling prescriptive regulation.[14] This role has gone, on the whole, unchallenged in the "good times" of the past fifteen years. Recent stresses in the system have tested this understanding, especially by highlighting the extent to which the existing system encouraged "herd behavior" and thus can exasperate a crisis. Indeed, the "new" problems (liquidity and solvency problems, linked to significant write-offs related to subprime products and associated lack of confidence in market mechanisms) that financial institutions faced in the period of 2008–09 and the ways in which they have and are being addressed by the transnational governance network will add further useful insights.

Implications for global governance: building legitimacy in a time of crisis?

In examining the legitimacy of global financial governance arrangements, it may be useful to distinguish between the legitimacy of policy priorities and that of the actors in charge. The empirical analysis of this chapter supports the claim that the policies that make up global financial governance are accepted and adopted primarily as a result of the technical definition of the issues and the high level of expertise involved in the policy process, as seen in the transnational financial governance network in question. Students of legitimacy will recognize that this is not a sufficient condition for making these policy priorities legitimate. The network has long identified efficiency, innovation and stability as the key goals of its activities. This in and by itself offers only a narrow set of preoccupations. Yet what is also important is the extent to which the above set of priorities prevents other issues, related to social and distributive justice, to be actively considered, let alone promoted. Inevitably, therefore, these policy priorities produce winners and losers. In other aspects of economic governance, policy outcomes in terms of winners and losers are more easily apparent;[15] the identification of losers in the politics of banking regulation and supervision has, until recently, been much more problematic. We could see how securitization and financial innovation moved an increasing number of financial activities off the balance sheet, thus raising concerns about the capacity of institutions to stay on top of their obligations in a time of crisis. We could also observe a high level of individual involvement in global finance (especially in the Anglo-American systems) through the so-called "democratization of finance," yet also identify the many shortfalls of these developments in terms of an individual's competence to effectively function in the system over a sustained period of time (Ertuk *et al.* 2007). The credit crisis clearly showed the pitfalls of the de-politicization of finance,[16] as well as the problems that may arise from viewing the risks of transnational financial regulation mostly as administrative and not political (Holzer 2007).

The legitimacy of actors in existing arrangements is equally problematic. As the analysis in this chapter has shown, global financial governance is essentially governance by network, the latter being a strongly cohesive and coherent actor when it comes to articulating, promoting and adopting standards and practices that are too closely linked to private sector interests. This has consequences for the legitimacy of public actors: "when states delegate effective authority to actors in private markets, both the act of delegation and the future performance of those actors have implications for their own continued legitimacy" (Pauly 1997: 18). The state's relations with its non-financial constituencies are thus compromised. This has been particularly apparent in the context of the credit crisis; in the United States, the repercussions of the crisis have been felt at the level of banking and other financial institutions but, importantly, the crisis has also been obviously manifest in the number of foreclosures affecting home-owners, the restriction of credit to individuals and businesses alike and the related repercussions on the real economy. Governments, and public agencies, have thus found themselves balancing the needs of different types of constituencies in a way that they have not done in recent times. The question "why is anyone that surprised?" demands serious answers and highlights the extent to which business actors have held a particularly privileged position in the current governance arrangements as well as the degree of "capture" of the public regulatory agencies (though, in my reading, this is not capture as a result of a deliberate strategy). It is important to distinguish this account from explanations relying on blame games – while the credit crisis has been serious enough to have generated a discourse of culpability and punishment, the key point is that in understanding how financial governance is generated, we are in a better position to identify how policy options have been defined and what governance gaps exist in the quest for financial reform.

Indeed, this state of affairs matters in particular when we are looking at the opportunities for change or reform of the system: the relevant actors have acted as gatekeepers in this process, and continue to do so. Substantial alternatives have not come through and, for the most part, concerns about the bail-out of institutions that are generally deemed "too big to fail" because of fears of systemic contagion and the moral hazard that inevitably ensues long remained academic. This is our first real opportunity to observe how this transnational financial governance network can react to a crisis. In the first phase of the crisis, the response indicated that (i) politics still matters, in a way, however, that increased the moral hazard in the system and did not penalize irresponsible risk-taking, as indicated by the Federal Reserve-supported takeover of Bear Stearns in March 2008; (ii) the network was quick to identify regulatory oversight gaps, focusing almost exclusively on the role of mortgage brokers and not on the activities of its own institutions (Russo 2008), thus leaving some of its own practices unchallenged; and (iii) the first voices for reform of the system actually came from the private sector in the guise of the IIF, which advocated work on market best practice in issues such as risk management, rating agencies, underwriting standards, disclosure and remuneration; so far, so uncontroversial.[17]

In the second phase of the crisis, starting in August 2008, the transnational policy community as a whole responded in a more systemic manner, based on recommendations of the Financial Stability Forum on "Enhancing Market and Institutional Resilience" (Financial Stability Forum 2008). During an intensive period of crisis management, bail-outs and takeovers were orchestrated, with the important exception of Lehman Brothers which was allowed to fail with dire systemic consequences, thereby highlighting that market discipline amid a crisis can pose its own challenges. Cross-border cooperation was shown to work, as demonstrated in the instances of Fortis and Dexia and the involvement of Benelux and French authorities, or to fail, as revealed by British and Icelandic disagreements in the aftermath of the near-failure and subsequent nationalization of Landsbanki. Specific rescue plans were put in place, both in the United States and in Europe. Restoring confidence in the system, in terms of ensuring liquidity, safeguarding large institutions and insuring deposits, was the order of the day. At the same time, discussions of the effects of the crisis on the real economy became more central to analyses as the use of taxpayer funds needed to be explained and justified, and the spectre of recession in many industrialized countries called for renewed attention to the links between financial stability and monetary policy and the wider role of central banks. More broadly, the role of finance in the economy has been re-evaluated as the significance of finance for the economy as a whole has underlined the utility-like characteristics of the sector.

At the global institutional level, the focus has been on coordination and a (re)discovery of the institutions and fora available for managing the crisis and debating reform of the system. High expectations have been attached to the activities of the G-20, a group bringing together large advanced and emerging economies, and both the role of the International Monetary Fund and the potential of a more formal role for the now renamed Financial Stability Board are explored. These are important departures as, while it is the case that the institutional framework of global financial governance became more inclusive in the aftermath of the Asian financial crisis, core governance arrangements are still inhabited by a relatively small number of financial institutions and public authorities with a strong North American and European bias – these still form the bulk of the transnational financial governance network. This has further ramifications for what gets (and what does not get) on the agenda, as well as for the significant costs that policies such as Basel II place on the economies of emerging countries (Claessens *et al.* 2008).

Crisis management activities have undoubtedly been intense, with a plethora of initiatives debating the future of the financial system. As the crisis unfolded, however, the parameters for reform remained tight and defined by the same transnational governance network.[18] Most proposals have involved tweaking of current arrangements, often focusing on fairly technical matters. Within the European Union, following the exposure of weaknesses in cross-border arrangements, supervisory responsibilities are reconsidered, with the idea of a "College of Supervisors," the potential for a greater role for the European Central Bank and EU-level regulatory and supervisory coordination bodies more actively discussed. In the global arena, proposals have focused on adjustments to regulatory and supervisory provisions and the extension of oversight to non-banking financial institutions, greater transparency and international coordination (Group of 30 2009), with the Basel Committee putting forward enhancements to the Basel II framework.[19] The network is proving resilient.

Conclusions

Despite a plethora of information on the proliferation of forms of non-state governance in finance and elsewhere, there is still much to be said on the political and ideational process by which private actors "capture" governance of an issue area – where private actors emerge, get formalized, and find a policymaking niche that constitutes influence on regulatory outcomes. How are new actors developing their legitimacy and building political power? And is this (i) a failure of existing regulation; (ii) a process of market failure; (iii) deliberate strategies whereby private actors are doing their best to minimize state intervention; (iv) something altogether more complex?

The banking industry story shows a shift in public agency and private actor preferences for a more transnational form of governance, resulting in the emergence of a transnational governance network; existing literature does not always help to explain why that happens. In order to best understand financial governance arrangements, this chapter has offered an account of how the move to more market-oriented and more transnational forms of governance resulted in a process of capture by private interests of the crucial public policy functions of regulation and supervision.

Moreover, despite plenty of recognition that there are some important legitimacy and efficiency issues associated with non-state financial governance, we don't yet know how policy communities or governance networks try to deal with this at the global level or how significant a problem this is in a particular empirical setting over a significant period of time. Global finance in the context of the activities of large financial conglomerates is a case in point. The existing literature is also unclear on whether the isolation of non-governmental actors is really a good or a bad thing.

Studying these questions, and especially matters of responsibility, accountability and legitimacy, has been challenging, as while gaps have been identified, the standard distinctions between winners and losers (in times of prosperity but also in the context of the crises experienced in the past 20 years) have been less clear. Winners have been easy to spot – large financial institutions have helped shape a governance system that is tailor-made to their needs and aspirations. But how were "losers" to be identified? In many "private governance" stories, the contrast between winners and losers has been noticeable – but not so in the world of banks. This is a world that long benefited from a remarkably benign economic climate and, until recently, a great deal of trust in the wisdom of central bankers and other senior agency officials and awe inspired by the lucrative activities of those in the private sector. This is also a world where, significantly, the Asian crisis was not seen as a crisis at all, and where, until the subprime crisis hit in 2007, the closest the system came to be threatened was the near-collapse of the Long-Term Capital Management hedge fund in the late 1990s. Recent events have resurrected the question "who picks up the pieces when something goes wrong?" and the increased role of governments in the running of financial activity since 2007 has been a clear reminder that while financial banking activity is increasingly global, supervision is only trying to be global while crisis management solutions are firmly national, relying on the national tax base for the bail-outs and funerals of financial institutions. It remains to be seen whether the crisis will form the basis of considerable political capital for financial reform and, indeed, how the transnational governance network will evolve under stress.

Notes

1 The Basel Committee long comprised key regulators and supervisors of G-10 countries: Belgium, Canada, France, Germany, Italy, Japan, Luxembourg, the Netherlands, Spain, Sweden, Switzerland, the United Kingdom and the United States. For an overview of the Committee and its host institution, see Seabrooke (2006). Following calls for a more

representative institutional set-up in response to the credit crisis, membership of the Committee was extended, in the first place, to Australia, Brazil, China, India, Korea, Mexico and Russia, and subsequently to all G-20 non-members, Argentina, Indonesia, Saudi Arabia, South Africa and Turkey, as well as Hong Kong and Singapore.

2 See also King and Sinclair (2003).

3 The final document of the accord is the result of agreement among the relevant regulators and supervisors of Basel Committee-represented countries. As part of the consultation process, other regulatory authorities and several private actors (both individual private institutions and lobbying or representative associations) provided extensive feedback and advice.

4 This, in particular, is an important departure for many supervisory authorities in Europe. For an analysis of the implications of the supervisory review process and the resulting public–private (inter-organizational) building of knowledge resources, see Strulik (2006).

5 This was part of the overall consultative process which included four rounds of proposals and responses in the 1999–2004 period (all comments were published on the BIS website, www.bis.org). It should be noted that a majority of comments came from private sector institutions.

6 G-30 members include senior officials from regulatory and supervisory agencies (such as Central Bank governors and senior staff at the International Financial Institutions), the private sector (including directors of key financial conglomerates) and established academic economists. For more information on the G-30, including an up-to-date list of members and current projects, see the group's website, www.group30.org. For an earlier (and broader) analysis of the G-30 as an actor at the core of a transnational financial governance network, see Tsingou (2007).

7 This point is made in the introduction to the G-30 report in question but has been further corroborated in several interviews the author conducted with relevant public and private sector officials.

8 The IIF has, since its inception in 1993, cultivated and maintained strong relations with regulatory and supervisory bodies at the global level. It represents and articulates the interests of a large number of institutions across the world, including all banking institutions of a significant size. Importantly, it also has access to public bodies at the national level; interviews with officials in public regulatory and supervisory agencies in the United States indicate that individual US-based conglomerates often request that IIF proposals are reviewed and accepted as representative of large US bank positions.

9 In the case of the G-30, the network is indeed composed predominantly of men. While more women are now likely to be found in senior finance positions, their presence remains marginal, including at a time when economic and financial turmoil calls for fresh approaches and possibly different understandings of appropriate behavior and appetite towards risk. On the other hand, more progress has been made in terms of geographical representation. Though the bulk of the community is still located in North America and Europe, efforts have been made to include financial experts from other parts of the world, especially Asia and the Middle East; African officials remain a rarity, however.

10 The current credit crisis is doubtless providing ample evidence of these consequences, as well as clarification of the often tenuous links between finance and what we understand as the "real economy."

11 For new work on "revolving doors," see Seabrooke and Tsingou (2009).

12 See also Woll (2007) for an analysis of private sector influence which focuses instead on resource distribution as the most relevant component of such studies.

13 For a comprehensive analysis of the role of rating agencies, see Sinclair (2005). For an account of the process that led to the current accounting standards, see Perry and Nölke (2006).

14 For a recent, and controversial, example of the move towards a risk-based approach, the debate surrounding the "invention" of operational risk in Basel II is particularly illuminating – see Power (2005). For a discussion on the drawbacks of the risk-based system see also Persaud and Nugée (2007).

15 Note, for example, the case of global trade and intellectual property protection; cf. Sell (2003).

16 For earlier warnings, see Helleiner (1994) and Underhill (1995).

17 These proposals were publicly discussed at the 2008 spring meeting of the IIF; for more information, see www.iif.com – the recommendation to review remuneration structures attracted some attention in the financial press but, for the most part, there was a semblance of "business as usual." The proposals were further elaborated upon in a special IIF report (Institute of International Finance 2008) and were in line with discussions taking place in more formal fora such as the FSF (Financial Stability Forum 2008).

18 Reform recommendations at play have included the above-mentioned reports by the IIF, FSF and G-30, as well as the (private) Counterparty Risk Management Policy Group, the De Larosière report with EU-specific proposals, the Turner report, which focuses on the UK, issue-specific recommendations and a plethora of (mostly broad) proposals emerging from official summits and other meetings.

19 For updated information on adjustments to Basel II, see www.bis.org.

References

Abdelal, Rawi (2007) *Capital Rules: The Construction of Global Finance* (Cambridge, MA: Harvard University Press).

Basel Committee on Banking Supervision (2004) *International Convergence of Capital Measurement and Capital Standards – A Revised Framework* (Basel: Bank for International Settlements).

Blyth, Mark (2002) *Great Transformations – Economic Ideas and Institutional Change in the Twentieth Century* (Cambridge: Cambridge University Press).

Cerny, Philip G. (1996) "International Finance and the Erosion of State Policy Capacity," in Philip Gummett (ed.) *Globalization and Public Policy*, pp. 83–104 (Cheltenham: Edward Elgar).

—— (2002) "Webs of governance and the privatization of transnational regulation," in David M. Andrews, C. Randall Henning and Louis W. Pauly (eds) *Governing the World's Money*, pp. 194–215 (Ithaca: Cornell University Press).

Chwieroth, Jeff M. (2007) "Testing and Measuring the Role of Ideas: The Case of Neoliberalism in the International Monetary Fund," *International Studies Quarterly* 51(1): 5–30.

Claessens, Stijn, Underhill, Geoffrey and Zhang, Xiaoke (2008) "The Political Economy of Basle II: the costs for poor countries," *The World Economy* 31(3): 313–44.

Cohen, Edward S. (2008) "Constructing Power through Law: Private Law Pluralism and Harmonization in the Global Political Economy," *Review of International Political Economy* 15(5): 770–99.

Cutler, Claire A., Virginia Haufler and Tony Porter (eds) (1999) *Private Authority and International Affairs* (Albany: State University of New York).

Dolowitz, David P. and David Marsh (2000) "Learning from abroad: the role of policy transfer in contemporary policy-making," *Governance* 13(1): 5–24.

Drezner, Daniel (2007) *All Politics is Global – Explaining International Regulatory Regimes* (Princeton: Princeton University Press).

Ertuk, Ismail, Froud, Julie, Johal, Sukhdev, Leaver, Adam and Williams, Karel (2007) "The democratization of finance? Promises, outcomes and conditions," *Review of International Political Economy* 14(4): 553–75.

Financial Stability Forum (2008) *Enhancing Market and Institutional Resilience*, Basel: Financial Stability Forum.

Financial Times, The (2007) "The Bank loses a game of chicken" – opinion piece by Martin Wolf, 20 September.

Fuchs, Doris (2007) *Business Power and Global Governance* (Boulder and London: Lynne Rienner).

Graz, Jean-Christophe and Andreas Nölke (eds) (2008) *Transnational Private Governance and its Limits* (London and New York: Routledge).

Group of Thirty (1993) *Derivatives: Practices and Principles* (Washington, DC: Group of Thirty).

Group of Thirty (1997) *Global Institutions, National Supervision and Systemic Risk* (Washington, DC: Group of Thirty).

—— (2009) *Financial Reform – A Framework for Financial Stability* (Washington, DC: Group of Thirty).

Haas, Peter M. (1992) "Introduction: Epistemic Communities and International Policy Coordination," *International Organization*, Special Issue on Knowledge, Power, and International Policy Coordination, 46(1): 1–35.

Helleiner, Eric (1994) *States and the Reemergence of Global Finance: From Bretton Woods to the 1990s* (Ithaca: Cornell University Press).

Hewson, Martin and Timothy J. Sinclair (1999) "The Emergence of Global Governance Theory" in Martin Hewson and Timothy J. Sinclair (eds) *Approaches to Global Governance Theory*, pp. 3–22 (Albany: State University of New York Press).

Holzer, Boris (2007) "Governance without Politics? Administration and Politics in the Basel II process" in Torsten Strulik and Helmut Wilke (eds) *Towards a Cognitive Mode in Global Finance*, pp. 259–78 (Campus / The University of Chicago Press).

Institute of International Finance (1997) *Report of the Task Force on Conglomerate Supervision* (Washington, DC: Institute of International Finance).

—— (2008) *Final Report of the IIF Committee on Market Best Practices: Principles of Conduct and Best Practice Recommendations* (Washington, DC: Institute of International Finance).

Kapstein, Ethan (1991) "Supervising International Banks: Origins and Implications of the Basle Accord," *Essays in International Finance*, 185, December.

King, Michael R. and Timothy J. Sinclair (2003) "Private Actors and Public Policy: A Requiem for the New Basel Capital Accord," *International Political Science Review* 24(3): 345–62.

Marcussen, Martin (2007) "The Basel Committee as a Transnational Governance Network" in Martin Marcussen and Jacob Torfing (eds) *Democratic Network Governance in Europe*, pp. 214–31 (Basingstoke: Palgrave).

Morgan, Glenn (2001) "Transnational Communities and Business Systems," *Global Networks* 1(2): 113–30.

Pauly, Louis (1997) *Who Elected the Bankers?* (Ithaca: Cornell University Press).

—— (2002) "Global finance, political authority, and the problem of legitimation" in Rodney Bruce Hall and Thomas J. Biersteker (eds) *The Emergence of Private Authority in Global Governance*, pp. 76–90 (Cambridge: Cambridge University Press).

Perry, James and Andreas Nölke (2006) "The Political Economy of International Accounting Standards," *Review of International Political Economy* 13(4): 559–86.

Persaud, Avinash and John Nugée (2007) "Redesigning Financial Regulation" in Libby Assassi, Anastasia Nesvetailova and Duncan Wigan (eds) *Global Finance in the New Century – Beyond Deregulation*, pp. 207–19 (Basingstoke: Palgrave).

Picciotto, Sol and Jason Haines (1999) "Regulating Global Financial Markets," *Journal of Law and Society* 26(3): 351–68.

Power, Michael (2005) "The invention of operational risk," *Review of International Political Economy* 12(4): 577–99.

Russo, Thomas (2008) "Credit Crunch: Where Do We Stand?" *Occasional Paper* 76, Washington, DC: Group of Thirty.

Seabrooke, Leonard (2006) "Global Monitor: The Bank for International Settlements," *New Political Economy* 11(1): 141–49.

Seabrooke, Leonard and Eleni Tsingou (2009) "Revolving Doors and Linked Ecologies in the World Economy: Policy Locations and the Practice of International Financial Reform," *CSGR Working Paper* (260/09).

Sell, Susan K. (2003) *Private Power, Public Law* (Cambridge: Cambridge University Press).

Simmons, Beth A., F. Dobbins and Geoffrey Garrett (eds) (2008) *The Global Diffusion of Markets and Democracy* (Cambridge: Cambridge University Press).

Sinclair, Timothy J. (2005) *The Masters of Capital* (Ithaca: Cornell University Press).

Slaughter, Anne-Marie and David Zaring (2006) "Networking Goes International: An Update," *Annual Review of Law and Social Science* 2: 211–29.

Stone, Diane (1996) *Capturing the Political Imagination: Think Tanks and the Policy Process* (London: Frank Cass).

—— (2004) "Transfer agents and global networks in the 'transnationalization' of policy," *Journal of European Public Policy* 11(3): 545–66.

—— (2008) "Global Public Policy, Transnational Policy Communities and their Networks," *Policy Studies Journal* 36(1): 19–38.

Strulik, Torsten (2006) "Knowledge Politics in the Field of Global Finance? The Emergence of a Cognitive Approach in Banking Supervision," *CSGR Working Paper* (195/06).

Tsingou, Eleni (2007) "The role of policy communities in global financial governance: a critical examination of the Group of Thirty" in Torsten Strulik and Helmut Wilke (eds) *Towards a Cognitive Mode in Global Finance*, pp. 213–37 (Campus / The University of Chicago Press).

Underhill, Geoffrey (1995) "Keeping Governments out of Politics: Transnational Securities Markets, Regulatory Cooperation, and Political Legitimacy," *Review of International Studies* 21: 251–78.

Woll, Cornelia (2007) "Leading the Dance? Power and Political Resources of Business Lobbyists," *Journal of Public Policy* 27(1): 57–78.

Wood, Duncan (2005) *Governing Global Banking* (Aldershot: Ashgate).

8 Non-triad multinationals and global governance

Still a North–South conflict?

Andreas Nölke and Heather Taylor

Introduction

According to projections made by Goldman Sachs, by 2030 Brazil, China, Russia and India will collectively possess product and services markets substantially larger than the combined size of G7 countries today. It is further predicted that such dynamic growth will bring their collective gross national product (GNP) over the same time frame up to $41 trillion, only two trillion dollars below that of the projections made for the G7 for the same time frame (Van Agtmael 2007: 11). While these projections may have to be adjusted for the repercussions of the subprime economic crisis, we nevertheless may expect a substantially increased role for non-triad economies in the decades to come.

The role of home-grown firms, hereafter deemed "non-triad multinational companies" (NTMNCs),[1] will be crucial for these economies to realize these predictions. These firms will not only be responsible for pushing economic growth within their home countries, but, more importantly, their amplified presence and dominance in the global economy subsequently imply that their ability to shape, if not to articulate and dictate, global business regulation will steadily escalate. The core question motivating this contribution is whether the rise of NTMNCs will lead to a renewed North–South conflict, similar to those around demands for a New Economic World Order during the 1970s. In order to anticipate the global regulatory implications of the rise of NTMNCs, we first have to understand how these companies emerged and how they operate, with a specific focus on their domestic regulatory environment. More specifically, will they support the current regulatory environment, or will they prefer alternative forms of economic order?

In geographical terms, where do NTMNCs come from? In the absence of a comprehensive database on these companies we are relying on a variety of company rankings provided by academics, business journals and international organizations. Through cross-referencing six investment rankings to achieve a list of NTMNCs appearing on at least two of those rankings, the top home countries of NTMNCs are given by Figure 8.1.

As far as sectors in which NTMNCs are involved, we can distinguish four specific clusters: (1) conglomerate groups; (2) natural resources (fossil

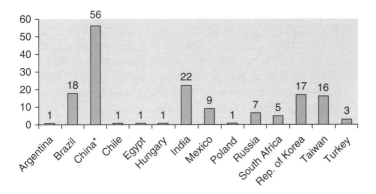

Figure 8.1 Non-triad multinationals per non-triad nation.
*China including Hong Kong

Source: Aguiar *et al.* 2006, 2007; *Business Week* 2005; *Forbes Magazine* 2007; *Fortune Magazine* 2007; UNCTAD 2005.

fuels and mining); (3) non-financial services (telecommunications, software and computer services, electrical and electronic equipment, air transport and seaports, construction); and (4) capital-intensive industrial commodities (motor vehicles, cement, food and beverages).

This is the third wave of NTMNCs to hit the global economy in the post-war period, whereby it is crucial to realize that this generation has managed to spark tension and anxiety in the triad at a more rapid and consequential pace than either of the preceding waves. Tensions have reached an all-time high as brownfield investments (i.e. acquisitions) have increasingly become the predominant mode of entry choice[2] into triad markets versus greenfield investments, which continue to be the main form of foreign direct investment (FDI) in non-triad markets. "During 2005 alone, emerging multinationals [NTMNCs] spent a record $42 billion in takeover deals in Europe (more than twice the previous year) and another $14 billion (in ninety-six separate deals) in the United States, well above the $10 billion previous peak in 2000" (*Wall Street Journal*, February 13, 2006, cited by Van Agtmael 2007: 25). The surge in brownfields in the triad has sparked anxiety precisely because it entails NTMNCs gaining access not only to triad markets but, also more importantly, to resources (both tangible and intangible assets, *inter alia* technology, knowledge, natural resources, manpower). Moreover, the close relationship many NTMNCs have with their home governments has done precisely the opposite of placating tensions.

In order to address – and possibly decrease – these tensions, this paper asks whether there is a structurally rooted conflict between triad and non-triad MNCs. In order to do so, it undertakes a theoretical discussion of how different business communities (i.e. NTMNCs in contrast to triad-MNCs) are likely to respond to global governance issues, both as subject and as likely opponent to existing global governance arrangements. In the absence of direct empirical evidence on NTMNCs' take on global governance issues, we take a more indirect approach in order to formulate theoretically grounded expectations for NTMNCs' response to global economic governance. As a first step we will ask whether NTMNCs are different and, if they are, in what sense. More particularly, do they have significantly different growth strategies or business models? We will do so in the next section on the basis of a review of the existing theoretical approaches on triad-MNCs and contrast those theories with the experience on NTMNCs. As a second step we take on the question whether the differences between the national business systems in which triad and non-triad MNC s are rooted do matter. For this purpose, in the following section we use , the Varieties of Capitalism approach as a heuristic device in order to identify the institutional preferences of NTMNCs. During a third and final step, we will contrast these preferences with the existing global governance institutions (as mainly shaped by the preferences and practices of triad-MNCs) and will chart the corresponding potential for future conflict.

Conventional theoretical approaches to (NT)MNCs

Broadly speaking, international business and economic scholars have primarily been the sources responsible for developing theories on MNC internationalization processes. In the last thirty years, there have been three such influential approaches: (1) the eclectic paradigm; (2) the product cycle model; and (3) the linking, leverage, learning (LLL) approach. Despite the strengths of each theory, one cannot ignore that fact that each is ridden with inherent weaknesses. In what follows below, we briefly outline the tenets and weaknesses of each of these theories.

The eclectic paradigm

The eclectic paradigm of international production (Dunning 1981, 1986, 1988a, 1988b, 1995, 1998) is by far the most widely accepted and utilized approach in international business for analyzing MNC internationalization. Its appeal stems from its dynamic take on internationalization as a process. This dynamic approach is achieved through the provision of two separate, yet interrelated, theoretical frameworks – the OLI and the IDP frameworks.

In short, the OLI framework outlines the conditions of MNC internationalization. It builds a theoretical approach around sequentially answering three questions pertaining to internationalization – why, where and how. On this basis, internationalization strategies are understood in terms of three categories of "advantages": (1) "O": ownership advantages[3] (why); (2) "L": locational advantages (where); and (3) "I" internalization advantages (how).[4] While all three variables are significant, O-advantages are *the* cornerstone variable. Internationalization is costly: upon initial entry into the market foreign firms will always be operationally disadvantaged compared to domestic firms. Internationalization should thus be a strategy reserved for firms possessing O-advantages. The ascendancy of

O-advantages is crucial in the framework as they foreordain *whether* and *why* a firm should internationalize.[5] Put simply, the "L" and the "I" in OLI are secondary advantages which can only be exploited if there is an "O."

The second theoretical component of the eclectic paradigm is the investment development path (IDP). While the OLI framework deals with firm strategy, the IDP places the internationalization process of firms within their home country stage of economic development. The main premise of the IDP suggests for any given country there exists a positive correlation between net income levels per capita and net foreign direct investment. Thus, growth income levels will be accompanies by an increase in net foreign direct investment. From here, the correlation for each country between the two variables is measured relative to the rest of the world. This comparison between the individual country and the rest of the world is used to determine the location of that country along the investment development trajectory. Thus, countries are catalogued according to stages that range from 1 to 5 based on measuring national net inward and outward investment levels and correlating it to national gross per capita income in a given economy relative to the rest of the world. As an economy moves upwards from stage 1 to stage 5,[6] the O-advantages, which are available for domestic firms to exploit through internationalization, will grow. In positing the stages of economic development, the IDP goes on to theorize that, if a country is facing a capital shortage because of a lack of foreign exchange reserves, it should foremost aim to pursue a policy that builds up reserves through importing capital. Moreover, capital importation should be aimed at attracting foreign-MNC inward foreign direct investment (FDI) in order to simultaneously build up national capital reserves and domestic firm capacity through transferring technology. An economy lacking capital and supporting domestic firm internationalization will head down a developmental path consisting of continuously poor and stunted growth rates because capital imports were not available to strengthen the specific competitive advantages of firm and comparative advantages of the country. The developmental stages of the IDP can, overall, be summarized as tracing the transformation of an economy from being a net capital importer into a net capital exporter.

The eclectic paradigm has certainly provided useful insights regarding MNC internationalization strategies. Nevertheless, it is not sufficiently equipped to provide a comprehensive account of NTMNCs due to its numerous pitfalls. It is perhaps the origins of the paradigm which pose the most fundamental quandary. Both frameworks in the paradigm were originally developed in the 1970s to explain the internationalization experiences of triad-MNCs, specifically Anglo-Saxon MNCs. Since then, neither framework has undergone any large modifications. Despite transformations within the global economy and the existence of a set of fundamentally different non-Anglo-Saxon MNCs operating in the global economy, the eclectic paradigm has remained true to its roots as an *ex post* explanation of Anglo-Saxon MNC internationalization strategies. Precisely because scholars utilizing the framework often openly assume that "the multinationalizing trend [is] widely recognized as similar in nature irrespective of the nationality of the parent company" (Vernon 1983; 12, cited by Wilkins

1986: 202), the paradigm has just been repetitively applied for nearly 30 years to all various sorts of MNCs and MNC internationalization strategies.

Regarding the pitfalls of each respective framework within the paradigm, the fundamental drawback of the OLI framework is its vertical compartmentalization of the three variables of the internationalization process in a sequentially ordered manner, which only allows for them to be dealt with on a one-by-one basis. Thus, internationalization becomes trapped within a static theoretical framework that ignores the dynamic and ongoing interaction between variables (Ramamurti 2008: 26). Furthermore, the OLI framework cannot readily explain how and why NTMNCs have successfully internationalized when lacking the cornerstone O-advantages. The approach cannot grasp that "when[NTMNCs] decide to invest overseas … they rarely have at hand resources such as proprietary technology, financial capital, brands and experienced management" (Bonaglia *et al*. 2006: 4) which are required O-advantages in the OLI framework. Along the same lines, it also cannot explain how these forms of NTMNC internationalization are then able to be successful, especially in terms of spawning value-creating synergies.

Coming to the IDP framework, its core dilemma relates to the rapid internation-alization strategies of NTMNCs that overtly receive support from home-country non-triad economies with scant capital reserves. Most recently, scholars have given "economic globalization" the blame for this empirically unsustainable theoretical conundrum. A final problem in the IDP, and indeed the paradigm as a whole, is the scant attention given to socio-economic and political institutions in the internationalization process. To be sure, the paradigm does indeed posit that institutions matter, and the IDP framework supposedly helps to theoretically outline how institutional capabilities are built within a national economy. Despite this recognition, neither the paradigm as whole, nor the IDP individually, has been able to successfully incorporate institutions into the analysis. Given that both the OLI and IDP frameworks implicitly assume that the MNC is an institution in itself and minimally shaped by, let alone dependent on, its domestic institutional environment, it is highly likely that institutions will remain a rather oblique concept in the eclectic paradigm and its corresponding frameworks.

The product cycle model

The product cycle model (Buckley and Casson 1976; Vernon 1966; 1977) postulates that firms innovate in response to demand and factor prices in their home markets. After creating a product, firms supply their home markets and then foreign markets similar to their own. Exporting should be the first internationalization strategy pursued by firms in these markets. Production facilities should be established in the host market when demand increases and alterations to the profit possibilities for the firm in the host market occur.[7] From here, as standardization in the product market slowly develops and as more companies gain access to the knowledge and technology required to produce, competition will become fiercer and primarily based on pricing.

In the early nineteen-eighties, Louis T. Wells (1981, 1983, 1986, 1998) stipulated that it is precisely at this point that NTMNCs enter the model. As such, NTMNCs will imitate standardized technology and processes for production and then later adapt and modify the product to sell in their home environments. Through organizational innovation[8] and lower input costs, the rise of NTMNCs at this stage in the model will encourage new investment patterns based on moving product manufacturing to non-triad markets and keeping product marketing and branding in triad markets.

The product cycle model has increasingly lost validity since many NTMNCs have become technology innovators. In 2006 alone, South Korea and Taiwan joined the ranks of the top fifteen R&D-spending countries (Department of Trade and Industry 2006). Furthermore, many NTMNCs have moved beyond manufacturing, becoming actively involved and highly profitable in branding, marketing and distribution of products and services in foreign markets. Examples of such firms include, *inter alia*, Wipro Technologies, the Tata Group and Zydus Cadila.

Like the eclectic paradigm, institutions are scantily mentioned in the model, especially with regard to NTMNCs' economies. Moreover, the model is incapable of explaining the rapid surge in NTMNC brownfield investments targeting the triad. In aiming to provide an innovative and comprehensive approach to NTMNCs, the central task of this contribution is indeed to underline the quintessential role of socio-economic institutional environment in the internationalization process as a coordinating mechanism, which guides and shapes NTMNC firm behavior and preferences.

The linking, learning, leverage approach

To date there has only been one approach particularly created on the basis of the NTMNC strategies alone: the linking, learning, leverage (LLL) approach (Mathews 2002; 2004; 2006). Most startling about this approach is that, unlike the afore mentioned theories, it is premised on the recognition that profound differences exist between triad-MNCs and NTMNCs, and between the current and former waves of NTMNCs. These differences have risen out of the unique characteristics that current NTMNCs possess. It is crucial to realize that rapid internationalization has not necessarily occurred by choice. Unlike the generations of triad-MNCs and NTMNCs between 1960 and 1990, today's NTMNCs have not been "pushed" into the global economy as standalone operators. Developments within the global economy over the last twenty years – i.e. economic globalization – have effectively ensured that integration of production, distribution and marketing networks is spread across the globe. As a result, an integrated global economy has "pulled" current NTMNCs into stepping up their involvement in the global economy and global networks. Thus, current NTMNCs have rapidly "gone global" and linked up with triad partners in foreign markets. Linking provides initial access to the foreign market and access to the knowledge and technology of the partner firm. This in turn affords NTMNCs with the chance to leverage the knowledge and technology they have been exposed to in foreign markets. A series of feedback loops occurs during the process of leveraging, all aimed at internally incorporating, enhancing and/or altering the resources gained from linking. These feedback loops are in turn referred to as "learning" (Mathews 2006: 16–20).

The LLL approach is perhaps the most valuable of the aforementioned theories as it has been created on the basis of NTMNC experiences. Furthermore, it also acknowledges the key role of institutions and governments in supporting and shaping the strategies of NTMNCs. Nevertheless, *acknowledge* is the key word to realize here. The approach has only very minimally elaborated on the coordination mechanisms related to institutions and governments. Moreover, when it has managed to give details on institutions, these details are primarily concerned with South Korean and Taiwanese MNCs. Thus, we are still left with an immense lacuna regarding: (1) which institutions have been essential; (2) in what ways they have been essential (i.e. in shaping preferences, strategies etc.); and (3) how the institutions have evolved as the NTMNCs they have bred become stronger, more aggressive, and more active in global markets (i.e., what influence have the NTMNCs had on their domestic institutions?).

A "modified varieties of capitalism" explanation for the rise of NTMNCs

As mentioned before, a conundrum facing most theoretical approaches on NTMNC internationalization arises out of the mere reality that they have been created to understand experiences of triad-MNCs. Precisely because of their axiomatic understanding of "MNC" and "internationalization" they are incapable of considering NTMNCs as unique. Moreover, while "institutions matter," none of the approaches have the capacity to theoretically establish the link between the MNC strategies and preferences and the MNC–home-country institutional context. Indeed, why and how institutions matter has remained an unsolved mystery because, theoretically, NTMNCs and internationalization have remained two topics confined to evolving in a field that assumes that the MNC is an institution in itself. This chapter argues for the need to bring NTMNCs down into their socio-economic environment as it would enable a more comprehensive and unique approach to develop on them. In order to study these variances in the domestic institutional context, we turn to the "varieties of capitalism" approach.

The varieties of capitalism theoretical framework

During the last few years, the comparative capitalism perspective has become "canonical" among students of the political economy of Western societies (Blyth 2003: 215). Pioneered by scholars such as Shonfield (1965) and popularized by Albert (1993), the "varieties of capitalism" (VoC) approach as elaborated by Hall and Soskice (2001a) has particularly become the hallmark of the study of comparative capitalism. Although the VoC approach has primarily been employed to empirical assessments of economic success in the OECD world, we assume that it can also be adapted to non-triad economies. In adapting the VoC approach, the aforementioned theoretical approaches would be complemented with a more sociological and political approach to NTMNCs. The VoC approach is thus utilized below as a heuristic device with the capacity to provide us with categories that have to be addressed in order to explain the success of certain socio-economic systems. The primary focus is on domestic socio-economic institutional embeddedness of NTMNCs, since this entrenchment has allowed NTMNCs to develop specific competitive advantages and has also shaped their preferences and interests. Our analysis not only helps to better account for the rise of NTMNCs, but also helps to reduce some pitfalls of the VoC approach by broadening its empirical focus and overcoming its overly strict dualism (Crouch 2005: chapter 2; Hancké *et al.* 2007: 4–9; Jackson and Deeg 2006: 37–39).

Despite numerous alternatives (e.g. Amable 2003), the most widely utilized version of the comparative capitalism research program is that developed by Hall and Soskice (2001a). Indeed, most authors still prefer to depart from the coordinated market economies (CME) and liberal market economies (LME) juxtaposition. Besides offering a balanced and inclusive framework, its parsimony remains the quintessential advantage of the typology (Hancké *et al.* 2007: 16; Jackson and Deeg 2006: 31–32). Granted that the two basic models are clearly unable to give full justice to the intricacies of, for example, British, French or Italian capitalism, by providing a comprehensive account of the differences between Anglo-Saxon and Rhenish capitalism the approach is quite useful since it gives us the basis for developing a theoretical framework with the capacity to understand the manner in which domestic institutions interact and shape MNC behavior and preferences.

The main theoretical task of the CME/LME juxtaposition is to explain the marked differences in the competitive advantages of advanced capitalist economies. These advantages are most easily demonstrated if we focus on the different types of innovation process central to the two production systems (Hall and Soskice 2001b: 38–44). CMEs, such as Germany or Austria, are assumed to have a premium on incremental innovation. This is particularly important for producing capital goods such as machine tools and company equipments, consumer durables, engines, and specialized transport equipment. "The problem is to maintain the high quality of an established product line, to devise incremental improvements to it that attract consumer loyalty, and to secure continuous improvements in the production process in order to improve quality control and hold down costs" (ibid.: 39). LMEs, such as the US and the UK, in contrast, are supposed to focus on radical innovation. This is important in fast-moving technology sectors (e.g. biotechnology or software development), and in the provision of complex system-based products and services (e.g. financial services). Of course, these patterns of specialization do not comprise the whole economy. Basic services, for example, are produced throughout all economies, but are hardly covered by any VoC model (Blyth 2003: 223). Furthermore, equating an entire industry with a specialization pattern in innovation remains problematic since an industry, at any one time, is composed of more and less innovative activities (Crouch 2005: 31).

The VoC approach hypothesizes that the inherent institutional complementarities of the two respective market economies help explain these broadly conceived innovation patterns. Each element of the two basic types has strong institutional complementarities with other elements of the same model, and differs clearly from the functional equivalent of the other model. Usually, five interdependent elements can be highlighted (Hall and Soskice 2001b 17–33; see also Jackson and Deeg 2006: 11–20), namely (1) the financial system, i.e. the primary means to raise investments, (2) corporate governance, i.e. the internal structure of the firm, (3) the pattern of industrial relations, (4) the education and training system, and (5) the preferred mode for the transfer of innovations within the economy.

(1) The primary means of raising capital for investment in the LME system are bonds and equities to be issued on international capital markets. In CMEs, domestic bank lending plays a much bigger role, together with retained earnings. The two different modes of financing clearly differ regarding the importance of current returns and of publicly available information. Companies in LME economies are strongly dependent on publicly available information and on current earnings for terms of investments. Dispersed and fluid investors need this information in order to value the quality of bonds and shares. In CMEs, balance sheet criteria are less important since investors have alternative sources of information, either as owners or based on long-term business (banking) relationships, together with diverse channels for reputational monitoring, such as business associations.

(2) Correspondingly, there is a stark difference between corporate governance systems in the two models. The LME model focuses on outsider control by dispersed owners, based on active markets for corporate control (mergers and acquisitions, including hostile takeovers). Managers enjoy a considerable freedom of maneuver, being controlled via incentives that are strongly geared towards share prices, e.g. via share options. The CME model, in contrast, has rather strong disincentives for hostile takeovers, and is primarily based on insider control by major shareholders (blockholders). Managers have to find the consensus of their supervisory boards for major decisions and therefore have to involve blockholders and labor representatives.

(3) Generally, the relationship between business and labor is far more consensual within CMEs, being based on a corporatist system of industrial relations including industry-level wage bargaining and powerful company-level works councils. This is a necessity for production strategies based on continuous improvements in product lines and production processes and on highly skilled labor. Management needs motivated labor to keep productivity high, whereas labor needs protection against lay-offs in order to invest into company-specific skills. The LME pattern of industrial relations, in contrast, relies heavily on the market as a coordinating mechanism. Management has full autonomy to hire and fire, based on highly fluid labor markets. Labor, in return, has few incentives to invest in company-specific skills, and instead focuses on general skills that are transferable across firms.

(4) Education and training systems in CMEs are geared towards the provision of skilled workers with highly industry- or company-specific skills. Correspondingly, business invests strongly into the human capital of its staff. CMEs have a comprehensive apprenticeship system and a strong focus on vocational training. Powerful employer associations prevent free riding of individual firms on the training effort of others. Given the fluidity of labor markets in LMEs, in contrast, there are only very limited incentives to invest in industry- or company-specific skills. Companies would not be able to benefit from their investments because workers might be lured away by competitors, whereas workers depend on acquiring skills that can be used in many different locations. Correspondingly, the education system is geared towards the provision of general skills.

(5) All capitalist varieties rely on the speedy transfer of innovations throughout the economy. Within LMEs, this transfer most frequently takes place by hiring qualified staff from other companies, or by acquiring the company responsible for that particular innovation. These options are both supported by rather fluid labor law and active markets for corporate control. In CMEs, these options are not readily available, given long-term labor contracts and protection against hostile takeovers. Instead, innovations are transferred by a host of inter-company relationships, including business associations or R&D joint ventures. This specific innovation system complements very well with sector-wide training schemes that focus on industry-specific skills.

In sum, the two models differ in particular regarding the basic mechanisms for solving coordination problems within national economies. In LMEs, the most important form of coordination is competitive market arrangements and formal contracts. In CMEs, non-market forms of coordination such as inter-firm networks and national or sector associations play a crucial role (Hall and Soskice 2001b: 8, 33–36).

Both models, however, tend to leave the state completely out of the picture. This leads to shortcomings regarding analyses of state-centered market economies such as France, Spain or Italy. Furthermore, it tends to underestimate the role of state regulation within LMEs and CMEs. Thus, we suggest complementing the Hall/Soskice model by incorporating the role of the state in general and that of the regulatory environment in particular.

While the varieties of capitalism framework usually is applied to explain the comparative advantages of whole national production systems, it can also be put to use in explaining the competitive advantages of individual multinational companies. In *The Myth of the Global Corporation*, Doremus *et al.* (1998) have conducted path-breaking research for precisely this purpose. Situated in the context of the debate on economic globalization and erosion of national differences, they demonstrate the enduring influence of national historical legacies on MNCs in Germany and the USA. Indeed, they utilize a remarkably similar approach to the VoC approach outlined above, although it does not elaborate a comparatively encompassing theoretical framework. Doremus and colleagues provide us with the capacity to interlink the national institutionalist VoC approach with our focus on competitive advantages of NTMNCs. Thus, we can use the VoC findings on triad capitalist institutions and relate those to the (multinational) company level.

Varieties of capitalism: NTMNC institutional foundations

To be sure, just as with triad-MNCs, NTMNCs are not a homogeneous group of firms. As a heterogeneous group, NTMNCs possess a wide array of competitive advantages. These competitive advantages include lower input costs[9] in comparison to their triad incumbents (Aguiar *et al.* 2006). Another major competitive advantage of NTMNCs has arisen out of operating experience in adverse market conditions, which allows them a considerable upper hand in sectors with a somewhat opaque regulatory environment or with a poor logistical situation (Goldstein 2007; Mathews 2006: 14; Van Agtmael 2007: 28–29). A third competitive advantage is related to superior access to natural resources in home and host economies, as exemplified by companies such as Gazprom or Petróleos de Venezuela. From a VoC perspective, the existence of a wide array of competitive advantages can partially be explained by the socio-economic institutions supporting NTMNCs. As will be demonstrated below, these institutions are quite different from the CME and LME varieties documented above. Due to the early stage of research on NTMNCs, however, we can merely provide anecdotal evidence to furnish empirical backing for these arguments. Furthermore, we will only provide a rather general account, since we cannot give full justice to the situation of each individual company.

(1) The financial system

In contrast to LME-based multinationals (and an increasing number of CME-based as well), most NTMNCs are less dependent on international capital markets. Instead, they frequently rely on internally generated funds or bank loans. Correspondingly, they are less pressed to look for short-term shareholder value. This allows NTMNCs to build up a reserve of slack resources as a financial cushion for the case of unforeseen crises in turbulent markets. Furthermore, NTMNCs frequently can make use of some kind of direct or indirect state financing, including fiscal incentives, financial guarantees and credits from state-owned banks (Goldstein 2007: 98). Particularly, this state involvement is responsible for the fact that many NTMNCs have access to cheaper finance than their competitors (ibid.: 127). Therefore the role national institutions play in promoting the creation of NTMNCs that can compete on the global level must not be understated.

Here a mechanism created by the Brazilian national development bank, BNDES, is a good example. In 2002, the bank established "a special credit line to support OFDI, which is granted on the condition that within six years the beneficiary increases its exports by an amount equal to the credit" (ibid.: 95). This provides evidence of the financial leverage offered to NTMNCs through their national structures, which helps secure the means to invest as well as access to the knowledge necessary to guide and successfully choose investments abroad.

(2) Corporate governance

Closely linked to corporate finance is the dominant mode of corporate governance. NTMNCs are not typically dominated by dispersed shareholders and the organized forces of global capital markets, but are rather family-owned or state-controlled. Family and state ownership might even be counted among the "distinguishing features" of NTMNCs (ibid.: 148). The absence of an open market for corporate control helps NTMNCs to avoid the short-term pressures of global capital markets. Only a few companies have chosen to list themselves on triad stock exchanges, examples including Concha y Toro (Chilean) on the New York Stock Exchange and SABMiller (South African) on the London Stock Exchange. Similar observations can be made for a few Russian firms that list in London because of improved legal safety (ibid.: 130).

An increasing number of NTMNCs have begun listing on their home markets' exchanges, whereby in most of these firms strategic investors (not dispersed minority shareholders) play a key role in steering the company. There is an outstanding number of state-owned and state-controlled companies in mainland China, whereby there is also a special role played by strategic investors in the latter case. This also tends to be the case in nearly all natural resource industries, especially with regard to those in Russia. (Aguiar *et al*. 2006: 8–9) In conclusion, the corporate governance of NTMNCs is quite different from those of LME and is rather based on insider control, including some parallels with CME. Moreover, "...different corporate governance rules and behaviors, especially in case of state-owned and family-controlled companies, respectively, means that EMNCs [Emerging Market Multinational Companies] may have less trouble and more flexibility in accessing capital than listed MNCs that are restricted by the volatile will of shareholders, market regulators, or analysts" (Goldstein 2007: 146). In a similar vein, numerous Asian NTMNCs are supported by inter-personal networks particularly based on ethnic ties (ibid: 117–22); these networks reduce information costs by the provision of trust and other forms of (social) capital. Among the most well-known of these networks are the Chaebol in South Korea and the Guanxi Chixe in Taiwan (Feenstra and Hamilton 2006).

(3) The pattern of industrial relations

The international business literature that dominates the debate on NTMNCs has not given much attention to industrial relations. However, from what is available in terms of information we have to highlight the weak role of organized labor, e.g. in terms of the overabundance of human capital and flexible production systems. As a result, many NTMNCs rely on human capital rather than machinery. A low-cost workforce not only benefits Chinese NTMNCs that base their business model on price competition in mature industries, but also Korean and Taiwanese NTMNCs that have made extensive use of low labor costs elsewhere in the region (Goldstein 2007: 76–78).

(4) The education and training system

Given the still somewhat inferior level of technological innovation of many (though not all) NTMNCs, they continue to heavily rely on large-scale public investment in skill formation and establishment of public research institutions (Goldstein 2007: 95; Ramamurti 2008). For example, the success of the pharmaceutical industries in India, as well as the computer and software industries, would not have been possible without the presence of institutions set up by the Indian government across the country which strongly support the training and education of the future workforce.

(5) The transfer of innovations within the economy

As an increasing number of NTMNCs are becoming innovators in knowledge and technology, it is indeed crucial to look at the significant role socio-economic institutions have played in patterning the manner in which innovations are transferred in an economy. Indeed, as in the other institutional spheres, the socio-economic institutions supporting the transfer of innovation within non-triad economies are not homogeneous. Nevertheless, in the midst of heterogeneity, there is indeed one quintessential element that is similar across the board in all non-triad economies, namely the role of the state in supporting the transfer of innovations within the economy.

In Taiwan, for example, a public laboratory was created to push small firms to collaborate within an R&D consortium. The consortium receives a considerable amount of funding from private organizations, government ministries, trade associations, as well as the public research institute Industrial Technology Research Institute (Mathews 2004: 42). In comparison, in India, the government has set up a number of R&D programs in order to encourage innovation specifically in IT and business solutions as well as in the pharmaceutical and biotechnology industries.

In more general terms, the latecomer status of NTMNCs is responsible for their strong focus on inter-firm cooperation (partnerships, joint ventures) for the spread of innovations, since these networks provide a crucial mode for the acquisition of technology (Goldstein 2007: 119). In a later stage of development, NTMNCs use acquisitions – in particular in countries of the triad – in order to improve their innovative capacity (ibid: 2).

Generally speaking, NTMNCs have often grown in an environment in which a rather generous version of competition policy was applicable to domestic firms in comparison to the more stringent competition policy applied to foreign firms, something which still remains a reality across many of the non-triad economies. Indeed, while some variations between non-triad economies exist, a significant portion – particularly in Latin America and East Asia – have used competition policies to support NTMNCs (ibid.: 99–104) through the creation of "national champions" and the consolidation of industries, even the creation of national monopolies, not only for the transfer of innovation in the economy, but also to be able to accumulate extra profits on the national markets in order to invest abroad.

(6) The regulatory environment and the role of the state

Generally, support by the state and its public policies have been crucial factors for NTMNCs, as already discussed regarding financial support, innovation and competition policies. To be sure, these three areas do not by any means exhaust the list of public support measures for NTMNCs. Other factors consist of lax property right enforcement, stringent inward investment regulation, regulatory policies (e.g. post-privatization) or public support for access to natural resources.

Some NTMNCs have developed competitive advantages due to operational experiences in difficult institutional environments within their home markets. In particular, "multilatinas" have superior knowledge of policy innovations such as public–private partnerships that have been important during post-privatization regulatory politics (Goldstein 2007: 3, 69). NTMNCs have learned the rules of the trade before they were introduced in the triad and thus have been empowered with an imperative competitive advantage. As an example, Goldstein has pointed out that public service companies from Latin America were confronted with pro-market regulatory regimes (enforced by the Bretton Woods Institutions) while companies in the triad were still state-owned monopolies and therefore were at a disadvantage when competing with NTMNCs in third country markets.

In addition, national resource companies, particularly in the oil sector, rely on direct state support in getting access to new resources. "Political considerations have traditionally played a key role in driving deals and determining contractual conditions in the extraction industries" (ibid.: 105). China in particular frequently uses its economic diplomacy, including the provision of development assistance, to support its NTMNCs, for example by tying development assistance to the use of Chinese companies (ibid.: 76f). Chinese NTMNCs are also infamous for rather aggressive searches for natural resources, including in "unsavory markets where more socially responsible companies fear to tread" (Pegg 2003:103, cited by Goldstein 2007: 105).

In general, "there is no doubt that many EMNCs have closer ties with their governments than their OECD peers" (Goldstein 2007: 150; Ramamurti 2008). We can, thus, with certainty highlight that the state – as an institutional entrepreneur and institutional builder (Chang 1995: 37) – is more important for NTMNCs than for multinationals based in either LMEs or CMEs. Throughout our discussion above we have concretely elucidated the supporting role of the state in the creation and maintenance of several crucial institutions that have fostered NTMNCs. And yet, surprisingly, it is here, despite the overwhelming empirical evidence, where established theories on (triad) MNCs are found wanting and consequently inefficiently equipped to explain the rise of NTMNCs (Goldstein 2007: 94).

Conclusion

Together, the socio-economic institutions analyzed above contribute to an explanation of the rise of NTMNCs and their competitive advantages. Moreover, these institutions are mutually interdependent: a system of corporate finance relying heavily on state or family ownership works well with a system of corporate governance focused on insider control. Also, the financial cushion built up by many NTMNCs supports their ability to weather potential crises in turbulent regulatory environments. Finally, if we identify competitive market arrangements and formal contracts as characteristic of MNCs in LMEs, and non-market forms of coordination such as inter-firm networks and national or sector associations as typical for CME MNCs, we may identify an important supporting role for the state as the most significant common denominator for NTMNCs.

Implications for global governance: charting future conflict and cooperation potential

In using the VoC approach to contextualize NTMNCs, we have highlighted the domestic political, social and institutional contexts that have conditioned their ascent and shaped their preferences. However, global expansion also entails confronting the international institutions and agreements that govern the global economy. How are NTMNCs mediating this confrontation? What preferences have NTMNCs developed with regard to how the global economy should optimally be regulated? To what extent are current global governance institutions, arrangements and mechanisms broadly in line with the needs and preferences of NTMNCs?

The VoC approach as such is of limited use here. It has been developed with a neglect of the global institutional context. This is hardly surprising, given its background in comparative economic sociology and comparative politics. Thus we need to extrapolate from our findings above how the rise of NTMNCs may affect global governance institutions. In the following, we provide a broad outline that focuses on discussing how the existing global governance institutions have enabled the rise of NTMNCs and on looking at the possible demands of NTMNCs regarding the future evolution of global governance institutions and the potential conflicts with other stakeholders that may arise in this context. In operationalizing this "dependent variable," we particularly focus on the potential convergence versus a continued divergence in the regulatory preferences of triad-MNCs and NTMNCs, Moreover, attention is also given to assessing the extent to which NTMNCs are likely to refute the current liberal economic order, inducing a structural shift in favor of a more mercantilist one. Given the recent character of the phenomenon, this section takes a somewhat speculative character.

(1) The financial system

As outlined above, NTMNCs have usually grown through systems of company finance that do not fully cater to the demands of global financial markets. Based on family or state ownership/support, they have maintained a high degree of stability and an orientation towards the long term, thereby neglecting issues such as the protection of minority shareholders. Given that most global institutions, such as the IMF, IBRD, WTO or the OECD, are focused on a further expansion of LME-like standards in financial market regulation, we may expect that an increasingly intensive conflict over these issues will turn towards accommodating the needs of global financial markets. Evidencing this is the WTO decision in 2000 deeming the Proex subsidy, created by the Brazilian government specifically to support Embraer, illegal and subsequently forcing the government to abolish the subsidy program. Despite this example, for the time being most of these conflicts are not being played out in the open; that is, as the case of accounting regulation has demonstrated, where NTMNCs do not oppose the dominant global regulation (e.g. by lobbying within the IASB, or not adopting IFRS at all), but rather selectively implement global standards.

(2) Corporate governance regulation

Corporate governance issues are not regulated by a powerful global regime like, for example, the WTO. Instead, these issues are quite loosely institutionalized. Most regulations are in the form of voluntary codes, such as those issued by the OECD. Similar to the issue area of corporate finance, in corporate governance debates we expect that the roles of strategic investors, the state, and controlling families will cause a significant opposition to arise if and when financial market-driven (LME) standards are too forcefully imposed on the global place.

However, the debate might become more complex due to the recent wave of western concerns about the increasing influence of non-triad sovereign wealth funds working within global capitalism. NTMNCs prefer less restrictive takeover regulations, given that they have increasingly relied on brownfield investments in the triad to acquire market access, higher profit margins, brand recognition etc. Nevertheless, some triad governments are increasingly becoming wary of market-friendly standards and have started introducing institutions that protect against takeover by non-triad state funds.[10] Correspondingly, we expect increasing tensions and a growing importance of institutions such as CFIUS (Goldstein 2007: 143).

(3) Industrial relations

In the field of industrial relations, NTMNCs usually are unwilling to accept comprehensive global labor regulation by the ILO, because of the corresponding threat to the low (labor) cost strategy that has helped them to expand. Furthermore, we witness increasing tensions with OECD unions when companies are taken over and local industrial relations models are not respected (Goldstein 2007.: 139–40, 143–44).[11] Finally, also in the field of corporate social responsibility, NTMNCs usually are less willing to accept stringent (self) regulation (ibid.: 133). However, there is also the perspective that upgrading CSR activity in the medium term would be possible if more companies strongly participate in global value chains or are directly confronted with (CSR-conscious) western customers (ibid.: 135).

(4) The education and training system

Education and training systems are perhaps least affected by comprehensive global regulation. NTMNCs and their home countries are still rather unrestrained in their strategies. Technical standards remain the primary issue here in terms of international regulation impacting production levels at the firm or national level. Here we are likely to witness a divergence in NTMNC preferences between firms involved in capital-intensive sectors and those firms that are rapidly becoming involved in more advanced service and technology industries. To date, the former have not pressed for standard specifications; however, as the number of firms active in the latter sector continues to grow they may begin to push for more stringent specifications. Given that technologically advanced industries are critically important in terms of their capacity for uplifting national economic development, these industries may gain an upper hand in dictating the preferences of the group at the international level.

(5) The transfer of innovations within the economy

On the basis of our assumptions about the basic institutions supporting the transfer of innovations for NTMNCs, two issue areas of global business regulation stand out: intellectual property rights (IPRs) and competition policy. In terms of IPRs, regulation through TRIPS and WIPO often coerced non-triad markets into *prematurely* embedding strict(er) IPR regulation legislatively by 2005, i.e. prior to normative acceptance. Given that many of the current NTMNCs have been enabled to flourish through lax IPR regulation, this will likely remain an area that non-triad governments will contest, as is currently evidenced through lax IPR legislative enforcement in the non-triad (Braithwaite and Drahos 2000; May 2007; Sell 1998, 2003). At the firm level, many NTMNCs are against strict(er) IPR regulations which may inhibit cross-border learning. Nevertheless, as more NTMNCs become involved in industries that thrive on strict(er) IPR regulation, significant contestation may arise not only *among* NTMNCs, but also *between* NTMNCs *and* small indigenous firms in their domestic markets. The former refers to conflicts between those wanting strict(er) IPR versus those against it, something which will be heavily conditioned by the degree to which NTMNCs continue to move up the global value chain (Goldstein 2007: 135).

Regarding global competition policy, we assume most NTMNCs prefer less restrictive policies than those favored by the International Competition Network, which is dominated by triad competition authorities, for two reasons: foremost, so as not to impede inter-firm linkages that allow for the transfer of innovation; and secondly, not to choke government protection of national champions.

(6) The regulatory environment and the role of the state

Trade and other public policies probably will become the most controversial topics within global governance regarding the rise of NTMNCs. Indeed, it is in fact quite interesting to note that during the same time frame of 2001–08 we have witnessed not only numerous failed attempts to conclude the WTO's Doha round of negotiations, but also a substantial surge in NTMNC OFDI – especially triad-destined OFDI. Indeed, it is quite curious, especially when compared with the experiences of non-triad governments during TRIPS negotiations, and plausible given that NTMNCs have strongly risen in the last eight years, that they have provided their governments with the strength to stick to their guns during international negotiations.

On a more general note, non-triad trade policies have been geared towards sheltering domestic markets to build up NTMNC domestic strength, but also towards providing NTMNCs with the leverage needed to expand into foreign markets. These policies have stimulated aggressive OFDI expansion aimed at gaining resources and have supported economic development. Demonstrating the latter is the fact that between 1995 and 2005, South–South investment increased by $30 billion, from $15 to $45 billion (Santiso 2007: 3). This increase has also been accompanied by NTMNCs becoming a critical driving force pushing South–South cooperation, in schemes such as the Sao Paulo Round of the Global System of Trade Preferences among Developing Countries and the Trilateral Business Council (India, Brazil, South Africa/IBSA). NTMNCs have been key supporters of regional cooperation (ASEAN, Mercosur etc.), something explained by the large number of NTMNCs oriented towards regional and pan-regional expansion. Given the increasing importance of preferential trade and investment treaties (PTIAs), we may expect a change of global trade and investment patterns in favor of more South–South cooperation. However, South–South cooperation on trade and investment matters is at times just as controversial as North–South cooperation, as is indicated by increasing tensions over the role of Telmex and América Móvil in Latin America (Clifton *et al.* 2007: 17).

Finally, we expect commercial diplomacy to become an increasingly contested issue area within global business regulation, as already witnessed by the geopolitical clashes over oil resources and the increasingly controversial role of China in Africa that may be weakening the leverage of the international financial institutions about their lending countries (Goldstein 2007: 135).[12] Again, these tensions are most obvious in the field of resource extraction, as witnessed by the non-implementation of the OECD Convention on "Combating Bribery of Foreign Public Officials in International Business Transactions," the "Extractive Industries Transparency Initiative" and the "Publish What You Pay" campaign by many NTMNCs (ibid.: 106). Furthermore, given that Chinese firms have steadily increased their presence in Latin America, whereby "in 2005 the region was the second largest recipient of Chinese FDI" (Santiso 2007: 8), we may witness future conflicts not only between triad and non-triad-MNCs, but also among NTMNCs.

Concluding remarks

In conclusion, our extrapolation (from a VoC perspective) of how potential North–South conflicts are being played out within global governance has not yet led to a clear picture. While we have noted numerous areas where we expect intensified conflict in the near future, in other areas we rather assume that the preferences of triad-MNCs and NTMNCs may gradually converge. Indeed, we have found several cases where NTMNCs appear to take on similar preferences as triad-MNCs over time. However, we also identified a number of cases where NTMNCs operate in far more close collaboration with national governments than triad-MNCs, thus indicating that the potential push for a more mercantilist form of global governance may be one of the most visible conflicts to come in the future. Which of these trajectories in the end will gain the upper hand is difficult to say at the moment – much more research on NTMNCs and their position towards global governance is needed.[13] While our contribution has not yet provided firm answers, it has presented strategies for developing these answers in the future.

Notes

1 Non-triad multinationals encompass all multinationals located outside the traditional triad (North America, Europe and Japan/Australia). This term has taken precedence over others, such as "emerging market multinationals" or "challenger companies," given that: (a) it is the least "loaded" per se; and (b) it also incorporates firms from South Korea, Singapore and Taiwan – three economies neither perceived as emerging markets nor as part of the triad. As such, we assume these economies and their firms may have very different preferences with regard to global governance from those of triad MNCs, thereby justifying their inclusion into our overall analysis.

2 "Choice" is being used here to highlight that numerous NTMNC takeover bids in the triad have failed.

3 Examples of ownership-specific advantages include firm size, proprietary technology, trade mark and brand name power, flexible production systems, etc.

4 "How" refers to whether a firm should choose to export, participate in a joint venture, establish a sales subsidiary, establish a manufacturing plant, acquire a pre-existing firm, etc.

5 "Why" can refer to either of the following two things: (1) to reap monetary benefits of an O-advantage; or (2) to augment and strengthen current O-advantages.

6 Ranging from stage 1 to stage 5 relates, for instance, to no outward or inward FDI in stage 1 all the way up to stage 5 in which levels of net outward and inward investment converge (Sim and Pandian 2003; Tolentino 1993).

7 For instance, because of decreasing costs, increasing rents, or when protecting its export markets from local competitors.

8 Referring to things like small scale, input costs, etc.

9 For instance, lower costs associated with labour, raw materials, property, equipment or capital.

10 This has become a particularly conflict-ridden issue area in light of the sub-prime crisis and numerous defaults of western banks which have enabled 'non-transparent' sovereign wealth funds to cheaply and rapidly invest large sums in triad markets. Although this conflict has arisen as a result of sovereign wealth funds from China and the Middle East, it is expected that stricter regulations will impact all non-triad markets.

11 One example that has further exasperated these tensions is Taiwan's Benq, which in 2005 acquired the handset unit of Siemens (Germany) and subsequently closed the subsidiary in 2006. After enough time had passed to leverage all the resources the subsidiary possessed, bankruptcy was declared, and this was done directly after the expiration date of all contracts of the roughly 6,000 workers they inherited.

12 We do not deal with the utilization of NTMNCs as foreign policy instruments, e.g. the case of Chavez and PDVSA (Goldstein 2007: 107–9).
13 This research is currently being carried out in a collaborative project involving the authors as well as partners from nine other universities across Europe. By each project focusing on a specific region(s), industry(ies), company(ies) and issue area(s), we collectively aim to establish concretely what implications NTMNCs have had on the multitude of global governance arrangements and mechanisms.

References

Aguiar, M. *et al.* (2006) "The New Global Challengers: How 100 Top Companies from Rapidly Developing Economies are Changing the World," Boston Consulting Group.

Aguiar, M. *et al.* (2007) "The 2008 BCG 100 New Global Challengers," Boston Consulting Group.

Albert, M. (1993) *Capitalism Against Capitalism* (London: Whurr Publishers).

Amable, B. (2003) *The Diversity of Modern Capitalism* (Oxford: Oxford University Press).

Blyth, M. (2003) "Same as it Never Was: Temporality and Typology in the Varieties of Capitalism," *Comparative European Politics* 1(2): 215–25.

Bonaglia, F., Goldstein, A. and Mathews, J.A. (2006) "Accelerated Internationalisation by Emerging Multinational: The Case of the White Goods Sector," Universita' Politecnica delle Marche (I), Dipartimento di Economia Working Papers 270.

Braithwaite, J. and Drahos, P. (2000) *Global Business Regulation* (Cambridge: Cambridge University Press).

Buckley, P.J. and Casson, M. (1976) *The Future of the Multinational Enterprise* (London: Palgrave Macmillan).

Business Week (2005) "The BusinessWeek Global 1200," <http://www.businessweek.com/pdfs/2005/0552_global.pdf> (1 April 2007).

Chang, H.J. (1995) "Entrepreneurship and Conflict Management," in Chang, H.J. and Rowthorn, R. (eds) *The Role of the State in Economic Change*, pp. 31–47 (Oxford: Clarendon Press).

Clifton, J., Comin, F. and Fuentes, D.D. (2007) "Transforming Network Services in Europe and the Americas: From Ugly Ducklings to Swans?" in Clifton, J., Comin, F. *et al.* (eds) *Transforming Public Enterprise in Europe and North America*, pp. 3–15 (New York: Palgrave Macmillan).

Crouch, C. (2005) *Capitalist Diversity and Change* (Oxford: Oxford University Press).

Department of Trade and Industry (DTI) (2006) "The Top 800 UK and 1250 Global Companies by R&D Investment," (London: Department for Business Enterprise and Regulatory Reform).

Doremus, P.N., Keller, W.W., Pauly, L.W. and Reich, S. (1998) *The Myth of the Global Corporation* (Princeton: Princeton University Press).

Dunning, J.H. (1981) "Explaining Outward Direct Investment of Developing Countries: in Support of the Eclectic Theory of International Relations," in Kumar, K. and McLeod, M.G. (eds) *Multinationals from Developing Countries*, pp. 1–22 (Lexington: Lexington Books, D.C. Heath and Company).

—— (1986) "The Investment Development and Third World Multinationals," in Khan, K.M. (eds) *Multinationals of the South: New Actors in the International Economy* (London: Palgrave Macmillan).

—— (1988a) "The Eclectic Paradigm of International Production: A Restatement and Some Possible Extensions," *Journal of International Business Studies* 19(1): 1–25.

—— (1988b) "Trade, Location of Economic Activity and the Multinational Enterprise. A Search for an Eclectic Approach," in Dunning, J.H. *Explaining International Production*, pp. 13–140 (London: Unwin Hyman).

—— (1995) "Reappraising the Eclectic Paradigm in an Age of Alliance Capitalism," *Journal of International Business Studies* 26(3): 461–91.

—— (1998) "Location and the Multinational Enterprise: A Neglected Factor," *Journal of International Business Studies* 29(1): 45–66.

Feenstra, R.C. and Hamilton, C.G. (2006) *Emergent Economies, Divergent Paths* (New York: Cambridge University Press).

Forbes Magazine (2007) "The Global 2000," <http://www.forbes.com/2004/03/24/04f2000land.html> (1 April).

Fortune Magazine (2007) "Global Fortune 500," <http://money.cnn.com/magazines/fortune/global(500/2007)/> (1 April).

Goldstein, A. (2007) *Multinational Companies from Emerging Economies* (New York: Palgrave Macmillan).

Hall, P.A. and Soskice, D. (eds) (2001a) *Varieties of Capitalism: The Institutional Foundations of Comparative Advantage* (Oxford: Oxford University Press).

—— (2001b) "A Introduction to Varieties of Capitalism," in Hall, P.A. and Soskice, D. (eds) *Varieties of Capitalism: The Institutional Foundations of Comparative Advantage*, pp. 1–70 (Oxford: Oxford University Press).

Hancké, B., Rhodes, M. and Thatcher, M. (eds) (2007) *Beyond Varieties of Capitalism. Conflict, Contradictions and Complementarities in the European Economy* (Oxford: Oxford University Press).

Jackson, G. and Deeg, R. (2006) "How Many Varieties of Capitalism? Comparing the Comparative Institutional Analyses of Capitalist Diversity," *MPI*fG Discussion Paper (06/02), Cologne: Max Planck Institute for the Social Sciences.

Mathews, J.A. (2002) "Competitive Advantages of the Latecomer Firm: A Resource-based Account of Industrial Catch-Up Strategies," *Asia Pacific Journal of Management* 19: 467–88.

—— (2004) "Catchup Strategies and the Latecomer Effect: World Industrial Development in the 21st Century," MGSM Working Paper 2004–18.

—— (2006) "Dragon Multinationals: New Players in 21st Century Globalization," *Asia Pacific Journal of Management* 23: 5–27.

May, C. (2007) "The Hypocrisy of Forgetfulness: The Contemporary Significance of Early Innovations in Intellectual Property," *Review of International Political Economy* 14(1): 1–25.

Pegg, S. (2003). "Globalization and natural-resource conflicts", The New Strategic Environment 56(4) 82–96.

Ramamurti, Ravi (2008) "What Have We Learned about Emerging-Market MNEs?" Paper prepared for Conference on *Emerging Market Multinationals: Outward FDI from Emerging and Developing Economies*, 9–10 October 2008, Copenhagen: Copenhagen Business School.

Santiso, J. (2007) "The Emergence of Latin Multinationals," Deutsche Bank Research, www.dbresearch.com (13 March 2007).

Sell, S.K. (1998) *Power and Ideas: North–South Politics of Intellectual Property and Antitrust* (Albany: State University of New York Press).

—— (2003) *Private Power, Public Law: The Globalization of Intellectual Property Rights* (Cambridge: Cambridge University Press).

Shonfield, A. (1965) *Modern Capitalism* (London, New York: Oxford University Press).

Sim, A.B. and Pandian, J. (2003) "Emerging Asian MNEs and their Internationalization Strategies – Case Study Evidence on Taiwanese and Singaporean Firms," *Asia Pacific Journal of Management* 20: 27–50.

Tolentino, P.E.E. (1993) *Technological Innovation and Third World Multinationals* (London: Routledge).

UNCTAD (2005) The Top 100 Non-Financial TNCs from Developing Countries Ranked by Foreign Assets, New York /Geneva: United Nations.

Van Agtmael, A. (2007) *The Emerging Market Century* (London: Simon & Schuster).

Vernon, R. (1966) "International Investment and International Trade in the Product Cycle," *Quarterly Journal of Economics* 80(2): 190–207.

Vernon, R. (1983) *Two hungry giants: The US and Japan in the quest for oil and ores.* (Cambridge): Harvard University Press)

—— (1977) *Storm Over the Multinationals: The Real Issues* (London: George Allen & Unwin).

Wells, L.T. (1981) "Foreign Investors from the Third World," in Kumar, K. and McLeod, M.G. (eds) *Multinationals from Developing Countries*, pp. 23–36 (Lexington: Lexington Books, D.C. Heath and Company).

—— (1983) *Third World Multinationals: The Rise of Foreign Investment from Developing Countries* (Cambridge, MA: The MIT Press).

—— (1986) "New and Old Multinationals: Competitors or Partners," in Khan, K.M. (ed.) *Multinationals of the South: New Actors in the International Economy* (London: Palgrave).

—— (1998) "Multinationals and the Developing Countries," *Journal of International Business Studies* 29(1): 101–14.

Wilkins, Mira (1986) "Japanese Multinational Enterprises before 1914," *Business History Review* 60(2): 199–232.

Part III

Business as partner in global governance

9 Rethinking multilateralism

Global governance and public–private partnerships with the UN

Benedicte Bull

Introduction

Among the increasingly important roles of business in global governance is that of being a partner to governments and international organizations. This may take many forms, but recently increased significance has been put on the formation of public–private partnerships (PPPs). These have raised important theoretical and normative questions. Related to the formation of such PPPs with the United Nations' (UN) organizations, concerns have particularly been voiced about how such PPPs affect the legitimacy and accountability of the UN (Bull et al. 2004, Martens 2007) and of transnational governance more broadly (Börzel and Risse 2005). Critics have argued that such PPPs imply a co-optation of the multilateral organizations by global capital (Richter 2002, 2003), and that they fragment international cooperation and undermine efforts for cooperation and equity among states (Zammit 2003). Indeed, one extreme position is that PPPs imply a 'privatization' of international and transnational governance.

There is at the moment a general consensus that, rather than a privatization, we see a transformation of inter- and transnational relations in which the states still play an important part. But how can we best describe these relations, and what role do the PPPs play in them? The starting point for this paper is the notion of multilateralism as formulated by John G. Ruggie and Robert Cox (Ruggie 1982, 1993, Cox 1983, 1992). Both theorize the multilateral system in the context of the broader post-war political economic order. They also view the breakdown of this order as the main reason for recent changes in multilateral collaboration. These changes have made Ruggie's definition of multilateralism as 'an institutional form that coordinates relations among three or more states on the basis of generalized principles of conduct' (Ruggie 1993: 11), increasingly obsolete. However, new forms of complex multilateral collaboration are emerging (O'Brian *et al.* 2000), although not yet well defined.

This paper aims to contribute to an understanding of the new form of multilateralism through an analysis of the form and purpose of the PPPs.[1] Based on an empirical analysis of key partnerships, the paper analyzes the premises for the new kind of multilateralism, what forms of legitimacy it is based on, the extent to which it is suitable for addressing the problems that the multilateral institutions were established to solve, and its inherent limitations. The argument is that PPPs are examples of what may be termed 'market multilateralism'. In terms of process, it describes the emergence of a system that coordinates relations not only between states, but also between private for-profit and non-profit actors. The boundaries of this collaboration tend to be set by the interests of key market actors, that is: large corporations. Goals of the collaboration or means to achieve commonly agreed goals that run counter to the interests of the corporations are 'ruled out' or kept off the agenda. Mechanisms employed to reach the goals of the collaboration also relate to the market: either making up for market failures, for regulatory failures, or for the detrimental consequences of oligopolistic market structures. This form of multilateralism is based on multiple forms of legitimacy and authority, implying that traditional formal legitimacy has been rendered a secondary role.

The argument of this paper is based on in-depth case studies of PPPs with the multilateral organizations aimed at achieving four development goals: 'health for all', 'bridging the digital divide', 'water for all' and 'abolition of child labor'.[2] The paper is outlined as follows. The first section discusses the rise of public–private partnerships in the multilateral system and presents a typology of partnerships. The second section details the theoretical argument of this paper. The third section presents two examples of market multilateralism drawn from case studies: the GAVI alliance and the partnership between UNESCO and Microsoft.

Public–private partnerships in the United Nations system

The concept of public–private partnerships (PPPs) is one of several – including, among others, 'multistakeholder initiatives' and 'policy networks'[3] – that are aimed at describing new forms of multi-actor collaboration at the global level. For the purpose of this paper, PPPs are defined as: 'voluntary and collaborative relationships between various parties, both State and non-State, in which all participants agree to work together to achieve a common purpose or undertake a specific task and to share risks and responsibilities, resources and benefits' (UN General Assembly 2005: 4).

In the UN system, PPPs have gained increasing prevalence. They have gained increasing attention in inter-governmental bodies such as various World Summits, the UN General Assembly and the respective governing bodies of the specialized UN organizations (Bull and McNeill 2007: ch 1; Martens 2007). The inter-governmental discussions have often responded to broader processes of change in the climate between business and the UN. Among the milestones in this story are: first, the burial of the efforts to develop binding codes of conduct for multinational enterprises under the UN Conference on Trade and Development (UNCTAD) in 1993, which improved the climate between the UN and corporations (Hummel 2005); second, the historic gift of one billion US dollars given by Time Warner vice-chairman Ted Turner to the UN, which led to the establishment of the United Nations Foundation (UNF) and the United Nations Fund for International Partnerships (UNFIP), aimed at encouraging further partnerships with the UN;

Table 9.1 Types of public–private partnerships

	Goals	*What does the UN contribute?*	*What does business contribute?*
Resource mobilization partnerships	Fundraising Public–private investment	Expertise Image Policy networks	Money In-kind donations
Advocacy partnerships	PR campaigns Advocacy	Expertise Legitimacy	Technology Access to media
Policy partnerships	Change of policy Development of standards/norms	Expertise Policy networks	Access to policy actors
Operational partnerships	Long-term procurement Product development	Coordination of resources to create markets Policy networks	Technology Production facilities

and third, the appointment of business-friendly, Kofi Annan as general secretary in 1997 and his launch of the Global Compact in 1999. Later in 1999/2000 the secretary general's office produced a series of reports on partnerships and finally it presented the UN Guidelines for Cooperation with the Business Community upon the request from the General Assembly.[4]

By 2005 Broadwater and Kaul (2005) had identified 400 partnerships between private actors and the UN organizations, while admitting that there could easily exist more. These PPPs were of a diverse nature. There are many different typologies of partnerships (see for example Tesner with Kell 2000; UN General Assembly 2003, 2005, Witte and Reinecke 2005, Börzel and Risse 2005). The fourfold typology summarized in Table 9.1 essentially groups partnerships on the basis of their goals.

Resource mobilization partnerships seek to mobilize private resources either by direct fund-raising or by promoting and facilitating foreign direct investment (FDI) flows to poorer countries. The primary aim of *advocacy partnerships* is to raise awareness concerning the global issues addressed by the UN, or to add a further issue to the global agenda. *Policy partnerships* typically establish both formal and informal dialogue and knowledge sharing between the UN and the private sector, with the aim of changing the policy of international organizations, governments or corporations. One main function of such networks is the development of norms and standards. *Operational partnerships* are often formed in order to compensate for market imperfections, information failures and political hurdles against provision of essential goods and services.

In pure monetary terms the direct contributions by corporations to the UN is negligible. There exist no global numbers, but examples from individual UN organizations show that the private sector contributes less than 1 per cent of the budget. There are some exceptions, for example UNICEF, which receives 3.4 per cent of its budget from business, in addition to business contributions to national committees. The latter contribute approx. 28 per cent of the UNICEF budget, but how much of that is business contributions is unclear. Private foundations contributed significantly to specific areas of UN operations, but by any measures the governments are still the most important contributors to the UN. Nevertheless, PPPs may have important implications for multilateral collaboration, as will be discussed below.

PPPs and multilateralism

John Ruggie has defined multilateralism as 'an institutional form that coordinates relations among three or more states on the basis of generalized principles of conduct' (Ruggie 1993: 11). According to Ruggie, the organizing principles of multilateralism – indivisibility, generalized principles of conduct, and diffuse reciprocity[5] – are a feature of the Westphalian state system. Thus this is a descriptive definition, referring to process rather than outcome and to what Ikenberry has called the 'basic level of multilateralism', namely the basic organizing principles of the state system (Ikenberry 2003).

However, Ruggie was also concerned with the particular multilateral system emerging after the Second World War, referring thus to the 'intermediate level of multilateralism' (Ikenberry 2003). He related post-war multilateralism to the quest for a sustained framework for the operation of a global market. This framework rested on the bargain of 'embedded liberalism': the sustaining of a liberal international infrastructure of global economic management, predicated on the domestic interventions for social protection by the modern capitalist state (Ruggie 1982).

A major limitation of Ruggie's account of the post-war compromise is that it describes the situation only in a part of the world. As Ruggie himself notes, the benefits of embedded liberalism were never fully extended to developing countries, since they were exposed to the demands of openness towards international markets but ill-equipped to provide buffers against the negative effects. This resulted in various attempts at forging a new compromise at the international level. In analyzing this, Robert Cox argues that multilateralism is 'in part the institutionalization and regulation of existing order, and in part the site of struggle between conservative and transformative forces' (Cox 1992: 514). Multilateralism embodies the rules which facilitate the expansion of the existing order, it ideologically legitimates its norms and it co-opts and absorbs counter hegemonic ideas (Cox 1983). As such, it may be associated with sustaining the global market, as discussed by Ruggie. However, multilateralism is also the site of struggle between conservative and transformative forces (Cox 1992: 514). This function is symbolically located in the UN General Assembly, which is perceived by powerful states as harboring an unfriendly Third World majority. The UN General Assembly was intended to correct the inequities in the world economy, and it has, among other things, brought forward the demand for the aforementioned codes of conduct for multinational enterprises.

The weakening of state protection of vulnerable sectors at the domestic level, and the transnationalization of the economy, led to both the breakdown of embedded liberalism and the weakening of initiatives to create new international compromises (see e.g. Ruggie 1997, 2004). The period in question is also characterized by the increased size and global spread of large corporations and their increased role in politics and policy making (Harrod 2006). The rise of PPPs must be understood against this background; rather than attempting to regulate business at the national or global levels, corporations are intended to be brought in as collaborative partners at the global level.

However, this immediately raises issues of the legitimacy and authority of the multilateral system. When private actors are given a say in multilateral matters, this reduces to some extent the *formal-legal legitimacy* of the multilateral system, which is derived from the fact that the multilateral institutions are established by, and run according to, rules made and interpreted by legitimate states. Some would also argue that it reduces their *democratic legitimacy* which depends on the governance structure that, at least in the case of the United Nations, was designed to partially correct the discrepancy of power between the large and powerful countries and the smaller, less powerful ones (Martens 2007, Utting and Zammit 2006). Thus, some authors view PPPs mainly as a threat to democratic legitimacy and look at ways that this can be restored, avoiding the emergence of 'elite multilateralism' (Martens 2007).

This paper takes a different approach. It aims rather to describe the kind of multilateralism that is emerging in the place of the old multilateralism and what forms of legitimacy and authority it may come to rest on.

Market multilateralism: legitimacy and authority

I argue that a new form of multilateralism has emerged, which we can label 'market multilateralism'.[6] In terms of process it describes the emergence of a system that coordinates relations not only between states but also between private for-profit and non-profit organizations. However, privileged among these are key market actors, mostly large corporations, and foundations and organizations that are closely linked to those. In this system norms and rules for collaboration evolve. Thus the behavior of the corporations is guided not only by short-term profit, but also by norms emerging in the collaboration with multilateral institutions. However, the boundaries of this collaboration tend to be set by the interests of large corporations. Also, where there is a consensus about goals, means to achieve those goals that run counter to the interests of the corporations are 'ruled out' or kept off the agenda. This form of multilateralism is set out to support the global capitalist system rather than challenge it, and initiatives that make use of business methods and market mechanisms will have a greater chance of succeeding than those that do not. Another feature of corporate multilateralism is that multilateral institutions tend to mimic the corporations in their way of operating.

The use of the term 'market' has been criticized on many fronts. Harrod (2006) argues that as most sectors today are organized as oligopolies and dominated by a handful of large corporations, the notion of a market as used in neo-classical theory is an illusion that mostly serves to disguise the power of the corporation. However, in spite of the domination of large corporations, these still compete with each other. Thus, they *are* market actors, though also political actors and social institutions: although they are able to postpone surplus generation in favor of power-seeking, the long-term goal is always surplus generation. Thus, one can argue that corporations are at the same time profit-seeking market actors and power-seeking political actors. The term 'market multilateralism' is thus not meant to convey that this is a form of multilateralism that operates according to classical market principles or benefits from the workings of free markets. Rather, the term is chosen because (i) it involves key market actors, (ii) it intends to make use of market mechanisms and creates mechanisms that make use both of a market logic and of classical principles of multilateralism, and (iii) it tends to produce a certain 'assimilation' between multilateral institutions and key market actors (corporations).

This form of multilateralism is criticized by many for lacking legitimacy. However, the view on that depends on our concept of legitimacy. A main premise for the following discussion is that the legitimacy of any institution is constructed. Legitimacy is based on the normative belief held by an actor that the rule of this institution ought to be obeyed. It is a subjective quality, relational between actor and institution, and defined by the actor's perception of the institution in question (Hurd 1999: 5). Authority may be defined as the legitimate exercise of power.

There are at least three alternative sources of legitimacy to the ones discussed above (formal legal legitimacy and democratic legitimacy). The first of these is *expertise*. The significance of knowledge and expertise as a source of authority within the multilateral system has long been acknowledged, and there has been an upsurge of research on the topic in recent years, perhaps because the construction of expertise-based authority has been a conscious strategy of several multilateral institutions (Bøås and McNeill 2004). The second additional source of legitimacy is *moral standing*. The UN has traditionally enjoyed significant such legitimacy based on its stated aims to work for impartial pursuit of peace and development. The third possible source of legitimacy is *goal achievement*. Quite irrespective of their expertise and moral standing, their formal dependence on legitimate states or democratic governance structure, institutions may gain legitimacy if they actually manage to achieve what are considered to be legitimate goals. And, as a corollary,: only if they fail to deliver on their promises will questions be raised about their accountability, transparency or expertise.

However, these sources of legitimacy may be more contested and context-dependent than the formal-legal and democratic legitimacy. What gives an institution legitimacy among one group may detract from its legitimacy in another. In the context of an ever-expanding global capitalism, institutions that convey the image of operating in accordance with the ideals of global corporations, collaborating with private sector partners and benefiting from business expertise may be considered to have a higher 'moral standing', be more efficient in achieving goals and have a higher level of expertise. Such views are clearly contested.

However, they may be prevalent in circles that are of importance for multilateral institutions.

Viewing legitimacy as essentially constructed also allows for a larger role for the multilateral *organizations* and their executive heads.[7] In a state-centred view of multilateralism, the multilateral organizations understood as the international bureaucracies were viewed as at best formal implementing agencies for the collective decisions of states, and at worst bureaucratic quagmires hampering efficient execution of such decisions. Mouritzen (1990, p. 24, quoted in Jönsson 1995: 5) expresses the latter view very well, describing the international bureaucracies as the 'twining plants of international cooperation': they are too weak to keep upright without support; they look beautiful and often serve to hide ugly walls, and they are almost impossible to get rid of. To the extent that any autonomy has been granted to international organizations in the literature, it is as a result of 'agency slack' derived from antinomic delegation (the delegation of tasks with partly incompatible goals) and 'mission creep' (the mushrooming of new institutional goals without a corresponding reduction in old goals) (Gutner 2005).

However, with a constructivist starting point one should also consider how these organizations construct their own legitimacy and room for action. Through their production of knowledge and framing of discourses they increasingly shape their environment and define multilateral collaboration (e.g. Bøås and McNeill 2004; Stone 2000; Finnemore 1997).

Another way of doing that is through taking advantage of existing power relations. The early writings of Robert Cox focus on the ability of the executive heads to exercise strategic 'sailors' skills' to navigate between the constraints and pressures faced by the organizations and thereby gain a certain degree of autonomy (Cox 1969 [1996]: 317). In a world were heads of leading corporations are included in policy forums alongside heads of states, and where corporations control a large share of the technology and resources needed to fulfil the mandates of the multilateral institutions, it is only natural that the executive heads of multinational institutions will include corporations in their efforts to exercise strategic 'sailors' skills' and increase the authority and autonomy of their own institutions.

In the following I will discuss two different cases of 'market multilateralism' and intend to show how they both (i) were initiated and governed by a group of multiple actors in which private corporations, foundations and officials of multilateral organizations have played a key role, (ii) have resulted in the emergence of norms for collaboration, and (iii) at the same time are aimed at accommodating the interests of the corporations. The concluding section returns to the issue of legitimacy and authority of the multilateral system.

Cases of market multilateralism

Vaccines and immunization: GAVI, Gates and big pharma

Health and the environment are the two sectors that have attracted most PPPs. Broadwater and Kaul (2005) find that of a sample of 100 registered partnerships

29 per cent are in health (followed by 24 per cent in environment). In 2004, there were 92 health partnerships registered in the Initiative for Public Private Partnership for Health (IPPPH) database (www.ippph.org), and multilateral organizations were involved in 35 of them.

The Global Alliance for Vaccines and Immunization (GAVI) is prominent among the partnerships due to its generous funding and high public profile. This is a partnership between the World Health Organization (WHO), UNICEF, the World Bank, donor governments, private foundations (the Bill and Melinda Gates Foundation) and private pharmaceutical companies. It encompasses several of the categories outlined in table 9.1.

The background for the GAVI partnership is the perceived decline of vaccination rates of traditional children's vaccines from the early 1990s and the slow take-up of new biotech-based vaccines (Hib, Hepatitis B and Yellow Fever), due to a combination of lack of political will and inadequate vaccination systems at the country level, together with the lack of adequate vaccines for developing countries, prohibitive prices, and a supply crisis of vaccines at the global level (UNICEF 2004). The problems were aggravated by the drop in governmental funding for basic research, and the pressures towards an increasingly strict patent regime as agreed under the TRIPS agreement under the WTO.

The vaccine industry is characterized by being both an oligopoly and an oligopsony (the presence of only a few purchasers in the market). At the supply side, the pharmaceutical industry has been labelled a 'networked knowledge-based oligopoly' (Mytelka and Delapierre 1999), with a handful of dominating vaccine producers that are also responsible for most product development (Muraskin 1998). The UN is a major purchaser of vaccines. In the UN system, the responsibility for vaccines is shared between the WHO, which sets quality and safety standards, collaborates on research and development, mobilizes and channels funds to specific research projects and public vaccination programs, and UNICEF, which purchases 40 per cent of the total global volume of vaccine doses (UNICEF 2004).

From the early 1990s, several attempts were made at establishing partnerships between the UN and corporations to increase the vaccination rates (Muraskin 1998). When it finally succeeded, it was due to the entrepreneurship of the executive heads of multilateral organizations and the availability of foundation money on a large scale. More concretely, the initiative to form GAVI was taken by former WHO director Gro Harlem Brundtland jointly with World Bank President James Wolfensohn and UNICEF director Carol Bellamy. However, from the start they were in close dialogue with the Bill and Melinda Gates foundation that had already expressed its interest in funding such initiatives. GAVI was launched during the 30th World Economic Forum in 2000 at Davos, along with a Global Fund for Children's Vaccines (later renamed the Vaccine Fund) to support GAVI's activities. At this occasion a $750 million donation to it by the Bill and Melinda Gates Foundation was announced. Later, several other governments came on board. By 2007 the Vaccine Fund had raised and committed more than

US$ 2.2 billion for vaccines. Currently the United Kingdom is the largest donor. The only significant private donor is the Gates Foundation, which accounts for 49 per cent of the resources committed to GAVI and is granted a seat on the board.[8]

The private pharmaceutical industry was intended to participate in vaccine supply and R&D. It was granted two seats on the Executive Board – one for the multinational R&D-based companies and one for developing country industry, mainly producing generic drugs. The industry also has one seat in the Working Group set up to implement the board's decisions, and it has been represented in the various task forces set up to elaborate specific issues.

However, the private actor that has shaped the GAVI the most is the Gates Foundation. This foundation had an immediate effect on the willingness of the companies to participate, since it ensured predictable, long-term funding of programs under which significant amounts of vaccines will be purchased. This induced companies to make the kind of long-term commitment that is necessary in order to develop or produce vaccines.

The Gates Foundation also played a key role in shaping GAVI's operational structure. In general, it differs in two ways from other foundations: it has been less bureaucratic, being significantly affected by the 'hands on' management style of the Gates family (Bill, Melinda and Bill Gates Sr), and it has a technology bias – being specifically concerned to bring new technology to developing countries. This also made GAVI more attractive to the big R&D-based pharmaceutical companies that are the main proprietors of new technology in the health sector.

GAVI was created with five objectives: (i) to improve access to sustainable immunization services; (ii) to expand the use of all existing cost-effective vaccines; (iii) to accelerate the development and introduction of new vaccines (focusing on Hep B, Hib and Yellow Fever); (iv) to accelerate research and development efforts on vaccines and related products specifically needed by developing countries; and (v) to make immunization coverage an integral part of the design and assessment of health systems and international development efforts (World Health Organization 2000).

In sheer numbers, the achievements of GAVI have been impressive. By 2007 approximately 28 million additional children had been protected with basic vaccines (against diphtheria, tetanus and pertussis), and approximately 138 million additional children had been protected with new vaccines. But how has the GAVI alliance changed multilateral cooperation in health and what may be the outcome of this multilateralism? Have the companies taken actions in the pursuit of public health goals rather than their own short-term profit?

A first issue that may shed light on the questions above is whether GAVI has managed to drive down prices on essential drugs, and contributed to drug security – defined as the uninterrupted, sustainable supply of affordable commodities of accepted quality standards (Caines *et al.* 2004: 24). One strategy to achieve this is to secure sustained funding for such drugs and thereby create a long-term market, which will induce more producers to enter, thus encouraging competition and driving prices down. Given the close collaboration with the pharmaceutical industry, there were high hopes attached to GAVI's potential to drive down vaccine prices. But although the prices of some vaccines have fallen, the prices of GAVI vaccines have, in general, risen. This is partly because mature products tend to fall in price, and since the strategy of GAVI has been to focus on new vaccines, they are almost per definition not mature.[9] Moreover, GAVI decided to purchase combination vaccines rather than monovalent vaccines in response to receiving countries' requests. Another important reason for the price increase of the GAVI vaccines is that GlaxoSmithKline holds a patent on two combination vaccines.[10] As a result, the total cost of immunizing a child has risen (Kaddar *et al.* 2004).

A second issue is whether the industry has deviated from its normal practice and devoted resources to the development of products for which there is a need but not necessarily a market. For the industry, R&D partnerships are among the most demanding ways in which to participate in PPPs, as they may require that companies commit to long-term involvement and take a significant amount of risk. GAVI has so far not had much success in making the industry take on such risk. Indeed, it is interesting to note that although GAVI emphasizes partnerships with industry in most of its operations, until recently the R&D efforts undertaken under GAVI have not involved industry directly. Moreover, GAVI's efforts are focused not on discovery, but on the less demanding and less risky process of making already available drugs suitable for the Third World (Nwaka and Ridley 2003). After finalizing the work of the R&D task force in 2003, the board decided to open the window of the Vaccine Fund for R&D on two of the selected diseases: rotavirus and pneumococcal disease. The strategy is to work with multinational firms that already hold late-stage products ('picking the low hanging fruits'), through implementing the Accelerated Development and Introduction Plan (ADIP) – a comprehensive plan to speed up the introduction of an almost finished product. The aim was to avoid what happened with, for example, the HepB vaccine, which took 10 years to bring from development to common use. The board gave US$ 30 million over five years to support the development of these vaccines. However, so far these efforts have not resulted in any new vaccines.

In 2007, a new mechanism to accelerate product development was launched, administered by GAVI, which more directly involves business. The so-called Advance Market Commitment (AMC) is a 'pull mechanism' that aims to encourage pharmaceutical companies to set off resources to develop vaccines for developing countries. Companies that are interested may enter into a contract with the AMC board and when the vaccine is ready for the market it will be guaranteed a subsidy that makes up for the low purchasing power in the intended markets. The first pilot-AMC is for an improved pneumococcal vaccine for which a subsidy of US$3 billion is promised. However, as this is an existing vaccine on which the two companies that got the contract (Whyeth and GlaxoSmithCline) already make good money, the companies take no significant risk. Thus the pilot is not really an AMC but rather a huge subsidy of 'big pharma'. Moreover, GAVI has set an extraordinarily generous price on the vaccine. Whereas internationally renowned experts have estimated the price to be between 1 and 2 US$, GAVI pays the companies USD 5 (Light 2007; Farlow *et al.* 2005). The main reason for choosing this was suggested to be that the donors needed a quick success story in order not to lose the interest of Gates.[11]

Thus, vaccine experts who for decades have worked on how to raise vaccination rates experience that when this has finally happened it has occurred simultaneously to an increased commercialization and corporate control over vaccine initiatives (Hardon and Blume 2005).

However, that does not mean that the big pharmaceutical companies have learned nothing from participating in multilateral initiatives. From interviews we received mixed messages. On the one hand, it is emphasized that the big pharmaceutical companies have not changed much in terms of their basic orientation. On the other hand, it is reported that participation in PPPs has improved their understanding of the constraints faced by the multilateral institutions in their work, for example the weaknesses of developing country health systems that constitute a major impediment to effectiveness in disease prevention, cure and care.

In sum, how is GAVI an example of 'market multilateralism'? It was initiated by a multiple set of actors but, particularly, Bill Gates and executive heads of multilateral organizations played key roles. The governing structure of GAVI includes non-state actors as well as governments. Regarding the outcome, we do not find a shift among the for-profit actors involved towards an altruistic promotion of 'health for all'; but nor are the PPPs simply assemblies of self-interested actors seeking maximum benefit. Rather, we are witnessing a process in which some mutual learning does occur, and where some shared norms of collaborative behavior are emerging. This process involves a degree of convergence: the multilateral system (including PPPs) is increasingly operating according to the logic of the large corporations, while in the pharmaceutical companies there are instances of behavior that is not solely oriented towards short-term profit. Nevertheless, the basic rules of the game are still set by profit motives and the interests of the large corporations.

UNESCO between FOSS and Microsoft

The UNESCO–Microsoft partnership differs from GAVI on most accounts. Whereas GAVI is a broad partnership that spans many of the categories listed in Table 9.1, the UNESCO–Microsoft partnership is essentially an operational partnership focusing on technical and equipment contributions from Microsoft. Unlike GAVI, which is singled out as a separate entity, the UNESCO–Microsoft partnership is located in UNESCO proper. Furthermore, it is a much more limited partnership in terms of funding and scope and, perhaps most importantly, the main private sector partner is a corporation, not a foundation, although, ironically, the key figure is the same person: Bill Gates.

However, the UNESCO–Microsoft partnership shares some main features with GAVI and provides yet another illustration of 'market multilateralism'.

The background for the agreement was a strategic shift agreed in intergovernmental processes, but yet the initiative was taken by the combined effort of corporate heads and leaders of a multilateral organization. Until the mid 1990s, UNESCO was among the UN organizations that was least inclined to collaborate with the private sector (Coate 1992). When the strategy changed, it was due to: first, the withdrawal of the United States from the organization in 1984, which contributed to a slump in funding and no growth in the regular budget between the mid 1980s and 2005; and second, the challenges raised by the ICT revolution. The glaring inequalities in access to computers and software across the world came to be seen not only as a problem in itself, but also as an impediment to reaching many of UNESCO's other goals, among them 'education for all'. In response to this, the UN Secretary General's office launched an ICT Task Force in 2001. From the start, the ICT task force focused on partnerships with the private sector as a means to bridge the digital divide. As argued by Kofi Annan: "Fortunately, the use of ICT for development is one of the areas where the long-term interests of the international community, governments and private business most obviously coincide [...] Private companies can, in short, 'do well by doing good' ".[12] When the United States rejoined UNESCO in 2003, it made it clear that it intended to strongly encourage partnerships with the private sector. The increasingly 'business-friendly' rhetoric employed by Director General Kolchiro Matsuura[13] was viewed by many as serving to facilitate the smooth return of the United States.

Thus, UNESCO increasingly sought agreements with corporations. However, the process leading to the signing of the Microsoft agreement began with a contact between Microsoft and a UNESCO field officer in Cairo. The process quickly reached the Director-General's office, which contacted the Information and Communication (IC) department in order to give the agreement content. Only towards the end of this rapid process was the Private Sector Department involved. And, in spite of the fact that the majority of the components of the agreement relate to education, the education sector was not consulted at all.[14]

Thus, in accordance with our definition of 'market multilateralism', the process leading up to the agreement included mainly a multilateral organization's executive heads and private sector representatives. But how about its content and impact? Did it involve norm-governed behavior by the private sector? Did it make business contribute to the goals of UNESCO? Or rather, did it move UNESCO further towards the interests of key market actors?

Looking first at the formal agreement, this has broad objectives that were generally in accordance with UNESCO's 2002–7 Medium-Term Strategy (UNESCO 2002). The agreement listed a number of 'areas of collaboration', but the concrete activities mentioned were for the most part limited to existing projects initiated in the context of Microsoft's own corporate social responsibility (CSR) program, and in which it is relatively unclear what role UNESCO was to play. The only three projects that were not pre-existing parts of Microsoft's CSR program were pre-existing UNESCO projects – mostly in education – to which Microsoft should contribute with technology. Microsoft also made some financial contributions, but the total sum stipulated did not exceed US$ 200,000.

Thus, Microsoft's contribution in concrete terms to reaching UNESCO's goals is modest, and in financial terms it is negligible.[15] Yet, the agreement may still have significant effects. One of those is that significantly more emphasis is put on ICT in education than what is stipulated in UNESCO's program. More importantly, the agreement signifies a shift of strategy related to Free and Open Source Software (FOSS), which challenges the near-monopoly of Microsoft's Windows operating system and compatible software.[16] Unlike the World Trade Organization (WTO) and the World Intellectual Property Rights Organization (WIPO), UNESCO has for a long time been viewed as a supporter of FOSS.[17] UNESCO started to lend its support to the FOSS in 2001 as a part of the ICT for development agenda (ICT4D) and the efforts to promote 'knowledge societies'. From 2001, UNESCO hosted a free software internet portal,[18] facilitated the development of key software tools for processing information, and promoted their utilization. The leader of the IC department, Philippe Quéau, was a high-profile defender of knowledge and information literacy as a public good, and had on several occasions criticized the patent protection regime for software products (Quéau 2000, 2002).

The FOSS community was therefore highly critical when UNESCO signed the partnership with Microsoft (Da Silveira *et al.* 2005), a short time after Quéau had been reassigned to the Moscow office and replaced with a leader with experience from the corporate sector. The agreement does not exclude the use of FOSS in UNESCO projects or inhibit it from supporting a FOSS initiative (UNESCO 2005a: 2). However, it is clear that the Microsoft partnership will weaken UNESCO's role as a staunch defender of FOSS as a tool to bridge the digital divide.

Thus, to a significant extent, the content of the agreement is in accordance with the interest of one of the world's largest corporations, Microsoft. In interviews, furthermore, it was made clear that adjustments were made in the way in which UNESCO was operating in order to accommodate the interests of the corporations. The introduction of resource-based management and monitoring (Medium Term Strategy 31/C4 – UNESCO 2002), and the conscious 'mimicking' of the private sector, had rendered the organizational culture of UNESCO more similar to that of their private partners.

Conclusion

The increasing role of business as a partner to multilateral organizations is one aspect of a significant process of change in the multilateral system. This raises theoretical as well as normative questions, and we have suggested the term 'market multilateralism' to describe the functioning of this system.

However, some words of caution are in place. First, the conclusions reached here emerge out of a study of development issues. 'Market multilateralism' does not claim to be equally fit as a description of security-related activities by the United Nations. Although private companies are also increasingly included in security operations, the decision-making process in security may be significantly different from the ones sketched above. Second, by pointing to the way corporations influence the system I do not suggest that the states are no longer the key actors. The argument is rather that the multilateral system's formal, hierarchical way of operating is complemented by other structures that involve non-state actors and governments in new ways. For example, the executive heads of multilateral organizations are frequently former governmental representatives. However, they influence the PPPs not on the basis of their legitimacy as heads of state, but rather on the basis of their networks and expertise. Third, I do not claim that the multilateral institutions always accommodate the interests of corporations. Rather, I argue that there is some mutual learning and the emergence of norms. However, there are also certain boundaries for the operations by the new PPPs.

Analyzing PPPs from a perspective of multilateralism is important in several ways. First, it requires us to analyze the PPPs within a broader context of ideological and material changes. The emergence of PPPs in some parts of the multilateral system cannot be understood without also taking into account developments in the global framework for the market established in other parts of the multilateral system (e.g., TRIPs of the WTO, WIPO, etc.). Moreover, it must be understood on the background of ideological changes favoring the private sector modes of operation (e.g., new management models) and policy changes at the domestic level. However, this framework also leads us to focus on the multilateral organizations as actors that may get the most out of the context in which they are operating in order to reach their goals.

Returning then to the issue of legitimacy: how may the legitimacy of the multilateral institutions be affected by the emergence of market multilateralism? It is difficult to measure legitimacy, particularly in the three alternative forms suggested here. However, it is plausible to argue that as long as the PPPs achieve their stated goals, and that the goals are legitimate, corporate multilateralism will not have a major impact on the legitimacy of the multilateral institutions. UNESCO was for a long time generally considered to be among the most bureaucratic and least efficient of the UN organizations, suffering from an unclear mandate, political conflicts and almost constant US opposition. In spite of having formal-legal and democratic legitimacy, its legitimacy was nevertheless constantly questioned. With the Microsoft agreement, UNESCO's legitimacy has waned in the eyes of the FOSS community, but if it makes progress in its pursuit of bridging the digital divide it may still achieve greater legitimacy. Regarding the GAVI and the multilateral institutions in health, the picture is more complex. GAVI has made strong progress in accelerating vaccination rates. However, since GAVI is not a part of any multilateral organization (although physically hosted by UNICEF), it is not obvious how that will reflect on the legitimacy of the multilateral system. What seems clear by now is that the deep involvement by large corporations and the relatively generous deals that GAVI grants them is not going to take away the legitimacy gained through goal achievement and expertise, a matter which explains the lack of public attention to the revelations of huge amounts of donor funds going straight into the already well filled coffers of 'big pharma' through the AMC.

Notes

1 The paper is based on a book on the same topic by Bull and McNeill (2007).
2 The case studies are described in further detail in Bull and McNeill (2007). The method employed was qualitative: it included the study of documents and extensive interviews with officials of the multilateral organizations and their partners conducted in New York, Geneva, Paris and Washington.
3 For accounts of these concepts, see Reinecke and Deng (2000); Witte and Reinecke (2005).
4 http://www.un.org/partners/business/otherpages/guide.htm.
5 The term 'indivisibility' derives from the theorizing of security communities and refers to the understanding that an action against one partner is an action against everybody. The term 'diffuse reciprocity' is based on Keohane (1989, ch. 6) and refers to the giving of something without a specific expectation of what is to be returned.
6 Bäckstrand (2007) also employs this term, but without actually defining it.
7 A multilateral organization is a formal organizational entity, characterized by a permanent location and postal address, distinct headquarters, staff and secretariat. This differs from a multilateral *institution*, which is more broadly interpreted to include also associated rules and practices.
8 http://www.gavialliance.org/resources/Total_Contributions_1999_June_2007_2.xls
9 The monovalent Hepatitis B is a mature product, and the prices have decreased significantly over the last years and are expected to continue to fall. However, the prices of Hib vaccines have remained high and the price of Yellow Fever vaccine has increased (from $0.34 in 2002 to $0.80 in 2004, with a forecast of $0.97 in 2006 [Fife 2003; UNICEF 2004, 2005]). Some of the price increase was due to a change in vial size.
10 To give the new vaccines in combination with the traditional DTP vaccine would minimize the extra burden on the health systems. Two new vaccines – DTP+HepB and DTP−Hep3+Hib – were made available especially to GAVI. These are significantly more expensive than the monovalent vaccines and prices are increasing: DTP-HepB was available at $1.10 in 2001, and was forecast to increase to $1,25 in 2005. The comparable prices for DTP−HepB+Hib were $3.50, $3.65 and $3.60 (Fife 2003, UNICEF 2004, 2005).
11 Roy Widdus, former Manager of IPPPH in Aftenposten, 3 March 2008.
12 UN Secretary General, Kofi Annan, speech at the launching of the ICT Task Force, 20 November 2001.
13 See e.g. UNESCO (2003).
14 This description is based on interviews with officials of several different offices in UNESCO.
15 According to UNESCO, the lack of mention of money in the agreement was due to Microsoft's preference to avoid expressions of collaboration in terms of funding levels in order to avoid common accusations that they buy their partners (UNESCO 2005b).
16 The fact that a program is based on FOSS does not necessarily mean that it does not cost anything. However, it comes with many benefits compared to licensed software for poor countries. See (http://www.fsf.org).
17 Interview with Frédérique Couchet, President, Free Software Foundation (FSF), France, and Benôit Sibaud, President, L'Association pour la Promotion et la Recherche en Informatique Libre (APRIL), Paris, 7 June 2005.
18 http://portal.unesco.org/ci/en/ev.php-URL_ID=12034&URL_DO=DO_TOPIC& URL_SECTION=201.html

References

Bäckstrand, K. (2007) 'Accountability of Networked Climate Governance: The Rise of Transnational Climate Partnerships', paper presented to the Amsterdam Conference on Earth System Governance, May 24–26, 2007.

Bøås, M. and McNeill, D. (ed.) (2004) *Global Institutions and Development: Framing the world?* London and New York: Routledge.

Börzel, T. and Risse, T. (2005) 'Public–Private Partnerships: Effective and Legitimate Tools of Transnational Governance?', in E. Grande and L.W. Pauly (eds) *Complex Sovereignty: Reconstituting Political Authority in the Twenty-first Century*, Toronto: University of Toronto Press, pp. 195–216.

Broadwater, I. and Kaul, I. (2005) Global Public–Private Partnerships: The Current Landscape, prepared for the Book Project: The New Public Finance: Responding to Global Challenges: New York: UNDP, February 2005. Online. Available HTTP: <http://www.thenewpublicfinance.org/background/current_landscape.pdf>, accessed 19 June 2009.

Bull, B., Bøås, M. and McNeill, D. (2004) 'Private Sector Influence in the Multilateral System: a Changing Structure of World Governance?', *Global Governance*, 10(4): 481–498.

Bull, B. and McNeill, D. (2007) *Development Issues in Global Governance: Public–Private Partnerships and Market Multilateralism*, London and New York: Routledge.

Caines, K., Buse, K., Carlson, C., Druc, N., Grace, C., Pearson, M., Sancho, J. and Sadanandan, R. (2004) *Assessing the Impact of Global Health Partnerships*, London: DFID Health Resource Centre.

Coate, R. (1992) 'Changing Patterns of Conflict: The United States and UNESCO', in M.P. Karns and K.A. Mingst (ed.) *The Untied States and Multilateral Institutions*, Merson Center Series on International Security and Foreign Policy, Volume V, London and New York: Routledge.

Cox, R.W. (1969) 'The executive head: an essay on leadership in international organization', reprinted in R.W. Cox with T.J. Sinclair (1996), *Approaches to world order*, Cambridge: Cambridge University Press.

—— (1983) 'Gramsci, hegemony, and international relations: an essay in method', reprinted in R.W. Cox with T.J. Sinclair (1996), *Approaches to world order*, Cambridge: Cambridge University Press.

—— (1992) 'Multilateralism and world order', reprinted in R.W. Cox with T.J. Sinclair (1996), *Approaches to world order*, Cambridge: Cambridge University Press.

Da Silveira, S., Sibaud, B. and Couchet, F. (2005) 'Bill Gates à la conquête du Sud, Liberación', 5 January 2005, Online. Available at HTTP <http://www.liberation.fr/page.php?Article=265884> Accessed 10.12.2008.

Farlow, A., Light D., Mahoney, R.T. and Widdus, R. (2005), 'Concerns regarding the Center for Global Development report *"Making Markets for Vaccines"*' Submission to: Commission on Intellectual Property Rights, Innovation and Public Health, WHO, 29 April 2005.

Fife, P.R. (2003) 'The Vaccine Provision Project (VPP): Lessons Learned from the Pilot Phase', July 03–October 03, GAVI.

Finnemore, M. (1997) 'Redefining Development at the World Bank'. in F. Cooper and R. Packard (eds) *International Development and the Social Sciences. Essays on the History and Politics of Knowledge*, Berkeley: University of California Press.

Foundation Center, The (2004) *Foundation Growth and Giving Estimates*, New York: The Foundation Center.

—— (2005), Top 100 U.S. Foundations by Asset Size. Online. Available HTTP: <http://fdncenter.org/research/trends_analysis/top100assets.html> Accessed 19.6.2009.

Gutner, T. (2005) Explaining the gaps between Mandate and Performance: Agency Theory and World Bank Environmental Reform, *Global Environmental Politics*, 5:2, May, pp. 10–37.

Hardon, A. and Blume, S. (2005), Shifts in global immunisation goals (1984–2004): unfinished agendas and mixed results, *Social science & medicine*, 60(2), pp. 345–56.

Harrod, J. (2006), 'The Century of the Corporation', in C. May (ed.) *Global Corporate Power*, International Political Economy Yearbook, Vol. 15, Boulder and London: Lynne Rienner Publishers, pp. 23–46.

Hummel, H. (2005), The United Nations and Transnational Corporations', paper for the conference 'Global Governance and the Power of Business', Dec. 8–10, 2005, Wittenberg, Germany.

Hurd, I. (1999) 'Legitimacy and authority in international politics, *International Organization*, 53(2): 379–408.

Ikenberry, G.J. (2003) 'Is American Multilateralism in Decline?', *Perspectives on Politics*, 30(1): 533–50.

Jönsson, C. 'An Interorganization Approach to the Study of Multilateral Institutions: Lessons from Previous Research on International Cooperation', Research Programme on Multilateral Development Assistance, Fridtjof Nansen Institute, Oslo, working paper no. 1, 1995.

Kaddar, M., Lydon, P. and Levine, R. (2004) 'Financial challenges of immunization: a look at GAVI', *Bulletin of the World Health Organization*, 82(9): 697–702.

Keohane, R.O. (1989) *International Institutions and State Power: Essays in International Relations Theory*, Boulder, San Francisco and London: Westview Press.

Light, D. (2007) 'Is G8 putting profits before the world's poorest children?' *The Lancet*, vol. 370, July 28, pp. 297–98.

Martens, K. (2007) 'Multistakeholder Partnerships – Future Models of Multilateralism?' *Dialogue on Globalization, Occasional Papers*, No. 29, January, Berlin: Friedrich Ebert Stiftung.

May, C. (2005) 'Intellectual Property Rights', in D. Kelly and W. Grant (eds), *The Politics of International Trade in the Twenty-First Century: Actors, Issues and Regional Dynamics*, International Political Economy Series, Houndmills, Basingstoke, Hampshire and London: Palgrave Macmillan.

Mouritzen, H (1990) *The International Civil Service. A Study of Bureaucracy: International Organizations*, Aldershot UK: Dartmouth Publishing Company, pp. 150.

Muraskin, W. (1998) *The Politics of International Health: The Children's Vaccine Initiative and the Struggle to Develop Vaccines for the Third World*, New York: State University of New York Press.

Mytelka, L.K. and Delapierre, M. (1999)' Strategic Partnerships, Knowledge-Based Networked Oligopolies, and the State', in A.C. Cutler, V. Haufler and T. Porter, *Private authority in international affairs*, New York: New York State University Press.

Nwaka, S. and Ridley, R.G. (2003) 'Virtual drug discovery and development for neglected diseases through public–private partnerships', *Nature Reviews*, 2, November, 919–28.

O'Brian, R., Goetz, A.M., Scholte, J.A. and Williams, M. (2000) *Contesting Global Governance: Multilateral Economic Institutions and Global Social Movements*, Cambridge: Cambridge University Press.

Quéau, P. (2000) 'Defining the World's Public Property: Who owns knowledge?' *Le Monde Diplomatique*, January.

—— (2002) 'La formation à l'informatión: un bien publique mundial', online. Available at HTTP: <http://www.nclis.gov/libinter/infolitconf&meet/papers/queau-francaisefullpaper.pdf> Accessed 10.12.2008.

—— and Deng, F. (2000) *Critical Choices: The United Nations, Networks, and the Future of Global Governance*, Ottawa: International Development Research Centre.

Richter, J. (2002) 'Codes in Context: TNC Regulation in an Era of Dialogues and Partnerships', *The Corner House Briefing* 26. Online. Available HTTP: <www.thecornerhouse.org.uk/pdf/briefing/26codes.pdf> Accessed 19.6.2009.

Ruggie, J.G. (1982) 'International Regime, Transactions, and Change: embedded Liberalism in the Postwar Economic Order', *International Organization*, 36, Spring: 379–415.

—— (1993) 'Multilateralism: The Anatomy of an Institution', in J.G. Ruggie (ed.) *Multilateralism Matters: The Theory and Praxis of an Institutional Form*, New York: Columbia University Press.

—— (1997) 'Globalization and the Embedded Liberalism Compromise: The End of an Era?' Max Planck Institute for the Study of Societies, Working Paper 97/1, January 1997, online, available HTTP: http://www.ciaonet.org/wps/ruj01.

—— (2004) 'Reconstituting the Global Public Domain – Issues, Actors, and Practices', *European Journal of International Relations*, 10(4): 499–531.

Sander, A. and Widdus, R. (2004) 'The emerging landscape of public–private partnerships for product development', Paper prepared for the workshop of the Initiative on Public–Private Partnerships for Health 'Combating Diseases Associated with Poverty: Financing Strategies for Product Development and the Potential Role of Public–Private Partnerships, London, 15–16 April 2004.

Stone, D. (ed.) (2000) *Banking on Knowledge: the Genesis of the Global Development Network*, London: Routledge.

Tesner, S. with Kell, G. (2000) *The United Nations and Business: A Partnership Recovered*, New York: St. Martin's Press.

UN General Assembly (2003) 'Enhanced cooperation between the United Nations and all relevant partners, in particular the private sector', Report of the Secretary-General, A/58/227, United Nations General Assembly.

—— (2005) 'Enhanced cooperation between the United Nations and all relevant partners, in particular the private sector', Report of the Secretary-General, A/60/214, United Nations General Assembly.

UNESCO—— 'Medium-Term Strategy 2002-2007', 31C/4

—— (2003) 'Introduction by the Director General to the Debate on Items 3.1 and 3.2', Executive Board, 167 EX/INF.7, Paris, 16 September 2003.

—— (2005a) 'UNESCO's Position on Free and Open Source Software (FOSS)', Briefing Notes & Frequently Asked Questions, The CI Sector, UNESCO, April 2005.

—— (2005b) 'Cooperation Agreement Between UNESCO & Microsoft', Briefing Notes & Frequently Asked Questions, The CI Sector, UNESCO, February 2005.

UNICEF (2004) *Vaccine projections 2004*. Online. Available HTTP: <http://www.unicef.org/supply/index_7991.html>

—— (2005) *Vaccine projections 2005*. Online. Available HTTP: http://www.unicef.org/supply/index_7991.html Accessed 19.6.2009.

Utting, P and Zammit, A. (2006), *Beyond Pragmatism: Appraising UN–Business Partnerships*, Geneva: UNRISD (Program on Markets, Business and Regulation, Paper No. 1).

Witte, J.M. and Reinicke, W. (2005) 'Business Unusual: Facilitating United Nations Report Through Partnerships', Report commissioned by the United Nations.

World Health Organization (2000) 'Global Alliance for Vaccines and Immunization. Report by the Secretariat', EB {105/43}, 25 January 2000.

Zammit, A. (2003) *Development at Risk: Rethinking UN–Business Partnerships*, Geneva: South Centre and UNRISD.

10 ISO and the success of regulation through voluntary consensus[1]

Craig N. Murphy and JoAnne Yates

Current efforts at mobilizing business as a partner in global governance often rely on voluntary consensus standard setting. This institution has a long history that began before 1900 with efforts by engineers to set industrial standards. Because this process is now migrating to other areas, including environmental governance and norms for corporate social responsibility, it is of interest to ask "Why has this process proven so successful?" Our answer combines two strands of theory. One is concerned with the nature of the knowledge community and social movement of "standardizers," a focus that leads us to adopt some of Pierre Bourdieu's concepts. A second set of theories helps us see members of that social movement as leaders who help competing companies and sectors overcome impediments to strategic cooperation and collaboration.

Our empirical focus is the International Organization for Standardization (usually just called "ISO," which is often treated as a word, not as an acronym), which stands at the apex of a global network of agencies involved in voluntary consensus standard setting. ISO is a non-governmental organization composed of national standard-setting bodies, some of which are entirely public, some are private, and some are mixed. ISO produces standards for business and has strong business participation in all of its work. For both of these reasons, ISO's voluntary consensus standard setting is unusually relevant for business and for global governance, especially because ISO has begun to take on standard setting in fields that are central to most firms, including quality management and corporate social responsibility.

Champions of voluntary consensus standard setting have long believed that its openness, as well as its aim of achieving solutions that are "scientific" or "technical" rather than "political," assures the legitimacy of the resulting standards and, hence, their widespread adoption. The Fabian social theorists Sidney and Beatrice Webb (1920: 56) wrote that it was "impossible to over-rate the importance in the control of industry of this silent but all-pervading determination of processes." They hoped for the "further development" of such organizations in "the public service." More recently, the World Bank's Vice President for Europe published a lively book that called for solving the world's twenty most urgent global problems, from global warming to falling labor standards, by applying ISO's voluntary consensus process (Rischard 2002).

ISO has, in fact, taken on some of the tasks that have proven too difficult for governments or the UN. These include environmental regulation (where the voluntary ISO standard, ISO 14000, may have had more impact than any of the UN-sponsored agreements of the 1990s), and questions of corporate responsibility for human rights (including core labor rights), where the new ISO 26000 could prove more successful than the UN-sponsored Global Compact.

Our primary concern here is with how and why the ISO process "works," how it creates standards that are widely adopted and enforced. ISO's insistence on the *voluntary* nature of its standards – for example, the ISO website states that, *"ISO itself does not regulate or legislate"* (ISO 2009a) – obscures a more complex reality of an organization that has grown to play a central role in global governance. This chapter introduces ISO's history and current operations before offering a preliminary theory of the process and the impact – the "how" and the "so what" – of voluntary consensus standard setting.

Gaining capacity, building a world market, and expanding scope

ISO was formed immediately after the Second World War, which had highlighted the need for greater international standardization; differences between British and American standards for screw threads alone had added at least £25 million to the cost of the war (UNSCC 1945). Many of those who created ISO lived to see it develop the capacity to be the global standard setter that they had imagined. That major transition, which allowed ISO to help build a world market, took place between 1964 and 1986, a period that coincides with the predominance within the organization of a Swedish standard setter, Olle Sturén, who chaired the committee that systematically redirected ISO's work in the mid-1960s and then served as the organization's chief from 1969 through 1986. After Sturén's retirement, ISO continued to grow and to expand the scope of its activities into fields far removed from the nuts and bolts work of its origin.

Gaining capacity, 1947–64

In 1964, ISO was largely a European organization. Although its membership consisted of national standard-setting bodies throughout the world, fewer than half of these bodies, almost all of them from Europe, participated in large numbers of ISO's technical committees, the groups that set standards. If we consider those that contributed the most staff, this picture is even clearer. ISO relies upon its member organizations to provide the secretariats of the different committees. Taken together, just two bodies, BSI (the British Standards Institution) and the French standards association (AFNOR) provided almost half (92 of 227) of the secretariats of the technical committees and their subcommittees; other Western European countries took on tasks equally disproportionate to their populations (ISO 1964).

In 1958, a relatively young Olle Sturén – who at 38 had just become head of the Swedish Standards Institute (SIS) – wrote that Western Europe had a much greater interest in having global standards than the US or Eastern Europe did because, unlike them, Western Europeans had to sell to global markets (Sturén 1958: 161). In 1969, shortly after he became ISO Secretary General, Sturén looked back and concluded that ISO had done much of global significance under Western Europe's special tutelage. The organization had finally established a globally accepted common terminology of measurements and nomenclature as well as common ways of testing different basic materials, including steel, cement, and plastics. Problems of mechanical incompatibilities were becoming a thing of the past (Sturén 1969).

Building a world market, 1964–86

Nevertheless, by 1969, there was a much larger agenda that Sturén knew well. He had first became heavily involved in ISO in 1964, when he was asked to chair a study group to respond to a challenge laid down by the Dutch standardizers who were convinced that the world economy was about to enter a new phase, what we would now call the phase of "globalization." Political nationalism and even economic nationalism might exist for many generations, but, as Sturén (1969: 13) put it, "[O]ne must face the fact that industrial nationalism is about to disappear." Sturén's group was concerned with three key responsibilities. They were to figure out how ISO could (1) stop the duplication of effort – there was no reason for the Dutch to create a standard for plastic milk bottles if one had already been created by the Swiss; (2) reduce the time needed to create standards in new technological fields; and (3) cooperate more effectively with the European Economic Community, with increasingly vocal consumer groups, with the UN agencies that were promoting industrialization throughout the world, and with the GATT (the General Agreement on Tariffs and Trade), which was rapidly creating a global market in industrial goods. The group's recommendations about these topics became ISO's agenda for the next two decades.

By 1980, most of the duplication among national standards bodies had been eliminated. In fact, by the 1980s, most of the time and effort expended by many of the most active national bodies were directed toward the development of global standards, and many "national" or "European" standards were simply word-for-word adoptions of ISO documents (Sturén 1984). Also, by the early 1980s, ISO had developed very close relations with the UN, which often provided technical assistance for the establishment of national standards bodies. In the 1970s and 1980s, ISO also developed a close working relationship with the GATT. In 1979, in an effort to reduce non-tariff barriers to trade, GATT adopted a standards code that required its members to rely on international standards as the basis for their own technical regulations. This change did not necessarily mean that ISO standards automatically had the force of international law, but it did mean that GATT members had to develop very strong arguments if they did not adopt those standards as their own (Sturén 1980).

Many accounts of ISO during this second period – this era of building a world market – emphasize the organization's role in standardizing the physical infrastructure of today's global economy, especially ISO's impact on containerized shipping (Murphy and Yates 2009: 46–67). It was during this second era that ISO began affecting almost every sector of the global economy. The steady growth in ISO standards that began in the late 1960s tells part of the story, but, late in life, Sturén (1997) focused on two other facts in looking back. The first was that by 1977 ISO had gained the "de facto monopoly" on setting international industrial standards in almost all industrial sectors that it still has today. Second, and more significantly in Sturén's mind, most new industrial standards developed since 1980 had been international standards.

Expanding scope, 1987–2008

In the most recent era, the one that began in the late 1980s, ISO has entered new realms. It has come to play a major role in setting standards for quality management and extending their application into environmental fields and into the general field of corporate social responsibility. Today, ISO's webpage seems to define the organization as focusing on these topics. At the beginning of 2008, when the page still wished visitors "A Very Happy and Prosperous New Year," its three "Latest news" stories were about improving the quality of water services to consumers, fighting climate change, and improving quality management in the international oil and gas industries. Only ISO 9000 (the quality management standard), ISO 14000 (the environmental standard), and the still-to-be-finalized ISO 26000 on social responsibility (of ISO's more than 25,000 standards or standards-in-development) had direct links from the home page.

This new ISO has its roots in the second era. In Sturén's first address as Secretary General, in 1969, he insisted, "ISO should take on work on water and air pollution, and noise levels, without delay" (Sturén 1969) and the standard that would become ISO 9000 was already fully formulated by the late 1970s (Murphy and Yates 2009: 72–73).

ISO's current structure and operations

ISO (2009a) calls itself "a nongovernmental organization [NGO] that *forms a bridge between the public and private sectors* ... [M]any of its member[s] ... are part of the governmental structure of their countries ... [O]ther members have their roots uniquely in the private sector, having been set up by national partnerships of industry associations." About two-thirds of ISO's member organizations are part of their country's central government; the rest are private bodies.

ISO conducts almost all of its work through technical committees that focus on specific topics. Each of its about 230 committees and 500 subcommittees has a rotating secretariat provided by one of the ISO member bodies. The committees conduct much of their discussion electronically and, when they meet face-to-face, they usually do so only for a day or two at a time. In 2008, about one-third of

ISO's technical committees and sub-committees met in more than 90 cities spread across 34 countries and six continents (Murphy and Yates 2009: 25).

A 150-person secretariat in Geneva serves the large committee structure; the secretariat is much smaller than those of most of the UN Specialized Agencies based in the same city. Nonetheless, the vastness and complexity of ISO's decentralized structure means that the number of people actively working on establishing new international agreements throughout the ISO network is probably larger than the staff of the entire UN system.

ISO has 158 national standard-setting bodies, spread across the world, as members. Of these, about 35 unusually active members, which may be designated major member bodies, each take part in hundreds of different technical committees and their subcommittees. Together, this group provides almost all the secretariats. About twice as many member bodies, around 70 of the remaining 123, are more selectively active; they each take part in the limited number of technical committees that affect the economic sectors in which their country is the most involved. The remaining members are only marginally active.

Many of the regular members of ISO are organized in the same way that ISO is: they are organizations of organizations. Even some national bodies that are part of their central governments are organized this way. The standard-setting bodies at all levels tend to work in the same way: They bring together representatives of their members to work toward consensus on documents (literally, these documents *are* "standards") that define specific qualities of products (such as the sizes of nuts and bolts), services, or business practices. The aim is to provide standards that will be widely and *voluntarily* adopted by organizations that produce the specific product or service or engage in the specific business practice.

Most standard-setting bodies do their work through those "technical committees" that focus on a particular range of products, services, or practices. Many of the committees meet over many years, not only to set standards but to amend them as conditions change. The oldest of ISO's technical committees (TC-1 Screw threads) continues the work of groups that had been meeting for decades before ISO's formation. The most active of ISO's technical committees, JTC-1 Information technology, is a committee run jointly with the International Electrotechnical Commission (IEC); JTC-1 has published more than 2100 standards, more than twice the number of any other committee (ISO 2009b).

ISO's technical committees are made up of "national delegations" recruited by the member body. Each delegation is expected to include experts on the technology in question and to be broadly representative of a host of stakeholders: (1) industry and trade associations; (2) science and academia; (3) national governments and their regulatory agencies; and (4) relevant NGOs such as environmental groups.

ISO rules require each national delegation "to take account of the views of the range of parties interested in the standard under development [and] ... present a consolidated, national consensus position to the technical committee" (ISO 2009c). Within ISO technical committees, then, each national delegation must, in theory, come to a consensus and vote as a whole. In fact, because the committee as a whole also operates on consensus, at any point before the end of the discussion there are likely to be disagreements *within* national delegations and strong agreements among some members *across* delegations from different countries even when the official positions of their countries are at odds. Sturén, the longest-serving ISO Secretary General, often found the inability of national delegates to agree among themselves to be particularly vexing, especially when the issue was something as important as the size of freight containers or protocols for the electronic transfer of data (Sturén 1997).

Specific "consensus" rules differ a bit from one standard-setting body to the next, but the underlying principle is always the same. Harland Cleveland (2000: 55), a public administration expert who advocates using ISO methods to tackle a host of international problems, summarizes the norm: "Consensus" usually means "the acquiescence of those who care [about a particular decision] supported by the apathy of those who don't." ISO has a one-country, one-vote system. Two-thirds of the member bodies participating in a technical committee must vote in favor to send a draft standard forward. Under current rules, two-thirds of the member bodies participating in the committee must approve a standard and no more than one-quarter may actively oppose it.

Adherence to the standards published by ISO and similar bodies is officially voluntary, and that is the most important meaning of the word in the phrase "voluntary consensus standards." However, there are also important ways in which the work of the technical committees is "voluntary."

ISO's Central Secretariat neither organizes nor pays for all the management and record keeping that is necessary to maintain the hundreds of technical committees and subcommittees. Instead, different member organizations volunteer to act as the secretariats for specific committees or subcommittees. The same practice is replicated down the nested hierarchy of standard-setting organizations; e.g., different national trade associations or professional societies volunteer to be the secretariats of technical committees organized by a national standard setter. In ISO, the most active member bodies rotate the burden of such work among themselves.

Sometimes a decision to take on the cost of maintaining a secretariat has to do largely with what a country (or its key industries) might gain or lose. Thus, it may not be surprising that the Swiss regularly provide the secretariat for TC-114 Horology, since Swiss clock- and watchmakers have a precarious dominance of the global industry.

On the other hand, often volunteering seems to be a consequence of a country's identity – less a question of "what we might gain" and more a question of "who we are." For example, in ISO's early years, Nehru's India – the "modern nation" that Nehru *defined* in terms of its commitment to science and industrial progress – took on three committees and four sub-committees, a commitment as great as that of many states in Europe (Murphy and Yates 2009: 31). More recently, the 2004 decision of the Swedish and Brazilian standards bodies to act as co-conveners of the working group on ISO 26000, the standard on corporate social responsibility, seems to have reflected convictions in both countries that their firms had a commitment to social responsibility (consider the unusually rapid embrace of the UN's Global Compact by Brazilian firms) as well as the long-standing commitment of Sweden to improved relations between the First and the Third Worlds, a major purpose of the standard (Sandberg 2006).

This aspect of the "volunteerism" in nongovernmental standard setting is similar to, and may be related to, the *noblesse oblige* that convinced different nineteenth-century monarchs to act as sponsors and benefactors of the first generation of global intergovernmental organizations, including the ITU (International Telegraph Union) and ILO (International Labor Organization), often without the active support of their governments (Murphy 1994: 56–62).

The final, and perhaps most important, voluntary element of the global voluntary consensus standard system is the involvement of those who serve on the technical committees. One estimate put the number of people engaged in 2000 as over 100,000, at a time when ISO's paid staff numbered only 163. By this estimate the volunteer group would have been about as large as the paid staff of all the organizations within the UN system, the UN proper, and all the UN Specialized Agencies including those of the World Bank, ILO, and ITU (Mattli and Tim Büthe 2003: 7; compare Besen and Saloner 1988).

A Council and an annual meeting of the member bodies oversee ISO. The meeting elects a president and two vice presidents and appoints 18 member bodies to the ISO Council, which acts as the organization's governing board and meets at least twice each year. The membership of the Council rotates, but it always includes the major national standard-setting bodies such as AFNOR (the Association Française de Normalisation), ANSI (the American National Standards Institute), and BSI (the British Standards Institution). Immediately after World War II, ISO's original members agreed to give long-term seats to the standards bodies of the same Big Five powers that had been made permanent, veto-wielding members of the UN Security Council. However, the engineers who created ISO, unlike the diplomats who created the UN, decided that it would be good to remember that nothing is permanent – especially the relative prowess of industrialized countries – so ISO has always had a mechanism for reviewing its list of quasi-permanent Council members.

The Council appoints a rotating treasurer (who helps the Board monitor the financial decisions of the professional staff) and a permanent Secretary General, who is actually responsible for the day-to-day operation of ISO. The Council is advised by standing committees on finance and on strategy (i.e. long-term planning) and by less permanent committees on policy development. In 2008, these included the Committee on Conformity Assessment (CASCO) and committees concerned with consumer policy and the developing countries. CASCO studies ways to assess the degree to which products, processes, services, and management systems conform to published standards.

The Council also is advised by a handful of "strategic and technical advisory groups" that deal with issues that involve coordination across industrial sectors or fields in which ISO's long-term role has not yet been determined. One recent example is the field of information security.

The various advisory groups and ISO's technical committees ostensibly report to the Council, but they do so via the Technical Management Board, TMB.

This board holds most of the agenda-setting power in ISO. The TMB's ten members always include the most influential of the standard-setting bodies, those that provide the secretariats for the most significant technical committees and those associated with the largest economies. In 2008, the members were AFNOR, ANSI, and BSI along with the standard-setting bodies of Brazil, Canada, China, Germany, Japan, the Netherlands, Norway, Spain, and South Africa. The TMB is chaired by one of ISO's rotating vice-presidents.

In 2005, Ziva Patir, who was chair of the TMB and Director General of the Standards Institution of Israel, explained that the TMB's purpose was to assure ISO's continued "global relevance" by entering new fields and by establishing working relationships with other standard setters who were also involved in the same areas. She pointed to seven fields in which ISO was beginning to focus aggressively: (1) security; (2) social responsibility; (3) management systems; (4) food safety; (5) tourism; (6) nanotechnology; and (7) second-hand goods (Patir 2005).

This is a grab bag of issues. Some are on the global agenda due to the concerns of consumers (food safety) and progressive NGOs (social responsibility). One item on the list is a fundamentally new industrial field (nanotechnology), while another (management systems) is a maturing field where an absence of some interoperability standards is causing widely recognized problems – the traditional sort of problem dealt with by voluntary consensus standard setters. The others are just sectors experiencing rapid growth (security, tourism, and second-hand goods). What links these fields is Patir's, and the TMB's, sense that these are areas in which ISO *may* have a role to play in standard setting, and that, perhaps even more significantly, if ISO does not stake out a claim to being the primary standard setter in these fields, other organizations will.

Given the agenda-setting significance of the TMB, the vice president who chairs it can play an important role in shaping what ISO becomes. The same is true of the heads of the most active member bodies. Because ISO's presidents (who serve for only two years) often come from the most influential member bodies, they, too, can play a powerful role, but the source of their power is not the ISO presidency itself, which can sometimes just be an honor given to an important standard setter for a lifetime of work – something in the same way that the presidency of many academic associations honors the achievements of a senior scholar.

The ISO Secretary General is also potentially quite powerful due to the position's unique role in connecting the member bodies and standard setters around the world. Sturén began the current practice of the Secretary General traveling widely; he typically visited more than 10 member bodies on three continents every year (Sturén n.d.). His successors benefited from the establishment, in the 1990s, of seven regional groupings of ISO members (originally for Africa, the Americas, the Arab region, Europe, the Pacific Rim, Southeast Asia, and a "Euro-Asiatic" region covering the former Soviet sphere). The meetings of these groups, according to the man who replaced Sturén, Lawrence Eicher (1997: 10), provided him with "greatly increased opportunities for communication and dialogue," a much wider range of face-to-face meetings than his predecessor had enjoyed.

The Secretary General's power comes more from these connections than from the position at the head of the modest Central Secretariat in Geneva. The secretariat coordinates the standard-setting work being done by the separate technical committees, oversees the (now largely electronic) voting on draft standards, and completes the final editing of new standards. Staff members also publish and sell ISO standards and conduct public relations campaigns.

Of course, the way in which those campaigns define ISO's mission and place in the world could, indeed, have a great deal of influence over the long-term direction of the organization. ISO's information campaigns can create expectations among members and among larger publics about what ISO is and what it can do. The ISO 9000 series of quality management standards has long been the focus of a very successful campaign. More recently, Ziva Patir (2005: 12) made a great deal of a program of "Promoting Standards through Art" in this regard, but it is not clear that thist program has even been as successful as a much older campaign to encourage the celebration of "World Standards Day" (14 October). That campaign at least convinced a dozen countries to issue celebratory postage stamps between 1970 and 1995 (Hilger 2008). Even ISO's newest public relations materials – such as its 2007 attempt to rebrand itself as "the Interesting Stories Organization" – have a slightly geeky quality that may limit their ability to mobilize new demand for ISO services (see, e.g., ISO 2007).

The greatest influence of members of the ISO secretariat may come from the fact that it is apparently a relatively congenial organization in which to work; people stay a long time, and they develop a strong, specialized organizational memory that must be invaluable to member organizations' representatives who are apt to change much more rapidly. For example, the official ISO history ends with a chapter by Roseline Barchietto (1997), a 40-year employee, who reports a widespread affection within the organization and among standard setters in general. Similarly, in 2008, Ole Sturén's widow, Nalle, summarized a life of experience in the field by saying "Either only nice people work in standardization, or standardization makes you nice," (Murphy and Yates 2009: 88).

In sum, the ISO of today is an unusually decentralized global network organization that has been developed by practitioners of voluntary consensus standard setting over many decades. Early ISO standards have had an impact on the structure of global markets and on the development of some of today's leading industries. How has that been possible and what has been the nature of that impact?

The development and adoption of specific standards: toward a theory of the international standards movement and its impact

Assessments similar to those of Roseline Barchietto and Nalle Sturén are peculiarly commonplace among people who are involved in voluntary consensus standard setting at all levels. Is this why so many volunteer to take part in technical committees? Perhaps that is part of the story.

Well, for many, "volunteering" is a part of their job. They are working for companies that a proposed standard will affect and they are paid by the company to sit as a representative of one of the stakeholders. Mark Nottingham, a computer standards' professional in California, has set up a humorous Amazon.com webpage for prospective "volunteers" of this sort. "So You'd Like to be a Standards Geek" lists all the books and other paraphernalia you need to take part in the electronic discussion and roam the world attending the endless round of meetings. The second item on the list is Machiavelli's *Prince*, "It's short, sweet (well, not really) and gets you in the proper frame of mind for doing battle, er, gathering consensus" (Nottingham n.d.).

Of course, the company stakeholder representatives are not the only members of the technical committees. Some of the women and men on the committees, especially those placed there as "neutral experts" by the constituent standard-setting bodies, are likely to be *believers* in standard setting *per se*, members of a social movement of standard setters that has existed for more than a century. They may also view their role as important in reinforcing their expertise and stature in relevant technical communities. Even company representatives are likely to be "standards geeks," otherwise they probably would have wormed their ways into a more comfortable jobs; as Nottingham points out, "One of the perks and millstones of being a standards person is constant travel. It's fun for a while, but separation from your family and familiarity with the Boeing and Airbus corporations' products wear quite quickly" (Nottingham n.d.). A generation earlier, Olle Sturén registered a similar complaint:

> Anyone who thinks that attendance at technical committee meetings is a comfortable, touristic experience is mistaken. Standards making is a hard profession and makes tremendous demands on participants if the standard is to be good and welcome for worldwide application. When sitting on an ISO committee you are often in the company of the best brains in the relevant industry, and somebody who is not completely confident technically may hesitate before contributing the mildest comment.
>
> (Sturén 1981: 4)

All of which is to say that many different motivations are at play in any technical committee. Moreover, as we explain below, these many different motivations help explain why the voluntary consensus process seems to work.

In theory, ISO's standard setting is demand driven. The organization is expected to set up new technical committees, approve new subcommittees, and suggest new areas of work when there is significant demand, say, from the companies that produce incompatible products, or, more likely, from the companies that purchase them! In fact, as the current grab bag of TMB interests suggests, ISO also plays an entrepreneurial role; it helps create the demand for the services it can provide. The Secretary General, vice presidents, and the leaders of major national bodies are constantly looking for areas in which new standards might prove useful, especially fields in which ISO's deliberative process would have an advantage over other ways in which standards might be set.

Moreover, some very important ISO standards actually have been "supply driven." Consider ISO's entry into the quality management field through ISO 9000. Standards guru Carl Cargill (2003: 204) calls ISO 9000 "a retread of an old US military standard on quality management and quality assurance from the 1960s that was rewritten by the British and then sold to ISO as the first of a series of 'management standards.'" There is an almost religious dispute about the earliest origins of ISO 9000, but no one contests that the standard ISO adopted was essentially the one that BSI had designed and heavily promoted.

Whatever the impetus for a particular ISO standard, its production goes through a series of stages in which proposals are drafted and debated within a technical committee. The secretariat of the committee, the national body that has taken on that role, is responsible for organizing meetings, assigning particular drafting tasks, and conducting voting, much of which can now be done through the electronic system maintained by the Central Secretariat.

During technical committee discussions, the secretariat is required to be neutral and "disassociate itself from the national point of view" (ISO 2005: 9), while each national delegation is expected to come to a consensus position even though it must include people reflecting fundamentally different interests. Under current ISO rules, the ability of national delegations to achieve an internal consensus may be aided by the fact that many trade associations and other interest groups can now be directly represented within technical committees by more than 600 national and international NGOs, government bureaus, and intergovernmental organizations that need not be part of national delegations. Thus, for example, the Office Québécois de la Langue Française contributes to TC-37 Terminology and other language and content resources, the European Cork Federation takes part in the work of TC-87 Cork, and the American Oil Chemists' Society (a food oils group) works with three of the subcommittees of TC-34 Food products (ISO 2009d).

After the members of a technical committee have agreed on a draft standard, it is made available to all member bodies, who have five months to comment and to vote on it. If no member objects, the technical committee merely has to respond to any comments and the standard is then published and distributed by the ISO Central Secretariat. If some members object, there is an additional period of two months for comment and voting. Assuming two-thirds of the members on the committee still support the standard, and no more than one-quarter oppose, it is published.

In the late 1980s, the production of a new standard within a technical committee typically took 72 months or six years. By 2002, that time had been reduced to 51 months (closer to four years), even though the average amount of documentation for each new ISO standard (the number of published pages it required) had almost tripled. This improvement may be attributable to the IT (information technology) explosion in the 1990s, when ISO committees began to be able to carry out much their discussion and exchange of documents electronically (Bryden 2003).

Past participants in ISO technical committees and scholars who have studied voluntary consensus standard setting have offered a series of plausible and compatible explanations of why such committees are so often able to reach consensus despite the many interests involved. One of the main arguments is that the committees provide a straightforward way to solve two kinds of problems that are faced by all standard setters.

The first, and simpler, kind arises when almost all producers or potential producers of a product or service (or users of a process) are convinced that there is a need for a standard: think of the nineteenth-century producers of nuts and bolts and all the manufacturers of mechanical equipment who had to rely on those parts. In this kind of case, the *particular* standard used for interconnection is not all that important; what is important is that there be *some* standard. These sorts of "coordination problems" can be solved relatively easily if those with technical expertise can agree on what they think is the "best" – or, at least, an "acceptable" – technology (Calvert 1992: 9). In fact, in the early days of the standards movement, many standard setters believed that the *only* problems that required their attention were such problems of coordination that could be solved by "expertise." This was one reason why many engineers felt it would just make things more complicated, it would muddy the waters, if the mere "users" of standards were brought into the voluntary consensus processes. Many engineers believed that they could do it by themselves, without representatives of the companies that were expected to adopt the standard (Yates and Murphy, 2007).

The men who created the nongovernmental bodies that became part of ISO realized that they needed to include representatives of interested companies (e.g., delegates of their trade associations), if for no other reason than to help pay for the national bodies' central secretariats! Nonetheless, many of these new stakeholders were interested in more than just coordination problems. They were concerned with the kinds of problems that might lead one to consider Machiavelli's *Prince* as one of the most important books for every standards geek to know. Game theorists call these problems of "cooperation" rather than of mere coordination. In the short term, many producer companies are perfectly happy with the solution, the "equilibrium," of incompatible standards.

Back when videotape players were new, the companies who owned the patents on VHS wanted the chance to make money on their technology and so did Sony, who owned Betamax. Whenever there are incompatible standards, every company involved knows that there will be a quantifiable cost associated with moving to a single standard, at least for those companies that have to move, that "lose" a "standards war." Each company will want to minimize that cost, or find other ways to gain a competitive edge over its rivals.

Yet Randall Calvert, a political scientist who investigates cooperation problems, argues that, in the real world, most such problems are unusually complex, but that actually can make them *easier* to solve. In the complexity of the real world's "repeated games" the "players [e.g., potential users of a standard] face the problem of mutually identifying which of numerous possible 'good' equilibria to pursue." This creates what Calvert (1992: 12) calls "a *derived coordination problem*."

Consider companies like Sony back in the days of the Beta/VHS war or Apple in the early days of the personal computer; both of them may be thought of as having "lost" a major "standards war," but, in the long run, that "war" turned out just to be a temporary battle in a much longer conflict. A new business environment (created by VHS's dominance of videotape and Microsoft's ability to place its operating system on most personal computers) meant that the companies had to search for new products elsewhere, and it is difficult to say whether the Apple or Sony of 2010 would be "better off" had they won their standards battle of 1970. Given that fact, it may even have been better had they not "fought the battle" (in the courts and in the marketplace) in the first place. It may have been advantageous if they had accepted a standard created by an ISO committee.

Of course, Sony and Apple did not know that at the time. Calvert wants us to think about the kinds of people who can convince parties that are facing such complex cooperation problems to choose to compete on one set of battlegrounds and not on others. In the case of standard setting, this "derived" or "second order" coordination problem is one of finding people who can convince all key stakeholders that they really do have an interest in, or a desire for, some shared standard.

In both the more complex situation and the less complex one, Calvert points to *leadership* as providing the solution to the problem. In the less complex case, participants in a consensus standards meeting can defer to any person or a small group that identifies something as "the standard" to which they should adhere. In the more complex case, the meeting's leaders may not only have to identify a common focal point, they may also have to act as mediators – private channels of messages from one party to another – as well as sources of suggested compromises. They might also, Calvert argues, have to act as "moral, inspirational, or 'transformational' " leaders, ones who promote different norms and different goals to the ones that the parties bring to the table. Contemporaries of many of the early leaders of the standard-setting movement often described them in these terms (Yates and Murphy 2008).

Such leaders still exist. The information technology "standards guru" Carl F. Cargill is someone often described in these terms. He is the one person whose *Open Systems Standardization* Mark Nottingham's "So You'd Like to be a Standards Geek" lists as even more essential than Machiavelli's *Prince* (Nottingham n.d.). That makes sense, because the secret of the success of technical committees is that the inspired vision of a guru can trump short-term *Realpolitik* of a Machiavelli: a persuasive reframing of the problem can turn an intractable conflict among self-seeking company representatives into a deliberatively reached agreement on a technically viable solution that may shift competition in a socially valuable way.

What are the sources of the power of the leaders who take part in standard-setting committees?

In the first case, when there is strong agreement on the need for a standard, it is most likely the perceived *expertise* of those committee members who are there due to their technical skills: " If a standard is desirable, let's go with the one suggested by the experts" (especially if the experts have taken into account all of the objections and suggestions offered by those of us who will be affected by the standard).

In the second case, where a more transformative, goal-changing kind of leadership may be needed, the ability to provide such transformative goals often derives from the active engagement of some of the standardizers in the larger "standards movement." Cargill, for example, is a "guru" not because he serves the interests of his employer, Sun Microsystems, particularly well, but because his vision extends beyond those interests. He has developed a new, historically embedded theory of contemporary voluntary consensus standard setting (Cargill 2003) and it is in this context that historian Andrew Russell (2005) says that Cargill became a "guru."

To understand the deference that companies have given to engineers and other kinds of experts, and why those experts would voluntarily take part in such work, it may be useful to think of standardization as taking place within the kind of social field described by sociologist Pierre Bourdieu. Within that field are business leaders in the newest industries, men made powerful by their control of *economic capital* and bent on its further accumulation. Next to this group, and only slightly overlapping it, are more inter-related groups of scientists and engineers, holders of particular forms of *cultural capital*, of credentials and expertise, that they guard and try to augment. Taking part in important standardizing committees is not only a way to build cultural capital (a new credential that adds to an engineer's prestige *vis-à-vis* other engineers and even scientists); the engineer's expertise provides the kind of solution to which business people can easily defer.

The historian of the Australian standards movement, Winton Higgins, makes a similar claim about the motivations of the participants in technical committees, and relates it to a larger claim. According to Higgins, the transformative vision that sometimes solves problems faced by technical committees is not something that is limited to a few "gurus." Instead, the "democratic" process itself gives everyone the opportunity to see beyond their narrow interests or even the disciplinary blinders of their expertise:

> By sitting on standards committees, many people enhance their professional competence and business contacts. They also take the opportunity to push the particular interest they represent on the committee in question. But beyond that, they immerse themselves in civic culture – the discipline of open discussion and argument between equals, compromise, and accepting the experience of being outvoted by one's peers. For those who come from hierarchical institutions, this experience is both novel and essential training for citizenship in a free society … Jürgen Habermas has revealed one of the secret strengths of the kind of deliberative decision-making that these standards bodies deploy. "Communicative rationality" – the outcome of open discussion and debate between equal individuals with different backgrounds – represents a superior rationality compared to the conclusions reached by experts and senior administrators in isolation, ones untested

in debate. The standards produced by the typical standards body crystallise the communicative rationality that Habermas has in mind.

(Higgins 2005: 28–29)

Higgins might be overstating the case. However, for over a century, many of those involved in the standards movement have emphasized its decision-making process as a main cohesive element of the movement, as the reason, in Nalle Sturén's words, that it might just be that "standardization makes you nice." Standardizers and their admirers since the beginning – from the Fabian Webbs to that recent World Bank Vice President – have also focused on that decision-making process as one of the great social values of the movement, the reason the Webbs hoped for the "further development" of standard setting in "the public service." In that sense, the central role of the standardizing movement's "democratic principles" makes it surprisingly similar to a number of more typical, non-elite social movements that the sociologist Francesca Polletta discusses in her path-breaking *Freedom is an Endless Meeting* (Polletta 2002).

Not surprisingly, many standard setters do speak and write about holding a kind of "public trust" when they take part in the work of ISO and its member bodies. Moreover, ISO's rules – especially the rule that national bodies are, themselves, expected to reach consensus before taking active part in global discussions, even though conflicting interests are represented at the national level – encourage standard setters to think of themselves as trustees for a more general interest. The 1946 Nobel Peace Prize lecture given by the eminent activist economist Emily Greene Balch called the "conception of a public trustee," a fruitful new idea that was beginning to play a role in "world cooperation in different fields." Balch pointed to its parallel in domestic affairs:

> In the United States, hospitals, colleges, all sorts of undertakings for the public welfare are carried on by boards of trustees entrusted with their administration, and they have an honorable record of devotion to their trust. The same man, who, trading in Wall Street, prides himself on his skill in making money, conceives of himself when he finds himself trusted to carry on a public service, as a public servant, and devotes his ability no longer to making money for himself but to the welfare of the park, or the research foundation, or other matter with which he now identifies himself.
>
> (Balch 1946)

It is certainly true that, moving beyond any individual committee, the larger work of standard setting brings engineers and business people into larger social networks that enhance the third of Bourdieu's forms of capital, *social capital*, "the sum of the resources, actual or virtual, that accrue to an individual by virtue of possessing a durable network of more or less institutionalised relationships of mutual acquaintance and recognition"(Bourdieu and Wacquant 1992: 119).

That larger social network was, from the beginning, a transnational movement. The norms and rhetoric of that movement, in turn, have continued to be useful resources deployed by leaders within those technical committees in which the issues are particularly contentious or complex. The existence of the standards movement is one important reason why ISO committees "work," why they actually produce consensus standards. In other words, to summarize the preceding analysis, the institutional form of voluntary standard setting has been successful because the stakeholder meetings themselves provide opportunities for engineers or other actors who are deeply committed to standard setting to suggest reasonable solutions to complex cooperation problems that businesses and other stakeholders would not be able to solve in other forums. Moreover, the long-established social movement of standard setters has reproduced the type of leaders that work effectively within ISO committees.

Note

1 This chapter is part of a larger project and relies on arguments presented in Murphy and Yates 2009. We are grateful to Harvard's Radcliffe Institute for Advanced Study, MIT, and Wellesley College for research support, to our research assistants Naa Ammah-Tagoe, Honor McGee, and Maria Nassén and, for archival help, to Beatrice Frey at ISO, Stacy Leistner at ANSI, Robert C. McWilliam in the United Kingdom, and Lars and Lolo Sturén for giving us access to the papers of their father, Olle.

References

Balch, Emily Greene (1946) "Toward Human Unity or Beyond Nationalism," Nobel Peace Prize Lecture for 1946, nobelprize.org/nobel_prizes/peace/laureates/1946/balch-lecture. html.

Barchietto, Roseline (1997) "The Work of the Central Secretariat," in Jack Latimer (compiler) *Friendship Among Equals: Recollections from ISO's First Fifty Years.* Geneva: ISO Central Secretariat.

Besen, Stanley M. and Garth Saloner (1988) "Compatibility Standards and the Market for Telecommunications Services," in Robert W. Crandall and Kenneth Flamm (eds) *Changing the Rules: Technological Change, International Competition, and Regulation in Telecommunications.* Washington, DC: The Brookings Institution.

Bourdieu, Pierre and Loïc J.D. Wacquant (1992) *An Invitation to Reflexive Sociology.* Chicago: University of Chicago Press.

Bryden, Alan (2003) Report of the Secretary-General, 26th ISO General Assembly, SG/PRD/ID 13237769, 5 September 2003.

Calvert, Randall L. (1992) "Leadership and its Basis in Problems of Social Coordination," *International Political Science Review*, vol. 13, no. 1, pp. 7–24.

—— (2003) "Standardization as a Guardian of Innovation," unpublished paper, 27 January.

Cargill, Carl F. (1997) *Open System's Standardization: A Business Approach.* Upper Saddle River, NJ: Prentice Hall PTR.

Cleveland, Harland (2000) "Coming Soon: The Nobody-in-Charge Society," *The Futurist*, vol. 34, no. 5, 52–56.

Eicher, Lawrence D. (1997) Foreword to Jack Latimer (compiler) *Friendship Among Equals: Recollections from ISO's First Fifty Years.* Geneva: ISO Central Secretariat.

Higgins, Winton (2005) *Engine of Change: Standards Australia since 1922.* Blackheath, Australia: Brandl & Schlesinger Book Publishers.

Hilger, Don (2008) "ISO World Standards Day," www.cira.colostate.edu/cira/RAMM// hillger/standards.htm.

ISO (1964) "The ISO Technical Committees Shown in Figures 1947–64." ISO/GA-1964-8.

—— (2005) "My ISO Job: Guidance for Delegates and Experts." Geneva: ISO Central Secretariat.

—— (2007) "ISO 14001: The World's Environmental Management Standard." Geneva: ISO.

—— (2009a) "The ISO brand," www.iso.org/iso/about/discover-iso_meet-iso/discover-iso_the-iso-brand.htm.

—— (2009b) "List of ISO technical committees," www.iso.org/iso/standards_development/technical_committees/list_of_iso_technical_committees.htm.

—— (2009c) "Who develops ISO standards," www.iso.org/iso/about/discover-iso_meet-iso/discover-iso_who-develops-iso-standards.htm.

—— (2009d) "Organizations in cooperation with ISO," http://www.iso.org/iso/about/organizations_in_liaison.htm.

Mattli, Walter and Tim Büthe (2003) "Setting International Standards: Technical Rationality or the Primacy of Power?" *World Politics*, vol. 56, no. 1, 1–42.

Murphy, Craig N. (1994) *International Organization and Industrial Change: Global Governance since 1850.* New York: Oxford University Press.

Murphy, Craig N. and JoAnne Yates (2009) *The International Organization for Standardization (ISO): Global Governance through Voluntary Consensus.* London: Routledge.

Nottingham, Mark (n.d.) "So You'd Like to be a Standards Geek," www.amazon.com/gp/richpub/syltguides/fullview/1OL709EFLT7Y0.

Patir, Ziva (2005) "Demystifying the ISO/TMB," Presentation to the ANSI Conference on US Leadership in ISO and the IEC, Phoenix, AZ.

Polletta, Francesca (2002) *Freedom is an Endless Meeting.* Chicago: University of Chicago Press.

Rischard, J.F. (2002) *High Noon: Twenty Global Problems: Twenty Years to Solve Them.* New York: Basic Books.

Russell, Andrew (2005) "The American System: A Schumpeterian History of Standardization," *Progress on Point*, Periodic Commentaries on the Policy Debate from the Progress and Freedom Foundation, Release 12 (18 September): 3–6.

Sandberg, Kristina (2006) "ISO 26000 – Social Responsibility," Paper presented to the ISO Working Group, Stockholm, 24 February.

Sturén, Olle (n.d.) "Notebook listing travel, 1953–87." [Sturén papers.]

—— (1958) "Standardization and Variety Reduction as a Contribution to a Free European Market," in Committee for Scientific Management (CIOS), *Report of the European Management Conference, Berlin.* Geneva: CIOS.

—— (1969) Typescript, "1969" [Minutes of a meeting of the ISO Council], 12. [Papers of Olle Sturén collected by him for a projected memoir.]

—— (1980) "Responding to the Challenge of the GATT Standards Code," Speech to ANSI, Washington, DC, March. [Sturén papers.]

—— (1981) "Collaboration in International Standardization between Industrialized and Developing Countries," Speech to the German Institute for Standardization. [Sturén papers.]

—— (1984) Speech to the American Society of Mechanical Engineers, New Orleans, LA, December. [Sturén papers.]

—— (1997) "The Scope of ISO," Speech to the Standards Council of Canada, Ottawa, Ont., June. [Sturén papers.]

UNSCC (1945) *Economist*, vol. 148 (3 March), 286–87.

Webb, Sidney and Beatrice Webb (1920) *A Constitution for a Socialist Commonwealth of Great Britain.* London: Longmans, Green and Co.

Yates, JoAnne and Craig N. Murphy (2007) "Coordinating International Standards: The Formation of the ISO," MIT Sloan Research Paper No. 4638–07.

—— (2008) "Charles Le Maistre: Entrepreneur in International Standardization," *Enterprises et Histoire*, no. 51(June): 10–57.

11 Beyond the boardroom

"Multilocation" and the business face of celebrity diplomacy

Andrew F. Cooper

Introduction

At first glance, the personae of profit-seeking corporate elites and that of peace-seeking diplomats may seem worlds apart. Certainly their motivations and priorities appear to be at odds with one another. Business leaders are interested in selling goods and services, generating personal wealth, and eliminating borders or obstacles to the free movement of products and capital in the global economy. In contrast, diplomats advance ideas and policies, generate discussion and consensus, and pride sovereignty and national boundaries as founding principles of their trade. Despite their differences, elements of these two seemingly intractable world views have collided through the rise of global advocacy and mega philanthropy.

Over even just the last decade, an influential set of new and active global players has emerged – coming from a variety of backgrounds and possessing unconventional skill sets – challenging the established toolkit of theories used to decipher world events. These individuals have transcended the business/diplomacy dichotomy by championing global, revenue-negative campaigns on health, poverty reduction and democratization, among others. Their abilities to leverage material resources and entrepreneurial innovation into successful development-focused initiatives outside of the state-based system mark some of business's most significant contributions to contemporary global governance. While the influence of the business dimension on international advocacy and philanthropy is increasingly demonstrable, much more research on the political economy of these trends is needed. This chapter expands on empirical observations and advances the concept of "multilocation" as a useful theoretical explanation for the hybrid activity of mega philanthropists.

In theory and practice

Orthodox approaches to the study of international relations (IR) appear to have lost their ability to explain or predict activity on the world stage. As Marieke de Goede (2003: 79) observes, a new wave of scholars has critically contested the central principles of IR, including "the state, rational man and the separation between the domestic and the international spheres," in an attempt to open the discipline to broader concerns like "the cultural representation of political practices and the politics of everyday life." However, as she continues to identify, the international political economy (IPE) tradition, despite its preoccupation with critical reflection on IR and the state/market dichotomy, has yet to address a number of important questions raised in this poststructuralist vein (ibid.: 80).

The representation of business in IPE highlights the deficiencies of the "economism" of orthodox approaches. Mainstream IPE has traditionally viewed business through a hyper-structural framework. Liberal internationalism, in privileging the notion of complex interdependence, prioritizes the system over the practice of agents. Indeed, the corporate world is treated as a uniform group, one in which business practitioners rarely have unique identities or are even named social actors. Robert Keohane (1984), for example, puts the connection between politics and economics in the international system at the center of his oft-cited book *After Hegemony*, yet makes no mention of business practitioners or the influence of individuals.

Gramscians, with their heavy emphasis on the power of social control or conditioning, do locate some faces of dynastic corporate power. The Rockefeller family, for example, is cast with some accuracy as the main force behind the rise of the Trilateral Commission. Stephen Gill (1990: 140) goes so far as to say that "the Trilateral Commission without David Rockefeller is as unimaginable as Hamlet without the Prince."

Nevertheless, the role of business leaders is still cast as part of a structural understanding and not as part of a multi-dimensional critical narrative. There is no attempt to explore the cultural or personal dimensions of this type of social force. In this literature there is no space for individual personalities to emerge from a structural typecasting. The network of Rockefeller interests is privileged for their connections with "east coast banking and financial interests" (ibid.: 132). Giovanni Agnelli is cast starkly as "the Fiat tycoon" (ibid.: 137). And the Ushiba family in Japan merits attention for its links "Mitsubishi, Sony and Nippon Credit Bank" (ibid.: 150). Overall, firms represented in the Trilateral Commission are depicted as being "at the apex of world economic hierarchies and at the vanguard of the transnationalization process" (ibid.: 155).

Students of business or corporate affairs, it should be added, push in the opposite direction, devoting considerable energy to the nature of personalistic leadership. To be sure, some of the literature takes on a Carlyle-like orientation with the focus on business supermen (whether Lee Iacocca of Chrysler, Jack Welsh of GE, Jeff Bezos of Amazon, or even Donald Trump). However, the monopoly of interest in this literature is on successful leadership in the corporate domain, whether for personal gain or for the material benefit of their shareholders. Little or no attention is paid to non-corporate forms of entrepreneurialism of either an ideational or a social nature.

Throughout the literature, business leaders are either rendered largely as cogs in a bigger machine of capitalistic enterprise or set up in a stereotyped image as dynamic champions of innovation in the private sector. In both their personal experiences as well as in the shifting cultural/social context, the theme of social purpose as a driving or motivating force for business leaders is severely under-researched.[1]

An exception to the rule may be judged to be the accentuated focus on individual corporate business leaders in terms of their role in corporate social responsibility (CSR). But again, these much contested initiatives accent the division between the structural emphasis in the IPE literature and the hyper-individualism among the students of business. Advocates of CSR place great weight on an expanded consciousness of individual corporate leaders in these particular activities (with the positive branding opportunities linked to the mantra of the Global Compact).

My perspective is that an expanded framework must be utilized to capture the tendency of business leaders to stretch their boundaries, or sites of activity, beyond the boardroom to some substantial areas of transnational social advocacy. A useful starting point here is Ulrich Beck's (2000) notion of "multilocation" of personal lives or biographies, where an appreciation of the extended breadth of lives and activities is brought to the fore. What Beck categorizes as "grand multidimensional narratives" – with attendant ambiguities – is useful for exploring everyday lives across the spectrum of society. But it is particularly useful for breaking down the tendency in mainstream IPE to treat business leaders in a one-dimensional or enclave manner.

Akin to political leaders, members of the corporate elite cannot be typecast. Indeed, it is no exaggeration to say that the bigger they are, the more the individual psychological/experiential differences among them are salient. This is true both when the referent is business leaders as part of the corporate elite and as transnational social advocates.

Beck's approach suggests that, in an exaggerated fashion, business leaders may go through some process of "inner mobility" between these different worlds (ibid.: 76). Although this paper is more of a mapping exercise of "multilocation" as traced through the activities of specific business leaders, it does implicitly raise (if not answer) some grander conceptual questions. What is the process by which this "multilocation" takes place? Are there complements or contradictions in moving their activities beyond the boardroom? And what are the positives and negatives of this complex and controversial process?

One increasingly important aspect of the makeup (and daily lives) of the leading business elite is their representation as celebrity icons, not simply because of their success as business leaders but as transnational advocates. Another component is the connection between these members of the corporate elite and other elements from the world of entertainment, as represented by their work on global social issues. Together they make up a distinctive network where the relationship is constituted by their positions within society.

Select members of the corporate elite have become increasingly embedded in this wider process that I term "celebrity diplomacy" (Cooper 2007). From this perspective, George Soros and Bill (and Melinda) Gates share common attributes with Bono and Angelina Jolie, including a distinct ability to connect to wide audiences and to grab the attention of important international leaders. Both sides of this phenomenon challenge some of the traditional fixtures of IPE theory, most notably the centrality of the state and a separation between the private and public spheres. But corporate celebrity diplomacy remains distinctive in a variety of ways. Unlike Angelina Jolie and other celebrity diplomats from the world of entertainment, they do not need to locate their activities within formal institutional settings such as the United Nations or the G8. Nor, unlike Bono's organization DATA, do they need to raise material resources from external sources. Gates and Soros, in particular, have an autonomous capability which separates them from the entertainment side of celebrity diplomacy. They fundamentally shape, rather than embellish, the agenda of key sites of celebrity diplomacy, such as the World Economic Forum (WEF) at Davos, Switzerland.

The expanding world of the celebrity diplomat

The notion of celebrity involvement in the world of diplomacy is by no means new or unique to the twenty-first century. Benjamin Franklin's assiduous work for the French Court of Louis XVI (*PBS* 2002), Lawrence of Arabia's connection to the Paris Peace Conference of 1919, and the stunning range of prominent actors, writers, poets, and entertainers – including Shirley Temple Black, Pablo Neruda, and Octavio Paz – who have represented their countries as ambassadors, all indicate the long association of celebrity with the modern world of diplomacy.

Yet, if not completely new, the enmeshment of late-twentieth-century and early-twenty-first-century celebrities in diplomacy is quite different in nature, scope, and intensity. The selection of Bono and Bill and Melinda Gates as *Time* magazine's 2005 persons of the year serves only as the most visible measure of how new types of celebrities performing an expanded range of activities are being recognized on the international stage. Their enhanced role demonstrates the interplay between the domestic and the global in a very obvious fashion. Diplomacy has become porous not only in terms of formal structures but in terms of the fusion of informal elite dynamics as well. As celebrities push for recognition and support by becoming plugged into transnational policy making, the political elite use celebrities to boost their own popular credibility. This interplay is consolidated by the combination of publicity and symbolic and material resources that only celebrities can generate.

The elevated role taken on by celebrities reveals the cracks in the rigidities of the modern Westphalian state-centric system. As Morten Ougaard observes (2008: 387–88), the disaggregation of state power and the growing role of personal and business networks act as push–pull factors in "a general movement away from state-as-unitary-actor-centred ontologies of the international realm." Celebrity diplomacy emphasizes global reach and connectivity in terms of problem solving, pushing for activity when and where it is needed. The Latin root of ambassador, *ambactiare* (meaning to go on a mission) has effectively become the mantra of diplomacy used by celebrities. All push hard against the constraints of the fixed way of doing things. All blend enthusiasm with outrage. All privilege a transnational trajectory over national sensibilities.

The current wave of celebrities squarely targets the arenas of global governance, global equity, and global regulatory issues. Efforts to end global poverty, to cancel debt, to expand programs of official development assistance, and to focus on HIV/AIDS and other pandemic health issues, all of which are heavily concentrated on Africa, would be at the top of most current lists of celebrity activism. As one campaigner suggests, celebrities lend their names to issues and initiatives absent in mainstream media, thereby attracting widespread attention through a "redistribution of cameras" (Buston 2008).

In regard to the milieu, globalization is privileged along with the transformation of information technology. Celebrity diplomats have hitched a ride on this technical revolution, or what Bob Geldof terms "an electronic loop around the planet" (Vallely 1995). Cutting through the complications associated with negotiations and protocol, celebrities can connect immediately with a range of audiences. MTV and other mechanisms – including both text messaging and a proliferation of blogs about Bono and other celebrity diplomats – provide a multitude of connections to a global audience beyond the imagination of a few decades ago. Select celebrities have a reach around the world far beyond what could have possibly been contemplated even at the time of a mega-event such as Live Aid in the mid-1980s.

Bringing in the business dimension

The distinctive business dimension of celebrity diplomacy is increasingly full of corporate celebrities that operate beyond the boardroom (and sometimes, preemptively, beyond the grave).Warren (the "Oracle of Omaha") Buffett, whose net worth is reportedly more than $52 billion (Forbes 2007), has established a posthumous agreement with the Gates Foundation, setting amongst its conditions that Bill and Melinda "remain active in the policy setting agreement" and that the foundation continue to spend 5 per cent of its net worth annually on top of his generous gift ($37 billion). Richard Branson, entrepreneur and luminary of the Clinton Global Initiative (CGI) forum, made a multibillion-dollar investment into renewable energy initiatives to tackle global warming at the September 2006 CGI and is commonly heralded – along with musician Peter Gabriel – as the mind behind the global Elders' Group, comprising Nelson Mandela, Kofi Annan, Jimmy Carter, and numerous other international leaders.

Ted Turner, who has consistently championed the cause of the UN, is another particularly good example. Though Turner's celebrity roots are in sports and he has attracted some added attention and controversy because of his marriage to Jane Fonda, his links to the entertainment world went well beyond these images. Because of his ownership of CNN, Turner had not only a deep connection with the media world but the deep pockets to indulge his philanthropic enthusiasms. Significantly, the UN became the partner in a long and caring love affair with Turner. Advocating the need for a "Third World Marshall Plan" well before the idea was in vogue, Turner turned his maverick energy level to a number of UN activities. Along with Fonda, he went to Cairo to attend the UN's International Conference on Population and Development in 1994. Using his control of CNN as a lever, he ordered the channel to cover this type of event "from gavel to gavel" (Burkeman 2002).

In 1998, the media mogul raised the stakes further by setting up the United Nations Foundation/Better World Fund and offering $1 billion to the UN over ten years for humanitarian programs – the recipients for the initial sum of $22 million being UNFPA and UNICEF. In the same year, both Turner and Fonda were selected as UN ambassadors for UNFPA. Although his material resources were sapped by the fall in value of his AOL Time Warner stock – which had bought CNN – the impact of his efforts continued to reverberate. The creation of his foundations was given some credit for loosening up US congressional funds to make up the arrears of more than $1 billion owed to the UN. Further, Turner was in the forefront of a series of new global health initiatives, supporting the campaign to eradicate polio in Africa through his own foundations and, in partnership with Vodafone, contributing to initiatives on fighting measles and HIV/AIDS. This work was significant not only as a personal contribution but as a valuable guide to other celebrity entrepreneurs, above all Bill Gates.

Ultimately, in combining the ability of the Hollywood elite – in some cases affiliating directly with them – to play to the media and generate buzz on targeted issues, with the commercial bite inherent to unrivaled economic endowment and a recognized ability to mobilize resources, corporate celebrities are particularly well positioned to play the role of a "new sort of individual" and challenge the purpose and practice of global governance. The unique blend of a theatrical process, an immense economic benefaction and the presence of big, but diverse, personalities situate Davos as a prime location for celebrity diplomacy. As a result, this small Swiss mountain village provides a concentrated physical station from which to explore the expanding role of this corporate celebrity diplomat.

Davos and the "shifting power equation"

Most commonly viewed as a narrowly framed and restrictive annual event, the World Economic Forum at Davos is taken to be the exemplar of a hyper-driven globalized capitalism in which the disciplined model of a competitive ethos trumps all else. The participants are identified as members of the top layer of the world's economic elite, driving the process of market-driven globalization.

The best-known criticisms of the Davos culture – and the ascendancy of the so-called "Davos man" – are reactions to this image. Transnational anti-globalizers, or social justice advocates, condemn Davos as both an insidious and a defective site. The menu on offer is simply a variant of orthodox neoliberalism with a rigid focus on getting incentives right in the marketplace, with the inevitability of differentiated outcomes between winners and losers. Defenders of nationalism – and national interests – bemoan the "stateless" attributes of Davos. The stalwart of this latter camp continues to be the Harvard University professor

Samuel Huntington, who wrote that the homogeneous ethos of Davos (or, more accurately, the "Davos culture") stripped away territorial loyalties at the elite level without an appreciation of the array of cultural differentiation at the mass level (see Huntington 1996).

Davos reveals the immense capacity of business-driven diplomacy to adjust when and where there is a need to do so. So long as the new economy – epitomized by the high-tech boom – powered along, the original menu of Davos was highly palatable. The problem came when the political/economic atmosphere was transformed in a manner that threatened to pull down the "temple of capitalist narcissism" (Keegan 2005: 8). The Asian/IMF financial crisis of 1997–98, the dot-com crash, and the massive financial and accounting scandals involving Enron, WorldCom, and other companies were bad enough. But the tragedy of 9/11 and the buildup to the Iraq war exacerbated matters tremendously. All of the "isms" that were anathema to Davos came back onto the global agenda with a vengeance: nationalism, unilateralism, and terrorism.

Moreover, Davos was not only judged to be wrong in its economic calculations, it was also seen as being out of sync with geopolitical realities. The danger for Davos and for its highly successful originator, Klaus Schwab (who had started the event in 1971 as the European Management Forum before switching the name in 1987) was that this site would go from being the subject of intense contestation as an elite and normatively compromised project to being a venue of insignificance and/or ridicule. Davos could live – albeit uncomfortably – with its critics from alternative forums, including the World Social Forum (WSF). It could not survive, though, if judged to be irrelevant (Krugman 2000). Sensing this vulnerability, critics on the outside honed in on this theme. Public intellectuals such as John Ralston Saul (2005: 66) were derisive of Davos, declaring its concept out of date as hyper-globalization became discredited. In his words, while "classic plays have their fool, globalization had Davos." A writer from the Bible of counterculture, the *Village Voice*, added his own mocking kick to Davos through the charge that the transformation in global fundamentals "makes the World Economic Forum look like a dinosaur from a bubbly time" (Jones 2002).

Rescuing Davos meant recovering the aura of excitement associated with the event. From its outset, Davos has been star-struck. A good part of its appeal came through the production of the type of celebrities that its core constituency wanted to see and hear. As one participant judged, the stakes in getting the right mix were high: "The World Economic Forum still 'lives or dies on the buzz generated by Davos ... particularly [it is] the celebrities and newsmakers who give Davos its extra dash of glamour. It's a matter of survival. If it was a series of middling leaders from African countries the CEOs would reconsider their involvement' " (Landler 2005).

One component of this approach was to place the accent on those prominent members of the business community who could combine buzz with the attributes of commercial bite. Faced with the shakeouts of the high-tech bust and the financial crises at the end of the twentieth century, this cohort was made up of only a few rare individuals, the dominant figures being Bill Gates and George Soros.

Although many high-flying CEOs attended Davos, it is only these two that took on a profile within the Davos orbit that meshed with the model of celebrity diplomacy.

With the consolidation of stars from the business elite came a stretching out of the categories of other celebrities who took part in this forum. Davos was resited to accommodate different sources of glamour that contributed to the atmosphere of buzz. In any analysis of this resiting, a thorough appreciation of the contribution of stars, whether from Hollywood or the world of rock music, is necessary. The sustainability of Davos hinged on the unanticipated but highly effective blending of voice and material capabilities, stylistic performances, and operational delivery. In this light, it seems particularly appropriate that the forum's main theme in 2007 was "The Shifting Power Equation."

The novelty of Davos has been to mix and match celebrities from diverse professional backgrounds and to connect some aspects of their worlds. Although the CEOs, and indeed other attendees, wanted to meet their peer group at Davos, they also wanted to be excited and engaged by big ideas and personas from other walks of life. Davos could do this as a one-stop shop, mixing buzz and bite. Sir Martin Sorrell, the chief executive of the WPP Group (the world's largest advertising agency), captured the essence of this comparative advantage from an instrumental point of view: Davos is "incredibly efficient because so many people are there" (Pfanner 2004). And, from a more personal perspective, Wangari Maathai, the Kenyan deputy environment minister and 2004 Nobel Peace Prize winner, added: "You can bump into all these people you wouldn't normally meet, like presidents, royalty and celebrities" (Browne 2005).

The power of commercial bite: Gates and Soros

Many corporate executives – and, for that matter, individual business entrepreneurs – engage in high-stakes commercial diplomacy. Almost all these activities are of a highly instrumental nature: the maximization of profit. To give just one illustration, Hank Paulson, the Goldman Sachs chief executive turned US treasury secretary, visited China alone some seventy times over a fifteen-year period for investment banking purposes (Guerrera and Tucker 2006).

By this criterion, what are we supposed to make of Bill Gates and George Soros stretching out the contours of their activities? Both enjoy formidable reputations as hardheaded businessmen. As giant players in their respective areas of enterprise – Gates in high-tech via Microsoft (by 2000 the largest company in the world by market capitalization) and Soros in financial and currency transactions through his original Quantum Fund or, subsequently, the Soros Management Fund – they accumulated massive material resources and an attendant cult of celebrity. Neither dropped their main games from their Davos repertoire. Gates continued to speak on topics related to the future of technology, and Soros provided an annual assessment of currency markets.

Where Gates and Soros differed from most of their corporate counterparts at Davos was in the "multilocation" manner in which their embrace of diplomatic techniques took shape. Moving beyond the traditional deal-making business style associated with Davos, Gates and Soros became principal agents of celebrity diplomacy.

Temperamentally, neither Gates nor Soros can be considered ideal candidates for this shift in identity as actors. They could be admired for their high-stakes risk taking, but they were both feared for their rapacious commercial practices. Gates has been constantly criticized throughout his business career as an evil monopolist, charges given added credence by the antitrust actions brought against Microsoft not only by the US government but also by the EU. As the quintessential commercial "Davos man," any recognition (never mind endorsement) of Gates as a celebrity diplomat had to contend with the conventional and contradictory image that his "presence on the world stage is symptomatic of the new hegemony of global brands, which enjoy ... power unmatched by politicians" (Pitcher 2005: 31).

Gates reinforced these oversized personality traits even as he rebranded himself as a celebrity diplomat. Davos had to contend with Gates making demands to be on the program both as technological guru and as a supercharged activist on global social and economic issues. As a very frustrated managing director commented to the media in the context of Gates's demand in 2005 that he wanted to be on another panel with Bill Clinton, "I've already scheduled two major sessions for Bill Gates, and ... that's it ... he seems to want more and more" (Landler 2005: C1).

Soros had an even more tainted reputation.[2] A cunning speculator, he remained best known as the currency trader who had "broken" the Bank of England, and gained $1 billion in the process, by forcing the UK out of the European Exchange Rate Mechanism on what became known as "Black Wednesday" (16 September 1992). Following the Asian financial crisis five years later, the long-serving Malaysian prime minister, Mahathir Mohamad, was an especially harsh critic, accusing Soros of wanting to cause another financial shockwave in the region (see *Washington Post* 1998).

Further, Soros's attachment to controversy was not limited to the financial world. He had a confrontational relationship with a wide number of leaders around the world, a group that included President Vladimir Putin of Russia and President Islam Karimov of Uzbekistan. Both were considered by Soros to be enemies of his ideal of "the open society." His highly visible and well-resourced opposition to President George W. Bush polarized opinion about him in the United States. To sympathizers in MoveOn.org and other anti-Bush groups he was a champion of resistance not only to the war in Iraq but to an incipient authoritarian state at home. To his detractors, he was portrayed as a dangerous maverick: full of material resources but with no sense of responsibility.

If more inclined by disposition to be placed in the anti-diplomat category, both Gates and Soros reflect (in exaggerated form) the general shift by the commercial Davos elite toward "multilocation" and prominent roles in celebrity diplomacy. This move comes through far more explicitly in Soros's voice and attitude on global issues. By instinct, Soros remained a firm supporter of a new form of multilateralism. Unlike the hyper-globalists in the business community, he sought to bring fundamental reform to the core institutions at the center of the international order: the international financial institutions and the World Trade Organization (WTO). Equally, unlike the ultranationalists (or neoconservatives) so formidable in the US debate, he preferred diplomatic solutions to those attempted and/or imposed by coercive means. The retired commander of the North Atlantic Treaty Organization (NATO) and 2004 Democratic presidential hopeful, General Wesley Clark, described this aspect of Soros's ethos in bold strokes: "He understands that it's diplomacy first. It's building common bridges and common interests between people and cultures that makes the world safe and that makes it prosperous for all of us, not conquering territory at the point of a bayonet. That's the last resort when everything else has failed" (Soros *et al.* 2004).

Gates shared Soros's distaste for unilaterally imposed state-centric solutions. He was a sharp critic, for instance, of the tightening of the US visa restrictions in the post-9/11 environment. His preference continued to be for a thickening of globalism, with a diffusion of responsibilities in the management of international public policy. A good international citizenship approach by national governments was still taken to be important if this networked approach on display at Davos was to find traction. And, in pursuit of this model, he put a premium on the United States becoming as generous in its global responsibilities as "countries like Norway, Denmark, Sweden and the Netherlands" (Singer 2006). However, Gates was equally adamant that governments alone could not solve what he identified as the problems of primary importance: those related to health (both generally and in regard to the eradication of pandemic diseases such as HIV/AIDS, malaria, and tuberculosis). His main message was that "companies needed to get this on their agenda" in order to combat "a real market failure ... a failure of visibility, a failure of incentives, a failure of cooperation that has led to a very disastrous situation" (cited in *Pharma Marketletter* 2001: 17).

Despite marked contrasts in their backgrounds, with Gates a product of a comfortable mainstream Seattle upbringing and Soros a Jewish Hungarian double refugee from Nazi and communist occupations, they share some fundamental characteristics as celebrity diplomats. Both bring a formidable degree of intensity – or even velocity – to their engagement with public policy issues. Soros was quick to respond on a global basis to any issue of interest to him, with particular reference to the cultural advance toward open societies in states transitioning from authoritarian to democratic regimes. Gates simply turned his bulldozer instincts and an obsession with "winning" from the commercial to the health arena. As one journalistic profile highlighted this thrust of his character: "The way [Gates] talked about wiping out malaria was how he used to talk about wiping out Netscape" (Heilemann 2006).

Another mark of similarity was in the shape of their motivation. If their embrace of a social diplomatic purpose paralleled the initiative launched through the UN's Corporate Social Responsibility campaign, the activities taken on by Gates and Soros maintained an autonomous edge. They had no wish to be involved in any cause that smacked of froth. What they wanted were the results that, to their immense frustration, did not seem to be produced through conventional routes, whether national or supranational. Both conveyed a distinctive form of emotional instrumentalism. As U2's front-man (and archetype celebrity diplomat) Bono characterized this problem-solving attitude on the part of Gates: "This isn't about compassion. … Bill Gates is not into nice sentimental efforts or whimsical support of hopeless causes. When Bill walks into the room, we are not expecting a nice warm fuzzy feeling" (quoted in Specter 2005).

This competitive spirit spilled over into the relationship between Soros and Gates. In September 2006, Soros departed from his typical script of democracy-building programs, pledging $50 million to the Jeffrey Sachs-led Millennium Promise, the aim of which was to help eradicate extreme poverty in Africa. Soros still made it clear that he considered his own core agenda of democracy promotion to be of a much higher magnitude of operational sensitivity. At the 2007 WEF, Soros stated that although public health programs were important, they were "like apple pie" in that a consensus existed concerning their value (Norris 2007).

When either Soros or Gates talked at Davos, the other participants listened. But, unlike Bono and the celebrity diplomats from Hollywood, this power of attraction was not based on a buzz derived from glamour or an engaging voice. What celebrity Soros and Gates enjoyed came from the bite attached directly to their material wealth. Soros's deep pockets can be seen in the global reach of his Open Society Institute (OSI) and his wider network of foundations, which operate in some fifty countries with annual budgets between $400 and $500 million. On individual projects designed to build and embed democratic regimes within open, tolerant, and self-critical societies, his resources more often than not surpassed those brought to bear by the traditional dominant actor in democracy promotion: the United States. In the two years leading up to the so-called Orange Revolution in Ukraine in 2004, the United States targeted about $58 million on Ukraine. Soros, through his International Renaissance Foundation, spent millions more to allow for a change in government through a fair electoral process, topped up by a promise made at Davos of other resources to consolidate democracy in Ukraine.[3]

The donations promised by Gates toward global health programs, which have often been made public in announcements at Davos, were in keeping with the extraordinary material resources (rising to some $34 billion by 2006) of the Bill and Melinda Gates Foundation. Some perspective on these dimensions can be captured when it is considered that the yearly dispensation of grants by this private foundation (some $1.4 billion in 2005) exceeds the annual budget of the World Health Organization (WHO) (Jack 2006b).

From the time the foundation was established in 2000 (when Gates stepped down as CEO to become chair and chief software architect of Microsoft), Gates's sense of emotional embrace grew, sentiments that can be grasped by the type of language he began using in the public sphere: "I refuse to sit here and say, 'O.K. next problem, this one doesn't bother me.' It does bother me. Very much. And the only way for that to change is to stop malaria. So that is what we are going to have to do" (quoted in Specter 2005).

Those emotions translated easily into a series of enormous financial commitments that reflected the approach of his foundation. At Davos in 2001, the Gates Foundation pledged $100 million to the International AIDS Vaccine Initiative. In 2005 in the same venue, the Gates Foundation – in tune with the ethos of "saving lives now" – provided $750 million for targeting child immunization programs such as the GAVI Alliance (formerly known as the UN Global Alliance for Vaccines and Immunization).[4] At the 2006 WEF, Gates announced that he would triple his donation to $900 million for the Global Plan to Stop Tuberculosis.

It is tempting to inflate the transformative role played by Soros and Gates as celebrity diplomats. Media stories cast Soros as the chief agent not only for bringing about the Orange Revolution in Ukraine but also for the peaceful overthrow in Georgia of Eduard Shevardnadze's government through the so-called Rose Revolution in 2003.

A more nuanced portrayal sees them less as architects of any master plan and more as entrepreneurs who use material resources to build networks of influence to facilitate delivery in issue-specific areas. This pattern of activity has a distinctive top-down quality. Gates drew close to a number of influential politicians in the course of the re-siting of Davos and his own rebranding, including UK prime minister Gordon Brown, with whom he teamed up for a well-publicized "war on TB" (Jack 2006a). Soros, in a similar vein, supported Brown's proposals for shaking up the global financial architecture.

Yet, the horizontal as well as vertical contours of this type of activity must also be noted. Notwithstanding the Gates Foundation's pivotal position in terms of resources, it remained on some issues at least as much a follower as a leader. Its push on immunization for neglected diseases, for example, mirrored closely the approach initiated by Médecins Sans Frontières. If Soros's voice could be used as a blunt instrument, his material resources were usually deployed in an indirect manner: going around traditional channels of official interaction with funds directed via societal actors across national boundaries. As his longtime friend Mark Malloch Brown – the former administrator of the United Nations Development Program (UNDP) and former deputy secretary-general to Kofi Annan – put it: "Soros has helped launch nongovernmental organizations that challenge … governments and spoken out against leaders whose policies, he maintained, harmed citizens" (quoted in Harman 2004: 11).[5]

As in the dominant commercial sides of their lives, Gates and Soros have faced fierce criticism for their intrusive behavior. Detractors of Gates – and there have been many – challenged both his motivations and his mechanisms. His conversion away from the orthodox neoliberal Davos model was portrayed as either a ploy to gain tax benefits via the establishment of his foundation and/or a device to soften his "take-no-prisoners, hyper-competitive" image in the Rockefeller/Carnegie tradition before him.[6] His model of operation was viewed as flawed in a number of ways. It favored a research design that placed the onus on early-stage science, developing vaccines and drugs instead of relying on existing medicines and technology proven to be useful on the front lines of delivery to those in need (Jack 2006c). It privileged a model of partnerships under conditions where the

Gates Foundation held the advantage in terms of financial backing. As one critical study illustrates, "The Gates Foundation, as a 'majority shareholder' of the GAVI Fund, virtually maintains a veto right on all important decision making, which is further consolidated by its position as a permanent Alliance Board member" (Martens 2007: 41).

The negative judgments on Soros had at least as much sting and were far more varied in their origins. Autocrats under threat from the transnational networked approach countered that it was a strategy intended to bring into power actors loyal to Soros. Unfortunately, some of his more creative proposals, such as the joint venture with UNDP to split the cost of salaries for a wide variety of state officials within the new government of President Mikheil Saakashvili in Georgia, reinforced this impression. While intended to provide salaries that would be sufficient to deter bribes, the plan signaled to many critical observers that the government was being "paid by Soros." Left-wing critics joined in this chorus, instinctively suspicious that a currency speculator could be promoting innovations in governance: "George Soros: The billionaire trader has become Eastern Europe's uncrowned king and the prophet of 'the open society.' But open to what?" (Clark 2003: 32).

Still, valuable compensation for both Gates and Soros came in the form of diplomatic access and recognition that spread well beyond the Davos site. Although it is too far-fetched to say that Soros is a global statesman with an all-encompassing approach, his bite lent him enormous profile and, at least in some areas, clout. Some appreciation of this celebrity presence is garnered in Malloch Brown's somewhat offhand remark: that he would be hard-pressed to think of a "nongovernmental figure in the U.S. today – except perhaps Oprah ... who has as much power or influence overseas ... as does Soros" (quoted in Harman 2004: 11).

Bill Gates, or more accurately, Bill and Melinda Gates (as Melinda Gates has had a more substantial role in the day-to-day running of the foundation) shared with Soros a huge amount of access to policy players around the world.[7] The only difference came in their treatment as diplomatic actors. Upping the ante on even Soros, some of the Gates' tours of health programs sponsored by the foundation took on the character of state visits. One trip to Bangladesh, profiled in the *Financial Times*, featured a ten-car entourage, complete with a military escort and an ambulance, as well as roadblocks and snipers (Jack 2006b). Another to Vietnam in April 2007 included a meeting with Prime Minister Nguyen Tan Dung (a leader who had made his initial appearance at the WEF at the beginning of the same year) as well as representatives from the WHO, United Nations Children's Fund (UNICEF), and charitable organizations.

Multilocational images and impact

The international presence of Buffett, Branson, Turner and, in particular, Gates and Soros serves to illustrate the significant transference between business and celebrity. As business leaders stretch their boundaries beyond the boardroom to substantial areas of transnational social advocacy, pushing, with hefty material power, on the issues that they see as important, they attain celebrity status and, often, celebrity benefaction. Again, the cover of *Time*, in which Bono is sandwiched by the Gates, is only the most visual display of this "multilocational" phenomenon. At the same time, when celebrities like Jolie and Bono, whose mode of operation is decidedly populist in style, practice their unconventional public diplomacy and address issues of global significance, they are heralded for their business skills and commonly receive corporate benefaction. Bono serves as the prime example of this other category of "multilocation." In an article highlighting the many profitable facets of "Bono's empire," he and his band are even described as "arch-capitalists" (Tomlinson and O'Brien 2007). This business–celebrity hybridism, whether personal or through affiliation, combines an ability to play to the media and generate buzz on targeted issues with virtually unrivaled economic endowment and capability to mobilize resources, putting these dynamic celebrities in a position to challenge the purpose and practice of global governance.

This transference, between business, celebrity and global governance, points to the need for an expanded appreciation of business actors in IPE and IR more generally. The enhanced and multidimensional roles taken on by both entertainment and corporate celebrities reveal the cracks in the rigidities of the modern Westphalian state-centric system. Celebrity diplomats emphasize global reach in terms of problem solving, forcing action when and where it is needed. All fervently challenge the constraints of the fixed way of doing things. All privilege a transnational trajectory over national sensibilities. The fixtures of orthodox IPE theory then, like state-centrism, do not fit this model. At the same time, its flavor of historical materialism cannot simply be discarded in exchange for the Carlylean historicism espoused by many students of corporate affairs. The "great man" tendencies of this discipline do not account for the larger networks that empower these influential individuals, nor the structural shifts in the international stage that harbor them.

On a fundamental level, philanthropy-led non-state activity presents some potential difficulty for the instruments of global governance over the long term. Private foundations can be seen as an expression of the ascendancy of private authority on global public policy, and the tacit reliance on mega philanthropists to conduct social policy in lieu of legitimate authority is one thing. The question of accountability and the representative form of this activity emerges as another issue altogether. These matters become ever more complicated in times of economic crisis, when philanthropic contributions fall off and states have limited capital to share outside their borders for development assistance, basic health provisions, climate adjustment, and state-building initiatives (see Preston 2008).

Important works, such as Keohane's and Gill's, have emphasized the inter-connection between politics and economics in the international system, which is increasingly apparent to the public. These well-known scholars have illustrated the end of hegemonic world order and the growing influence and importance of international regimes with regard to cooperation and global governance. However, the degree to which this interconnected, decentralized environment has given rise to exceptional individuals with exceptional networks of influence is thoroughly under-researched. This is particularly true in terms of these corporate entrepreneurs who employ celebrity status to stretch their boundaries of influence into areas of international social change. In essence, celebrity diplomacy is the decisive product of the "after-hegemony" global order. It is an important nexus of private enterprise and public advocacy; of interconnectivity and individual agency; of business and global governance, which underscores the importance of viewing corporate leaders beyond a one-dimensional or enclave manner. These individuals have expanded their sites of activity far beyond the boardroom and deserve to be taken seriously as part of a more comprehensive research agenda in IPE.

Notes

This paper expands on my earlier work, *Celebrity Diplomacy* (Paradigm Publishers, 2007). I want to thank James Munro and Andrew Schrumm for research assistance. An earlier version of this paper was presented at the International Studies Association Annual Convention 2008, San Francisco, 26–29 March 2008.

1 However, the recent book by Doris Fuchs (2007: 139–58) highlights the "power of ideas" of business, along with its political mobilization and structural power.
2 For the contradictory elements in Soros's character, see Frankel (1999).
3 The International Renaissance Foundation spent $15,078,000 in the Ukraine between 2002 and 2004 (see Soros Foundations Networks 2003, 2004).
4 This contribution amounted to about half of GAVI's resources, although the alliance itself was made up of UN agencies, corporate representatives, and a set of national governments (see *Economist* 2005).
5 Kaufman (2002: 292) notes that both Malloch Brown and Morton Abramowitz were "allies and advisors" to Soros. He also adds that Soros hired a former State Department official (John Fox) to serve as an "ambassador," operating out of the OSI office in Washington, DC.
6 This negative image was compounded by charges that the Gates Foundation had been involved in unethical investment practices that contradict the organization's purpose (see Piller 2007).
7 The role of Melinda Gates – like that of Ali Hewson – deserves more attention. She is often termed the "most powerful woman you know next to nothing about" (Collins 2006).

References

Beck, Ulrich (2000) *What is Globalization?* (Cambridge: Polity Press).
Browne, Anthony (2005) "Meeting of minds can turn talk into action," *The Times*, 31 January.
Burkeman, Oliver (2002) "Ted's Tears," *Guardian*, 18 June.
Buston, Oliver (2008) "Winning Hearts and Minds: Celebrities in Action," Keynote address, *Celebrity Diplomacy: Unconventional International Politics*. Clingendael Institute, The Hague, Netherlands, 30 October.
Clark, Neil (2003) "NS Profile: George Soros," *New Statesman*, 2 June.
Collins, Clayton (2006) "Behind the Golden Gates," *Christian Science Monitor*, 31 July.
Cooper, Andrew F. (2007) *Celebrity Diplomacy*. (Boulder: Paradigm Publishers).

de Goede, Marieke (2003) "Beyond Economism in IPE," *Review of International Studies* (23), pp. 79–97.

Economist, The (2005) "Global Health: The World's Richest Charity Confronts the Health of the World's Poorest People," 29 January, p. 84.

Forbes (2007) "The World's Billionaires: #2 Warren Buffett," 3 August.

Frankel, Jeffrey A. (1999) "Soros's Split Personality," *Foreign Affairs*, 78(2), pp. 124–30.

Fuchs, Doris (2007) *Business Power in Global Governance*. (Boulder: Lynne Rienner).

Gill, Stephen (1990) *American Hegemony and the Trilateral Commission*. (Cambridge: Cambridge University Press).

Guerrera, Francesco and Sundeep Tucker (2006) "Jet-Set Diplomacy Forges Strong Ties with China," *Financial Times*, 1 June.

Harman, Danna (2004) "Mr. Soros Goes to Washington," *Christian Science Monitor*, 25 August.

Heilemann, John (2006) "The Softening of a Software Man," *New York Times Magazine*, 3 January.

Huntington, Samuel P. (1996) *The Clash of Civilizations and the Remaking of World Order*. (New York: Simon and Schuster).

Jack, Andrew (2006a) "Gates and Brown back New Global War on TB," *Financial Times*, 28 January.

—— (2006b) "The Casual-Trousered Philanthropists: the Bill and Melinda Gates Foundation is the world's largest charity and spends more each year on health and education than the World Health Organization," *Financial Times*, 11 March.

—— (2006c) "Gates learns that even in charity there can be controversy," *Financial Times*, 13 June.

Jones, Sasha Frere (2002) "Schmooze Operators: Inside the World Economic Forum," *Village Voice*, 5 February.

Kaufman, Michael T. (2002) *Soros: The Life and Times of a Messianic Billionaire*. (New York: Random House).

Keegan, William (2005) "Summit Hope for a Pro-Bono Gesture," *Observer*, 30 January, p. 8.

Keohane, Robert O. (1984) *After Hegemony*. (Princeton: Princeton University Press).

Krugman, Paul (2000) "Davos Man needs to Resolve an Image Problem," *International Herald Tribune*, 24 January.

Landler, Mark (2005) "Guess who's Coming to Davos," *New York Times*, 20 January, p. C1.

Martens, Jens (2007) "Multistakeholders Partnerships – Future Models of Multi-lateralism?" Dialogue on Globalization Occasional Papers, 29. Berlin: Friedrich Ebert Stiftung.

Norris, Floyd (2007) "George Soros backs Obama (but Hedges his Bets)," *New York Times*, 27 January.

Ougaard, Morten (2008). "Private Institutions and Business Power in Global Governance," *Global Governance*, 14(3), pp.387–403.

PBS (2002) "Benjamin Franklin – World of Influence, Celebrity," [internet], available at: http://www.pbs.org/benfranklin/l3_world_celebrity.html [accessed 11 April 2007].

Pfanner, Eric (2004) "Leaders in Davos are Hoping for more than Just a Talkfest," *International Herald Tribune*, 21 January.

Pharma Marketletter (2001) "Bill Gates Slams Govts and Industry over Poverty Funding 'Failure'," 31 January.

Piller, Charles (2007) "Money Clashes with Mission," *Los Angeles Times*, 8 January.

Pitcher, George (2005) "Can a Young Bill Succeed where Uncle Sam Failed?" *Marketing Week*, 3 February.

Preston, Caroline (2008) "International Charities say Donations could Drop by 15%," *The Chronicle of Philanthropy* [internet], 15 December. Available at: http://philanthropy. com/news/updates/index.php?id=6565 [accessed 16 December 2008].

Saul, John Ralston (2005) *The Collapse of Globalism and the Reinvention of the World*. (Toronto: Viking Canada).

Singer, Peter (2006) "What Should a Billionaire Give – and What Should You?" *New York Times*, 17 December, Sec. 6, p. 58.

Soros, George, Arthur Harman and Wesley Clark (2004) "Bush Policies on Iraq and the War on Terror," News Conference, National Press Club, Washington, DC, 28 September.

Soros Foundations Networks (2003) "Building Open Societies: 2002 Report," Open Societies Institute.

—— (2004) "Building Open Societies: 2003 Report," Open Societies Institute.

Specter, Michael (2005) "What Money can Buy: Millions of Africans die needlessly of disease each year. Can Bill Gates change that?" *New Yorker*, 24 October.

Tomlinson, Richard and Fergal O'Brien (2007) "Bono Inc.," *Bloomberg Markets*, March, pp. 68–74.

Vallely, Paul (1995) "All he wants now is a Life to Call his Own," *The Independent*, 15 July.

Washington Post (1998) "Asia's Financial Crisis: Asian Economies Report," [internet] available at: http://www.washingtonpost.com/wp-srv/business/longterm/asiaecon/timeline.htm [accessed 11 April 2007].

12 Variations in corporate norm-entrepreneurship

Why the home state matters[1]

Annegret Flohr, Lothar Rieth,
Sandra Schwindenhammer and Klaus Dieter Wolf

Introduction

A major focus of the current discussions in International Relations (IR) research about new forms of governance beyond the state (Brozus *et al.* 2003; Wolf 2006, 2008; Zürn 1998) lies on the role of non-state actors, their changing relationships with public actors and the conditions under which transnational corporations (TNCs), in particular, are gaining political authority (Cutler *et al.* 1999; Haufler 2001). In fact, global governance researchers have already discovered TNCs as potent partners for solving collective action problems that call for the extension of traditional public policy approaches beyond the state realm (Higgott *et al.* 2000; Reinicke 1998; Reinicke and Deng 2000).

A growing body of literature reflects the emergence of new governance patterns, including private standard-setting institutions which have taken on authoritative roles and regulatory functions previously primarily ascribed to the state (Cutler *et al.* 1999; Hall and Biersteker 2002). Corporations are found to engage in such governance arrangements and in different forms of norm-related behavior, for instance by addressing social or environmental standard setting.

According to the framework set out in this volume, such new patterns of corporate behavior fit within an understanding of *business as partner*, raising questions about the extent to which and the conditions under which corporations take responsibility for serving the public interest and providing public goods. Both of these directions for research – relating to the causes as well as to the desirability of corporate engagement in global governance – are of high political importance in an increasingly transnationalizing world.

The focus of this chapter, however, mainly lies on the causal analysis of conditions under which corporations can be expected to take part in global governance processes. Observing that TNCs, increasingly, become proponents of norms or behavioral standards for their own behavior and advocates of these norms within global public–private or purely private self-regulatory fora, we inquire the reasons for these – seemingly counterintuitive – activities. Our explanation goes against manifold approaches that, on the one hand, view the state as increasingly losing influence and significance in the age of globalization (Ohmae 1995; Strange 1996), and that, on the other hand, conceptualize TNCs as fully stateless entities oriented "purely to their own bottom lines – without regard to any national or local interest" (Korten 1995: 127). In contrast, we argue that *the state still matters* and, more specifically, that opening this black box will confirm state influence in more subtle and indirect ways than traditionally expected. Moreover, this influence does not only refer to command and control relations as legal scholars postulate (Muchlinski 1995; Zerk 2006).

Our theoretical approach confirms that an understanding and self-perception of business as partner in global governance is not only possible but is the result of – unconscious – socialization processes that corporations are undergoing within national (cooperative) institutions. We therefore explain cross-national variations in corporate contributions to global governance by combining a constructivist logic with a modified Varieties of Capitalism (VoC) approach, with the latter underlining the importance of national institutions for business–government interactions. Following the argument about the significance of institutional differences between capitalist systems, we go beyond the classic differentiation between Coordinated and Liberal Market Economies and introduce a continuum ranging from cooperative to confrontative relationships between the state and business actors to explain corporate behavior on the international level. The underlying assumption is that corporations will take on the same behavioral roles they "learnt" at the national level when engaging within international self-regulatory fora. The significant national institutions therefore are those which enable or disable cooperation or partnership between business and public actors and which facilitate active participation of business actors in rule-setting processes. Habitualization into the execution of public functions will also lead corporations to engage in rule advocacy in the fields of human rights, social standards, environmental protection and anti-corruption policies on the international level.

This chapter proceeds as follows. The second section offers a conceptual framework for distinguishing two types of corporate contributions to governance: norm-entrepreneurship and norm-consumership. The third section introduces a quantitative puzzle of national variations in the levels of corporate norm-entrepreneurship within two global governance arrangements, the UN Global Compact (GC) and the Global Reporting Initiative (GRI). In the fourth section we look for possible explanations for these cross-country variations by examining various schools of thought in the existing literature and showing that they are not able to explain our empirical findings. In the fifth section, therefore, an alternative approach is introduced which brings national institutional settings back in. It suggests that the dominant type of business–government relations in a given national environment has a significant impact on corporate behavior. In the sixth section, the constructivist logic behind this argument is explicated, arguing that different types of national institutional environments shape the identity of business actors and socialize them into adhering to different types of procedural norms. Depending on the procedural norm dominant in its home state, a company takes on the role of either a norm-entrepreneur or a norm-consumer. Finally, the seventh section summarizes the findings and sketches future steps for research.

The concept of corporate norm-entrepreneurship

This section highlights the analytical concept of norm-entrepreneurship and thereby follows a new typology of corporate contributions to governance introduced by the authors in an earlier publication (Flohr *et al.* 2010). We differentiate between two general patterns of corporate behavior that are significant for global governance: norm-entrepreneurship and norm-consumership. The former points to a gap in the constructivist literature on norm- or moral-entrepreneurs because it ignores that corporations, too, can engage in the redefinition of "an activity as a problem" (Nadelmann 1990: 482) and can act as "meaning managers" by creating new "cognitive frames" and establishing "new ways of talking about and understanding issues" (Finnemore and Sikkink 1998: 897). We therefore distinguish such proactive behavior early in a norm's life cycle from the reactive role classically foreseen for corporations – meaning the mere implementation of norms that have been created by other types of actors, which we conceptualize as norm-consumership. The decisive distinction is that norm-entrepreneurs are no longer the object of rulemaking as *rule-takers*, but have rather become subjects of rulemaking and therefore *rule-takers* themselves.

Two specific patterns of behavior indicate norm-entrepreneurship: norm setting and norm development. Corporations can support the setting or institutionalization of an entirely new norm by lobbying for it among their peers or by engaging in the creation of a collective self-regulatory initiative. But even after a norm has already reached a certain level of acceptance and institutionalization, a corporation can still engage as a norm-entrepreneur through norm development activities, for example by further specifying a norm's implied requirements. These two types of corporate behavior stand in contrast to the classic role of norm-consumers, whose behavioral options can be distinguished as either norm acceptance or norm implementation.

The remainder of this chapter will focus on norm-entrepreneurs and will seek to establish in how far certain characteristics of a corporation's home state foster corporate norm-entrepreneurship.

The puzzle – cross-national variations in corporate norm-entrepreneurship

Our claim that the home state matters for fostering norm-entrepreneurship rests on the observation of significant cross-country variation in the numbers of corporate norm-entrepreneurs[2] versus norm-consumers within two important international self-regulatory fora – the UN Global Compact (GC)[3] and the Global Reporting Initiative (GRI)[4] (Flohr *et al.* 2008).

Figures 12.1 and 12.2 show the ratio of norm-entrepreneurs to norm-consumers in the Global Compact and the Global Reporting Initiative, respectively. Taking these observations together, intuitively one might be surprised to find only Germany and the UK consistently showing high ratios of norm-entrepreneurs to norm-consumers, while the US ranks only in the intermediate quantile together

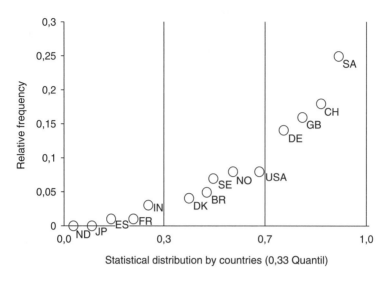

Figure 12.1   Ratio of norm-entrepreneurs to norm-consumers in the Global Compact.

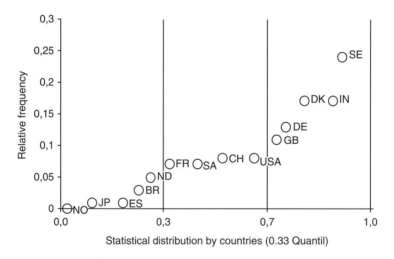

Figure 12.2   Ratio of norm-entrepreneurs to norm-consumers in the Global Reporting Initiative.

with countries such as Switzerland, Sweden, Norway or South Africa. A third group of countries shows disproportionately low results in both self-regulatory initiatives, including Japan, Spain and the Netherlands – but France also hardly reaches the intermediate level. Although both self-regulatory initiatives allow for norm-consumership and norm-entrepreneurship by all corporations independent of their origin, some corporate home states show significantly higher degrees of norm-entrepreneurship than others. How can this puzzle of cross-country variation be explained? In the next section some possible explanations are examined.

Possible explanations

When home state characteristics are employed to account for behavioral differences of (transnational) companies, classic explanations often refer to the level of regulation and the VoC approach. But even though both of these theoretical approaches explicitly focus on a company's home state as an explanation for variation in corporate behavior, neither of the two, as will be shown subsequently, can sufficiently explain the varying levels of corporate engagement in norm setting and norm development processes.

Corporate law literature claims that the level of regulation has an influence on corporate behavior and that it defines the scope and boundaries of corporate activities (Braithwaite and Drahos 2000). Again, assuming that corporations are influenced most of all by home state characteristics, a hypothesis could be that the level of regulation prevailing in the home state influences corporate behavior even outside the home state and that corporations from highly regulated home states participate more actively in norm setting and norm development. Since their being subject to extensive regulation might result in a competitive disadvantage internationally, they seek to make similar regulations applicable to their competitors in order to level the (global) playing field. Yet, when applying rankings that compare national levels of regulation, such as the Environmental Regulatory Regime Index (ERRI) which summarizes the overall comprehensiveness of the environmental regulatory system in a country, it becomes clear that these are not able to provide a sufficient explanatory account for varying levels of corporate norm-entrepreneurship across countries. ERRI identifies significant differences between levels of regulation in countries that show similar ratios in corporate norm-entrepreneurship (Esty and Porter 2002, 2005). Obviously, these findings contradict the hypothesis that a high degree of (environmental) regulation leads to high levels of norm-entrepreneurship, since countries with high levels of regulation can be found among all three clusters with low, medium and high levels of corporate norm-entrepreneurship.

In contrast to a pure level of regulation hypothesis, the VoC approach involves a broad range of variables to differentiate between capitalist systems and emphasizes inherent institutional complementarities, such as between the financial system, corporate governance, industrial relations, etc. (Hall and Soskice 2001: 17f; Jackson and Deeg 2006: 11f). The VoC typology introduced by Hall and Soskice (2001) classifies capitalist systems as either Coordinated Market Economies (CMEs), in which interaction between different political and economic actors is based on coordination, long-lasting relations and strategic partnership, or Liberal Market Economies (LMEs), in which actors use solely market-based mechanisms to interact. Among the large OECD nations, six are classified as LMEs – the USA, the UK, Australia, Canada, New Zealand, Ireland – and another ten as CMEs – Germany, Japan, Switzerland, the Netherlands, Belgium, Sweden, Norway, Denmark, Finland and Austria (Hall and Soskice 2001: 21). However, the authors themselves acknowledge that several states do not neatly fit onto the CME–LME continuum. Therefore, they introduce a third category, Mediterranean capitalisms, to classify six countries with ambiguous characteristics – France, Italy, Spain, Portugal, Greece and Turkey (ibid.: 21).

If the VoC approach were applicable to our empirical findings from the GC and GRI analysis, we would expect corporate home states that show either a high or a low level of corporate norm-entrepreneurship to belong to one and the same category of market economies. In opposition to this assumption, we do not find the classic differentiation between CMEs and LMEs valid to provide any analytical added value when analyzing the home state as an independent variable. We found countries that represent different varieties of capitalism, such as Germany (CME) and the UK (LME), ranking similarly high in the number of norm-entrepreneurs. Equally, highly diverse types of capitalist countries, such as the US (LME) and France (Mediterranean CME), rank close to one another in their degree of norm-entrepreneurship.

Therefore, as an intermediate result, we find neither the level of regulation within a home state nor the VoC approach valid for providing a comprehensive explanation for the cross-national differences between the proactive behavior of TNCs coming from the UK and Germany and the comparatively low engagement of those from France and the US.

However, in the following we still draw on the VoC approach for determining our case selection. We focus on those countries usually taken as ideal typical examples of the VoC typology to explicate clearly where we deviate from the approach: the UK and the US as prime LMEs, Germany representing CMEs and France as a representative of the Mediterranean CMEs. Selecting countries from all three categories allows us to modify the traditional VoC approach in order to focus on the institutional differences with significant explanatory power for our specific puzzle while at the same time providing the advantage of representing economically and politically important countries some of which are also homes to the comparatively highest numbers of TNCs in the world.

Business–government relations: an alternative explanation?

So far we have discussed possible explanatory approaches and established their invalidity with regard to the empirical findings presented above. The question remains why there are such apparent cross-national differences between the behavior of corporations from the UK and Germany, and those from France and the US. Why are some corporations, namely those from the UK and Germany, more willing to take on governance functions, thereby setting norms for their own and others' corporate behavior at the transnational level? By offering an alternative theoretical argument we will broaden the perspective and take up earlier attempts in IR to explain the policy impact of transnational actors in world politics by reference to domestic factors (Risse-Kappen 1995). Relying on the notion that different national institutional environments allocate responsibility for social and ecological issues differently (Matten and Moon 2004), we argue that domestic structures may indeed have an influence on corporate contributions to governance. Instead of focusing on state structures versus societal structures, we will rather extend the policy network concept that links state and society, especially by focusing on particular business–government relations (Risse-Kappen 1995: 22).

The alternative approach: cooperative versus adversarial business–government relations

In searching for an alternative explanation for the cross-national variation, we combine the assumption that the home state and its institutions indeed matter (Doremus *et al.* 1999) with an explicit constructivist argument (Hall and Taylor 1996): As opposed to the widespread opinion that corporations will always have a natural stance of opposing any kind of regulation – regardless of the character of such regulation, whether it consists of binding national law or voluntary self-regulation – we assume that such features of a corporation's identity are not exogenously given but can be subject to change. The direction of such change and identity formation will depend on the kind of *socialization* the company experiences at home over time. This argument refers to Wendt's constructivist approach to identity formation on the basis of intersubjective understandings and the mutual constitution of structure and agency (Wendt 1999). We argue that such socialization and the ensuing development of the company's identity will depend largely, though not exclusively, on the national institutional environment a company is embedded in. National institutions will play an important role as socializing agencies and might therefore also influence the behavior of corporations acting on the international level (Checkel 1997; Doremus *et al.* 1999: 15f; Hooghe 2005). More specifically, we presume the degree to which a company is used to taking on public functions and to participating in political processes *at home* will influence the likeliness of also taking on such functions *away from home*, including in transnational arenas. How far a company is ready to engage in norm setting processes, without doubt one of the most prominent public functions, at the transnational level by acting as a norm-entrepreneur within self-regulatory initiatives will therefore depend on the degree to which it is already used to doing so on the national level. Accordingly, in order to analyze the importance of the type of interaction within the national institutional environment, we will take a closer look at policy styles, decision-making procedures and mechanisms for societal involvement within a country to be able to test under which conditions TNCs take on a public role.

In contrast to the VoC approach which, as exemplified most prominently by Hall and Soskice (2001), generally presents the UK and Germany as opposite extreme cases of CMEs and LMEs respectively, we are looking for similarities between the UK and Germany that allow for an explanation of the comparatively high level of norm-entrepreneurship by companies coming from both states. Such similarities rather than differences between institutions in these two countries are stipulated by research on neo-corporatism. As an analytical concept, the corporatist approach usually focuses on one or both aspects of two related phenomena: the degree to which interest intermediation is organized and centralized within a national economy, and the degree to which these organized interests are regularly consulted in legislative processes (Lijphart 1999: 171; Schmitter 1982: 262f). The latter aspect is referred to as concertation and is contrasted to an opposite mode of policy making, "pressure", where interest groups remain outside the policy process (Schmitter 1982: 263). This literature, and especially the concept of institutionalized cooperation or concertation between business and government, is closely linked to our argument because it looks at the degree to which national decision-making foresees tripartite interactions in non-hierarchical fora and therefore corporate involvement with norm setting processes.[5] Katzenstein further differentiates between liberal and social types of corporatism, with either capital or labor being the dominant interest group (Katzenstein 1985: 104f). Crouch describes the corporatist state – in contrast to both the free-market and the interventionist state – as one that shares public order functions so that civil society groups help to bear the burden of the state and become "staatstragende Kräfte", meaning indispensable actors that support the state in carrying out public functions (Crouch 1993: 6f).

All of these descriptions of corporatist politics underline characteristics of *national* economies that are likely able to explain the cross-national difference in corporate participation in processes of international norm setting and norm development: They stress the different degrees to which corporations in different countries are used to act in partnership with government in a cooperative manner and to take on public functions. Corporatist systems are differentiated from liberal systems – where interactions between business and government are not institutionalized but, at the most, the outcome of political competition and bargaining – and from interventionist systems – where the state dominates business–government relations significantly by enforcing strict policies unilaterally. Even though there are differences in and disputes about the typologies created by this research, it provides several clear arguments for why Germany and the UK can be considered similar cases in this regard and should be differentiated from countries such as France and the US, because corporatist structures in the two former countries are significantly stronger than in the latter where liberal competition or state intervention dominate.

A closely connected argument, though it is usually treated within a different line of literature, focuses on the type of relationship that dominates business–government interactions within a given national economy and on ensuing types of business regulation. Departing from the observation of "adversarial legalism" that characterizes these relationships in the US, this literature first of all differentiates the US from non-adversarial economies, such as the UK, where corporations act in partnership with government entities (Vogel 1986). This differentiation has already been employed by Kollmann and Prakash to explain the cross-national variation in business acceptance rates for the voluntary eco-management schemes EMAS and ISO 14000. They also made the case for further differentiating the US from the German type of adversarial economy – because, in the latter, a consensual style of policy-making dominates most issue areas, maybe with the exemption of environmental policy where stringent laws seem to characterize a more adversarial relationship (Kollman and Prakash 2001: 418–20).

In the following we transfer this logic to the cases of the UK, Germany, the US and France in order to make a similar argument about the influence of national business–government relations on the behavior of corporations on the international level. But instead of using it as an explanation for the level of corporate adoption and implementation rates of prescribed policies, we seek to explain corporate participation in governance, therefore focusing on rule-making rather than on rule-taking. An argument pointing in the same direction has been made by Newman and Bach, who explain different styles of self-regulation prevalent in the digital economy by pointing to national variations in the shadow of public power. Specifically, they differentiate between a state's carrot and stick capacities as two distinct ways of inducing collective action by corporations and stipulate that these will result either in cooperative or legalistic versions of self-regulation respectively (Newman and Bach 2004).

In a similar vein, according to our assumption about business–government relations as institutions of socialization at the national level, we expect those countries showing a high level of corporate norm-entrepreneurship to be dominated by cooperative interactions between business and government, whereas countries with a low level should be characterized by adversarial business–government relations. By not providing for a constructive role in the policy-making process, adversarial business–government relations bring forward corporations that also remain passive beyond the state. Whereas corporatist notions of business–government relations further support the readiness of corporations to become norm-entrepreneurs, interventionist types of state regulation hamper corporations from taking on this function – because their *socialization* has only taught them a passive role in regulatory processes which are heavily dominated by the state.

United Kingdom (UK)

Companies from the UK show, similarly to the German case, a high degree of norm-entrepreneurship. Corporatist theory alone, however, will not help us to understand this phenomenon because the UK is usually presented as a case of low centralization and power of trade associations. The institutional representation of business interests is comparatively weak and underdeveloped (Grant 1993: 104f). Business organizations as well as labor unions are fragmented in size, sector and territory and lack public law status as well as personal, financial and political resources.[6] Though typologies sometimes disagree on the location of the UK on the corporatist–liberal continuum, it cannot be seen as a prime example of institutionalized interaction between business and government in policy-making. But, nevertheless, there is a surprisingly strong partnership between government and individual corporations, which is described in terms of a so-called British "company state" (Grant 2004: 411), which is characteristic of the UK style of business regulation (Vogel 1986). The UK system of regulation is based profoundly on mutual trust between business and government. Legislation in the UK encourages business self-regulation, for example in the case of environmental regulation, which is not done through precise emission limits or generally stringent binding laws but through non-binding guidelines that can flexibly be adapted to local conditions by individual administrative or regulatory agencies (Kollmann and Prakash 2001: 420f). UK business associations insist heavily on preserving Britain's regulatory style against persistent EU attempts at harmonization (Vogel 1986: 21). The British government prefers direct consultation with individual corporations (Coen and Grant 2006: 23) and thereby offers business the permanent chance to directly influence UK policies in short-term, issue-specific arrangements. UK business has a substantial interest in more engagement of the British government with binding regulation – which is coherent to the business's interest – as a sort of trade threshold against competitors from emerging markets. But, until now, government is still trapped in the traditional Anglo-Saxon reluctance toward interventions in the marketplace: "UK plc. is ill-served by lowest-common-denominator lobbying" (Ward and Smith 2006: 36f).

In sum, UK business is used to a cooperative approach to policy-making with government as an individual partner – which above all stands in contrast to the US style of business–government relations. Therefore, British corporations are more likely to adopt the same expectations and style when interacting on the international level. Thus, they do not perceive regulatory measures as generally evil but rather appreciate the possibility of contributing to their making. As a result, the corporations' Corporate Social Responsibility (CSR) performance, including their role as norm-entrepreneurs, has reached a superior level (Bertelsmann Foundation 2007: 10, 32f).

Germany

Corporations based in Germany have participated in norm setting and norm development processes at the transnational level to a comparatively high extent. Germany is generally characterized as a highly regulated economy, especially in regulatory areas that are considered to be most relevant to and therefore probably most influential upon corporate social behavior, such as workers' rights and environmental protection. In terms of the participation of business in policy-making and the institutions enabling it, Germany is typically portrayed as an ideal example of corporatist policy-making, including not only a high degree of interest group centralization but, above all, concertation mechanisms that make trilateral consultation on policy-making the rule rather than the exception – though there are no statutory entitlements granting rights to such consultations (Lehmbruch 1982: 20). Even though the German policy style might be termed partly "adversarial" in so far as it usually relies on complex legalistic rules, these rules are usually made in consultation with or even by industry actors themselves via institutions that facilitate government–industry cooperation (Kollmann and Prakash 2001: 418–20). Some authors point out Germany's traditional patterns of cooperative economic governance (Esser 1995) and its flexibility within stable institutions (Katzenstein 1989). For our argument, we can therefore conclude that due to corporatist decision-making processes and institutions German corporations are highly used to participating in the setting of prescriptive rules for their own behavior within the German national context. This makes it likely that they have internalized such functions over time and accepted them as part of their identity. As a result, they engage in the setting of rules for corporate behavior at the international level. Although corporate CSR behavior has not reached its full potential, German business–government relations provide a solid foundation for norm-entrepreneurship and CSR engagement in general (Habisch *et al.* 2005).

USA

As stated earlier, though high levels of regulation are a distinct feature of the American economy – at least in certain areas – American companies show relatively little engagement in processes of norm-entrepreneurship within international self-regulatory fora. Interest group theory helps us to understand this phenomenon because interest intermediation in the US is classically portrayed as highly liberal, with a variety of small rather than big interest groups competing rather than cooperating in terms of their public policy goals. Due to Americans' historical mistrust of corporate power and suspicion of business–government cooperation, government officials have been reluctant to justify particular policies on the grounds of their benefits to a particular industry (Vogel 1986: 94). Tripartite concertation is rather unheard of in the US, which is probably due to the most distinct feature of American business–government relations for which the term "adversarial legalism" was originally coined (Kagan 1991).[7]

American regulation is not only not based upon partnership policy style, it also shows virtually no flexibility or discretion on the part of administration; it rather consists of fully classic command-and-control mechanisms. Regulatory rule-making in the US entails many more legal formalities: public notice and comment, open hearings, restrictions on informal contracts, legalistically specified evidentiary and scientific standards, mandatory official findings, and responses to interest group arguments (Kagan and Axelrad 1997: 153).

Probably most importantly, any new type of regulation is more often than not challenged in court by industries addressed by it, showing the stark contrast between confrontation in the US and collaboration in the UK and Germany (Vogel 1986). This underlines the non-collaborative interaction mode in business–government relations in the US. It leads to the preliminary conclusion that US companies have no history of working in collaboration with government and of taking on public functions, such as setting of CSR rules for their own behavior. Accordingly, companies will also be less proactive in forging such corporate engagement in international processes.

France

French companies have shown even less engagement in norm setting and norm development processes than American companies – which we explain by French business–government relations being of an interventionist nature: French business–government relations operate within the context of a historical background that takes for granted a close relationship between government and industry, that accepts that the state should articulate historical priorities and expects that such priorities will continue to maintain an almost "mercantilist" concern with French economic interests (Cawson *et al.* 1987: 10). Because of the accepted monopoly of the state and the strong belief in its responsibility for the common welfare, there is a deep mistrust in intermediary organizations. The traditional understanding of how to divide private and public responsibilities has been characterized by public authority enjoying a high degree of legitimacy, whereas the market has suffered from weak legitimacy.[8]

France is a country where the executive is strong, the legislature weak, the bureaucracy predominant, where interest group politics and lobbying are often seen as illegitimate (Schmidt 1996: 179) and where providing social welfare is predominantly in the state's responsibility (Blasco and Zølner 2008: 25). Corporatist research finds France to be only weakly corporatist in nature because, despite strongly organized interest groups, concertation does not lead to consensus and the ideologies of the different sectors remain rather adversarial (Lehmbruch 1982: 22). The French environment of trade unions, business associations and labor organizations is described as highly specialized and decentralized and, in general, with a low degree of organization (Jansen 2001: 129).

France is characterized as having "limited pluralism" or "weak corporatism" with a "statist" tradition that characterizes a polity in which the state is "strong" and autonomous (Schmidt 1996: 46). The role of the French state in business–government relations is described as predominantly "interventionist" or "dirigiste" (Schmidt 1996: 46f), and French government today still continues to intervene in business, albeit in a more limited, supply-side way through laws and incentives intended not only to make the economy more competitive but also to "moralize" business and labor relations (Schmidt 2003: 547). All this underlines the non-collaborative interaction mode in French business–government relations and leads to the preliminary conclusion that French companies have no history of working in collaboration with government and therefore are less proactive in norm setting and norm development processes.

In sum, these four case studies illustrate different national environments along a continuum from cooperative to adversarial business–government relations. These domestic constellations provide differently strong encouragements for corporations to engage in processes of norm setting and norm development within collective self-regulatory initiatives at the transnational level. Whereas levels of national regulation or national types of capitalist institutions seem unable to explain the different engagement of corporations from different countries, the alternative hypothesis presented here can: Within international self-regulatory fora, corporations are indeed taking on the same roles that they have become used to in business–government relations at the national level.

A constructivist explanation: national environments and business identity

We have argued that cooperative business–government relations at the national level enhance the likelihood of corporations taking on a proactive role on the transnational level whereas adversarial relations or those dominated by heavy government intervention inhibit such behavior. Our database of 71 corporations that are active as norm-entrepreneurs within six self-regulatory initiatives shows strong evidence of such correlations – companies from Germany or the UK are to a considerably higher degree active as norm-entrepreneurs than companies from France or the US. It remains to be shown what specific causal path connects the supposed explanatory variable, business–government relations prevailing in a given home state, and the dependent variable, the engagement of companies as norm-entrepreneurs within self-regulatory initiatives at the international level. We have already tentatively stated that we believe the causal argument to be of a constructivist nature. In what follows we will seek to outline how such a constructivist causal mechanism works.

Having originally departed from the assumption that corporations will usually be opposed to or at least not be interested in taking on public regulatory functions, we have observed that these preferences, and also certain aspects of the social identity of corporations, apparently have been altered in certain countries. We suggest that this alteration happened as a result of cooperative interaction between business and government. In contrast, in countries with adversarial relations and clear-cut hierarchical top-down approaches to regulation, corporate preferences – in so far as they can be delineated from corporate action, or rather non-action, with regard to norm-entrepreneurship – remain the same; no identity change seems to have taken place. In other words, it is suggested that business–government relations function as institutions of socialization at the national level, capable of altering the preferences and identity of the actors being socialized – in our case, corporations (see Figure 12.3).

We apply an understanding of socialization analogous to that of international socialization used in IR research, where actors are socialized into a new community by being "taught" the norms constitutive of and applied in that community (Finnemore 1996; Schimmelfennig 2003: 406). We take the subject of socialization (the socialization agency) and the content of the socialization (the norms and scripts of the community) as the basis for our analysis. However, and differing from current socialization research, we are not looking at the socialization of state actors into an international community, but we apply the concept of socialization to national institutional environments impacting on corporate actors as the subjects of socialization (see also Checkel 1997). In our case, the socialization agency is the national environment, defined as national business–government relations. Finally, regarding the content of socialization, the

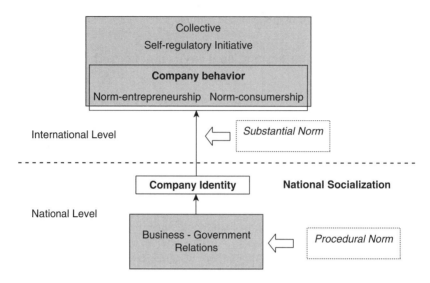

Figure 12.3 Causal   mechanism: business–government   relations   and   norm-
           entrepreneurship.

distinction between procedural and substantial norms (Hurrell 2002: 143) enables
us to establish that, at the national level, companies have been socialized into a
procedural norm that tells them how regulations should be set and how public
goods should be provided – either in cooperation between public and private
actors or by confrontational interaction. This procedural norm will therefore
influence the corporate expectations about how the process of norm setting
should be designed on the global level and will determine the ensuing corporate
behavior.

By differentiating between procedural and substantial norms, we are also able
to disentangle the presumed influence on the identity of a company in a broad
sense into its influence on more specific and separate aspects of that identity.
Procedural norms determine a company's beliefs about its relationship to other
groups – which ought to be separated from its normative beliefs and practices. The
latter would be affected by substantial norms about appropriate corporate behavior
in specific social contexts rather than by the procedural socialization process at the
national level (Johnston 2005: 1032). We therefore argue that when a company
is confronted with new substantial norms addressed to it from the outside world,
such as emerging CSR norms, its reaction will depend on the procedural norms it
has been socialized into nationally and its ensuing identity. This type of behavior
has also been called "stickiness", which implies a certain sense of obligation to a
social group and its social values (Johnston 2005: 1031).

National socialization, therefore, depending on its form and process, first has
an influence on an actor's behavior as a norm-entrepreneur or norm-consumer
at the transnational level (procedural norm). But national socialization can also

have an effect in enabling or inhibiting processes of transnational socialization of corporate actors, understood – in analogy to IR research – as learning to implement substantial norms generated at the transnational level (Checkel 1997, 2001; Hooghe 2005). This differentiation has related our findings to those of Sell and Prakash (2004), who seek to show the limits of constructivism's distinction between transnational networks that are motivated either by principled ideas or by instrumentalist goals. While stipulating that both NGO as well as business networks can be driven by normative ideals and material concerns, these authors demonstrate that the strategies employed by both for the framing of international norms and regimes do not differ along the lines of the assumed motivations. In analogy, our argument also does not prejudice the question whether corporations engage in international norm setting processes for instrumental or normative reasons, but rather supposes that only companies that have been socialized nationally in a certain way will engage at all.

We do therefore assume the existence of an at least two-stage process of socialization of corporate actors into transnational norm setting: At the end of the first, national stage, the company enters the transnational arena as an actor whose identity has been shaped by specific procedural norms in the national arena and who now has to decide whether or not to participate in processes of norm formation and norm development within international self-regulatory initiatives. It would be only at the end of this second stage of – now transnational – socialization that a corporation might become a norm-abiding actor in international society who actually implements its norms. At this stage, the content of socialization would be a substantial CSR norm and the socializing institution could be the collectivity of corporations or multiple stakeholders active in the respective self-regulatory initiative. Again, structure and agency are mutually influencing and co-determining each other.

While we find strong evidence that national business–government relations are capable of altering business's preferences and therefore, business's behavior at the international level, we also have to concede that by far not all corporations from such cooperative national environments engage in norm-entrepreneurship at the transnational level. In fact, many engage in norm-related behavior only very sporadically.

At the same time, we find a considerable number of actors from these cooperative national environments that engage extensively in such processes on basically every occasion they get. Such frequency and intensity in application of the – seemingly – *learnt* behavior we find to be analogous to sustained implementation of community norms, which is usually taken as an indication in IR research that internalization and persuasion rather than mimicking and role-playing are at work (Schimmelfennig 2005: 839). We therefore suggest that corporations that engage intensively in norm-entrepreneurship have actually internalized the procedural norm of cooperation in norm setting, whereas those who remain passive in self-regulatory initiatives have only engaged in role-playing based on processes of habitualization and imitation at the national level (Schimmelfennig 2003: 415). This strong argument, according to which corporations acting as (systematic) norm-entrepreneurs have internalized procedural norms of cooperation through a process of national socialization, can be supported by taking a look at the conditions under which national socialization took place – which generally conform with those identified by constructivist researchers as prerequisites for persuasion and learning (Checkel 2001; Risse 2000): Interaction between business and government, for example in corporatist Germany, usually takes place in "in camera" institutions where actors meet without much public attention and where state authorities will not act as "lecturers" but will rather engage in argumentation (Checkel 2001: 562f). As regards the procedural norm, therefore, a case could be made for internalization.

However, the same reasoning can lead to the opposite hypothesis regarding the potential reactions of corporations to new substantial norms addressed to them in international self-regulatory initiatives where, instead of persuasion, role-playing could more likely be expected: For this latter type of behavior Powell and DiMaggio (1991) have coined the term "institutional isomorphism." They stress the impact of situations of insecurity which leads a company to follow a familiar pattern of behavior. In case of the emergence of a new norm, in this case a CSR norm, companies might be confused about how to react to rising expectations of new stakeholder groups such as civil society organizations or also – to some degree – of additional market actors. In addition, such self-regulatory initiatives are usually rather public and politicized, making persuasion even less likely, and it seems therefore probable that if companies resort to the same type of behavior they are habituated to on the national level this will rather take a form of unintentional role-playing. With the help of this excursion into empirical constructivist theory (Risse 2003), we can conclude that despite good reasons to suspect constructivist causal mechanisms of socialization – especially into procedural norms – and identity change to be at work, further qualitative research needs to be undertaken to confirm these conjectures. In any case it has to be noted that the causal variable identified here, the national business–government relations, must not be understood as deterministic but rather as enabling causes, because by far not all corporations from a given environment show the behavior the value of the variable would suggest. Such variation in behavior despite the presence of an identical variable may be attributed to the presence or absence of certain other conditions characterizing the actors, rather than their environments. Indeed, several have been found to be necessary conditions for norm-entrepreneurship within the overall research project – such as the heterogeneity of the regulatory environments, the visibility of the company and transnational activist pressure (Flohr *et al.* 2010).

Conclusion

In sum, we can conclude that different national environments seem to promote or prevent corporations from engaging in processes of norm setting and norm development within collective self-regulatory initiatives at the transnational level. Whereas levels of national regulation or national types of capitalist institutions seem unable to explain, in particular, the starkly different engagement of corporations from Germany and the UK as opposed to those from France and the US, our presented alternative hypothesis, seeking to typologize business–government relations on the national level, seems to be highly significant. The underlying assumption is that corporations will take on the same behavioral roles within international self-regulatory fora that they are already used to at the national level. The significant national institutions therefore are those that enable or disable cooperation between business and government and an active participation of business actors in rule-setting processes and the execution of public functions. Different stances in comparative research have already identified such institutions. We draw on these to categorize the types of business–government relations prevalent in certain countries on a scale ranging from cooperative to adversarial relations. We suggest that non-corporatist, adversarial or interventionist national economies that do not provide cooperative roles for business actors at the national level will not foster corporate norm-entrepreneurship at the international level. In contrast, political systems described as corporatist, non-adversarial and non-interventionist are usually characterized by cooperative relations between business and government. Corporations socialized in such systems will also be more likely to adopt an active role in norm setting and norm development. We therefore argue that corporations are not *per se* opposed to any kind of rules and regulation but rather that their identity in this regard is constructed by the social institutions and procedural norms they are *used to* at the national level.

Notes

1 This chapter presents findings from the research project "Corporations as Norm-Entrepreneurs? Potential and Limitations of Private Self-regulation in Global Governance" at Darmstadt University of Technology funded by the German Research Foundation (DFG). For a more comprehensive analysis of the project's results see Flohr et al. 2010. The authors wish to thank Martina Borusewitsch, Kristian Lempa, Linda Wallbott, Julia Ebling, Iman Sakkaki and Samuil Simeonov for their research assistance.

2 The research project 'Corporations as norm-entrepreneurs?' generated a database identifying 256 corporate norm-entrepreneurs on the basis of 27 indicators for norm setting and norm development within six different self-regulatory initiatives. These corporations were further differentiated into 185 random norm-entrepreneurs fulfilling only one indicator for norm-entrepreneurship and therefore being of less interest to this study, 71 sporadic norm-entrepreneurs being active as such at least twice and 10 systematic norm-entrepreneurs engaging in norm setting or norm development in at least three of the six initiatives. The following empirical puzzle and analysis rests on comparisons of systematic and sporadic norm-entrepreneurship to norm-consumership.

3 The GC provides a learning and dialogue platform in which corporations as well as trade unions, civil society organizations and various UN organizations and programs can participate (Nelson 2002; Rieth 2004). Each participating company has the responsibility to translate the GC principles into business strategies and operations, thereby accepting norms as applicable to their behavior which are not otherwise legally binding upon them (Kell 2003). By sending a letter to the Secretary General of the United Nations, expressing support for the GC and its ten principles, a company can demonstrate that it is committed to the most basic principles of human rights, labor standards, protection of the environment and anti-corruption. By either being a founding member of the GC,

having been a member of the Advisory Board or having actively taken part in other GC engagement mechanisms such as the Annual Learning Forum, companies can contribute to norm setting and norm development.

4 The GRI seeks to establish a globally accepted framework for corporate sustainability reporting (Kolk 2003, 2004). All norms of this reporting framework are developed in an ongoing, formal and highly institutionalized review procedure (Global Reporting Initiative 2002, 2006). The prevailing mode of governance is discursive and consensus seeking, but the "label" provided to companies reporting "in accordance with" GRI also functions as a market incentive. Although the GRI allows for all four types of corporate contributions to governance, TNCs predominantly engage in norm development: by submitting their input, comments and suggestions on the content of the reporting guidelines in a formal three-phase norm-development process (Gee and Slater 2005), they participate in the continuous improvement of the norm inventory.

5 We are aware of potential problems in applying the neo-corporatist approach to the analysis of TNCs and therefore equating them with the business associations of which they are members, but we are optimistic that the logic remains equally applicable to our argument.

6 For instance, the leading business organization Confederation of British Industry (CBI) has been constrained by broad membership, an internal structure of special committees and, most importantly, a policy of the lowest common denominator, and is thus generally more reactive than active in driving its interests (Grant 1993: 105, 111). The CBI has the strong advantage of a cooperative relationship with New Labour despite a tighter net of regulation, because of the UK's blocking position to EU regulation which might impact on business competition (Grant 2004: 417).

7 First, adversarial legalism differs from informal methods of resolving disputes or making policy decisions, such as mediation, expert professional judgment, or bargaining among political authorities. Second, in adversarial legalism, litigants and their lawyers play active roles in the policy implementation and decision-making process; hence the style differs from governance that is legally formal but more hierarchical or bureaucratic (Kagan and Axelrad 1997: 152).

8 With regard to post-1789 France, scholars turn to different factors to explain this. First among these is French republicanism with its discourse on the "general interest" (*la morale de l'intérêt général*) which states that the state, standing beyond civil society and the market, can and should define rationally what is best for the nation and serve its interests. On the contrary, civil society and the market are considered to act in favor of their own particular interests rather than for the common good. Thus, private actors have enjoyed little legitimacy in comparison to the state (Blasco and Zølner 2008: 24).

References

Bertelsmann Foundation (2007) *CSR Navigator* (Gütersloh: Bertelsmann Foundation).

Blasco, M. and Zølner, M. (2008) "Corporate Social Responsibility in Mexico and France: Exploring the Role of Normative Institutions," in *Business & Society*, OnlineFirst, 30 January 2008.

Braithwaite, J. and Drahos, P. (2000) *Global Business Regulation* (Cambridge: Cambridge University Press).

Brozus, L., Take, I. and Wolf, K.D. (2003) *Vergesellschaftung des Regierens? Der Wandel nationaler und internationaler politischer Steuerung unter dem Leitbild der nachhaltigen Entwicklung* (Opladen: Leske+Brudrich).

Cawson, A., Holmes, P. and Stevens, A. (1987) "The Interaction between Firms and the State in France: The Telecommunications and Consumer Electronics Sector," in Wilks, S.

and Wright, M. (eds) *Comparative Government–Industry Relations. Western Europe, the United States, and Japan*, pp. 10–34 (Oxford: Clarendon Press).

Checkel, J.T. (1997) "International Norms and Domestic Politics: Bridging the Rationalist–Constructivist Divide," in *European Journal of International Relations*, 3:4, 473–95.

—— (2001) "Why Comply? Social Learning and European Identity Change," in *International Organization*, 55:3, 553–88.

Coen, D. and Grant, W. (2006) "Managing Business and Government Relations," in Coen, D. and Grant, W. (eds) *Business and Government. Methods and Practice*, pp. 13–32 (Opladen: Barbara Budrich Publishers).

Crouch, C. (1993) *Industrial Relations and European State Traditions* (Oxford: Clarendon Press).

Cutler, C., Haufler, V. and Porter, T. (1999) *Private Authority and International Affairs* (New York: State University of New York Press).

Doremus, P.N., Kelly, W.W., Pauly, L.W. and Reich, S. (1999) *The Myth of the Global Corporation* (Princeton: Princeton University Press).

Esser, J. (1995) "Germany: The Old Policy Style," in Hayward, J. (ed.) *Industrial Enterprise and European Integration: From National to International Champions in Western Europe*, pp. 48–75 (Oxford: Oxford University Press).

Esty, D.C. and Porter, M.E. (2002) "Ranking National Environmental Regulation and Performance: A Leading Indicator of Future Competitiveness?" in World Economic Forum (ed.) *The Global Competitiveness Report 2001–2002* (Davos: World Economic Forum).

—— (2005) "National environmental performance: an empirical analysis of policy results and determinants," in *Environment and Development Economics*, 10: 391–434.

Finnemore, M. (1996) *National Interests in International Society* (Ithaca, NY: Cornell University Press).

Finnemore, M. and Sikkink, K. (1998) "International Norm Dynamics and Political Change," *International Organization*, 52:4, 887–917.

Flohr, A., Rieth, L., Schwindenhammer, S. and Wolf, K.D. (2008) "Variations in Corporate Norm-Entrepreneurship: Why the Home State Matters," Paper presented at the 49th International Studies Association Convention, March 2008, San Francisco.

Flohr, A., Rieth, L., Schwindenhammer, S. and Wolf, K.D. (2010) *The Role of Business in Global Governance. Corporations as Norm-Entrepreneurs*. London: Macmillan.

Gee, C. and Slater, A. (2005) "Developing Next-Generation GRI Guidelines," in *Corporate Responsibility Management*, 1:5, 30–33.

Global Reporting Initiative (2002) *Sustainability Reporting Guidelines* (Amsterdam: Global Reporting Initiative).

—— (2006) *G3 Sustainability Reporting Guidelines* (Amsterdam: Global Reporting Initiative).

Grant, W. (1993) *Business and Politics in Britain* (London: Macmillan).

—— (2004) "Pressure Politics. The Changing World of Pressure Groups," in *Parliamentary Affairs*, 57:2, 408–19.

Habisch, A., Jonker, J. and Schmidtpeter, R. (eds) (2005) *Corporate Social Responsibility across Europe* (Berlin: Springer).

Hall, P.A. and Taylor, R.C.R. (1996) "Political Science and the Three New Institutionalisms," in *Political Studies*, 44, 936–57.

Hall, P.A. and Soskice, D. (2001) *Varieties of Capitalism, The Institutional Foundations of Comparative Advantage* (Oxford: Oxford University Press).

Hall, R.B. and Biersteker, T.J. (2002) "The Emergence of Private Authority in Global Governance," in Hall, R.B. and Biersteker, T.J. (eds) *The Emergence of Private Authority in Global Governance*, pp. 3–22 (Cambridge: Cambridge University Press).

Haufler, V. (2001) *A Public Role for the Private Sector. Industry Self-Regulation in a Global Economy* (Washington, DC: Carnegie Endowment for International Peace).

Higgott, R.A., Underhill, G.R.D. and Bieler, A. (2000) *Non-state Actors and Authority in the Global System* (London: Routledge).

Hooghe, L. (2005) "Several Roads lead to International Norms, but Few via International Socialization. A Case Study of the European Commission," in *International Organization*, 59:4, 861–98.

Hurrell, A. (2002) "Norms and Ethics in International Relations," in Carlsnaes, W., Risse, T. and Simmons, B.A. (eds) *Handbook of International Relations*, pp. 137–54 (London: Sage).

Jackson, G. and Deeg, R. (2006) "How many Varieties of Capitalism? Comparing the Comparative Institutional Analyses of Capitalist Diversity," in *MPIfG Discussion Paper*, (06/2), Köln.

Jansen, P. (2001) "Frankreich. Verbände – Eine Rechnung mit vielen Unbekannten," in Reutter, W. and Rütters, P. (eds) *Verbände und Verbandssysteme in Westeuropa*, pp. 125–50 (Opladen: Leske+Budrich).

Johnston, A.I. (2005) "Conclusions and Extensions: Toward Mid-range Theorizing and Beyond Europe," in *International Organization*, 59:4, 1013–44.

Kagan, R.A. (1991) "Adversarial Legalism and American Government," in *Journal of Policy Analysis and Management*, 10:3, 369–406.

Kagan, R.A. and Axelrad, L. (1997) "Adversarial Legalism. An International Perspective," in Nivola, P.S. (ed.) *Comparative Disadvantages? Social Regulations and the Global Economy*, pp. 146–202 (Washington, DC: Brookings Institute Press).

Katzenstein, P.J. (1985) *Small States in World Markets* (Ithaca, NY: Cornell University Press).

Katzenstein, P.J. (ed.) (1989) *Industry and Politics in West Germany, Toward the Third Republic* (Ithaca, NY: Cornell University Press).

Kell, G. (2003) "The Global Compact: Origins, Operations, Progress, Challenges," in *Journal of Corporate Citizenship*, 3:11, 35–49.

Kolk, A. (2003) "Trends in Sustainability Reporting by the Fortune Global 250," in *Business Strategy and the Environment*, 12, 279–91.

—— (2004) "A Decade of Sustainability Reporting: Developments and Significance," in *International Journal of Environment and Sustainable Development*, 3:1, 51–64.

Kollmann, K. and Prakash, A. (2001) "Green by Choice? Cross-National Variations in Firms' Responses to EMS-based Environmental Regimes," in *World Politics*, 53, 399–430.

Korten, D.C. (1995) *When Corporations Rule the World* (West Hartford, CT: Berrett-Koehler).

Lehmbruch, G. (1982) "Introduction: Neo-Corporatism in Comparative Perspective," in Lehmbruch, G. and Schmitter, Ph.C. (eds) (1982) *Patterns of Corporatist Policy-Making*, pp. 1–28 (London: Sage).

Lijphart, A. (1999) *Patterns of Democracy* (New Haven: Yale University Press).

Matten, D. and Moon, J. (2004) " 'Implicit' and 'Explicit' CSR: A Conceptual Framework for Understanding CSR in Europe," in *The Academy of Management Review*, 2:4, 404–24.

Muchlinski, P. (1995) *Multinational Enterprises and the Law* (Oxford: Oxford University Press).

Nadelmann, E. A. (1990) "Global Prohibition Regimes: The Evolution of Norms in International Society" in *International Organization*, 44:4, 479–526.

Nelson, J. (2002) *Building Partnerships. Cooperation between the United Nations System and the Private Sector* (New York: United Nations).

Newman, A.L. and Bach, D. (2004) "Self-Regulatory Trajectories in the Shadow of Public Power. Resolving Digital Dilemmas in Europe and the United States," in *Governance*, 17:3, 387–413.

Ohmae, K. (1995) *The End of the Nation-State. The Rise of Regional Economics* (New York: Free Press).

Powell, W.W. and DiMaggio, P.J. (eds) (1991) *The New Institutionalism in Organizational Analysis* (Chicago: University of Chicago Press).

Reinicke, W. (1998) *Global Public Policy: Governing without Government?* (Washington, DC: Brookings Institution Press).

Reinicke, W. and Deng, F. (2000) *Critical Choices: The United Nations, Networks, and the Future of Global Governance* (Washington, DC: Brookings Institution Press).

Rieth, L. (2004) "Der VN Global Compact: Was als Experiment begann," in *Die Friedenswarte*, 79:1–2, 151–70.

Risse, T. (2000) "'Let's argue!': Communicative Action in World Politics," in *International Organization*, 54:1, 1–39

Risse, T. (2003) "Konstruktivismus, Rationalismus und Theorien Internationaler Beziehungen – warum empirisch nichts so heiß gegessen wird, wie es theoretisch gekocht wurde," in Hellmann, G., Wolf, K.D. and Zürn, M. (eds) *Die neuen internationalen Beziehungen: Forschungsstand und Perspektiven in Deutschland*, pp. 99–132 (Baden-Baden: Nomos).

Risse-Kappen, T. (ed.) (1995) *Bringing Transnational Relations back in: Non-State Actors, Domestic Structures and International Institutions* (Cambridge: Cambridge University Press).

Schimmelfennig, F. (2003) "Internationale Sozialisation: Von einem 'erschöpften' zu einem produktiven Forschungsprogramm?" in Hellmann, G., Wolf, K.D. and Zürn, M. (eds) *Die neuen internationalen Beziehungen: Forschungsstand und Perspektiven in Deutschland*, pp. 401–27 (Baden-Baden: Nomos).

—— (2005) "Strategic Calculation and International Socialization: Membership Incentives, Party Constellations, and Sustained Compliance in Central and Eastern Europe," in *International Organization*, 59:4, 827–60.

Schmidt, V.A. (1996) *From State to Market? The Transformation of French Business and Government* (Cambridge: Cambridge University Press).

—— (2003) "French capitalism transformed, yet still a third variety of capitalism" in *Economy and Society*, 32:4, 526–54.

Schmitter, Ph.C. (1982) "Reflections on where the Theory of Neo-Corporatism has Gone and where the Praxis of Neo-Corporatism may be Going," in Lehmbruch, G. and Schmitter, Ph.C. (eds) *Patterns of Corporatist Policy-Making*, pp. 259–79 (London: Sage).

Sell, S.K. and Prakash, A. (2004) "Using Ideas Strategically: The Contest between Business and NGO Networks in Intellectual Property Rights," in *International Studies Quarterly*, 48, 143–75.

Strange, S. (1996) *The Retreat of the State: the Diffusion of Power in the World Economy* (Cambridge: Cambridge University Press).

Vogel, D. (1986) *National Styles of Business Regulation* (Ithaca, NY: Cornell University Press).

Ward, H. and Smith, C. (2006) "Corporate Social Responsibility at a Crossroads. Futures for CSR in the UK to 2015," *IIED Working paper*, London.

Wendt, A. (1999) *A Social Theory of International Politics* (Cambridge: Cambridge University Press).

Wolf, K.D. (2006) "Private Actors and the Legitimacy of Governance beyond the State," in Benz, A. and Papadopoulos, I. (eds) *Governance and Democracy, Comparing National, European and International Experiences*, pp. 200–27 (London: Routledge).

—— (2008) "Emerging Patterns of Global Governance, The New Interplay between the State, Business and Civil Society," in Scherer, A.G. and Palazzo, G. (eds) *Handbook of Research on Global Corporate Citizenship*, pp. 225–48 (Cheltenham: Edward Elgar).

Zerk, J.A. (2006) *Multinationals and Corporate Social Responsibility, Limitations and Opportunities in International Law* (Cambridge: Cambridge University Press).

Zürn, M. (1998) *Regieren jenseits des Nationalstaats, Globalisierung und Denationalisierung als Chance* (Frankfurt a.M.: Suhrkamp).

Index